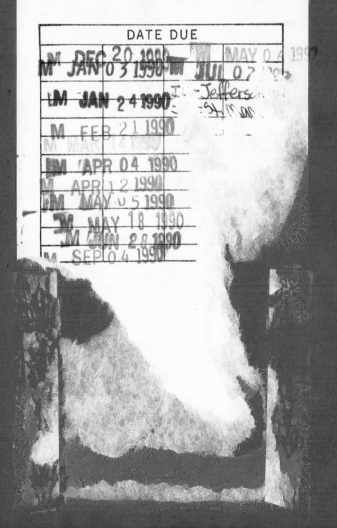

| DATE DUE | | |
|---|---|---|
| M DEC 20 1989 | M | MAY 0 6 1997 |
| LM JAN 0 3 1990 | M JUL 07 1997 |
| LM JAN 2 4 1990 | Jefferson |
| M FEB 21 1990 | SH man |
| M MAR 14 1990 | |
| LM APR 04 1990 | |
| M APR 12 1990 | |
| M MAY 05 1990 | |
| M MAY 18 1990 | |
| M JUN 2 8 1990 | |
| M SEP 0 4 1990 | |

# ASIMOV ON SCIENCE

## SCIENCE ESSAY COLLECTIONS BY ISAAC ASIMOV

### From *The Magazine of Fantasy and Science Fiction*

FACT AND FANCY
VIEW FROM A HEIGHT
ADDING A DIMENSION
OF TIME AND SPACE
  AND OTHER THINGS
FROM EARTH TO HEAVEN
SCIENCE, NUMBERS, AND I
THE SOLAR SYSTEM
  AND BACK
THE STARS IN THEIR
  COURSES
THE LEFT HAND OF THE
  ELECTRON
THE TRAGEDY OF THE
  MOON
ASIMOV ON ASTRONOMY
ASIMOV ON CHEMISTRY

OF MATTERS GREAT AND
  SMALL
ASIMOV ON PHYSICS
THE PLANET THAT WASN'T
ASIMOV ON NUMBERS
QUASAR, QUASAR,
  BURNING BRIGHT
THE ROAD TO INFINITY
THE SUN SHINES BRIGHT
COUNTING THE EONS
X STANDS FOR UNKNOWN
THE SUBATOMIC MONSTER
FAR AS HUMAN EYE
  COULD SEE
THE RELATIVITY
  OF WRONG
ASIMOV ON SCIENCE

### From Other Sources

ONLY A TRILLION
IS ANYONE THERE?
TODAY AND TOMORROW
  AND—
PLEASE EXPLAIN!
SCIENCE PAST—SCIENCE
  FUTURE
THE BEGINNING AND THE
  END

LIFE AND TIME
CHANGE!
THE ROVING MIND
THE DANGERS
  OF INTELLIGENCE
PAST, PRESENT, AND
  FUTURE

# ASIMOV
# on Science

## A 30-Year Retrospective

### Isaac Asimov

**DOUBLEDAY**
*New York • London • Toronto • Sydney • Auckland*

Published by Doubleday, a division of Bantam Doubleday Dell Publishing
Group, Inc., 666 Fifth Avenue, New York, New York 10103

DOUBLEDAY and the portrayal of an anchor with a dolphin are trademarks of
Doubleday, a division of Bantam Doubleday Dell Publishing Group, Inc.

Library of Congress Cataloging-in-Publication Data

Asimov, Isaac, 1920–
Asimov on science.

1. Science. I. Title.
Q126.8.A85   1989       500       88-33435
ISBN 0-385-26345-7

BG

The essays in this volume are reprinted from *The Magazine of Fantasy and Science Fiction*, having appeared in the indicated issues:

"The Dust of Ages" (November 1958); "The Ultimate Split of the Second" (September 1959); "A Piece of Pi" (May 1960); "Heaven on Earth" (May 1961); "The Egg and Wee" (June 1962); "You, Too, Can Speak Gaelic" (~~June 1962~~); "The Slowly Moving Finger" (February 1964); "Exclamation Point!" (July 1965); "I'm Looking over a Four-Leaf Clover" (September 1966); "Twelve Point Three Six Nine" (July 1967); "Knock Plastic!" (November 1967); "Uncertain, Coy, and Hard to Please" (February 1969); "The Luxon Wall" (December 1969); "Pompey and Circumstance" (May 1971); "Lost in Non-Translation" (March 1972); "The Ancient and the Ultimate" (January 1973); "Look Long upon a Monkey" (September 1974); "Thinking About Thinking" (January 1975); "Best Foot Backward" (November 1975); "The Subtlest Difference" (October 1977); "The Floating Crystal Palace" (April 1978); "Alas, All Human" (June 1979); "Milton! Thou Shouldst Be Living at This Hour" (August 1980); "And After Many a Summer Dies the Proton" (September 1981); "The Circle of the Earth" (February 1982); "What Truck?" (August 1983); "More Thinking About Thinking" (November 1983); "Far as Human Eye Could See" (November 1984); "The Relativity of Wrong" (October 1986); "A Sacred Poet" (September 1987); "The Longest River" (July 1988); "The Secret of the Universe" (March 1989).

Essays copyright © 1958, 1959, 1960, 1961, 1962, 1963, 1965, 1966, 1967, 1968, 1969, 1971, 1972, 1974, 1975, 1977, 1978, 1979, 1980, 1981, 1983, 1984, 1986, 1987, 1988, 1989, by Mercury Press, Inc.

Dedicated to the memory of Robert Park Mills (1920–1986), at whose invitation this series of essays was begun in 1958.

# Contents

# Introduction

Back in 1958, Robert P. Mills, then the editor of *The Magazine of Fantasy and Science Fiction*, asked me if I would be willing to write a monthly science column for the magazine. The terms were that I must meet the deadline every issue, and in return I would get a small sum of money (which was not important) and the privilege of writing about anything I wished, with neither suggestions nor objections from the editor (which was supremely important).

I accepted at once, with unconcealed glee. I had no way of knowing how long it would last, and it seemed quite probable that after a rather short time something might go wrong. The magazine might cease publication, or a new editor might arise who would not want my science column, or I would run out of subjects to write about, or run out of time, or run out of health. Who could know?

But none of that happened. As I write I am celebrating the 30th anniversary of my science column. I have never missed an issue. Neither Mills, nor his two successors, Avram Davidson and

Edward L. Ferman, have ever made suggestions or objections, nor have they made the slightest gesture of putting an end to it. My very first *F&SF* essay appeared in the November 1958 issue of the magazine. It was only 1,200 words or so long, because that was the length I was told to make it. Within a few months, I was asked to lengthen the essays to 4,000 words, which I think was a flattering development.

That first essay, "The Dust of Ages," ran as follows:

*One of the disheartening discoveries a housewife makes early in housewifery concerns the unbeatability of dust. No matter how clean a house is kept and how little activity is allowed within it and how thoroughly children and other filthy creatures are barred from the premises, a fine layer of dust coats everything as soon as you turn your back.*

*The atmosphere of Earth, particularly in cities, is just plain dusty; and a good thing, too, or there would be no blue skies and no softening of shadows.*

*And space, particularly within solar systems, is also dusty. It is loaded with individual atoms and with conglomerates of atoms. Many of the conglomerates range up to pinhead size or so; the so-called "micro-meteors" which, at the velocities at which they move, are large enough to do damage to a space vessel. (One of the functions of the artificial satellites is to measure the quantity of such micro-meteors in circumterrestrial space.)*

*Their numbers, we hope, will not be high enough to impede space travel, but they are high. The Earth sweeps up billions of them each day. They burn in the upper reaches of the atmosphere through friction-generated heat and never get within sixty miles of the Earth's surface. (The occasional large meteors that weigh pounds or tons are another story.) However, what is meant by "burn"?*

*In burning, the atoms composing the micro-meteors don't disappear, they merely vaporize with heat and then this vapor condenses to form an extremely fine dust. Slowly, this dust settles to Earth.*

*The most recent measurements of the atmosphere's meteoric dust (as far as I know) were reported by Hans Petterson in the February 1, 1958 issue of the British scientific journal,* Nature. *He traveled some two miles above sea level on the slopes of Mauna Loa in Hawaii (and another mountain on Kauai) and sieved the air, separating out the fine dust, weighing it and analyzing it. At a two-mile height in the middle of the Pacific Ocean one can expect the air to be pretty free of terrestrial dust. Furthermore, Petterson*

*paid particular attention to the cobalt content of the dust since meteoric dust
is high in cobalt whereas Earthly dust is low in it.*

*He found 14.3 micrograms (about one two-millionth of an ounce) of
cobalt in the dust filtered out of one thousand cubic meters of air. In meteors
some 2.5 percent of the atoms are cobalt, so Petterson calculated that the
total quantity of dust of meteoric origin in the atmosphere, up to a height of
60 miles, amounts to 28,600,000 tons.*

*This dust isn't just sitting there. Slowly, it is settling to Earth while new
dust is being added by the continuous entry of more micro-meteors into the
atmosphere. If the 28,600,000 tons is a steady figure, the same amount is
being added each year as is settling out, but how much is that?*

*Petterson went back to data concerning the 1883 explosion of the
Krakatoa volcano in the East Indies when tremendous quantities of the
very finest dust were liberated into the upper atmosphere and sunsets were
extra beautiful all over the world. Pretty nearly all that dust had settled
back to Earth after two years. If this two-year-settling figure holds for
meteor dust, too, then half the total—14,300,000 tons of such dust—
settles to Earth each year and 14,300,000 tons of new dust must enter the
atmosphere.*

*At this point Petterson ends his calculation and I begin mine—and the
speculations that result concern our industrial civilization and the problem
of landing on the Moon.*

*Naturally, 14,300,000 tons of dust per year seems like a large figure
and the thought, to any housewife, would be a sobering one. However,
spread out over the Earth it's not so bad. The Earth has a surface area of
about 197,000,000 square miles so the annual dust-fall per square mile is
only about 145 pounds, which is nothing compared to the dust generated by
the coal and oil we burn.*

*If we consider meteor dust to be mostly iron, 145 pounds is equivalent to
510 cubic inches (a cube eight inches on each side). Since a square mile
contains about 4,000,000,000 square inches, a year's accumulation of
dust spread out evenly over the square mile would pile up a dust layer about
0.00000013 inches thick. That's a little over a ten-millionth of an inch
and no one would worry about that.*

*Of course, this goes on year after year and the Earth has been in existence
as a solid body for a good long time; for as long as 4,600,000,000 years. If
through all that time, meteor dust had settled to Earth at the same rate it*

*does today, then by now, if it were undisturbed, it would form a layer 50 feet thick over all the Earth.*

*It does not remain undisturbed, however. It falls in the ocean. It is blown about. It is rained on. It is trampled underfoot. Leaves fall on it. And yet, this dust never disappears and it could be of the greatest importance to us. In comparison to the mass of the Earth, the 70,000,000,000,000,000 tons of dust collected in Earth's history is very little. It is only a hundred-thousandth of the Earth's mass. But—the dust is mostly iron, and that makes it rather special.*

*The Earth, you see, consists of two layers, a central core of iron and materials soluble in it, and an outer crust of silicates and materials soluble in it. This, presumably, dates back to the time when Earth was liquid and the two mutually immiscible liquids settled out, the dense one below and the lighter one above. In that case, though, why is there so much iron found in the Earth's crust among the silicates? Iron is actually the fourth commonest element in the crust.*

*Can this surface iron be, not Earth's original substance, but, at least in significant part, the accumulated meteoric dust of ages? According to my calculation, the dust would account for all the iron in the upper 1 1/2 miles of the Earth's solid crust, and certainly accounts, too, for all the iron we've managed to dig up. Can it be, then, that the modern technology of our Age of Steel feeds entirely on the accumulated dust of space, like whales feeding on plankton? I wonder.*

*But what about the Moon? It travels through space with us and although it is smaller and has a weaker gravity, it, too, should sweep up a respectable quantity of micro-meteors.*

*To be sure, the Moon has no atmosphere to friction the micro-meteors to dust, but the act of striking the Moon's surface should develop enough heat to do the job.*

*Now it is already known, from a variety of evidence, that the Moon (or at least the level lowlands) is covered with a layer of dust. No one, however, knows for sure how thick this dust may be.*

*It strikes me that if this dust is the dust of falling micro-meteors, the thickness may be great. On the Moon there are no oceans to swallow the dust, no winds to disturb it, or life forms to mess it up generally, one way or another. The dust that forms must just lie there, and, if the Moon gets anything like Earth's supply, it could be dozens of feet thick. In fact, the dust that strikes crater walls quite probably rolls down hill and collects at the bottom, forming drifts that could be 50 feet deep, or more. Why not? I get a picture, therefore, of the first spaceship, picking out a nice level place for landing purposes, coming slowly downward tail-first—and sinking majestically out of sight.*

I have never included this essay in one of my collections and I include it here in the introduction only for historic reasons. You see, it was not long before I decided I didn't like it. For one thing, I kept wondering how accurate Petterson's results might be. For another, I grew appalled at my assumption that all meteoric matter is mostly iron, when actually iron meteors make up only about 10 percent of the whole.

Finally, the landing on the Moon, eleven years after I wrote this essay, really knocked out the matter of thick layers of dust on the Moon. That notion had been advanced by Thomas Gold and it was plausible (or I wouldn't have fallen for it) but it was wrong. The thing is that the dust on the Moon is accumulating in a vacuum. In air, oxygen atoms layer the surface and keep the dust particles apart. In vacuum, the dust particles stick together so that the surface is something like crunchy snow. But you can't win them all.

As you will see, I have not run out of ideas and I don't think I am likely to. It is my intention to continue writing the articles until either the magazine or I, myself, come to an end.

After thirty years, however, I feel it is time for retrospection. So I have chosen one essay from every successive twelve and put together this volume as a celebration of longevity. I thank *F&SF*, Doubleday (which has hitherto published my essays in many volumes), and all my editors and readers.

# ASIMOV ON SCIENCE

# I

# The Ultimate Split
# of the Second

Occasionally, I get an idea for something new in science; not necessarily something important, of course, but new anyway. One of these ideas is what I will devote this chapter to.

The notion came to me some time ago, when the news broke that a subatomic particle called "xi-zero" (with "xi" pronounced "ksee," if you speak Greek, and "zigh" if you speak English) had been detected for the first time. Like other particles of its general nature, it is strangely stable, having a half-life of fully a ten-billionth ($10^{-10}$) of a second or so.

The last sentence may seem misprinted—you may think that I meant to write "unstable"—but no! A ten-billionth of a second can be a long time; it all depends on the scale of reference. Compared to a sextillionth ($10^{-23}$) of a second, a ten-billionth ($10^{-10}$) of a second is an aeon. The difference between those two intervals of time is as that between one day and thirty billion years.

You may grant this and yet feel an onset of dizziness. The world of split-seconds and split-split-split-seconds is a difficult one to visualize. It is easy to say "a sextillionth of a second" and just as easy to say "a ten-billionth of a second"; but no matter how easily we juggle the symbols representing such time intervals, it is impossible (or *seems* impossible) to visualize either.

My idea is intended to make split-seconds more visualizable, and I got it from the device used in a realm of measurement that is also grotesque and also outside the range of all common experience—that of astronomical distances.

There is nothing strange in saying, "Vega is a very nearby star. It's not very much more than a hundred fifty trillion ($1.5 \times 10^{14}$) miles away."

Most of us who read science fiction are well-used to the thought that a hundred fifty trillion miles is a very small distance on the cosmic scale. The bulk of the stars in our galaxy are something like two hundred quadrillion ($2 \times 10^{17}$) miles away, and the nearest full-sized outside galaxy is more than ten quintillion ($10^{19}$) miles away.

Trillion, quadrillion and quintillion are all legitimate number-words, and there's no difficulty telling which is larger and by how much, if you simply want to manipulate symbols. Visualizing what they mean, however, is another thing.

So the trick is to make use of the speed of light to bring the numbers down to vest-pocket size. It doesn't change the actual distance any, but it's easier to make some sort of mental adjustment to the matter if all the zeroes of the "-illions" aren't getting in the way.

The velocity of light in a vacuum is 186,274 miles per second or, in the metric system, 299,779 kilometers per second.

A "light-second," then, can be defined as that distance which light (in a vacuum) will travel in a second of time, and is equal to 186,274 miles or to 299,779 kilometers.

It is easy to build longer units in this system. A "light-minute" is equal to 60 light-seconds; a "light-hour" is equal to 60 light-minutes, and so forth, till you reach the very familiar "light-year," which is the distance which light (in a vacuum) will travel in a year. This distance is equal to 5,890,000,000,000 miles or 9,460,000,000,000 kilometers. If you are content with round numbers, you can consider a light-year equal to six trillion

$(6 \times 10^{12})$ miles or nine and one-half trillion $(9.5 \times 10^{12})$ kilometers.

You can go on, if you please, to "light-centuries" and "light-millennia," but hardly anyone ever does. The light-year is the unit of preference for astronomic distances. (There is also the "parsec," which is equal to 3.26 light years, or roughly twenty trillion miles, but that is a unit based on a different principle, and we need not worry about it here.)

Using light-years as the unit, we can say that Vega is 27 light-years from us, and that this is a small distance considering that the bulk of the stars of our galaxy are 35,000 light-years away and that the nearest full-sized outside galaxy is 2,100,000 light-years away. The difference between 27 and 35,000 and 2,100,000, given our range of experience, is easier to visualize than that between a hundred fifty trillion and two hundred quadrillion and ten quintillion, though the ratios in both cases are the same.

Furthermore, the use of the speed of light in defining units of distance has the virtue of simplifying certain connections between time and distance.

For instance, suppose an expedition on Ganymede is, at a certain time, 500,000,000 miles from Earth. (The distance, naturally, varies with time, as both worlds move about in their orbits.) This distance can also be expressed as 44.8 light-minutes.

What is the advantage of the latter expression? For one thing, 44.8 is an easier number to say and handle than 500,000,000. For another, suppose our expedition is in radio communication with Earth. A message sent from Ganymede to Earth (or vice versa) will take 44.8 minutes to arrive. The use of light-units expresses distance *and* speed of communication at the same time.

(In fact, in a world in which interplanetary travel is a taken-for-granted fact, I wonder if the astronauts won't start measuring distance in "radio-minutes" rather than light-minutes. Same thing, of course, but more to the point.)

Then, when and if interstellar travel comes to pass, making necessary the use of velocities at near the speed of light, another advantage will come about. If time dilatation exists and the experience of time is slowed at high velocities, a trip to Vega may seem to endure for only a month or for only a week. To the stay-at-homes on Earth, however, who are experiencing "objective time" (the kind of time that is experienced at low velocities—strictly speaking, at zero velocity), the trip to Vega, 27 light-years distant, cannot take place in less than 27 years. A round-tripper, no matter how quickly the journey has seemed to pass for him, will find his friends on Earth a minimum of 54 years older. In the same way, a trip to the galaxy of Andromeda cannot take less than 2,100,000 years of objective time, Andromeda being 2,100,000 light-years distant. Once again, time and distance are simultaneously expressed.

My idea, then, is to apply this same principle to the realm of ultra-short intervals of time.

Instead of concentrating on the tremendously long distances light can cover in ordinary units of time, why not concentrate on the tremendously short times required for light to cover ordinary units of distance?

If we're going to speak of a light-second as equal to the distance covered by light (in a vacuum) in one second and set it equal to 186,273 miles, why not speak of a "light-mile" as equal to the time required for light (in a vacuum) to cover a distance of one mile, and set that equal to $1/186,273$ seconds?

Why not, indeed? The only drawback is that 186,273 is such an uneven number. However, by a curious coincidence undreamed of by the inventors of the metric system, the speed of light is very close to 300,000 kilometers per second, so that a "light-kilometer" is equal to $1/300,000$ of a second. It comes out even rounder if you note that $3\frac{1}{3}$ light-kilometers are equal to just about 0.00001 or $10^{-5}$ seconds.

Furthermore, to get to still smaller units of time, it is only necessary to consider light as covering smaller and smaller distances.

Thus, one kilometer ($10^5$ centimeters) is equal to a million millimeters, and one millimeter ($10^{-1}$ centimeters) is equal to a million millimicrons. To go one step further down, we can say that one millimicron ($10^{-7}$ centimeters) is equal to a million fermis. (The name "fermi" has been suggested, but has not yet been officially adopted, as far as I know, for a unit of length equal to a millionth of a millimicron, or to $10^{-13}$ centimeters. It is derived, of course, from the late Enrico Fermi, and I will accept the name for the purposes of this chapter.)

So we can set up a little table of light-units for ultra-short intervals of time, beginning with a light-kilometer,* which is itself equal to only $1/300,000$ of a second.

| | | |
|---|---|---|
| 1 light-kilometer | = | 1,000,000 light-millimeters |
| 1 light-millimeter | = | 1,000,000 light-millimicrons |
| 1 light-millimicron | = | 1,000,000 light-fermis |

To relate these units to conventional units of time, we need only set up another short table:

| | | |
|---|---|---|
| 3⅓ light-kilometers | = | $10^{-5}$ seconds (i.e. a hundred-thousandth of a second) |
| 3⅓ light-millimeters | = | $10^{-11}$ seconds (i.e. a hundred-billionth of a second) |
| 3⅓ light-millimicrons | = | $10^{-17}$ seconds (i.e. a hundred-quadrillionth of a second) |
| 3⅓ light-fermis | = | $10^{-23}$ seconds (i.e. a hundred-sextillionth of a second) |

But why stop at the light-fermi? We can proceed on downward, dividing by a million indefinitely.

Consider the fermi again. It is equal to $10^{-13}$ centimeters, a ten-trillionth of a centimeter. What is interesting about this particular figure, and why the name of an atomic physicist should have been suggested for the unit, is that $10^{-13}$ centimeters is also the approximate diameter of the various subatomic particles.

A light-fermi, therefore, is the time required for a ray of light to travel from one end of a proton to the other. The light-fermi is the time required for the fastest known motion to cover the smallest tangible distance. Until the day comes that we discover something faster than the speed of light or something smaller than subatomic particles, we are not likely ever to have to deal with an interval of time smaller than the light-fermi. As of now, the light-fermi is the ultimate split of the second.

* If it will help, one mile equals 1⅗ kilometers, and one inch equals 25½ millimeters.

Of course, you may wonder what can happen in the space of a light-fermi. And if something did happen in that unimaginably small interval, how could we tell it didn't take place in a light-millimicron, which is also unimaginably small for all it is equal to a million light-fermis?

Well, consider high-energy particles. These (if the energy is high enough) travel with almost the speed of light. And when one of these particles approaches another at such a speed, a reaction often takes place between them, as a result of mutual "nuclear forces" coming into play.

Nuclear forces, however, are very short-range. Their strength falls off with distance so rapidly that the forces are only appreciable within one or two fermis distance of any given particle.

We have here, then, the case of two particles passing at the speed of light and able to interact only while within a couple of fermis of each other. It would only take them a couple of light-fermis to enter and leave that tiny zone of interaction at the tremendous speed at which they are moving. Yet reactions *do* take place!

Nuclear reactions taking place in light-fermis of time are classed as "strong interactions." They are the results of forces that can make themselves felt in the most evanescent imaginable interval, and these are the strongest forces we know of. Nuclear forces of this sort are, in fact, about 135 times as strong as the electromagnetic forces with which we are familiar.

Scientists adjusted themselves to this fact and were prepared to have any nuclear reactions involving individual subatomic particles take only light-fermis of time to transpire.

But then complications arose. When particles were slammed together with sufficient energy to undergo strong interactions, new particles not previously observed were created in the process and were detected. Some of these new particles (first observed in 1950) amazed scientists by proving to be very massive. They were distinctly more massive, in fact, than neutrons or protons, which, until then, had been the most massive particles known.

These super-massive particles are called "hyperons" (the prefix "hyper-" comes from the Greek and means "over," "above," "beyond"). There are three classes of these hyperons, distinguished by being given the names of different Greek letters. There are the lambda particles, which are about 12 percent heavier than the proton; the sigma particles, which are about 13 percent heavier; and the xi particles, which are about 14 percent heavier.

There were theoretical reasons for suspecting that there were one pair of lambda particles, three pairs of sigma particles, and two pairs of xi particles. These differ among themselves in the nature of their electric charge and in the fact that one of each pair is an "antiparticle." One by one, each of the hyperons was detected in bubble chamber experiments; the xi-zero particle, detected early in 1959, was the last of them. The roster of hyperons was complete.

The hyperons as a whole, however, were odd little creatures. They didn't last long, only for unimaginably small fractions of a second. To scientists, however, they seemed to last very long indeed, for nuclear forces were involved in their breakdown, which should therefore have taken place in light-fermis of time.

But they didn't. Even the most unstable of all the hyperons, the sigma-zero particle, must last at least as long as a quintillionth of a second. Put that way, it sounds like a satisfactorily short period of time—not long enough to get really bored. But when the interval is converted from conventional units to light-units, we find that a quintillionth of a second is equal to 30,000 light-fermis.

Too long!

And even so, 30,000 light-fermis represent an extraordinarily short lifetime for a hyperon. The others, including the recently-discovered xi-zero particle, have half-lives of about 30,000,000,000,000 light-fermis, or 30 light-millimeters.

Since the nuclear forces bringing about the breakdown of hyperons last at least ten trillion times as long an interval of time as that required to form them, those forces must be that much weaker than those involved in the "strong interactions." Naturally, the new forces are spoken of as being involved in the "weak interactions"; and they are weak indeed, being almost a trillion times weaker than even electromagnetic forces.

In fact, the new particles which were involved in "weak interactions" were called "strange particles," partly because of this, and the name has stuck. Every particle is now given a "strangeness number" which may be +1, 0, −1 or −2.

Ordinary particles such as protons and neutrons have strangeness numbers of 0; lambda and sigma particles have strangeness numbers of −1, xi particles have strangeness numbers of −2, and so forth. Exactly what the strangeness number signifies is not yet completely clear; but it can be worked with now and figured out later.

The path and the activities of the various hyperons (and of the other subatomic particles as well) are followed by their effects upon the molecules with which they collide. Such a collision usually involves merely the tearing off of an electron or two from the air molecules. What is left of the molecule is a charged "ion."

An ion is much more efficient as a center about which a water droplet can form, than is the original uncharged molecule. If a speeding particle collides with molecules in a sample of air which is supercharged with water vapor (as in a Wilson cloud chamber) or in liquid hydrogen at the point of boiling (as in a bubble chamber), each ion that is produced is immediately made the center of a water droplet or gas droplet, respectively. The moving particle marks its path, therefore, with a delicate line of water drops. When the particle breaks down into two other particles, moving off in two different directions, the line of water gives this away by splitting into a Y form.

It all happens instantaneously to our merely human senses. But photograph upon photograph of the tracks that result will allow nuclear physicists to deduce the chain of events that produced the different track patterns.

Only subatomic particles that are themselves charged are very efficient in knocking electrons out of the edges of air molecules. For that reason, only charged particles can be followed by the water traceries. And, also for that reason, in any class of particles, the uncharged or neutral varieties are the last to be detected.

For instance, the neutron, which is uncharged, was not discovered until eighteen years after the discovery of the similar, but electrically charged, proton. And in the case of the hyperons, the last to be found was xi-zero, one of the uncharged varieties. (The "zero" means "zero charge.") Yet the uncharged particles can be detected by the very absence of a trace. For instance, the xi-zero particle was formed from a charged particle, and broke down, eventually, into another type of charged particle. In the photograph that finally landed the jackpot (about seventy thousand were examined), there were lines of droplets separated by a significant gap! That gap could not be filled by any known uncharged particle, for any of those would have brought about a different type of gap or a different sequence of events at the conclusion of the gap. Only the xi-zero could be made to fit; and so, in this thoroughly negative manner, the final particle was discovered.

And where do the light-units I'm suggesting come in? Why, consider that a particle traveling at almost the speed of light has a chance, if its lifetime is about 30 light-millimeters, to travel 30 light-millimeters before breaking down.

The one implies the other. By using conventional units, you might say that a length of water droplets of about 30 millimeters implies a half-life of about a trillionth of a second (or vice versa), but there is no obvious connection between the two numerical values. To say that a track of 30 millimeters implies a half-life of 30 light-millimeters is equally true, and how neatly it ties in. Once again, as in the case of astronomical distances, the use of the speed of light allows one number to express both distance and time.

A group of particles which entered the scene earlier than the hyperons are the "mesons." These are middleweight particles, lighter than protons or neutrons, but heavier than electrons. (Hence their name, from a Greek word meaning "middle.")

There are three known varieties of these particles, too. The two lighter varieties are also distinguished by means of Greek letters. They are the mu-mesons, discovered in 1935, which are about 0.11 as massive as a proton, and the pi-mesons, discovered in 1947, which are about 0.15 as massive as protons. Finally, beginning in 1949, various species of unusually heavy mesons, the K-mesons, were discovered. These are about 0.53 as massive as protons.

On the whole, the mesons are less unstable than the hyperons. They have longer half-lives. Whereas even the most stable of the hyperons has a half-life of only 30 light-millimeters, the meson half-lives generally range from that value up through 8,000 light-millimeters for those pi-mesons carrying an electric charge, to 800,000 light-millimeters for the mu-mesons.

By now, the figure of 800,000 light-millimeters ought to give you the impression of a long half-life indeed, so I'll just remind you that by conventional units it is the equivalent of $1/400,000$ of a second.

A short time to us, but a long, lo-o-o-ong time on the nuclear scale.

Of the mesons, it is only the K-variety that comes under the heading of strange particles. The K-plus and K-zero mesons have a strangeness number of $+1$, and the K-minus meson, a strangeness number of $-1$.

The weak interactions, by the way, recently opened the door to a revolution in physics. For the first eight years or so after their discovery, the weak interactions had seemed to be little more than confusing nuisances. Then, in 1957, as a result of studies involving them, the "law of conservation of parity" was shown not to apply to all processes in nature.

I won't go into the details of that, but it's perhaps enough to say that the demonstration thunderstruck physicists; that the two young Chinese students who turned the trick (the older one was in his middle thirties) were promptly awarded the Nobel Prize; and that a whole new horizon in nuclear theory seems to be opening up as a result.

Aside from the mesons and hyperons, there is only one unstable particle known—the neutron. Within the atomic nucleus the neutron is stable; but in isolation, it eventually breaks down to form a proton, an electron and a neutrino. (Of course, antiparticles such as positrons and antiprotons are unstable in the sense that they will react with electrons and protons, respectively. Under ordinary circumstances this will happen in a millionth of a second or so. However, if these antiparticles were in isolation, they would remain as they were indefinitely, and that is what we mean by stability.)

The half-life of the neutron breakdown is 1,010 seconds (or

about 17 minutes), and this is about a billion times longer than the half-life of the breakdown of any other known particle.

In light-units, the half-life of the neutron would be 350,000,000 light-kilometers. In other words, if a number of neutrons were speeding at the velocity of light, they would travel 350,000,000 kilometers (from one extreme of Earth's orbit to the other, plus a little extra) before half had broken down.

Of course, neutrons as made use of by scientists don't go at anything like the speed of light. In fact, the neutrons that are particularly useful in initiating uranium fission are very slow-moving neutrons that don't move any faster than air molecules do. Their speed is roughly a mile a second.

Even at that creep, a stream of neutrons would travel a thousand miles before half had broken down. And in that thousand miles, many other things have a chance to happen to them. For instance, if they're traveling through uranium or plutonium, they have a chance to be absorbed by nuclei and to initiate fission. And to help make the confusing and dangerous—but exciting—world we live in today.

## AFTERWORD

Naturally, my favorite science essays are those which, in one way or another, are unusual. Simply reporting on something in science may be interesting and useful, and I am satisfied to do that, and nothing more, at times. However, when I can present something that is original with me (or that I am under the impression is original with me), I feel a much greater sense of achievement. Wouldn't anyone?

As I said in the first sentence of the foregoing essay, I was presenting something new—a method describing ultra-short periods of time in such a way as to make them more understandable and useful. I was very proud of myself for doing this and, in the thirty years that have elapsed since then, no one has written to me to tell me that, in actual fact, this idea was advanced years earlier. So I *still* think it's original with me.

But, in the last thirty years, no one has adopted the idea, either. Its use remains confined to the foregoing essay. Too bad —for I still think it's a great notion, and what bothers me is that someday someone will think of it again, and that it will then come into use and no one will remember that I thought of it first.

And, incidentally, my discussion of subatomic particles is way out of date, naturally.

# 2

# A Piece of Pi

In my essay "Those Crazy Ideas," which appeared in *Fact and Fancy*, I casually threw in a footnote to the effect that $e^{\pi i} = -1$. Behold, a good proportion of the comment which I received thereafter dealt not with the essay itself but with that footnote (one reader, more in sorrow than in anger, proved the equality, which I had neglected to do).

My conclusion is that some readers are interested in these odd symbols. Since I am, too (albeit I am not really a mathematician, or anything else), the impulse is irresistible to pick up one of them, say $\pi$, and talk about it.

In the first place, what is $\pi$? Well, it is the Greek letter *pi* and it represents the ratio of the length of the perimeter of a circle to the length of its diameter. *Perimeter* is from the Greek *perimetron*, meaning "the measurement around," and *diameter* from the Greek *diametron*, meaning "the measurement through." For some obscure reason, while it is customary to use perimeter in the case of polygons, it is also customary to switch to the Latin *circumference* in speaking of circles. This is all right, I suppose (I am no purist) but it obscures the reason for the symbol π.

Back about 1600 the English mathematician William Oughtred, in discussing the ratio of a circle's perimeter to its diameter, used the Greek letter π to symbolize the perimeter and the Greek letter δ (delta) to symbolize the diameter. They were the first letters, respectively, of *perimetron* and *diametron.*

Now mathematicians often simplify matters by setting values equal to unity whenever they can. For instance, they might talk of a circle of unit diameter. In such a circle, the length of the perimeter is numerically equal to the ratio of perimeter to diameter. (This is obvious to some of you, I suppose, and the rest of you can take my word for it.) Since in a circle of unit diameter the perimeter equals the ratio, the ratio can be symbolized by π, the symbol of the perimeter. And since circles of unit diameter are very frequently dealt with, the habit becomes quickly ingrained.

The first top-flight man to use π as the symbol for the ratio of the length of a circle's perimeter to the length of its diameter was the Swiss mathematician Leonhard Euler, in 1737, and what was good enough for Euler was good enough for everyone else.

Now I can go back to calling the distance around a circle the circumference.

But what *is* the ratio of the circumference of a circle to its diameter in actual numbers?

This apparently is a question that always concerned the ancients even long before pure mathematics was invented. In any kind of construction past the hen-coop stage you must calculate in advance all sorts of measurements, if you are not perpetually to be calling out to some underling, "You nut, these beams are all half a foot too short." In order to make the measurements, the universe being what it is, you are forever having to use the value of π in multiplication. Even when you're not dealing with circles, but only with angles (and you can't avoid angles) you will bump into π.

Presumably, the first empirical calculators who realized that the ratio was important, determined the ratio by drawing a circle and actually measuring the length of the diameter and the circumference. Of course, measuring the length of the circumference is a tricky problem that can't be handled by the usual wooden foot-rule, which is far too inflexible for the purpose.

What the pyramid-builders and their predecessors probably did was to lay a linen cord along the circumference very carefully, make a little mark at the point where the circumference was completed, then straighten the line and measure it with the equivalent of a wooden foot-rule. (Modern theoretical mathematicians frown at this and make haughty remarks such as "But you are making the unwarranted assumption that the line is the same length when it is straight as when it was curved." I imagine the honest workman organizing the construction of the local temple, faced with such an objection, would have solved matters by throwing the objector into the river Nile.)

Anyway, by drawing circles of different size and making enough measurements, it undoubtedly dawned upon architects and artisans, very early in the game, that the ratio was always the same in all circles. In other words, if one circle had a diameter twice as long or 1 5/8 as long as the diameter of a second, it would also have a circumference twice as long or 1 5/8 as long. The problem boiled down, then, to finding not the ratio of the particular circle you were interested in using, but a universal ratio that would hold for all circles for all time. Once someone had the value of π in his head, he would never have to determine the ratio again for any circle.

As to the actual value of the ratio, as determined by measurement, that depended, in ancient times, on the care taken by the person making the measurement and on the value he placed on accuracy in the abstract. The ancient Hebrews, for instance, were not much in the way of construction engineers, and when the time came for them to build their one important building (Solomon's temple), they had to call in a Phoenician architect.

It is to be expected, then, that the Hebrews in describing the temple would use round figures only, seeing no point in stupid and troublesome fractions, and refusing to be bothered with such petty and niggling matters when the House of God was in question.

Thus, in Chapter 4 of 2 Chronicles, they describe a "molten sea" which was included in the temple and which was, presumably, some sort of container in circular form. The beginning of the description is in the second verse of that chapter and reads: "Also he made a molten sea of ten cubits from brim to brim, round in compass, and five cubits the height thereof; and a line of thirty cubits did compass it round about."

The Hebrews, you see, did not realize that in giving the diameter of a circle (as ten cubits or as anything else) they automatically gave the circumference as well. They felt it necessary to specify the circumference as thirty cubits and in so doing revealed the fact that they considered $\pi$ to be equal to exactly 3.

There is always the danger that some individuals, too wedded to the literal words of the Bible, may consider 3 to be the divinely ordained value of $\pi$ in consequence. I wonder if this may not have been the motive of the simple soul in some state legislature who, some years back, introduced a bill which would have made $\pi$ legally equal to 3 inside the bounds of the state. Fortunately, the bill did not pass or all the wheels in that state (which would, of course, have respected the laws of the state's august legislators) would have turned hexagonal.

In any case, those ancients who were architecturally sophisticated knew well, from their measurements, that the value of $\pi$ was distinctly more than 3. The best value they had was $22/7$ (or $3 1/7$, if you prefer) which really isn't bad and is still used to this day for quick approximations.

Decimally, $22/7$ is equal, roughly, to $3.142857$ . . . , while $\pi$ is equal, roughly, to $3.141592$. . . . Thus, $22/7$ is high by only 0.04 percent or 1 part in 2500. Good enough for most rule-of-thumb purposes.

Then along came the Greeks and developed a system of geometry that would have none of this vile lay-down-a-string-and-measure-it-with-a-ruler business. That, obviously, gave values that were only as good as the ruler and the string and the human eye, all of which were dreadfully imperfect. Instead, the Greeks went about deducing what the value of $\pi$ must be once the perfect lines and curves of the ideal plane geometry they had invented were taken properly into account.

Archimedes of Syracuse, for instance, used the "method of exhaustion" (a forerunner of integral calculus, which Archimedes might have invented two thousand years before Newton if some kind benefactor of later centuries had only sent him the Arabic numerals via a time machine) to calculate $\pi$.

To get the idea, imagine an equilateral triangle with its vertexes on the circumference of a circle of unit diameter. Ordinary geometry suffices to calculate exactly the perimeter of that triangle. It comes out to $3\sqrt{8}/2$, if you are curious, or 2.598076. . . . This perimeter has to be less than that of the circle (that is, than the value of $\pi$), again by elementary geometrical reasoning.

Next, imagine the arcs between the vertexes of the triangle divided in two so that a regular hexagon (a six-sided figure) can be inscribed in the circle. Its perimeter can be determined also (it is exactly 3) and this can be shown to be larger than that of the triangle but still less than that of the circle. By proceeding to do this over and over again, a regular polygon with 12, 24, 48 . . . sides can be inscribed.

The space between the polygon and the boundary of the circle is steadily decreased or "exhausted" and the polygon approaches as close to the circle as you wish, though it never really reaches it. You can do the same with a series of equilateral polygons that circumscribe the circle (that lay outside it, that is, with their sides tangent to the circle) and get a series of decreasing values that approach the circumference of the circle.

In essence, Archimedes trapped the circumference between a series of numbers that approached $\pi$ from below, and another that approached it from above. In this way $\pi$ could be determined with any degree of exactness, provided you were patient enough to bear the tedium of working with polygons of large numbers of sides.

Archimedes found the time and patience to work with polygons of ninety-six sides and was able to show that the value of $\pi$ was a little below 22/7 and a little above the slightly smaller fraction 223/71.

Now the average of these two fractions is 3,123/994 and the decimal equivalent of that is 3.141851. . . . This is more than the true value of $\pi$ by only 0.0082 percent or 1 part in 12,500.

Nothing better than this was obtained, in Europe, at least, until the sixteenth century. It was then that the fraction 355/113 was first used as an approximation of $\pi$. This is really the best approximation of $\pi$ that can be expressed as a reasonably simple

fraction. The decimal value of 355/113 is 3.14159292 . . . , while
the true value of $\pi$ is 3.14159265. . . . You can see from that
that 355/113 is higher than the true value by only 0.000008 percent, or by one part in 12,500,000.

Just to give you an idea of how good an approximation 355/113
is, let's suppose that the Earth were a perfect sphere with a
diameter of exactly 8,000 miles. We could then calculate the
length of the equator by multiplying 8,000 by $\pi$. Using the approximation 355/113 for $\pi$, the answer comes out 25,132.7433
. . . miles. The true value of $\pi$ would give the answer
25,132.7412 . . . miles. The difference would come to about
11 feet. A difference of 11 feet in calculating the circumference
of the Earth might well be reckoned as negligible. Even the
artificial satellites that have brought our geography to new
heights of precision haven't supplied us with measurements
within that range of accuracy.

It follows then that for anyone but mathematicians, 355/113 is as
close to $\pi$ as it is necessary to get under any but the most unusual
circumstances. And yet mathematicians have their own point of
view. They can't be happy without the true value. As far as they
are concerned, a miss, however close, is as bad as a megaparsec.

The key step toward the true value was taken by François
Vieta, a French mathematician of the sixteenth century. He is
considered the father of algebra because, among other things,
he introduced the use of letter symbols for unknowns, the famous $x$'s and $y$'s, which most of us have had to, at one time or
another in our lives, face with trepidation and uncertainty.

Vieta performed the algebraic equivalent of Archimedes' geometric method of exhaustion. That is, instead of setting up an
infinite series of polygons that came closer and closer to a circle,
he deduced an infinite series of fractions which could be evalu-
ated to give a figure for $\pi$. The greater the number of terms used
in the evaluation, the closer you were to the true value of $\pi$.

I won't give you Vieta's series here because it involves square
roots and the square roots of square roots and the square roots
of square roots of square roots. There is no point in involving
one's self in that when other mathematicians derived other series

of terms (always an infinite series) for the evaluation of π; series much easier to write.

For instance, in 1673 the German mathematician Gottfried Wilhelm von Leibniz derived a series which can be expressed as follows:

$$\pi = \frac{4}{1} - \frac{4}{3} + \frac{4}{5} - \frac{4}{7} + \frac{4}{9} - \frac{4}{11} + \frac{4}{13} - \frac{4}{15} \ldots$$

Being a naïve nonmathematician myself, with virtually no mathematical insight worth mentioning, I thought, when I first decided to write this essay, that I would use the Leibniz series to dash off a short calculation and show you how it would give π easily to a dozen places or so. However, shortly after beginning, I quit.

You may scorn my lack of perseverance, but any of you are welcome to evaluate the Leibniz series just as far as it is written above, to $\frac{4}{15}$, that is. You can even drop me a postcard and tell me the result. If, when you finish, you are disappointed to find that your answer isn't as close to π as the value of $\frac{355}{113}$, don't give up. Just add more terms. Add $\frac{4}{17}$ to your answer, then subtract $\frac{4}{19}$, then add $\frac{4}{21}$ and subtract $\frac{4}{23}$, and so on. You can go on as long as you want to, and if any of you find out how many terms it takes to improve on $\frac{355}{113}$, drop me a line and tell me that, too.

Of course, all this may disappoint you. To be sure, the endless series *is* a mathematical representation of the true and exact value of π. To a mathematician, it is as valid a way as any to express that value. But if you want it in the form of an actual number, how does it help you? It isn't even practical to sum up a couple of dozen terms for anyone who wants to go about the ordinary business of living; how, then, can it be possible to sum up an infinite number?

Ah, but mathematicians do not give up on the sum of a series just because the number of terms in it is unending. For instance, the series:

$$\frac{1}{2} + \frac{1}{4} + \frac{1}{8} + \frac{1}{16} + \frac{1}{32} + \frac{1}{64} \ldots$$

can be summed up, using successively more and more terms. If you do this, you will find that the more terms you use, the closer you get to 1, and you can express this in shorthand form by saying that the sum of that infinite number of terms is merely 1 after all.

There is a formula, in fact, that can be used to determine the sum of any decreasing geometric progression, of which the above is an example. Thus, the series:

$$3/10 + 3/100 + 3/1,000 + 3/10,000 + 3/100,000 \ldots$$

adds up, in all its splendidly infinite numbers, to a mere 1/3, and the series:

$$1/2 + 1/20 + 1/200 + 1/2,000 + 1/20,000 \ldots$$

adds up to 5/9.

To be sure, the series worked out for the evaluation of $\pi$ are none of them decreasing geometric progressions, and so the formula cannot be used to evaluate the sum. In fact, no formula has ever been found to evaluate the sum of the Leibniz series or any of the others. Nevertheless, there seemed no reason at first to suppose that there might not be some way of finding a decreasing geometric progression that would evaluate $\pi$. If so, $\pi$ would then be expressible as a fraction. A fraction is actually the ratio of two numbers and anything expressible as a fraction, or ratio, is a "rational number." The hope, then, was that $\pi$ might be a rational number.

One way of proving that a quantity is a rational number is to work out its value decimally as far as you can (by adding up more and more terms of an infinite series, for instance) and then show the result to be a "repeating decimal"; that is, a decimal in which digits or some group of digits repeat themselves endlessly.

For instance, the decimal value of 1/3 is 0.33333333333 . . . , while that of 1/7 is 0.142857 142857 142857 . . . , and so on endlessly. Even a fraction such as 1/8 which seems to "come out even" is really a repeating decimal if you count zeros, since its decimal equivalent is 0.125000000000. . . . It can be proved mathematically that every fraction, however complicated, can be expressed as a decimal which sooner or later becomes a repeating one. Conversely, any decimal which ends by becoming a repeating one, however involved the repetitive cycle, can be expressed as an exact fraction.

Take any repeating decimal at random, say 0.373737373737373737. . . . First, you can make a decreasing geometrical progression out of it by writing it as:

$$37/100 + 37/10{,}000 + 37/1{,}000{,}000 + 37/100{,}000{,}000 \ldots$$

and you can then use the formula to work out its sum, which comes out to 37/99. (Work out the decimal equivalent of that fraction and see what you get.)

Or suppose you have a decimal which starts out nonrepetitively and then becomes repetitive, such as 15.21655555555555. . . . This can be written as:

$$15 + 216/1{,}000 + 5/10{,}000 + 5/100{,}000 + 5/1{,}000{,}000 \ldots$$

From 5/10,000 on, we have a decreasing geometric progression and its sum works out to be 5/9,000. So the series becomes a finite one made out of exactly three terms and no more, and can be summed easily:

$$15 + 216/1{,}000 + 5/90{,}000 = 136{,}949/9{,}000$$

If you wish, work out the decimal equivalent of 136,949/9,000 and see what you get.

Well, then, if the decimal equivalent of π were worked out for a number of decimal places and some repetition were discovered in it, however slight and however complicated, provided it could be shown to go on endlessly, a new series could be written to express its exact value. This new series would conclude with a decreasing geometric progression which could be summed. There would then be a finite series and the true value of π could be expressed not as a series but as an actual number.

Mathematicians threw themselves into the pursuit. In 1593 Vieta himself used his own series to calculate π to seventeen decimal places. Here it is, if you want to stare at it: 3.14159265358979323. As you see, there are no apparent repetitions of any kind.

Then in 1615 the German mathematician Ludolf von Ceulen used an infinite series to calculate π to thirty-five places. He found no signs of repetitiveness, either. However, this was so impressive a feat for his time that he won a kind of fame, for π is sometimes called "Ludolf's number" in consequence, at least in German textbooks.

And then in 1717 the English mathematician Abraham Sharp went Ludolf several better by finding π to seventy-two decimal places. Still no sign of repeating.

But shortly thereafter, the game was spoiled.

To prove a quantity is rational, you have to present the fraction to which it is equivalent and display it. To prove it is irrational, however, you need not necessarily work out a single decimal place. What you must do is to *suppose* that the quantity can be expressed by a fraction, *p/q*, and then demonstrate that this involves a contradiction, such as that *p* must at the same time be even and odd. This would prove that no fraction could express the quantity, which would therefore be irrational.

Exactly this sort of proof was developed by the ancient Greeks to show that the square root of 2 was an irrational number (the first irrational ever discovered). The Pythagoreans were supposed to have been the first to discover this and to have been so appalled at finding that there could be quantities that could not be expressed by any fraction, however complicated, that they swore themselves to secrecy and provided a death penalty for snitching. But like all scientific secrets, from irrationals to atom bombs, the information leaked out anyway.

Well, in 1761 a German physicist and mathematician Johann Heinrich Lambert finally proved that π was irrational. Therefore, no pattern at all was to be expected, no matter how slight and no matter how many decimal places were worked out. The true value can *only* be expressed as an infinite series.

Alas!

But shed no tears. Once π was proved irrational, mathematicians were satisfied. The problem was over. And as for the application of π to physical calculations, that problem was over and done with, too. You may think that sometimes in very delicate calculations it might be necessary to know π to a few dozen or even to a few hundred places, but not so! The delicacy of scientific measurements is wonderful these days, but still there are few that approach, say, one part in a billion, and for anything that accurate which involves the use of π, nine or ten decimal places would be ample.

For example, suppose you drew a circle ten billion miles across, with the Sun at the center, for the purpose of enclosing the entire Solar System, and suppose you wanted to calculate the length of the circumference of this circle (which would come to over thirty-one billion miles) by using 355/113 as the approximate value of π. You would be off by less than three thousand miles.

But suppose you were so precise an individual that you found an error of three thousand miles in 31,000,000,000 to be insupportable. You might then use Ludolf's value of π to thirty-five places. You would then be off by a distance that would be equivalent to a millionth of the diameter of a proton.

Or let's take a *big* circle, say the circumference of the known universe. Large radio telescopes under construction will, it is hoped, receive signals from a distance as great as 40,000,000,-000 light-years. A circle about a universe with such a radius would have a length of, roughly, 150,000,000,000,000,000,000,-000 (150 sextillion) miles. If the length of this circumference were calculated by Ludolf's value of π to thirty-five places, it would be off by less than a millionth of an inch.

What can one say then about Sharp's value of π to seventy-two places?

Obviously, the value of π, as known by the time its irrationality was proven, was already far beyond the accuracy that could conceivably be demanded by science, now or in the future.

And yet with the value of π no longer needed for scientists, past what had already been determined, people nevertheless continued their calculations through the first half of the nineteenth century.

A fellow called George Vega got π to 140 places, another called Zacharias Dase did it to 200 places, and someone called Recher did it to 500 places.

Finally, in 1873, William Shanks reported the value of π to 707 places, and that, until 1949, was the record—and small wonder. It took Shanks fifteen years to make the calculation and, for what that's worth, no signs of any repetitiveness showed up.

We can wonder about the motivation that would cause a man

to spend fifteen years on a task that can serve no purpose. Perhaps it is the same mental attitude that will make a man sit on a flagpole or swallow goldfish in order to "break a record." Or perhaps Shanks saw this as his one road to fame.

If so, he made it. Histories of mathematics, in among their descriptions of the work of men like Archimedes, Fermat, Newton, Euler, and Gauss, will also find room for a line to the effect that William Shanks in the years preceding 1873 calculated π to 707 decimal places. So perhaps he felt that his life had not been wasted.

But alas, for human vanity—

In 1949 the giant computers were coming into their own, and occasionally the young fellows at the controls, full of fun and life and beer, could find time to play with them.

So, on one occasion, they pumped one of the unending series into the machine called ENIAC and had it calculate the value of π. They kept it at the task for seventy hours, and at the end of that time they had the value of π (shades of Shanks!) to 2035 places.*

And to top it all off for poor Shanks and his fifteen wasted years, an error was found in the five hundred umpty-umpth digit of Shanks' value, so that all the digits after that, well over a hundred, were *wrong!*

And of course, in case you're wondering, and you shouldn't, the values as determined by computers showed no signs of any repetitiveness either.

## AFTERWORD

Naturally, some of my essays go out of date to a greater or lesser extent. At the time I first wrote the foregoing essay, "pi" had been calculated to ten thousand places, as I pointed out.

Mathematicians, however, didn't stop there. By 1988, the world had computers that were much faster and more capable than the pipsqueaks of the late 1950s. In early 1988, a Japanese

---

* By 1955 a faster computer calculated π to 10,017 places in thirty-three hours and, actually, there *are* interesting mathematical points to be derived from studying the various digits of π.

computer scientist named Yasumasa Kanada, of the University of Tokyo, ran a supercomputer for six hours and came up with a value of "pi" to 201,326,000 places.

Why bother, since the decimal representation of "pi" has no end and additional places don't teach you anything important mathematically? Well, for one thing, it's a convenient way of testing a new computer or a new program. Once you have definitely established a couple of hundred million places, then you can set any computer with a new program to calculating "pi." If it makes even the slightest mistake, there is a glitch either in its circuits or in the program.

# 3

# Heaven on Earth

The nicest thing about writing these essays is the constant mental exercise it gives me. Unceasingly, I must keep my eyes and ears open for anything that will spark something that will, in my opinion, be of interest to the reader.

For instance, a letter arrived today, asking about the duodecimal system, where one counts by twelves rather than by tens, and this set up a mental chain reaction that ended in astronomy and, what's more, gave me a notion which, as far as I know, is original with me. Here's how it happened.

My first thought was that, after all, the duodecimal system is used in odd corners. For instance, we say that 12 objects make 1 dozen and 12 dozen make 1 gross. However, as far as I know, 12 has never been used as the base for a number system, except by mathematicians in play.

A number which has, on the other hand, been used as the base for a formal positional notation is 60. The ancient Babylonians used 10 as a base just as we do, but frequently used 60 as an alternate base. In a number based on 60, what we call the units column would contain any number from 1 to 59, while what we call the tens column would be the "sixties" column, and our hundreds column (ten times ten) would be the "thirty-six hundred" column (sixty times sixty).

Thus, when we write a number, 123, what it really stands for is $(1 \times 10^2) + (2 \times 10^1) + (3 \times 10^0)$. And since $10^2$ equals 100, $10^1$ equals 10 and $10^0$ equals 1, the total is $100 + 20 + 3$ or, as aforesaid, 123.

But if the Babylonians wrote the equivalent of 123, using 60 as the base, it would mean $(1 \times 60^2) + (2 \times 60^1) + (3 \times 60^0)$. And since $60^2$ equals 3,600, $60^1$ equals 60 and $60^0$ equals 1, this works out to $3,600 + 120 + 3$, or 3,723 by our decimal notation. Using a positional notation with the base 60 is a "sexagesimal notation" from the Latin word for sixtieth.

As the word "sixtieth" suggests, the sexagesimal notation can be carried into fractions too.

Our own decimal notation will allow us to use a figure such as 0.156, where what is really meant is $0 + \frac{1}{10} + \frac{5}{100} + \frac{6}{1,000}$. The denominators, you see, go up the scale in multiples of 10. In the sexagesimal scale, the denominators would go up the scale in multiples of 60 and 0.156 would represent $0 + \frac{1}{60} + \frac{5}{3,600} + \frac{6}{216,000}$, since 3,600 equals $60 \times 60$, 216,000 equals $60 \times 60 \times 60$, and so on.

Those of you who know all about exponential notation will no doubt be smugly aware that $\frac{1}{10}$ can be written $10^{-1}$, $\frac{1}{100}$ can be written $10^{-2}$ and so on, while $\frac{1}{60}$ can be written $60^{-1}$, $\frac{1}{3,600}$ can be written $60^{-2}$ and so on. Consequently, a full number expressed in sexagesimal notation would be something like this: (15) (45) (2). (17) (25) (59), or $(15 \times 60^2) + (45 \times 60^1) + (2 \times 60^0) + (17 \times 60^{-1}) + (25 \times 60^{-2}) + (59 \times 60^{-3})$, and if you want to amuse yourself by working out the equivalent in ordinary decimal notation, please do. As for me, I'm chickening out right now.

All this would be of purely academic interest, if it weren't for the fact that we still utilize sexagesimal notation in at least two important ways, which date back to the Greeks.

The Greeks had a tendency to pick up the number 60 from the Babylonians as a base, where computations were complicated, since so many numbers go evenly into 60 that fractions are avoided as often as possible (and who wouldn't avoid fractions as often as possible?).

One theory, for instance, is that the Greeks divided the radius of a circle into 60 equal parts so that in dealing with half a radius, or a third, or a fourth, or a fifth, or a sixth, or a tenth (and so on) they could always express it as a whole number of sixtieths. Then, since in ancient days the value of π (pi) was often set equal to a rough and ready 3, and since the length of the circumference of a circle is equal to twice π times the radius, the length of that circumference is equal to 6 times the radius or to 360 sixtieths of a radius. Thus (perhaps) began the custom of dividing a circle into 360 equal parts.

Another possible reason for doing so rests with the fact that the Sun completes its circuit of the stars in a little over 365 days, so that in each day it moves about 1/365 of the way around the sky. Well, the ancients weren't going to quibble about a few days here and there and 360 is so much easier to work with that they divided the circuit of the sky into that many divisions and considered the Sun as traveling through one of those parts (well, just about) each day.

A 360th of a circle is called a "degree" from Latin words meaning "step down." If the Sun is viewed as traveling down a long circular stairway, it takes one step down (well, just about) each day.

Each degree, if we stick with the sexagesimal system, can be divided into 60 smaller parts and each of those smaller parts into 60 still smaller parts and so on. The first division was called in Latin *pars minuta prima* (first small part) and the second was called *pars minuta secunda* (second small part), which have been shortened in English to minutes and seconds respectively.

We symbolize the degree by a little circle (naturally), the minute by a single stroke, and the second by a double stroke, so that when we say that the latitude of a particular spot on Earth is 39° 17′ 42″, we are saying that its distance from the equator is 39 degrees plus 17/60 of a degree plus 42/3,600 of a degree, and isn't that the sexagesimal system?

The second place where sexagesimals are still used is in measuring time (which was originally based on the movements of heavenly bodies). Thus we divide the hour into minutes and seconds and when we speak of a duration of 1 hour, 44 minutes, and 20 seconds, we are speaking of a duration of 1 hour plus 44/60 of an hour plus 20/3600 of an hour.

You can carry the system further than the second and, in the Middle Ages, Arabic astronomers often did. There is a record of one who divided one sexagesimal fraction into another and carried out the quotient to ten sexagesimal places, which is the equivalent of 17 decimal places.

Now let's take sexagesimal fractions for granted, and let's consider next the value of breaking up circumferences of circles into a fixed number of pieces. And, in particular, consider the circle of the ecliptic along which the Sun, Moon, and planets trace their path in the sky.

After all, how *does* one go about measuring a distance along the sky? One can't very well reach up with a tape measure. Instead the system, essentially, is to draw imaginary lines from the two ends of the distance traversed along the ecliptic (or along any other circular arc, actually) to the center of the circle, where we can imagine our eye to be, and to measure the angle made by those two lines.

The value of this system is hard to explain without a diagram, but I shall try to do so, with my usual dauntless bravery (though you're welcome to draw one as I go along, just in case I turn out to be hopelessly confusing).

Suppose you have a circle with a diameter of 115 feet, and another circle drawn about the same center with a diameter of 230 feet, and still another drawn about the same center with a diameter of 345 feet. (These are "concentric circles" and would look like a target.)

The circumference of the innermost circle would be about 360 feet, that of the middle one 720 feet and that of the outermost 1,080 feet.

Now mark off 1/360 of the innermost circle's circumference, a length of arc 1 foot long, and from the two ends of the arc draw lines to the center. Since 1/360 of the circumference is 1 degree, the angle formed at the center may be called 1 degree also (particularly since 360 such arcs will fill the entire circumference and 360 such central angles will consequently fill the entire space about the center).

If the 1-degree angle is now extended outwards so that the arms cut across the two outer circles, they will subtend a 2-foot arc of the middle circle and a 3-foot circle of the outer one. The arms diverge just enough to match the expanding circumference. The lengths of the arc will be different, but the fraction of the circle subtended will be the same. A 1-degree angle with vertex at the center of a circle will subtend a 1-degree arc of the circumference of any circle, regardless of its diameter, whether it is the circle bounding a proton or bounding the Universe (if we assume a Euclidean geometry, I quickly add). The same is analogously true for an angle of any size.

Suppose your eye was at the center of a circle that had two marks upon it. The two marks are separated by 1/6 the circumference of the circle, that is by 360/6 or 60 degrees of arc. If you imagine a line drawn from the two marks to your eye, the lines will form an angle of 60 degrees. If you look first at one mark, then at the other you will have to swivel your eyes through an angle of 60 degrees.

And it wouldn't matter, you see, whether the circle was a mile from your eye or a trillion miles. If the two marks were 1/6 of the circumference apart, they would be 60 degrees apart, regardless of distance. How nice to use such a measure, then, when you haven't the faintest idea of how far away the circle is.

So, since through most of man's history astronomers had no notion of the distance of the heavenly objects in the sky, angular measure was just the thing.

And if you think it isn't, try making use of linear measure. The average person, asked to estimate the diameter of the full Moon *in appearance,* almost instinctively makes use of linear measure. He is liable to reply, judiciously, "Oh, about a foot."

But as soon as he makes use of linear measure, he is setting a specific distance, whether he knows it or not. For an object a foot across to look as large as the full Moon, it would have to be 36 yards away. I doubt that anyone who judges the Moon to be a foot wide will also judge it to be no more than 36 yards distant.

If we stick to angular measure and say that the average width of the full Moon is 31' (minutes), we are making no judgments as to distance and are safe.

But if we're going to insist on using angular measure, with which the general population is unacquainted, it becomes necessary to find some way of making it clear to everyone. The most common way of doing this, and to picture the Moon's size, for instance, is to take some common circle with which we are all acquainted and calculate the distance at which it must be held to look as large as the Moon.

One such circle is that of the twenty-five-cent piece. Its diameter is about 0.96 inches and we won't be far off if we consider it just an inch in diameter. If a quarter is held 9 feet from the eye, it will subtend an arc of 31 minutes. That means it will look just as large as the full Moon does, and, if it is held at that distance between your eye and the full Moon, it will just cover it.

Now if you've never thought of this, you will undoubtedly be surprised that a quarter at 9 feet (which you must imagine will look quite small) can overlap the full Moon (which you probably think of as quite large). To which I can only say: Try the experiment!

Well, this sort of thing will do for the Sun and the Moon but these, after all, are, of all the heavenly bodies, the largest in appearance. In fact, they're the only ones (barring an occasional comet) that show a visible disc. All other objects are measured in fractions of a minute or even fractions of a second.

It is easy enough to continue the principle of comparison by saying that a particular planet or star has the apparent diameter of a quarter held at a distance of a mile or ten miles or a hundred miles and this is, in fact, what is generally done. But of what use is that? You can't see a quarter at all, at such distances, and you can't picture its size. You're just substituting one unvisionable measure for another.

There must be some better way of doing it.

And at this point in my thoughts, I had my original (I hope) idea.

Suppose that the Earth were exactly the size it is but were a huge hollow, smooth, transparent sphere. And suppose you were viewing the skies not from Earth's surface, but with your eye precisely at Earth's center. You would then see all the heavenly objects projected onto the sphere of the Earth.

In effect, it would be as though you were using the entire globe of the Earth as a background on which to paint a replica of the celestial sphere.

The value of this is that the terrestrial globe is the one sphere upon which we can easily picture angular measurement, since we have all learned about latitude and longitude which *are* angular measurements. On the Earth's surface, 1 degree is equal to 69 miles (with minor variations, which we can ignore, because of the fact that the Earth is not a perfect sphere). Consequently, 1 minute, which is equal to 1/60 of a degree, is equal to 1.15 miles or to 6,060 feet, and 1 second, which is equal to 1/60 of a minute, is equal to 101 feet.

You see, then, that if we know the apparent angular diameter of a heavenly body, we know exactly what its diameter would be if it were drawn on the Earth's surface to scale.

The Moon, for instance, with an average diameter of 31 minutes by angular measure, would be drawn with a diameter of 36 miles, if painted to scale on the Earth's surface. It would neatly cover all of Greater New York or the space between Boston and Worcester.

Your first impulse may be a "WHAT!" but this is not really as large as it seems. Remember, you are really viewing this scale model from the center of the Earth, four thousand miles from the surface, and just ask yourself how large Greater New York would seem, seen from a distance of 4,000 miles. Or look at a globe of the Earth, if you have one and picture a circle with a diameter stretching from Boston to Worcester and you will see that it is small indeed compared to the whole surface of the Earth, just as the Moon itself is small indeed compared to the whole surface of the sky. (Actually, it would take the area of 490,000 bodies the size of the Moon to fill the entire sky, and 490,000 bodies the size of our painted Moon to fill all of the Earth's surface.)

But at least this shows the magnifying effect of the device I am proposing, and it comes in particularly handy where bodies smaller in appearance than the Sun or the Moon are concerned, just at the point where the quarter-at-a-distance-of-so-many-miles notion breaks down.

For instance, in Table 1, I present the maximum angular diameters of the various planets as seen at the time of their closest approach to Earth, together with their linear diameter to scale if drawn on Earth's surface.

I omit Pluto because its angular diameter is not well known. However, if we assume that planet to be about the size of Mars, then at its furthest point in its orbit, it will still have an angular diameter of 0.2 seconds and can be presented as a circle 20 feet in diameter.

TABLE 1    Planets to Scale

| Planet | Angular diameter (SECONDS) | Linear diameter (FEET) |
|--------|------------------|-----------------|
| Mercury | 12.7 | 1,280 |
| Venus | 64.5 | 6,510 |
| Mars | 25.1 | 2,540 |
| Jupiter | 50.0 | 5,050 |
| Saturn | 20.6 | 2,080 |
| Uranus | 4.2 | 425 |
| Neptune | 2.4 | 240 |

Each planet could have its satellites drawn to scale with great convenience. For instance, the four large satellites of Jupiter would be circles ranging from 110 to 185 feet in diameter, set at distances of 3 to 14 miles from Jupiter. The entire Jovian system to the orbit of its outermost satellite (Jupiter IX, a circle about 5 inches in diameter) would cover a circle about 350 miles in diameter.

The real interest in such a setup, however, would be the stars. The stars, like the planets, do not have a visible disc to the eyes. Unlike the planets, however, they do not have a visible disc even to the largest telescope. The planets (all but Pluto) can be blown up to discs even by moderate-sized telescopes; not so the stars.

By indirect methods the apparent angular diameter of some stars has been determined. For instance, the largest angular diameter of any star is probably that of Betelgeuse, which is

0.047 seconds. Even the huge 200-inch telescope cannot magnify that diameter more than a thousandfold, and under such magnification the largest star is still less than 1 minute of arc in appearance and is therefore no more of a disc to the 200-incher than Jupiter is to the unaided eye. And of course, most stars are far smaller in appearance than is giant Betelgeuse. (Even stars that are in actuality larger than Betelgeuse are so far away as to appear smaller.)

But on my Earth-scale, Betelgeuse with an apparent diameter of 0.047 seconds of arc would be represented by a circle about 4.7 feet in diameter. (Compare that with the 20 feet of even distantest Pluto.)

However, it's no use trying to get actual figures on angular diameters because these have been measured for very few stars. Instead, let's make the assumption that all the stars have the same intrinsic brightness the Sun has. (This is not so, of course, but the Sun is an average star, and so the assumption won't radically change the appearance of the universe.)

Now then, area for area, the Sun (or any star) remains at constant brightness to the eye regardless of distance. If the Sun were moved out to twice its present distance, its apparent brightness would decrease by four times but so would its apparent surface area. What we could see of its area would be just as bright as it ever was; there would be less of it, that's all.

The same is true the other way, too. Mercury, at its closest approach to the Sun, sees a Sun that is no brighter per square second than ours is, but it sees one with ten times as many square seconds as ours has, so that Mercury's Sun is ten times as bright as ours.

Well, then, if all the stars were as luminous as the Sun, then the apparent area would be directly proportional to the apparent brightness. We know the magnitude of the Sun (−26.72) as well as the magnitudes of the various stars, and that gives us our scale of comparative brightness, from which we can work out a scale of comparative areas and, therefore, comparative diameters. Furthermore, since we know the angular measure of the Sun, we can use the comparative diameters to calculate the comparative angular measures which, of course, we can convert to linear diameters (to scale) on the Earth.

But never mind the details (you've probably skipped the previous paragraph already), I'll give you the results in Table 2.

(The fact that Betelgeuse has an apparent diameter of 0.047 and yet is no brighter than Altair is due to the fact that Betelgeuse, a red giant, has a lower temperature than the Sun and is much dimmer per unit area in consequence. Remember that Table 2 is based on the assumption that all stars are as luminous as the Sun.)

So you see what happens once we leave the Solar System. Within that system, we have bodies that must be drawn to scale in yards and miles. Outside the system, we deal with bodies which, to scale, range in mere inches.

TABLE 2   Stars to Scale

| Magnitude of star | Angular diameter (SECONDS) | Linear diameter (INCHES) |
|---|---|---|
| −1 (e.g. Sirius) | 0.014 | 17.0 |
| 0 (e.g. Rigel) | 0.0086 | 10.5 |
| 1 (e.g. Altair) | 0.0055 | 6.7 |
| 2 (e.g. Polaris) | 0.0035 | 4.25 |
| 3 | 0.0022 | 2.67 |
| 4 | 0.0014 | 1.70 |
| 5 | 0.00086 | 1.05 |
| 6 | 0.00055 | 0.67 |

If you imagine such small patches of Earth's surface, as seen from the Earth's center, I think you will get a new vision as to how small the stars are in appearance and why telescopes cannot make visible discs of them.

The total number of stars visible to the naked eye is about 6,000, of which two thirds are dim stars of 5th and 6th magnitude. We might then picture the Earth as spotted with 6,000 stars, most of them being about an inch in diameter. There would be only a very occasional larger one; only 20, all told, that would be as much as 6 inches in diameter.

The average distance between two stars on Earth's surface would be 180 miles. There would be one or, at most, two stars in New York State, and one hundred stars, more or less, within the territory of the United States (including Alaska).

The sky, you see, is quite uncrowded, regardless of its appearance.

Of course, these are only the visible stars. Through a telescope, myriads of stars too faint to be seen by the naked eye can be made out and the 200-inch telescope can photograph stars as dim as the 22nd magnitude.

A star of magnitude 22, drawn on the Earth to scale, would be a mere 0.0004 inches in diameter, or about the size of a bacterium. (Seeing a shining bacterium on Earth's surface from a vantage point at Earth's center, 4,000 miles down, is a dramatic indication of the power of the modern telescope.)

The number of individual stars visible down to this magnitude would be roughly two billion. (There are, of course, at least a hundred billion stars in our Galaxy, but almost all of them are located in the Galactic nucleus, which is completely hidden from our sight by dust clouds. The two billion we do see are just the scattering in our own neighborhood of the spiral arms.)

Drawn to scale on the Earth, this means that among the 6,000 circles we have already drawn (mostly an inch in diameter) we must place a powdering of two billion more dots, a small proportion of which are still large enough to see, but most of which are microscopic in size.

The average distance between stars even after this mighty powdering would still be, on the Earth-scale, 1,700 feet.

This answers a question I, for one, have asked myself in the past. Once a person looks at a photograph showing the myriad stars visible to a large telescope, he can't help wondering how it is possible to see beyond all that talcum powder and observe the outer galaxies.

Well, you see, despite the vast numbers of stars, the clear space between them is still comparatively huge. In fact, it has been estimated that all the starlight that reaches us is equivalent to the light of 1,100 stars of magnitude 1. This means that if all the stars that can be seen were massed together, they would fill a circle (on Earth-scale) that would be 18.5 feet in diameter.

From this we can conclude that all the stars combined do not cover up as much of the sky as the planet Pluto. As a matter of fact, the Moon, all by itself, obscures nearly 300 times as much of the sky as do all other nighttime heavenly bodies, planets, satellites, planetoids, stars, put together.

There would be no trouble whatever in viewing the spaces outside our Galaxy if it weren't for the dust clouds. Those are really the only obstacle, and they can't be removed even if we set up a telescope in space.

What a pity the Universe couldn't really be projected on Earth's surface temporarily—just long enough to send out the Walrus's seven maids with seven mops with strict orders to give the Universe a thorough dusting.

How happy astronomers would then be!

## AFTERWORD

It's odd how imagination can stop short. In the foregoing essay, I had the really brilliant idea of mapping the heavens on the sphere of the Earth and having a new and startling way of understanding the comparative apparent sizes of heavenly bodies. (To be sure, no one has ever actually made use of the idea in any astronomy textbook, as far as I know—another one of my unsung pieces of ingenuity.)

On the other hand, I ended the piece by complaining about dust clouds and saying they prevent us from seeing what lies beyond them, and "they can't be removed even if we set up a telescope in space."

By 1961, of course, we had radio telescopes, for which dust clouds were no problem. Microwaves pass through the clouds as though they weren't there. However, radio telescopes, in those days, detected things much more fuzzily than optical telescopes did.

Unfortunately, I was unable to visualize the fact that a number of radio telescopes, widely separated, and maneuvered in unison by computerized methods would, in essence, behave like a single giant dish and would actually see matters *more* clearly and in *finer* detail than optical telescopes can. As a result, we can, for instance, study the radio wave activity of our Galactic center with enormous precision right through all the dust clouds that stand in the way.

# 4

# The Egg and Wee

Every once in a while, you will come across some remarks pointing up how much more compact the human brain is than is any electronic computer.

It is true that the human brain is a marvel of compactness in comparison to man-made thinking machines, but it is my feeling that this is not because of any fundamental difference in the nature of the mechanism of brain action as compared with that of computer action. Rather, I have the feeling that the difference is a matter of the size of the components involved.

The human cerebral cortex, it is estimated, is made up of 10,000,000,000 nerve cells. In comparison, the first modern electronic computer, ENIAC, had about 20,000 switching devices. I don't know how many the latest computers have, but I am quite certain they do not begin to approach a content of ten billion.

The marvel, then, is not so much the brain as the cell. Not only is the cell considerably smaller than any man-made unit incorporated into a machine, but it is far more flexible than any man-made unit. In addition to acting as an electronic switch or amplifier (or whatever it does in the brain), it is a complete chemical factory.

Furthermore, cells need not aggregate in fearfully large numbers in order to make up an organism. To be sure, the average man may contain 50,000,000,000,000 (fifty trillion) cells and the largest whale as many as 100,000,000,000,000,000 (a hundred quadrillion) cells, but these are exceptional. The smallest shrew contains only 7,000,000,000 cells, and small invertebrate creatures contain even less. The smallest invertebrates are made up of only one hundred cells or so, and yet fulfill all the functions of a living organism.

As a matter of fact (and I'm sure you're ahead of me here), there are living organisms that possess all the basic abilities of life and are nevertheless composed of but a single cell.

If we are going to concern ourselves with compactness, then, let's consider the cell and ask ourselves the questions: How compact can a living structure be? How small can an object be and still have the capacity for life?

To begin: How large is a cell?

There is no one answer to that, for there are cells and cells, and some are larger than others. Almost all are microscopic, but some are so large as to be clearly, and even unavoidably, visible to the unaided eye. Just to push it to an extreme, it is possible for a cell to be larger than your head.

The giants of the cellular world are the various egg cells produced by animals. The human egg cell (or ovum), for instance, is the largest cell produced by the human body (either sex), and it is just visible to the naked eye. It is about the size of a pinhead.

In order to make the size quantitative and compare the human ovum in reasonable fashion with other cells both larger and smaller, let's pick out a convenient measuring unit. The inch or even the millimeter (which is approximately 1/25.4 of an inch) is too large a unit for any cell except certain egg cells. Instead, therefore, I'm going to use the micron, which equals a thousandth of a millimeter or 1/25,400 of an inch. For volume, we will use a cubic micron, which is the volume of a cube one micron long on each side. This is a very tiny unit of volume, as you will understand when I tell you that a cubic inch (which is something that is easy to visualize) contains over 16,000,000,000,000,000 (sixteen trillion) cubic micra.

There are a third as many cubic micra in a cubic inch, then, as there are cells in a human body. That alone should tell us we have a unit of the right magnitude to handle cellular volumes.

Back to the egg cells then. The human ovum is a little sphere approximately 140 micra in diameter and therefore 70 micra in radius. Cubing 70 and multiplying the result by 4.18 (I will spare you both the rationale and the details of arithmetic manipulation), we find that the human ovum has a volume of a little over 1,400,000 cubic micra.

But the human ovum is by no means large for an egg cell. Creatures that lay eggs, birds in particular, do much better; and bird eggs, however large, are (to begin with, at least) single cells.

The largest egg ever laid by any bird was that of the extinct Aepyornis of Madagascar. This was also called the elephant bird, and may have given rise to the myth—so it is said—of the roc of the *Arabian Nights*. The roc was supposed to be so large that it could fly off with an elephant in one set of talons and a rhinoceros in the other. Its egg was the size of a house.

Actually, the Aepyornis was not quite that lyrically vast. It could not fly off with any animal, however small, for it could not fly at all. And its egg was considerably less than house-size. Nevertheless, the egg was nine and one-half inches wide and thirteen inches long and had a volume of two gallons, which is tremendous enough if you want to restrict yourself to the dullness of reality.

This is not only the largest egg ever laid by any bird, but it may be the largest ever laid by any creature, including the huge reptiles of the Mesozoic age, for the Aepyornis egg approached the maximum size that any egg, with a shell of calcium carbonate and without any internal struts or braces, can be expected to reach. If the Aepyornis egg is accepted as the largest egg, then it is also the largest cell of which there is any record.

To return to the here and now, the largest egg (and, therefore, cell) produced by any living creature is that of the ostrich. This is about six to seven inches in length and four to six inches in diameter; and, if you are interested, it takes forty minutes to hard-boil an ostrich egg. In comparison, a large hen's egg is about one and three-quarter inches wide and two and a half inches long. The smallest egg laid by a bird is that of a species of hummingbird which produces an egg that is half an inch long.

Now let's put these figures, very roughly, into terms of volume:

| *Egg* | *Volume (in cubic micra)* |
|---|---|
| Aepyornis | 7,500,000,000,000,000 |
| Ostrich | 1,100,000,000,000,000 |
| Hen | 50,000,000,000,000 |
| Hummingbird | 400,000,000,000 |
| Human being | 1,400,000 |

As you see, the range in egg size is tremendous. Even the smallest bird egg is about 300,000 times as voluminous as the human ovum, whereas the largest bird egg is nearly 20,000 times as large as the smallest.

In other words, the Aepyornis egg compares to the hummingbird egg as the largest whale compares to a medium-sized dog; while the hummingbird egg, in turn, compares to the human ovum as the largest whale compares to a large rat.

And yet, even though the egg consists of but one cell, it is not the kind of cell we can consider typical. For one thing, scarcely any of it is alive. The eggshell certainly isn't alive and the white of the egg serves only as a water store. The yolk of the egg makes up the true cell and even that is almost entirely food supply.

If we really want to consider the size of cells, let's tackle those that contain a food supply only large enough to last them from day to day—cells that are largely protoplasm, in other words. These non-yolk cells range from the limits of visibility downward, just as egg cells range from the limits of visibility upward.

In fact, there is some overlapping. For instance, the amoeba, a simple free-living organism consisting of a single cell, has a diameter of about two hundred micra and a volume of 4,200,000 cubic micra. It is three times as voluminous as the human ovum.

The cells that make up multicellular organisms are considerably smaller, however. The various cells of the human body have volumes varying from 200 to 15,000 cubic micra. A typical liver cell, for instance, would have a volume of 1,750 cubic micra.

If we include cell-like bodies that are not quite complete cells, then we can reach smaller volumes. For instance, the human red blood cell, which is incomplete in that it lacks a cell nucleus, is considerably smaller than the ordinary cells of the human body. It has a volume of only 90 cubic micra.

Then, just as the female ovum is the largest cell produced by human beings, the male spermatozoon is the smallest. The spermatozoon is mainly nucleus, and only half the nucleus at that. It has a volume of about 17 cubic micra.

This may make it seem to you that the cells making up a multicellular organism are simply too small to be individual and independent fragments of life, and that in order to be free-living a cell must be unusually large. After all, an amoeba is 2,400 times as large as a liver cell, so perhaps in going from amoeba to liver cell, we have passed the limit of compactness that can be associated with independent life.

This is not so, however. Human cells cannot, to be sure, serve as individual organisms, but that is only because they are too specialized and *not* because they are too small. There are cells that serve as independent organisms that are far smaller than the amoeba and even smaller than the human spermatozoon. These are the bacteria.

Even the largest bacterium has a volume of no more than 7 cubic micra, while the smallest have volumes down to 0.02 cubic micra. All this can be summarized as follows:

| *Non-yolk cell* | *Volume (in cubic micra)* |
| --- | --- |
| Amoeba | 4,200,000 |
| Human liver cell | 1,750 |
| Human red blood cell | 90 |
| Human spermatozoon | 17 |
| Largest bacterium | 7 |
| Smallest bacterium | 0.02 |

Again we have quite a range. A large one-celled organism such as the amoeba is to a small one-celled organism such as a midget bacterium, as the largest full-grown whale is to a half-grown specimen of the smallest variety of shrew. For that matter, the difference between the largest and smallest bacterium is that between a large elephant and a small boy.

Now, then, how on earth can the complexity of life be crammed into a tiny bacterium one two-hundred-millionth the size of a simple amoeba?

Again we are faced with a problem in compactness and we must pause to consider units. When we thought of a brain in terms of pounds, it was a small bit of tissue. When we thought of it in terms of cells, however, it became a tremendously complex assemblage of small units. In the same way, in considering cells, let's stop thinking in terms of cubic micra and start considering atoms and molecules.

A cubic micron of protoplasm contains about 40,000,000,000 molecules. Allowing for this, we can recast the last table in molecular terms:

| *Cell* | *Number of molecules* |
|---|---|
| Amoeba | 170,000,000,000,000,000 |
| Human liver cell | 70,000,000,000,000 |
| Human red blood cell | 3,600,000,000,000 |
| Human spermatozoon | 680,000,000,000 |
| Largest bacterium | 280,000,000,000 |
| Smallest bacterium | 800,000,000 |

It would be tempting, at this point, to say that the molecule is the unit of the cell, as the cell is the unit of a multicellular organism. If we say that, we can go on to maintain that the amoeba is seventeen million times as complicated, molecularly speaking, as the human brain is, cellularly speaking. In that case, the compactness of the amoeba as a container for life becomes less surprising.

There is a catch, though. Almost all the molecules in protoplasm are water; simple little $H_2O$ combinations. These are essential to life, goodness knows, but they serve largely as background. They are not *the* characteristic molecules of life. If we can point to any molecules as characteristic of life, they are the complex nitrogen-phosphorus macromolecules: the proteins, the nucleic acids and the phospholipids. These, together, make up only about one ten-thousandth of the molecules in living tissue.

(Now, I am *not* saying that these macromolecules make up only 1/10,000 of the *weight* of living tissue; only of the numbers of molecules. The macromolecules are individually much heavier than the water molecules. An average protein molecule, for instance, is some two thousand times as heavy as a water molecule. If a system consisted of two thousand water molecules and one average protein molecule, the *number* of protein molecules would only be 1/2,001 of the total, but the *weight* of protein would be 1/2 the total.)

Let's revise the table again, then:

| Cell | Nitrogen-Phosphorus macromolecules |
|---|---|
| Amoeba | 17,000,000,000,000 |
| Human liver cell | 7,000,000,000 |
| Human red blood cell | 360,000,000 |
| Human spermatozoon | 68,000,000 |
| Largest bacterium | 28,000,000 |
| Smallest bacterium | 80,000 |

We can say, then, that the average human body cell is indeed as complex, molecularly speaking, as the human brain, cellularly speaking. Bacteria, however, are markedly simpler than the brain, while the amoeba is markedly more complex.

Still, even the simplest bacterium grows and divides with great alacrity and there is nothing simple, from the chemical standpoint, about growing and dividing. That simplest bacterium, just visible under a good optical microscope, is a busy, self-contained and complex chemical laboratory.

But then, most of the 80,000 macromolecules in the smallest bacterium (say 50,000 at a guess) are enzymes, each of which can catalyze a particular chemical reaction. If there are 2,000 different chemical reactions constantly proceeding within a cell, each of which is necessary to growth and multiplication (this is another guess), then there are, on the average, 25 enzymes for each reaction.

A human factory in which 2,000 different machine operations are being conducted, with 25 men on each machine, would rightly be considered a most complex structure. Even the smallest bacterium is that complex.

We can approach this from another angle, too. About the turn of the century, biochemists began to realize that in addition to the obvious atomic components of living tissue (such as carbon, hydrogen, oxygen, nitrogen, sulfur, phosphorus and so on) certain metals were required by the body in very small quantities.

As an example, consider the two most recent additions to the list of trace metals in the body, molybdenum and cobalt. The entire human body contains perhaps 18 milligrams of molybdenum and 12 milligrams of cobalt (roughly one two-thousandth of an ounce of each). Nevertheless, this quantity, while small, is absolutely essential. The body cannot exist without it.

To make this even more remarkable, the various trace minerals, including molybdenum and cobalt, seem to be essential to every cell. Divide up one two-thousandth of an ounce of these materials among the fifty trillion cells of the human body and what a miserably small trace of a trace is supplied each! *Surely,* the cells can do without.

But that is only if we persist in thinking in terms of ordinary weight units instead of in atoms. In the average cell, there are, very roughly speaking, some 40 molybdenum and cobalt atoms for every billion molecules. Let's, therefore, make still another table:

| Cell | Number of molybdenum and cobalt atoms |
|---|---|
| Amoeba | 6,800,000,000 |
| Human liver cell | 2,800,000 |
| Human red blood cell | 144,000 |
| Human spermatozoon | 27,200 |
| Largest bacterium | 11,200 |
| Smallest bacterium | 32 |

(Mind you, the cells listed are not necessarily "average." I am quite certain that the liver cell contains more than an average share of these atoms and the red blood cell less than an average share; just as earlier, the spermatozoon undoubtedly contained more than an average share of macromolecules. However, I firmly refuse to quibble.)

As you see, the trace minerals are not so sparse after all. An amoeba possesses them by the billions of atoms and a human body cell by the millions. Even the larger bacteria possess them by the thousands.

The smallest bacteria, however, have only a couple of dozen of them, and this fits in well with my earlier conclusion that the tiniest bacterium may have, on the average, 25 enzymes for each reaction. Cobalt and molybdenum (and the other trace metals) are essential because they are key bits of important enzymes. Allowing one atom per enzyme molecule, there are only a couple of dozen such molecules, all told, in the smallest bacterium.

But here we can sense that we are approaching a lower limit. The number of different enzymes is not likely to be distributed with perfect evenness. There will be more than a couple of dozen in some cases and less than a couple of dozen in others. Only one or two of the rarest of certain key enzymes may be present. If a cell had a volume of less than 0.02 cubic micra, the chances would be increasingly good that some key enzymes would find themselves jostled out altogether; with that, growth and multiplication would cease.

Therefore, it is reasonable to suppose that the smallest bacteria visible under a good optical microscope are actually the smallest bits of matter into which all the characteristic processes of life can be squeezed. Such bacteria represent, by this way of thinking, the limit of compactness as far as life is concerned.

But what about organisms still smaller than the smallest bacteria that, lacking some essential enzyme or enzymes, do not, under ordinary conditions, grow and multiply? Granted they are not independently alive, can they yet be considered as fully nonliving?

Before answering, consider that such tiny organisms (which we can call subcells) retain the potentiality of growth and multiplication. The potentiality can be made an actuality once the missing enzyme or enzymes are supplied, and these can only be supplied by a complete and living cell. A subcell, therefore, is an organism that possesses the ability to invade a cell and there, within the cell, to grow and multiply, utilizing the cell's enzymatic equipment to flesh out its own shortcomings.

The largest of the subcells are the rickettsiae, named for an American pathologist, Howard Taylor Ricketts, who, in 1909, discovered that insects were the transmitting agents of Rocky Mountain spotted fever, a disease produced by such subcells. He died the next year of typhus fever, catching it in the course of his researches on that disease, also transmitted by insects. He was thirty-nine at the time of his death; and his reward for giving his life for the good of man is, as you might expect, oblivion.

The smaller rickettsiae fade off into the viruses (there is no sharp dividing line) and the smaller viruses lap over, in size, the genes, which are found in the nuclei of cells and which, in their viruslike structure, carry genetic information.

Now, in considering the subcells, let's abandon the cubic micron as a measure of volume, because if we don't we will run into tiny decimals. Instead, let's use the "cubic millimicron." The millimicron is $1/1,000$ of a micron. A cubic millimicron is, therefore, $1/1,000$ times $1/1,000$ times $1/1,000$, or one-billionth of a cubic micron.

In other words, the smallest bacterium, with a volume of 0.02 cubic micra, can also be said to have a volume of 20,000,000 cubic millimicra. Now we can prepare a table of subcell volumes:

| Subcell | Volume (in cubic millimicra) |
|---|---|
| Typhus fever rickettsia | 54,000,000 |
| Cowpox virus | 5,600,000 |
| Influenza virus | 800,000 |
| Bacteriophage | 520,000 |
| Tobacco mosaic virus | 50,000 |
| Gene | 40,000 |
| Yellow-fever virus | 5,600 |
| Hoof-and-mouth virus | 700 |

The range of subcells is huge. The largest rickettsia is nearly three times the size of the smallest bacterium. (It is not size alone that makes an organism a subcell; it is the absence of at least one essential enzyme.) The smallest subcell, on the other hand, is only 1/3,500 as large as the smallest bacterium. The largest subcell is to the smallest one as the largest whale is to the average dog.

As one slides down the scale of subcells, the number of molecules decreases. Naturally, the nitrogen-phosphorus macromolecules don't disappear entirely, for life, however distantly potential, is impossible (in the form we know) without them. The very smallest subcells consist of nothing more than a very few of these macromolecules; only the bare essentials of life, so to speak, stripped of all superfluity.

The number of atoms, however, is still sizable. A cubic millimicron will hold several hundred atoms if they were packed with the greatest possible compactness, but of course, in living tissue, they are not.

Thus, the tobacco mosaic virus has a molecular weight of 40,000,000 and the atoms in living tissue have an atomic weight that averages about 8. (All but the hydrogen atom have atomic weights that are well above 8, but the numerous hydrogen atoms, each with an atomic weight of 1, pulls the average far down.)

This means there are roughly 5,000,000 atoms in a tobacco mosaic virus particle, or just about 100 atoms per cubic millimicron. We can therefore prepare a new version of the previous table:

| Subcell | Number of atoms |
|---|---|
| Typhus fever rickettsia | 5,400,000,000 |
| Cowpox virus | 560,000,000 |
| Influenza virus | 80,000,000 |
| Bacteriophage | 52,000,000 |
| Tobacco mosaic virus | 5,000,000 |
| Gene | 4,000,000 |
| Yellow-fever virus | 560,000 |
| Hoof-and-mouth virus | 70,000 |

It would seem, then, that the barest essentials of life can be packed into as few as 70,000 atoms. Below that level, we find ordinary protein molecules, definitely nonliving. Some protein molecules (definitely nonliving) actually run to more than

70,000 atoms, but the average such molecule contains 5,000 to 10,000 atoms.

Let's consider 70,000 atoms, then, as the "minimum life unit." Since an average human cell contains macromolecules possessing a total number of atoms at least half a billion times as large as the minimum life unit, and since the cerebral cortex of man contains ten billion such cells, it is not at all surprising that our brain is what it is.

In fact, the great and awesome wonder is that mankind, less than ten thousand years after inventing civilization, has managed to put together a mere few thousand excessively simple units and build computers that do as well as they do.

Imagine what would happen if we could make up units containing half a billion working parts, and then use ten billion of those units to design a computer. Why, we would have something that would make the human brain look like a wet firecracker.

Present company excepted, of course!

## AFTERWORD

I enjoy making comparisons, and considering properties of increasing or decreasing quantities, going stepwise to extremes— as I managed to do in the foregoing essays.

Eventually, I devoted an entire book to the exercise, writing one called *Measure of the Universe* (Harper & Row, 1983). I began with an ordinary measurement, say "1 meter," and worked upward in stages of half an order of magnitude. After 55 such steps I was at the circumference of the Universe. I then worked downward from 1 meter and, after 27 steps, reached the diameter of the proton.

I did it also for area, volume, mass, density, pressure, time, speed, and temperature, and I had more fun than I can easily describe.

# 5

## You, Too, Can Speak Gaelic

It is difficult to prove to the man in the street that one is a chemist. At least, when one is a chemist after my fashion (strictly armchair).

Faced with a miscellaneous stain on a garment of unknown composition, I am helpless. I say "Have you tried a dry cleaner?" with a rising inflection that disillusions everyone within earshot at once. I cannot look at a paste of dubious composition and tell what it is good for just by smelling it; and I haven't the foggiest notion what a drug, identified only by trade name, may have in it.

It is not long, in short, before the eyebrows move upward, the wise smiles shoot from lip to lip, and the hoarse whispers begin: "Some chemist! Wonder what barber college *he* went to?"

There is nothing to do but wait. Sooner or later, on some breakfast-cereal box, on some pill dispenser, on some bottle of lotion, there will appear an eighteen-syllable name of a chemical. Then, making sure I have a moment of silence, I will say carelessly, "Ah, yes," and rattle it off like a machine gun, reducing everyone for miles around to stunned amazement.

Because, you see, no matter how inept I may be at the practical aspects of chemistry, I speak the language fluently.

But, alas, I have a confession to make. It isn't hard to speak chemistry. It just looks hard because organic chemistry (that branch of chemistry with the richest supply of nutcracker names) was virtually a German monopoly in the nineteenth century. The Germans, for some reason known only to themselves, push words together and eradicate all traces of any seam between them. What we would express as a phrase, they treat as one interminable word. They did this to the names of their organic compounds and in English those names were slavishly adopted with minimum change.

It is for that reason, then, that you can come up to a perfectly respectable compound which, to all appearances, is just lying there, harming no one, and find that it has a name like para-dimethylaminobenzaldehyde. (And that is rather short, as such names go.)

To the average person, used to words of a respectable size, this conglomeration of letters is offensive and irritating, but actually, if you tackle it from the front and work your way slowly toward the back, it isn't bad. Pronounce it this way: PA-ruh-dy-METH-il-a-MEE-noh-ben-ZAL-duh-hide. If you accent the capitalized syllables, you will discover that after a while you can say it rapidly and without trouble and can impress your friends no end.

What's more, now that you can say the word, you will appreciate something that once happened to me. I was introduced to this particular compound some years ago, because when dissolved in hydrochloric acid, it is used to test for the presence of a compound called glucosamine and this was something I earnestly yearned to do at the time.

So I went to the reagent shelf and said to someone, "Do we have any para-dimethylaminobenzaldehyde?"

And he said, "What you mean is PA-ruh-dy-METH-il-a-MEE-noh-ben-ZAL-duh-hide," and he sang it to the tune of the "Irish Washerwoman."

If you don't know the tune of the "Irish Washerwoman," all I can say is that it is an Irish jig; in fact, it is *the* Irish jig; if you heard it, you would know it. I venture to say that if you know only one Irish jig, or if you try to make up an Irish jig, that's the one.

It goes: DUM-dee-dee-DUM-dee-dee-DUM-dee-dee-DUM-dee-dee, and so on almost indefinitely.

For a moment I was flabbergasted and then, realizing the enormity of having someone dare be whimsical at my expense, I said, "Of course! It's dactylic tetrameter."

"What?" he said.

I explained. A dactyl is a set of three syllables of which the first is accented and the next two are not, and a line of verse is dactylic tetrameter when four such sets of syllables occur in it. Anything in dactylic feet can be sung to the tune of the "Irish Washerwoman." You can sing most of Longfellow's "Evangeline" to it, for instance, and I promptly gave the fellow a sample:

"THIS is the FO-rest pri-ME-val. The MUR-muring PINES and the HEM-locks—" and so on and so on.

He was walking away from me by then, but I followed him at a half run. In fact, I went on, anything in iambic feet can be sung to the tune of Dvorak's "Humoresque." (You know the one—dee-DUM-dee-DUM-dee-DUM-dee-DUM-dee-DUM—and so on forever.)

For instance, I said, you could sing Portia's speech to the "Humoresque" like this: "The QUALiTY of MERcy IS not STRAINED it DROPpeth AS the GENtle RAIN from HEAV'N uPON the PLACE beNEATH."

He got away from me by then and didn't show up at work again for days, and served him right.

However, I didn't get off scot-free myself. Don't think it. I was haunted for weeks by those drumming dactylic feet. PA-ruh-dy-METH-il-a-MEE-noh-ben-ZAL-duh-hide-PA-ruh-dy-METH-il-a-MEE-noh—went my brain over and over. It scrambled my thoughts, interfered with my sleep, and reduced me to mumbling semimadness, for I would go about muttering it savagely under my breath to the alarm of all innocent bystanders.

Finally, the whole thing was exorcized and it came about in this fashion. I was standing at the desk of a receptionist waiting for a chance to give her my name in order that I might get in to see somebody. She was a very pretty Irish receptionist and so I was in no hurry because the individual I was to see was very masculine and I preferred the receptionist. So I waited patiently and smiled at her; and then her patent Irishness stirred that drumbeat memory in my mind, so that I sang in a soft voice (without even realizing what I was doing) PA-ruh-dy-METH-il-a-MEE-noh-ben-ZAL-duh-hide . . . through several rapid choruses.

And the receptionist clapped her hands together in delight and cried out, *"Oh, my, you know it in the original Gaelic!"*

What could I do? I smiled modestly and had her announce me as Isaac O'Asimov.

From that day to this I haven't sung it once except in telling this story. It was gone, for after all, folks, in my heart I know I don't know one word of Gaelic.

But what are these syllables that sound so Gaelic? Let's trace them to their lair, one by one, and make sense of them, if we can. Perhaps you will then find that you, too, can speak Gaelic.

Let's begin with a tree of southeast Asia, one that is chiefly found in Sumatra and Java. It exudes a reddish-brown resin that, on being burned, yields a pleasant odor. Arab traders had penetrated the Indian Ocean and its various shores during medieval times and had brought back this resin, which they called "Javanese incense." Of course, they called it that in Arabic, so that the phrase came out *"luban javi."*

When the Europeans picked up the substance from Arabic traders, the Arabic name was just a collection of nonsense syllables to them. The first syllable *lu* sounded as though it might be the definite article *(lo* is one of the words for *the* in Italian; *le* and *la* are *the* in French and so on). Consequently, the European traders thought of the substance as "the banjavi" or simply as "banjavi."

That made no sense, either, and it got twisted in a number of ways; to "benjamin," for instance (because that, at least, was a familiar word), to "benjoin," and then finally, about 1650, to "benzoin." In English, the resin is now called "gum benzoin."

About 1608 an acid substance was isolated from the resin and that was eventually called "benzoic acid." Then, in 1834, a German chemist Eilhart Mitscherlich converted benzoic acid (which contains two oxygen atoms in its molecule) into a compound which contains no oxygen atoms at all, but only carbon and hydrogen atoms. He named the new compound "benzin," the first syllable signifying its ancestry.

Another German chemist Justus Liebig objected to the suffix -*in*, which, he said, was used only for compounds that contained nitrogen atoms, which Mitscherlich's "benzin" did not. In this, Liebig was correct. However, he suggested the suffix -*ol*, signifying the German word for "oil," because the compound mixed with oils rather than with water. This was as bad as -*in*, however, for, as I shall shortly explain, the suffix -*ol* is used for other purposes by chemists. However, the name caught on in Germany, where the compound is still referred to as "benzol."

In 1845 still another German chemist (I told you organic chemistry was a German monopoly in the nineteenth century) August W. von Hofmann suggested the name *benzene*, and this is the name properly used in most of the world, including the United States. I say properly because the -*ene* ending is routinely used for many molecules containing hydrogen and carbon atoms only ("hydrocarbons") and therefore it is a good ending and a good name.

The molecule of benzene consists of six carbon atoms and six hydrogen atoms. The carbon atoms are arranged in a hexagon and to each of them is attached a single hydrogen atom. If we remember the actual structure we can content ourselves with stating that the formula of benzene is $C_6H_6$.

You will have noted, perhaps, that in the long and tortuous pathway from the island of Java to the molecule of benzene, the letters of the island have been completely lost. There is not a *j*, not an *a*, and not a *v*, in the word *benzene*.

Nevertheless, we've arrived somewhere. If you go back to the "Irish Washerwoman" compound, para-dimethylaminobenzaldehyde, you will not fail to note the syllable *benz*. Now you know where it comes from.

Having got this far, let's start on a different track altogether.

Women, being what they are (three cheers), have for many centuries been shading their eyelashes and upper eyelids and eye corners in order to make said eyes look large, dark, mysterious, and enticing. In ancient times they used for this purpose some dark pigment (an antimony compound, often) which was ground up into a fine powder. It had to be a *very* fine powder, of course, because lumpy shading would look awful.

The Arabs, with an admirable directness, referred to this cosmetic powder as "the finely divided powder." Only, once again, they used Arabic and it came out *"al-kuhl,"* where the *h* is pronounced in some sort of guttural way I can't imitate, and where *al* is the Arabic word for *the.*

The Arabs were the great alchemists of the early Middle Ages and when the Europeans took up alchemy in the late Middle Ages, they adopted many Arabic terms. The Arabs had begun to use *al-kuhl* as a name for any finely divided powder, without reference to cosmetic needs, and so did the Europeans. But they pronounced the word, and spelled it, in various ways that were climaxed with "alcohol."

As it happened, alchemists were never really at ease with gases or vapors. They didn't know what to make of them. They felt, somehow, that the vapors were not quite material in the same sense that liquids or solids were, and so they referred to the vapors as "spirits." They were particularly impressed with substances that gave off "spirits" even at ordinary temperatures (and not just when heated), and of these, the most important in medieval times was wine. So alchemists would speak of "spirits of wine" for the volatile component of wine (and we ourselves may speak of alcoholic beverages as "spirits," though we will also speak of "spirits of turpentine").

Then, too, when a liquid vaporizes it seems to powder away to nothing, so spirits also received the name *alcohol* and the alchemists would speak of "alcohol of wine." By the seventeenth century the word *alcohol* all by itself stood for the vapors given off by wine.

In the early nineteenth century the molecular structure of these vapors was determined. The molecule turned out to consist of two carbon atoms and an oxygen atom in a straight line. Three hydrogen atoms are attached to the first carbon, two hydrogen atoms to the second, and a single hydrogen atom to the oxygen. The formula can therefore be written as $CH_3CH_2OH$.

The hydrogen-oxygen group ($-OH$) is referred to in abbreviated form as a "hydroxyl group." Chemists began to discover numerous compounds in which a hydroxyl group is attached to a carbon atom, as it is in the alcohol of wine. All these compounds came to be referred to generally as alcohols, and each was given a special name of its own.

For instance, the alcohol of wine contains a group of two carbon atoms to which a total of five hydrogen atoms are attached. This same combination was discovered in a compound first isolated in 1540. This compound is even more easily vaporized than alcohol and the liquid disappears so quickly that it seems to be overwhelmingly eager to rise to its home in the high heavens. Aristotle had referred to the material making up the high heavens as "aether," so in 1730 this easily vaporized material received the name *spiritus aethereus,* or, in English, "ethereal spirits." This was eventually shortened to "ether."

The two-carbon-five-hydrogen group in ether (there were two of these in each ether molecule) was naturally called the "ethyl group," and since the alcohol of wine contained this group, it came to be called "ethyl alcohol" about 1850.

It came to pass, then, that chemists found it sufficient to give the name of a compound the suffix *-ol* to indicate that it was an alcohol, and possessed a hydroxyl group. That is the reason for the objection to *benzol* as a name for the compound $C_6H_6$. Benzene contains no hydroxyl group and is not an alcohol and should be called "benzene" and not "benzol." You hear?

It is possible to remove two hydrogen atoms from an alcohol, taking away the single hydrogen that is attached to the oxygen, and one of the hydrogens attached to the adjoining carbon. Instead of the molecule $CH_3CH_2OH$, you would have the molecule $CH_3CHO$.

Liebig (the man who had suggested the naughty word *benzol)* accomplished this task in 1835 and was the first actually to isolate $CH_3CHO$. Since the removal of hydrogen atoms is, naturally, a "dehydrogenation," what Liebig had was a dehydrogenated alcohol, and that's what he called it. Since he used Latin, however, the phrase was *alcohol dehydrogenatus.*

That is a rather long name for a simple compound, and chemists, being as human as the next fellow (honest!), have the tendency to shorten long names by leaving out syllables. Take the first syllable of *alcohol* and the first two syllables of *dehydrogenatus,* run the result together, and you have *aldehyde.*

Thus, the combination of a carbon, hydrogen, and oxygen atom ($-CHO$), which forms such a prominent portion of the molecule of dehydrogenated alcohol, came to be called the "aldehyde group," and any compound containing it came to be called an "aldehyde."

For instance, if we return to benzene, $C_6H_6$, and imagine one of its hydrogen atoms removed, and in its place a $-CHO$ group inserted, we would have $C_6H_5CHO$ and that compound would be "benzenealdehyde" or, to use the shortened form that is universally employed, "benzaldehyde."

Now let's move back in time again to the ancient Egyptians. The patron god of the Egyptian city of Thebes on the Upper Nile was named Amen or Amun. When Thebes gained hegemony over Egypt, as it did during the eighteenth and nineteenth dynasties, the time of Egypt's greatest military power, Amen naturally gained hegemony over the Egyptian gods. He rated many temples, including one on an oasis in the North African desert, well to the west of the main center of Egyptian culture. This one was well known to the Greeks and, later, to the Romans, who spelled the name of the god "Ammon."

Any desert area has a problem when it comes to finding fuel. One available fuel in North Africa is camel dung. The soot of the burning camel dung, which settled out on the walls and ceiling of the temple, contained white, salt-like crystals, which the Romans then called "sal ammoniac," meaning "salt of Ammon." (The expression "sal ammoniac" is still good pharmacist's jargon, but chemists call the substance "ammonium chloride" now.)

In 1774 an English chemist Joseph Priestley discovered that heating sal ammoniac produced a vapor with a pungent odor, and in 1782 the Swedish chemist Torbern Olof Bergmann suggested the name *ammonia* for this vapor. Three years later a French chemist, Claude Louis Berthollet, worked out the structure of the ammonia molecule. It consisted of a nitrogen atom to which three hydrogen atoms were attached, so that we can write it $NH_3$.

As time went on, chemists who were studying organic compounds (that is, compounds that contained carbon atoms) found that it often happened that a combination made up of a nitrogen atom and two hydrogen atoms ($-NH_2$) was attached to one of the carbon atoms in the organic molecule. The resemblance of this combination to the ammonia molecule was clear, and by 1860 the $-NH_2$ group was being called an "amine group" to emphasize the similarity.

Well, then, if we go back to our benzaldehyde, $C_6H_5CHO$, and imagine a second hydrogen atom removed from the original benzene and in its place an amine group inserted, we would have $C_6H_4(CHO)(NH_2)$ and that would be "aminobenzaldehyde."

Earlier I talked about the alcohol of wine, $CH_3CH_2OH$, and said it was "ethyl alcohol." It can also be called (and frequently is) "grain alcohol" because it is obtained from the fermentation of grain. But, as I hinted, it is not the only alcohol; far from it. As far back as 1661, the English chemist Robert Boyle found that if he heated wood in the absence of air, he obtained vapors, some of which condensed into clear liquid.

In this liquid he detected a substance rather similar to ordinary alcohol, but not quite the same. (It is more easily evaporated than ordinary alcohol, and it is considerably more poisonous, to mention two quick differences.) This new alcohol was called "wood alcohol."

However, for a name really to sound properly authoritative in science, what is really wanted is something in Greek or Latin. The Greek word for wine is *methy* and the Greek word for wood is *yli*. To get "wine from wood" (i.e., "wood alcohol"), stick the two Greek words together and you have *methyl*. The first to do this was the Swedish chemist Jöns Jakob Berzelius, about 1835, and ever since then wood alcohol has been "methyl alcohol" to chemists.

The formula for methyl alcohol was worked out in 1834 by a French chemist named Jean Baptiste André Dumas (no relation to the novelist, as far as I know). It turned out to be simpler than that of ethyl alcohol and to contain but one carbon atom. The formula is written $CH_3OH$. For this reason, a grouping of one carbon atom and three hydrogen atoms ($-CH_3$) came to be referred to as a "methyl group."

The French chemist Charles Adolphe Wurtz (he was born in

Alsace, which accounts for his Germanic name) discovered in 1849 that one of the two hydrogen atoms of the amine group could be replaced by a methyl group, so that the end product looked like this: $-NHCH_3$. This would naturally be a "methylamine group." If both hydrogen atoms were replaced by methyl groups, the formula would be $-N(CH_3)_2$ and we would have a "dimethylamine group." (The prefix *di-* is from the Greek *dis,* meaning "twice." The methyl group is added to the amine group twice, in other words.)

Now we can go back to our aminobenzaldehyde, $C_6H_4(CHO)$-$(NH_2)$. If, instead of an amine group, we had used a dimethylamine group, the formula would be $C_6H_4(CHO)(N(CH_3)_2)$ and the name would be "dimethylaminobenzaldehyde."

Let's think about benzene once again. Its molecule is a hexagon made up of six carbon atoms, each with a hydrogen atom attached. We have substituted an aldehyde group for one of the hydrogen atoms and a dimethylamine group for another, to form dimethylaminobenzaldehyde, but *which* two hydrogen atoms have we substituted?

In a perfectly symmetrical hexagon, such as that which is the molecule of benzene, there are only three ways in which you can choose two hydrogen atoms. You can take the hydrogen atoms of two adjoining carbon atoms; or you can take the hydrogens of two carbon atoms so selected that one untouched carbon-hydrogen combination lies between; or you can take them so that two untouched carbon-hydrogen combinations lie between.

If you number the carbon atoms of the hexagon in order, one through six, then the three possible combinations involve carbons 1,2; 1,3; and 1,4 respectively. If you draw a diagram for yourself (it is simple enough), you will see that no other combinations are possible. All the different combinations of two carbon atoms in the hexagon boil down to one or another of these three cases.

Chemists have evolved a special name for each combination. The 1,2 combination is *ortho* from a Greek word meaning "straight" or "correct," perhaps because it is the simplest in appearance, and what seems simple, seems correct.

The prefix *meta-* comes from a Greek word meaning "in the midst of," but it also has a secondary meaning, "next after."

That makes it suitable for the 1,3 combination. You substitute the first carbon, leave the next untouched, and substitute the one "next after."

The prefix *para-* is from a Greek word meaning "beside" or "side by side." If you mark the 1,4 angles on a hexagon and turn it so that the 1 is at the extreme left, then the 4 will be at the extreme right. The two are indeed "side by side" and so *para-* is used for the 1,4 combination.

Now we know where we are. When we say "para-dimethylaminobenzaldehyde," we mean that the dimethylamine group and the aldehyde group are in the 1,4 relationship to each other. They are at opposite ends of the benzene ring and we can write the formula $CHOC_6H_4N(CH_3)_2$.

See?

Now that you know Gaelic, what do you suppose the following are?

1) alpha-dee-glucosido-beta-dee-fructofuranoside
2) two,three-dihydro-three-oxobenzisosulfonazole
3) delta-four-pregnene-seventeen-alpha, twenty-one, diol-three, eleven, twenty-trione
4) three-(four-amino-two-methylpyrimidyl-five-methyl)-four-methyl-five-beta-hydroxyethylthiazolium chloride hydrochloride

Just in case your Gaelic is still a little rusty, I will give you the answers. They are:

> 1) table sugar
> 2) saccharin
> 3) cortisone
> 4) vitamin $B_1$

Isn't it simple?

## AFTERWORD

By scientific profession, I'm a chemist, but I don't often write essays on chemical subjects. I think that's quite understandable. I've spent years and years being filled up to here—no, higher, up to *here*—with chemistry, and I automatically find myself avoiding it, now and then.

Just the same, if I can find some aspect of chemistry which I find amusing, it becomes a pleasure to talk about it. And what is more maddening for non-chemists than all those funny names for chemicals? Except that those names have amusing historical backgrounds, and so I decided to write the essay.

# 6

# The Slowly
# Moving Finger

Alas, the evidences of mortality are all about us; the other day
our little parakeet died. As nearly as we could make out, it was a
trifle over five years old, and we had always taken the best of care
of it. We had fed it, watered it, kept its cage clean, allowed it to
leave the cage and fly about the house, taught it a small but
disreputable vocabulary, permitted it to ride about on our shoulders and eat at will from dishes at the table. In short, we encouraged it to think of itself as one of us humans.

But alas, its aging process remained that of a parakeet. During
its last year, it slowly grew morose and sullen; mentioned its
improper words but rarely; took to walking rather than flying.
And finally it died. And, of course, a similar process is taking
place within me.

This thought makes me petulant. Each year I break my own
previous record and enter new high ground as far as age is
concerned, and it is remarkably cold comfort to think that everyone else is doing exactly the same thing.

The fact of the matter is that I resent growing old. In my time I was a kind of mild infant prodigy—you know, the kind that teaches himself to read before he is five and enters college at fifteen and is writing for publication at eighteen and all like that there. As you might expect, I came in for frequent curious inspection as a sort of ludicrous freak, and I invariably interpreted this inspection as admiration and loved it.

But such behavior carries its own punishment, for the moving finger writes, as Edward FitzGerald said Omar Khayyám said, and having writ, moves on. And what that means is that the bright, young, bouncy, effervescent infant prodigy becomes a flabby, paunchy, bleary, middle-aged non-prodigy, and age sits twice as heavily on such as these.

It happens quite often that some huge, hulking, rawboned fellow, cheeks bristling with black stubble, comes to me and says in his bass voice, "I've been reading you ever since I learned to read; and I've collected all the stuff you wrote *before* I learned to read and I've read that, too." My impulse then is to hit him a stiff right cross to the side of the jaw, and I might do so if only I were quite sure he would respect my age and not hit back.

So I see nothing for it but to find a way of looking at the bright side, if any exists . . .

How long do organisms live anyway? We can only guess. Statistics on the subject have been carefully kept only in the last century or so, and then only for *Homo sapiens,* and then only in the more "advanced" parts of the world.

So most of what is said about longevity consists of quite rough estimates. But then, if everyone is guessing, I can guess, too; and as lightheartedly as the next person, you can bet.

In the first place, what do we mean by length of life? There are several ways of looking at this, and one is to consider the actual length of time (on the average) that actual organisms live under actual conditions. This is the "life expectancy."

One thing we can be certain of is that life expectancy is quite trifling for all kinds of creatures. If a codfish or an oyster produces millions or billions of eggs and only one or two happen to produce young that are still alive at the end of the first year, then the average life expectancy of all the coddish or oysterish youngsters can be measured in weeks, or possibly even days. I imagine that thousands upon thousands of them live no more than minutes.

Matters are not so extreme among birds and mammals where there is a certain amount of infant care, but I'll bet relatively few of the smaller ones live out a single year.

From the cold-blooded view of species survival, this is quite enough, however. Once a creature has reached sexual maturity, and contributed to the birth of a litter of young which it sees through to puberty or near-puberty, it has done its bit for species survival and can go its way. If it survives and produces additional litters, well and good, but it doesn't have to.

There is, obviously, considerable survival value in reaching sexual maturity as early as possible, so that there is time to produce the next generation before the first is gone. Meadow mice reach puberty in three weeks and can bear their first litter six weeks after birth. Even an animal as large as a horse or cow reaches the age of puberty after one year, and the largest whales reach puberty at two. Some large land animals can afford to be slower about it. Bears are adolescent only at six and elephants only at ten.

The large carnivores can expect to live a number of years, if only because they have relatively few enemies (always excepting man) and need not expect to be anyone's dinner. The largest herbivores, such as elephants and hippopotami, are also safe; while smaller ones such as baboons and water buffaloes achieve a certain safety by traveling in herds.

Early man falls into this category. He lived in small herds and he cared for his young. He had, at the very least, primitive clubs and eventually gained the use of fire. The average man, therefore, could look forward to a number of years of life. Even so, with undernourishment, disease, the hazards of the chase, and the cruelty of man to man, life was short by modern standards. Naturally, there was a limit to how short life could be. If men didn't live long enough, on the average, to replace themselves, the race would die out. However, I should guess that in a primitive society a life expectancy of 18 would be ample for species survival. And I rather suspect that the actual life expectancy of man in the Stone Age was not much greater.

As mankind developed agriculture and as he domesticated

animals, he gained a more dependable food supply. As he learned to dwell within walled cities and to live under a rule of law, he gained greater security against human enemies from without and within. Naturally, life expectancy rose somewhat. In fact, it doubled.

However, throughout ancient and medieval times, I doubt that life expectancy ever reached 40. In medieval England, the life expectancy is estimated to have been 35, so that if you did reach the age of 40 you were a revered sage. What with early marriage and early childbirth, you were undoubtedly a grandfather, too.

This situation still existed into the twentieth century in some parts of the world. In India, for instance, as of 1950, the life expectancy was about 32; in Egypt, as of 1938, it was 36; in Mexico, as of 1940, it was 38.

The next great step was medical advance, which brought infection and disease under control. Consider the United States. In 1850, life expectancy for American white males was 38.3 (not too much different from the situation in medieval England or ancient Rome). By 1900, however, after Pasteur and Koch had done their work, it was up to 48.2; then 56.3 in 1920; 60.6 in 1930; 62.8 in 1940; 66.3 in 1950; 67.3 in 1959; and 67.8 in 1961.

All through, females had a bit the better of it (being the tougher sex). In 1850, they averaged two years longer life than males; and by 1961, the edge had risen to nearly seven years. Non-whites in the United States don't do quite as well—not for any inborn reason, I'm sure, but because they generally occupy a position lower on the economic scale. They run some seven years behind whites in life expectancy. (And if anyone wonders why Negroes are restless these days, there's seven years of life apiece that they have coming to them. That might do as a starter.)

Even if we restrict ourselves to whites, the United States does not hold the record in life expectancy. I rather think Norway and Sweden do. The latest figures I can find (the middle 1950s) give Scandinavian males a life expectancy of 71, and females one of 74.

This change in life expectancy has introduced certain changes in social custom. In past centuries, the old man was a rare phenomenon—an unusual repository of long memories and a sure guide to ancient traditions. Old age was revered, and in some societies where life expectancy is still low and old men still exceptional, old age is still revered.

It might also be feared. Until the nineteenth century there were particular hazards to childbirth, and few women survived the process very often (puerperal fever and all that). Old women were therefore even rarer than old men, and with their wrinkled cheeks and toothless gums were strange and frightening phenomena. The witch mania of early modern times may have been a last expression of that.

Nowadays, old men and women are very common and the extremes of both good and evil are spared them. Perhaps that's just as well.

One might suppose, what with the steady rise in life expectancy in the more advanced portions of the globe, that we need merely hold on another century to find men routinely living a century and a half. Unfortunately, this is not so. Unless there is a remarkable biological breakthrough in geriatrics, we have gone just about as far as we can go in raising the life expectancy.

I once read an allegory that has haunted me all my adult life. I can't repeat it word for word; I wish I could. But it goes something like this. Death is an archer and life is a bridge. Children begin to cross the bridge gaily, skipping along and growing older, while Death shoots at them. His aim is miserable at first, and only an occasional child is transfixed and falls off the bridge into the cloud-enshrouded mists below. But as the crowd moves farther along, Death's aim improves and the numbers thin. Finally, when Death aims at the aged who totter nearly to the end of the bridge, his aim is perfect and he never misses. And not one man ever gets across the bridge to see what lies on the other side.

This remains true despite all the advances in social structure and medical science throughout history. Death's aim has worsened through early and middle life, but those last perfectly aimed arrows are the arrows of old age, and even now they never miss. All we have done to wipe out war, famine, and disease has been to allow more people the chance of experiencing old age.

When life expectancy was 35, perhaps one in a hundred reached old age; nowadays nearly half the population reaches it—but it is the same old old age. Death gets us all, and with every scrap of his ancient efficiency.

In short, putting life expectancy to one side, there is a "specific age" which is our most common time of death from inside, without any outside push at all; the age at which we would die even if we avoided accident, escaped disease, and took every care of ourselves.

Three thousand years ago, the psalmist testified as to the specific age of man (Ps. 90:10), saying: "The days of our years are threescore years and ten; and if by reason of strength they be fourscore years, yet is their strength labor and sorrow; for it is soon cut off, and we fly away."

And so it is today; three millennia of civilization and three centuries of science have not changed it. The commonest time of death by old age lies between 70 and 80.

But that is just the commonest time. We don't all die on our 75th birthday; some of us do better, and it is undoubtedly the hope of each one of us that we ourselves, personally, will be one of those who will do better. So what we have our eye on is not the specific age but the maximum age we can reach.

Every species of multicellular creature has a specific age and a maximum age; and of the species that have been studied to any degree at all, the maximum age would seem to be between 50 and 100 percent longer than the specific age. Thus, the maximum age for man is considered to be about 115.

There have been reports of older men, to be sure. The most famous is the case of Thomas Parr ("Old Parr"), who was supposed to have been born in 1481 in England and to have died in 1635 at the age of 154. The claim is not believed to be authentic (some think it was a put-up job involving three generations of the Parr family), nor are any other claims of the sort. The Soviet Union reports numerous centenarians in the Caucasus, but all were born in a region and at a time when records were not kept. The old man's age rests only upon his own word, therefore, and ancients are notorious for a tendency to lengthen their years. Indeed, we can make it a rule, almost, that the poorer the recording of vital statistics in a particular region, the older the centenarians claim to be.

In 1948, an English woman named Isabella Shepheard died at the reported age of 115. She was the last survivor, within the British Isles, from the period before the compulsory registration of births, so one couldn't be certain to the year. Still, she could not have been younger by more than a couple of years. In 1814, a French Canadian named Pierre Joubert died and he, apparently, had reliable records to show that he was born in 1701, so that he died at 113.

Let's accept 115 as man's maximum age, then, and ask whether we have a good reason to complain about this. How does the figure stack up against maximum ages for other types of living organisms?

If we compare plants with animals, there is no question that plants bear off the palm of victory. Not all plants generally, to be sure. To quote the Bible again (Ps. 103:15–16), "As for man his days are as grass: as a flower of the field, so he flourisheth. For the wind passeth over it, and it is gone; and the place thereof shall know it no more."

This is a spine-tingling simile representing the evanescence of human life, but what if the psalmist had said that as for man his days are as the oak tree; or better still, as the giant sequoia? Specimens of the latter are believed to be over three thousand years old, and no maximum age is known for them.

However, I don't suppose any of us wants long life at the cost of being a tree. Trees live long, but they live slowly, passively, and in terribly, terribly dull fashion. Let's see what we can do with animals.

Very simple animals do surprisingly well and there are reports of sea-anemones, corals, and such-like creatures passing the half-century mark, and even some tales (not very reliable) of centenarians among them. Among more elaborate invertebrates, lobsters may reach an age of 50 and clams one of 30. But I think we can pass invertebrates, too. There is no reliable tale of a complex invertebrate living to be 100 and even if giant squids, let us say, did so, we don't want to be giant squids.

What about vertebrates? Here we have legends, particularly

about fish. Some tell us that fish never grow old but live and grow forever, not dying till they are killed. Individual fish are reported with ages of several centuries. Unfortunately, none of this can be confirmed. The oldest age reported for a fish by a reputable observer is that of a lake sturgeon which is supposed to be well over a century old, going by a count of the rings on the spiny ray of its pectoral fin.

Among amphibia the record holder is the giant salamander, which may reach an age of 50. Reptiles are better. Snakes may reach an age of 30 and crocodiles may attain 60, but it is the turtles that hold the record for the animal kingdom. Even small turtles may reach the century mark, and at least one larger turtle is known, with reasonable certainty, to have lived 152 years. It may be that the large Galápagos turtles can attain an age of 200.

But then turtles live slowly and dully, too. Not as slowly as plants, but too slowly for us. In fact, there are only two classes of living creatures that live intensely and at peak level at all times, thanks to their warm blood, and these are the birds and the mammals. (Some mammals cheat a little and hibernate through the winter and probably extend their life span in that manner.) We might envy a tiger or an eagle if they lived a long, long time and even—as the shades of old age closed in—wish we could trade places with them. But do they live a long, long time?

Of the two classes, birds on the whole do rather better than mammals as far as maximum age is concerned. A pigeon can live as long as a lion and a herring gull as long as a hippopotamus. In fact, we have long-life legends about some birds, such as parrots and swans, which are supposed to pass the century mark with ease.

Any devotee of the Dr. Dolittle stories (weren't you?) must remember Polynesia, the parrot, who was in her third century. Then there is Tennyson's poem "Tithonus," about that mythical character who was granted immortality but, through an oversight, not freed from the incubus of old age so that he grew older and older and was finally, out of pity, turned into a grasshopper. Tennyson has him lament that death comes to all but him. He begins by pointing out that men and the plants of the field die, and his fourth line is an early climax, going, "And after many a summer dies the swan." In 1939, Aldous Huxley used the line as a title for a book that dealt with the striving for physical immortality.

However, as usual, these stories remain stories. The oldest confirmed age reached by a parrot is 73, and I imagine that swans do not do much better. An age of 115 has been reported for carrion crows and for some vultures, but this is with a pronounced question mark.

Mammals interest us most, naturally, since we are mammals, so let me list the maximum ages for some mammalian types. (I realize, of course, that the word "rat" or "deer" covers dozens of species, each with its own aging pattern, but I can't help that. Let's say the typical rat or the typical deer.)

| | | | |
|---|---|---|---|
| Elephant | 77 | Cat | 20 |
| Whale | 60 | Pig | 20 |
| Hippopotamus | 49 | Dog | 18 |
| Donkey | 46 | Goat | 17 |
| Gorilla | 45 | Sheep | 16 |
| Horse | 40 | Kangaroo | 16 |
| Chimpanzee | 39 | Bat | 15 |
| Zebra | 38 | Rabbit | 15 |
| Lion | 35 | Squirrel | 15 |
| Bear | 34 | Fox | 14 |
| Cow | 30 | Guinea Pig | 7 |
| Monkey | 29 | Rat | 4 |
| Deer | 25 | Mouse | 3 |
| Seal | 25 | Shrew | 2 |

The maximum age, be it remembered, is reached only by exceptional individuals. While an occasional rabbit may make 15, for instance, the average rabbit would die of old age before it was 10 and might have an actual life expectancy of only 2 or 3 years.

In general, among all groups of organisms sharing a common plan of structure, the large ones live longer than the small. Among plants, the giant sequoia tree lives longer than the daisy. Among animals, the giant sturgeon lives longer than the herring, the giant salamander lives longer than the frog, the giant alligator lives longer than the lizard, the vulture lives longer than the sparrow, and the elephant lives longer than the shrew.

Indeed, in mammals particularly, there seems to be a strong correlation between longevity and size. There are exceptions, to be sure—some startling ones. For instance, whales are extraordinarily short-lived for their size. The age of 60 I have given is quite exceptional. Most cetaceans are doing very well indeed if they reach 30. This may be because life in the water, with the continuous loss of heat and the never-ending necessity of swimming, shortens life.

But much more astonishing is the fact that man has a longer life than any other mammal—much longer than the elephant or even than the closely allied gorilla. When a human centenarian dies, of all the animals in the world alive on the day that he was born, the only ones that remain alive on the day of his death (as far as we know) are a few sluggish turtles, an occasional ancient vulture or sturgeon, and a number of other human centenarians. Not one non-human mammal that came into this world with him has remained. All, without exception (as far as we know), are dead.

If you think this is remarkable, wait! It is more remarkable than you suspect.

The smaller the mammal, the faster the rate of its metabolism; the more rapidly, so to speak, it lives. We might well suppose that while a small mammal doesn't live as long as a large one, it lives more rapidly and more intensely. In some subjective manner, the small mammal might be viewed as living just as long in terms of sensation as does the more sluggish large mammal. As concrete evidence of this difference in metabolism among mammals, consider the heartbeat rate. The following table lists some rough figures for the average number of heartbeats per minute in different types of mammal.

| Shrew | 1,000 | Sheep | 75 |
|---|---|---|---|
| Mouse | 550 | Man | 72 |
| Rat | 430 | Cow | 60 |
| Rabbit | 150 | Lion | 45 |
| Cat | 130 | Horse | 38 |
| Dog | 95 | Elephant | 30 |
| Pig | 75 | Whale | 17 |

For the fourteen types of animals listed we have the heartbeat rate (approximate) and the maximum age (approximate), and by appropriate multiplications, we can determine the maximum age of each type of creature, not in years but in total heartbeats. The result follows:

| | |
|---|---|
| Shrew | 1,050,000,000 |
| Mouse | 950,000,000 |
| Rat | 900,000,000 |
| Rabbit | 1,150,000,000 |
| Cat | 1,350,000,000 |
| Dog | 900,000,000 |
| Pig | 800,000,000 |
| Sheep | 600,000,000 |
| Lion | 830,000,000 |
| Horse | 800,000,000 |
| Cow | 950,000,000 |
| Elephant | 1,200,000,000 |
| Whale | 630,000,000 |

Allowing for the approximate nature of all my figures, I look at this final table through squinting eyes from a distance and come to the following conclusion: A mammal can, at best, live for about a billion heartbeats and when those are done, it is done.

But you'll notice that I have left man out of the table. That's because I want to treat him separately. He lives at the proper speed for his size. His heartbeat rate is about that of other animals of similar weight. It is faster than the heartbeat of larger animals, slower than the heartbeat of smaller animals. Yet his maximum age is 115 years, and that means his maximum number of heartbeats is about 4,350,000,000.

An occasional man can live for over 4 billion heartbeats! In fact, the life expectancy of the American male these days is 2.5 billion heartbeats. Any man who passes the quarter-century mark has gone beyond the billionth heartbeat mark and is still young, with the prime of life ahead.

Why? It is not just that we live longer than other mammals. Measured in heartbeats, we live *four times as long! Why??*

Upon what meat doth this, our species, feed, that we are grown so great? Not even our closest non-human relatives match us in this. If we assume the chimpanzee to have our heartbeat rate and the gorilla to have a slightly slower one, each lives for a maximum of about 1.5 billion heartbeats, which isn't very much out of line for mammals generally. How then do we make it to 4 billion?

What secret in our hearts makes those organs work so much better and last so much longer than any other mammalian heart in existence? Why does the moving finger write so slowly for us, and for us only?

Frankly, I don't know, but whatever the answer, I am comforted. If I were a member of any other mammalian species my heart would be stilled long years since, for it has gone well past its billionth beat. (Well, a *little* past.)

But since I am *Homo sapiens,* my wonderful heart beats even yet with all its old fire; and speeds up in proper fashion at all times when it should speed up, with a verve and efficiency that I find completely satisfying.

Why, when I stop to think of it, I am a young fellow, a child, an infant prodigy. I am a member of the most unusual species on Earth, in longevity as well as brain power, and I laugh at birthdays.

(Let's see now. How many years to 115?)

## AFTERWORD

I don't want to appear morbid, but this essay was written twenty-five years ago.

On the good side, I'm still here, despite having grown a year or two older in the quarter-century just past. And, of course, life expectancy has pushed up a little bit.

On the nervous-making side, I've added nearly a billion heartbeats to my record, and I've managed to throw in a few glitches, too. My coronary arteries insisted on getting clogged up and eventually I had to get around them by means of a triple-bypass operation.

But what the heck— Let's get back to the good side. I'm still here.

# 7

# Exclamation Point!

It is a sad thing to be unrequitedly in love, I can tell you. The truth is that I love mathematics and mathematics is completely indifferent to me.

Oh, I can handle the elementary aspects of math all right but as soon as subtle insights are required, she goes in search of someone else. She's not interested in me.

I know this because every once in a while I get all involved with pencil and paper, on the track of some great mathematical discovery and so far I have obtained only two kinds of results: 1) completely correct findings that are quite old, and 2) completely new findings that are quite wrong.

For instance (as an example of the first class of results), I discovered, when I was very young, that the sums of successive odd numbers were successive squares. In other words: $1 = 1$; $1 + 3 = 4$; $1 + 3 + 5 = 9$; $1 + 3 + 5 + 7 = 16$, and so on. Unfortunately, Pythagoras knew this too in 500 B.C., and I suspect that some Babylonian knew it in 1500 B.C.

An example of the second kind of result involves Fermat's Last Theorem.* I was thinking about it a couple of months ago when a sudden flash of insight struck me and a kind of luminous glow irradiated the interior of my skull. *I was able to prove the truth of Fermat's Last Theorem in a very simple way.*

When I tell you that the greatest mathematicians of the last three centuries have tackled Fermat's Last Theorem with ever increasingly sophisticated mathematical tools and that all have failed, you will realize what a stroke of unparalleled genius it was for me to succeed with nothing more than ordinary arithmetical reasoning.

My delirium of ecstasy did not completely blind me to the fact that my proof depended upon one assumption which I could check very easily with pencil and paper. I went upstairs to my study to carry that check through—stepping very carefully so as not to jar all that brilliance inside my cranium.

You guessed it, I'm sure. My assumption proved to be quite false inside of a few minutes. Fermat's Last Theorem was not proven after all; and my radiance paled into the light of ordinary day as I sat at my desk, disappointed and miserable.

Now that I have recovered completely, however, I look back on that episode with some satisfaction. After all, for five minutes, I was *convinced* that I was soon to be recognized as the most famous living mathematician in the world, and words cannot express how wonderful that felt while it lasted!

On the whole, though, I suppose that true old findings, however minor, are better than new false ones, however major. So I will trot out for your delectation, a little discovery of mine which I made just the other day but which, I am certain, is over three centuries old in reality.

However, I've never seen it anywhere, so until some Gentle Reader writes to tell me who first pointed it out and when, I will adopt the discovery as the Asimov Series.

First, let me lay the groundwork.

---

* I'm not going to discuss that here. Suffice it to say now that it is the most famous unsolved problem in mathematics.

We can begin with the following expression; $(1 + 1/n)^n$ where $n$ can be set equal to any whole number. Suppose we try out a few numbers.

If $n = 1$, the expression becomes $(1 + 1/1)^1 = 2$. If $n = 2$, the expression becomes $(1 + 1/2)^2$ or $(3/2)^2$ or $9/4$ or $2.25$. If $n = 3$, the expression becomes $(1 + 1/3)^3$ or $(4/3)^3$ or $64/27$ or about $2.3074$.

We can prepare Table 1 of the value of the expression for a selection of various values of $n$:

TABLE 1

| N | $(1 + 1/N)^n$ |
|---|---|
| 1 | 2 |
| 2 | 2.25 |
| 3 | 2.3074 |
| 4 | 2.4414 |
| 5 | 2.4888 |
| 10 | 2.5936 |
| 20 | 2.6534 |
| 50 | 2.6915 |
| 100 | 2.7051 |
| 200 | 2.7164 |

As you see, the higher the value of $n$, the higher the value of the expression $(1 + 1/n)^n$. Nevertheless, the value of the expression increases more and more slowly as $n$ increases. When $n$ doubles from 1 to 2, the expression increases in value by 0.25. When $n$ doubles from 100 to 200, the expression increases in value only by 0.0113.

The successive values of the expression form a "converging series" which reaches a definite limiting value. That is, the higher the value of $n$, the closer the value of the expression comes to a particular limiting value without ever quite reaching it (let alone getting past it).

The limiting value of the expression $(1 + 1/n)^n$ as $n$ grows larger without limit, turns out to be an unending decimal, which is conventionally represented by the symbol $e$.

It so happens that the quantity $e$ is extremely important to mathematicians and they have made use of computers to calculate its value to thousands of decimal places. Shall we make do with 50? All right. The value of *e* is: 2.7182818284590452353-6028747135266249775724709369995 . . .

You may wonder how mathematicians compute the limit of the expression to so many decimal places. Even when I carried *n* up to 200 and solved for $(1 + 1/200)^{200}$, I only got *e* correct to two decimal places. Nor can I reach higher values of *n*. I solved the equation for *n* = 200 by the use of five-place logarithm tables— the best available in my library—and those aren't accurate enough to handle values of *n* over 200 in this case. In fact, I don't trust my value for *n* = 200.

Fortunately, there are other ways of determining *e*. Consider the following series: $2 + 1/2 + 1/2 + 1/6 + 1/24 + 1/120 + 1/720$ . . .

There are six members in this series of numbers as far as I've given it above, and the successive sums are:

| | |
|---|---|
| $2 =$ | 2 |
| $2 + 1/2 =$ | 2.5 |
| $2 + 1/2 + 1/6 =$ | 2.6666 . . . |
| $2 + 1/2 + 1/6 + 1/24 =$ | 2.7083333 . . . |
| $2 + 1/2 + 1/6 + 1/24 + 1/120 =$ | 2.7166666 . . . |
| $2 + 1/2 + 1/6 + 1/24 + 1/120 + 1/720 =$ | 2.71805555 . . . |

In other words, by a simple addition of six numbers, a process for which I don't need a table of logarithms at all, I worked out *e* correct to three decimal places.

If I add a seventh number in the series, then an eighth, and so on, I could obtain *e* correct to a surprising number of additional decimal places. Indeed, the computer which obtained the value of *e* to thousands of places made use of the series above, summing thousands of fractions in the series.

But how does one tell what the next fraction in the series will be? In a useful mathematical series, there should be some way of predicting every member of the series from the first few. If I began a series as follows: $1/2 + 1/3 + 1/4 + 1/5$ . . . you would, without trouble, continue onward . . . $1/6 + 1/7 + 1/8$ . . . Similarly, if a series began $1/2 + 1/4 + 1/8 + 1/16$, you would be confident in continuing . . . $1/32 + 1/64 + 1/128$ . . .

In fact, an interesting parlor game for number-minded individuals would be to start a series and then ask for the next number. As simple examples consider:

2, 3, 5, 7, 11 . . .

2, 8, 18, 32, 50 . . .

Since the first series is the list of primes, the next number is obviously 13. Since the second series consists of numbers that are twice the list of successive squares, the next number is 72.

But what are we going to do with a series such as:

$2 + \frac{1}{2} + \frac{1}{6} + \frac{1}{24} + \frac{1}{120} + \frac{1}{720}$ . . . What is the next number?

If you know, the answer is obvious, but if you *hadn't* known, would you have been able to see it? And if you *don't* know, can you see it?

Just briefly, I am going to introduce a drastic change of subject.

Did any of you ever read Dorothy Sayers' *Nine Tailors*? I did, many years ago. It is a murder mystery, but I remember nothing of the murder, of the characters, of the action, of anything at all but for one item. That one item involves "ringing the changes."

Apparently (I slowly gathered as I read the book) in ringing the changes, you begin with a series of bells tuned to ring different notes, with one man at the rope of each bell. The bells are pulled in order: do, re, mi, fa, and so on. Then, they are pulled again, in a different order. Then, they are pulled again in a still different order. Then, they are pulled again—

You keep it up until all the possible orders (or "changes") in which the bells may be rung *are* rung. One must follow certain rules in doing so, such that no one bell, for instance, can be shifted more than one unit out of its place in the previous change. There are different patterns of shifting the order in the various kinds of change-ringing and these patterns are interesting in themselves. However, all I am dealing with here are the total number of possible changes connected with a fixed number of bells.

Let's symbolize a bell by an exclamation point (!) to represent its clapper, so that we can speak of one bell as 1!, two bells as 2! and so on.

No bells at all can be rung in one way only—by not ringing—so 0! = 1. One bell (assuming bells *must* be rung if they exist at all) can only be rung in one way—bong—so 1! = 1. Two bells, *a* and *b*, can clearly be rung in two ways, *ab* and *ba*, so 2! = 2.

Three bells, *a*, *b*, and *c*, can be rung in six ways: *abc*, *acb*, *bac*, *bca*, *cab*, and *cba*, and no more, so 3! = 6. Four bells, *a*, *b*, *c*, and *d*, can be rung in just twenty-four different ways. I won't list them all, but you can start with *abcd*, *abdc*, *acbd*, and *acdb* and see how many more changes you can list. If you can list twenty-five different and distinct orders of writing four letters, you have shaken the very foundations of mathematics, but I don't expect you will be able to do it. Anyway, 4! = 24.

Similarly (take my word for it for just a moment), five bells can be rung in 120 different changes and six bells in 720, so that 5! = 120 and 6! = 720.

By now I think you've caught on. Suppose we look again at the series that gives us our value of *e:* $2 + \frac{1}{2} + \frac{1}{6} + \frac{1}{24} + \frac{1}{120} + \frac{1}{720}$ . . . and write it this way:

$$e = \frac{1}{0!} + \frac{1}{1!} + \frac{1}{2!} + \frac{1}{3!} + \frac{1}{4!} + \frac{1}{5!} + \frac{1}{6!} \ldots$$

Now we know how to generate the fractions next in line. They are . . . $+\frac{1}{7!}, \frac{1}{8!}, + \frac{1}{9!}$, and so on forever.

To find the values of fractions such as $\frac{1}{7!}$, $\frac{1}{8!}$, and $\frac{1}{9!}$, you must know the value of 7!, 8!, and 9! and to know that you must figure out the number of changes in a set of seven bells, eight bells, and nine bells.

Of course, if you're going to try to list all possible changes and count them, you'll be at it all day; and you'll get hot and confused besides.

Let's search for a more indirect method, therefore.

We'll begin with four bells, because fewer bells offer no problem. Which bell shall we ring first? Any of the four, of course, so we have four choices for first place. For each one of these four choices, we can choose any of three bells (any one, that is, except the one already chosen for first place) so that for the first two places in line we have $4 \times 3$ possibilities. For each of these we can choose either of the two remaining bells for third place, so that for the first three places, we have $4 \times 3 \times 2$ possibilities. For each of these possibilities there remains only one bell for fourth place, so for all four places there are $4 \times 3 \times 2 \times 1$ arrangements.

We can say then, that $4! = 4 \times 3 \times 2 \times 1 = 24$.

If we work out the changes for any number of bells, we will reach similar conclusions. For seven bells, for instance, the total number of changes is $7 \times 6 \times 5 \times 4 \times 3 \times 2 \times 1 = 5,040$. We can say, then, that $7! = 5,040$.

(The common number of bells used in ringing the changes is seven; a set termed a "peal." If all seven bells are rung through once in six seconds, then a complete set of changes—5,040 of them—requires eight hours, twenty-four minutes . . . And ideally, it should be done without a mistake. Ringing the changes is a serious thing.)

Actually, the symbol "!" does not really mean "bell" (That was just an ingenious device of mine to introduce the matter.) In this case it stands for the word "factorial." Thus, 4! is "factorial four" and 7! is "factorial seven."

Such numbers represent not only the changes that can be rung in a set of bells, but the number of orders in which the cards can be found in a shuffled deck, the number of orders in which men can be seated at a table, and so on.

I have never seen any explanation for the term "factorial" but I can make what seems to me a reasonable stab at explaining it. Since the number $5,040 = 7 \times 6 \times 5 \times 4 \times 3 \times 2 \times 1$, it can be evenly divided by each number from 1 to 7 inclusive. In other words, each number from 1 to 7 is a factor of 5,040; why not, therefore, call 5,040 "factorial seven."

And we can make it general. All the integers from 1 to $n$ are factors of $n!$. Why not call $n!$ "factorial $n$" therefore.

We can see, now, why the series used to determine $e$ is such a good one to use.

The values of the factorial numbers increase at a tremendous rate, as is clear from the list in Table 2 of values up to merely 15!

As the values of the factorials zoom upward, the value of fractions with successive factorials in the denominator must zoom downward. By the time you reach $1/6!$, the value is only $1/720$, and by the time you reach $1/15!$, the value is considerably less than a trillionth.

Each such factorial-denominatored fraction is larger than the remainder of the series all put together. Thus $1/15!$ is larger than $1/16! + 1/17! + 1/18! \ldots$ and so on and so on forever, all put together. And this preponderance of a particular fraction over

TABLE 2   The Factorials

| 0! | 1 |
|---|---|
| 1! | 1 |
| 2! | 2 |
| 3! | 6 |
| 4! | 24 |
| 5! | 120 |
| 6! | 720 |
| 7! | 5,040 |
| 8! | 40,320 |
| 9! | 362,880 |
| 10! | 3,628,800 |
| 11! | 39,916,800 |
| 12! | 479,001,600 |
| 13! | 6,227,020,800 |
| 14! | 87,178,921,200 |
| 15! | 1,307,674,368,000 |

all later fractions combined increases as one goes along the series.

Therefore suppose we add up all the terms of the series through $1/14!$. The value is short of the truth by $1/15! + 1/16! + 1/17! + 1/18!$ etc, etc. We might, however, say the value is short of the truth by $1/15!$ because the remainder of the series is insignificant in sum compared to $1/15!$. The value of $1/15!$ is less than a trillionth. It is, in other words, less than 0.000000000001, and the value of *e* you obtain by summing a little over a dozen fractions is correct to eleven decimal places.

Suppose we summed all the series up to $1/999!$ (by computer, of course). If we do that, we are $1/1,000!$ short of the true answer. To find out how much that is, we must have some idea of the value of 1000!. We might determine that by calculating $1,000 \times 999 \times 998 \ldots$ and so on, but don't try. It will take forever.

Fortunately, there exist formulas for calculating out large factorials (at least approximately) and there are tables which give the logarithms of these large factorials.

Thus, *log* 1,000! = 2567.6046442. This means that 1,000! = 4.024 × $10^{2,567}$, or (approximately) a 4 followed by 2,567 zeroes. If the series for *e* is calculated out to $1/999!$, the value will be short of the truth by only $1/(4 \times 10^{2,567})$ and you will have *e* correct to 2,566 decimal places. (The best value of *e* I know of was calculated out to no less than 60,000 decimal places.)

Let me digress once again to recall a time I had personal use for moderately large factorials. When I was in the Army, I went through a period where three fellow sufferers and myself played bridge day and night until one of the others broke up the thing by throwing down his hand and saying, "We've played so many games, the same hands are beginning to show up."

I was terribly thankful, for that gave me something to think about.

Each order of the cards in a bridge deck means a possible different set of bridge hands. Since there are fifty-two cards, the total number of arrangements is 52!. However, within any individual hand, the arrangement doesn't matter. A particular set of thirteen cards received by a particular player is the same hand whatever its arrangement. The total number of arrangements of the thirteen cards of a hand is 13! and this is true for each of four hands. Therefore the total number of bridge-hand combinations is equal to the total number of arrangements divided by the number of those arrangements that don't matter, or:

$$\frac{52!}{(13!)^4}$$

I had no tables handy, so I worked it out the long way but that didn't bother me. It took up my time and, for my particular tastes, was much better than a game of bridge. I have lost the original figures long since, but now I can repeat the work with the help of tables.

The value of 52! is, approximately, 8.066 × $10^{67}$. The value of 13! (as you can see in the table of factorials I gave above) is approximately 6.227 × $10^9$ and the fourth power of that value is about $1.5 \times 10^{39}$. If we divide $8.066 \times 10^{67}$ by $1.5 \times 10^{39}$, we find that the total number of different bridge games possible is roughly $5.4 \times 10^{28}$ or 54,000,000,000,000,000,000,000,000,-000 or 54 octillion.

I announced this to my friends. I said, "The chances are not likely that we are repeating games. We could play a trillion games a second for a billion years, without repeating a single game."

My reward was complete incredulity. The friend who had originally complained said, gently, "But, pal, there are only fifty-two cards, you know," and he led me to a quiet corner of the barracks and told me to sit and rest awhile.

Actually, the series used to determine the value of *e* is only a special example of a general case. It is possible to show that:

$$e^x = x^0/0! + x^1/1! + x^2/2! + x^3/3! + x^4/4! + x^5/5! \ldots$$

Since $x^0 = 1$, for any value of *x,* and 0! and 1! both equal 1, the series is usually said to start: $e^x = 1 + x + x^2/2! + x^3/3! \ldots$ but I prefer my version given above. It is more symmetrical and beautiful.

Now *e* itself can be expressed as $e^1$. In this case, the *x* of the general series becomes 1. Since 1 to any power equals 1, then $x^2$, $x^8$, $x^4$ and all the rest become 1 and the series becomes:

$e^1 = 1/0! + 1/1! + 1/2! + 1/3! + 1/4! + 1/5! \ldots$ which is just the series we've been working with earlier.

But now let's take up the reciprocal of *e;* or, in other words, $1/e$. Its value to fifteen decimal places is $0.367879441171442 \ldots$

It so happens that $1/e$ can be written as $e^{-1}$, which means that in the general formula for $e^x$, we can substitute $-1$ for *x.*

When $-1$ is raised to a power, the answer is $+1$ if the power is an even one, and $-1$ if it is an odd one. In other words: $(-1)^0 = 1$, $(-1)^1 = -1$, $(-1)^2 = +1$, $(-1)^3 = -1$, $(-1)^4 = +1$, and so on forever.

If, in the general series, then, *x* is set equal to $-1$, we have:
$e^{-1} = (-1)^0/0! + (-1)^1/1! + (-1)^2/2! + (-1)^3/3! + (-1)^4/4! \ldots$ or $e^{-1} = 1/0! + (-1)/1! + 1/2! + (-1)/3! + 1/4! + (-1)/5! \ldots$ or $e^{-1} = 1/0! - 1/1! + 1/2! - 1/3! + 1/4! - 1/5! + 1/6! - 1/7! \ldots$

In other words, the series for $1/e$ is just like the series for *e* except that all the even terms are converted from additions to subtractions.

Furthermore, since 1/0! and 1/1! both equal 1, the first two terms in the series for 1/e — 1/0! — 1/1! — are equal to 1 — 1 = 0. They may therefore be omitted and we may conclude that:

$$e^{-1} = 1/2! - 1/3! + 1/4! - 1/5 + 1/6! - 1/7! + 1/8! - 1/9! + 1/10!,$$

and so on forever.

And now, at last, we come to my own personal discovery! As I looked at the series just given above for $e^{-1}$, I couldn't help think that the alternation between plus and minus is a flaw in its beauty. Could there not be any way in which it could be expressed with pluses only or with minuses only?

Since an expression such as $-1/3! + 1/4!$ can be converted into $-(1/3! - 1/4!)$, it seemed to me I could write the following series:

$$e^{-1} = 1/2! - (1/3! - 1/4!) - (1/5! - 1/6!) - (1/7! - 1/8!) \ldots$$

and so on.

Now we have only minus signs, but we also have parentheses, which again offer an esthetic flaw.

So I considered the contents of the parentheses. The first one contains $1/3! - 1/4!$ which equals $1/(3 \times 2 \times 1) - 1/(4 \times 3 \times 3 \times 1)$. This is equal to $(4 - 1)/(4 \times 3 \times 2 \times 1)$, or to $3/4!$. In the same way, $1/5! - 1/6! = 5/6!$; $1/7! - 1/8! = 7/8!$ and so on.

I was astonished and inexpressibly delighted for now I had the Asimov Series which goes:

$$e^{-1} = 1/2! - 3/4! - 5/6! - 7/8! - 9/10! \ldots \text{ and so on forever.}$$

I am certain that this series is at once obvious to any real mathematician and I'm sure it has been described in texts for three hundred years—but I've never seen it and until someone stops me, I'm calling it the Asimov Series.

Not only does the Asimov Series contain only minus signs (except for the unexpressed positive sign before the first term), but it contains all the digits in order. You simply can't ask for anything more beautiful than that. Let's conclude now, by working out just a few terms of the series:

| | |
|---|---|
| $1/2!$ | $= 0.5$ |
| $1/2! - 3/4!$ | $= 0.375$ |
| $1/2! - 3/4! - 5/6!$ | $= 0.3680555\ldots$ |
| $1/2! - 3/4! - 5/6! - 7/8!$ | $= 0.3678819\ldots$ |

As you see, by adding up only four terms of the series, I get an answer which is only 0.0000025 greater than the truth, an error of 1 part in a bit less than 150,000 or, roughly, $1/1500$ of 1 percent.

So if you think the "Exclamation Point" of the title refers only to the factorial symbol, you are wrong. It applies even more so to my pleasure and astonishment with the Asimov Series.

P.S. To get round the unexpressed positive sign in the Asimov Series some readers (after the first appearance in print of this chapter) suggested the series be written: $-(-1)/0! - 1/2! - 3/4!$ . . . All the terms would then indeed be negative, even the first, but we would have to step outside the realm of the natural numbers to include 0 and $-1$, which detracts a bit from the austere beauty of the series.

Another suggested alternative is: $0/1! + 2/3! + 4/5! + 6/7! + 8/9!$ . . . which also gives $1/e$. It includes only positive signs which are prettier (in my opinion) than negative signs but, on the other hand, it includes 0.

Still another reader suggested a similar series for $e$ itself; one that goes as follows: $2/1! + 4/3! + 6/5! + 8/7! + 10/9!$ . . . The inversion of the order of the natural numbers detracts from its orderliness but it gives it a certain touch of charming grace, doesn't it?

Oh, if only mathematics loved me as I love her!

## AFTERWORD

It is difficult for me to write essays on mathematical subjects for the simple reason that I'm not a mathematician. I don't mean that I don't know enough about mathematics (though that is also true) but that I have no *feel* for it. It's like not only being unable to play a musical instrument, but being tone-deaf as well.

And yet, for some obscure reason, I ache to write about math and every once in a while, I manage to think of something simple enough for me to write about without revealing my utter lack of talent.

Of all the mathematical essays I have written in the last thirty years, this one is my favorite. It *almost* makes me sound as though I know what I'm talking about. And I *did* end up with the Asimov series.

As I said in the essay, the Asimov series must be obvious at once to any real mathematician, and has probably been known for several centuries. I was sure, then, that hordes of people would write to me in order to tell me just who discovered it and when and how many treatises have been written on it, and so on.

But the fact is that not one letter like that ever arrived. It was as though every reader smiled indulgently and said, "Oh, let Isaac have his fun!"

# 8

## I'm Looking over a Four-Leaf Clover

History is full of apocryphal stories; stories about people saying and doing things they never really said and did—like George Washington chopping down the cherry tree, or Galileo dropping weights off the Leaning Tower of Pisa. Unfortunately, apocryphal stories are so much more interesting than the truth that it is impossible to kill them. And what's even more unfortunate for me, specifically, is that my memory is so selective that I never forget an apocryphal story, even though I frequently have trouble remembering facts.

For instance, here's a story, probably apocryphal (or I wouldn't remember it so tenaciously) about St. Augustine.

He was asked once, by a scoffer, "What did God spend His time doing before He created Heaven and Earth?"

And St. Augustine roared back, without hesitation, "Creating Hell, for those who ask questions like that!"

But I hope St. Augustine was just joshing when he said that, for I intend to go on to discuss my theories as to the birth and development of the Universe in the light of the conservation laws; and to do that I will (among other things) have to ask that unaskable question—what came before the beginning?

Some picture an oscillating Universe; one that first expands, then contracts, then expands, then contracts, and so on over and over again, with each cycle of expansion and contraction taking some eighty billion years, and with an extremely dense "cosmic egg" at the point of maximum contraction in each cycle.

In continuing the discussion, let's begin by asking whether all the cycles are identical, or whether there is some change from cycle to cycle; perhaps a steady, one-way change.

For instance, we might argue that as the Universe expands, it radiates massless particles—photons and neutrinos—constantly. These photons and neutrinos, we can say, move outward and are forever lost. When the Universe contracts again, the mass that comes together into a cosmic egg is smaller by the loss of the mass-equivalent of the energy represented by the lost radiation. This would continue with each cycle, each cosmic egg being less massive than the one before, until finally a cosmic egg is formed that possesses so little mass that it can no longer explode properly. When that happens the entire Universe is represented by one extremely large but slowly dying mass of condensed matter.

In that case, we would be living not merely in an oscillating Universe but in a damped oscillating one. The Universe, in that view, would be like a bouncing ball that is not very elastic. Each bounce is lower than the one before and finally the ball does not bounce at all but just lies there.

That is rather a neat picture for it produces a logical end, the kind of an end we are familiar with in ordinary life and one we might therefore be disposed to accept. But suppose we look backward in time? What about the cosmic egg that existed before the one that started the present expansion? That earlier one had to be larger than ours, and the one before that had to be even larger, and the one before that still larger. To move back in time and find ever-larger cosmic eggs, exploding with ever-greater violence is troublesome, for an endlessly increasing mass may be hard to handle. The damped oscillating Universe produces a neat overall end but no neat overall beginning.

Fortunately we don't have to complicate matters by picturing such a damped oscillation. Photons and neutrinos are not "forever lost." To be sure, they move outward from their source of radiation in a "straight line" but what do we mean by a "straight line"? Suppose we draw a straight line on the surface of the Earth. It might seem to us that if we extend that line with perfect straightness, it will go on and on forever and that a point traveling along it will be "forever lost" to anyone standing at the place of origin of the line. However, you know and I know that the Earth's surface is curved and that the "straight line" will eventually (if we assume the Earth to be a perfect sphere) come back to the place of origin.

In the same way, photons and neutrinos, in traveling a "straight line" by our local-neighborhood-of-the-Universe definition, are actually traveling in a grand circle and will return, roughly speaking, to the point of origin. The Universe of "curved space" has a finite volume and all it contains, matter and energy, must remain within that volume.

As the Universe contracts, not only matter, but also photons and neutrinos must be crowded together. The massless particles are still traveling in "straight lines" but these "straight lines" curve ever more sharply; and in the end all the contents of the previous cosmic egg are brought back into another cosmic egg, with nothing lost. Each cosmic egg is precisely like the one before and the one that will come after and there is no damping. In a strictly oscillating Universe of this sort, there is neither beginning nor end, nor, *on the whole,* any change. If this faces us with the uncomfortable concept of eternity, it is at least an essentially unchanging eternity.

Within a single cycle of the oscillation, of course, there is a beginning at one cosmic egg, an end at the next, and colossal change in between.

But what is the nature of the cosmic egg? That depends on the nature of the Universe. On the subatomic scale, our portion of the Universe is made up, in the main, of six kinds of particles: protons, electrons, neutrons, photons, neutrinos, and antineutrinos. The other particles that exist are present in vanishingly small traces on the whole and may be ignored.

The subatomic particles are associated into atoms at the moment and these atoms are associated into stars and galaxies. We can assume that the six kinds of particles that make up our part of the Universe make up all of it and that even the farthest galaxy is essentially similar in fundamental makeup to our own bodies.

As all the mass and energy of the Universe crunch together into the cosmic egg, the levels of organization of the Universe break down, one by one. The galaxies and stars come together in one contracting mass. The more complicated atoms decompose into hydrogen, absorbing neutrinos and photons as they do so. The hydrogen atoms break apart into protons and electrons, absorbing photons as they do so. The protons and electrons combine to form neutrons, absorbing antineutrinos as they do so.

In the end, the Universe has been converted into a cosmic egg made up of a mass of hard-packed neutrons—a mass of "neutronium."

Well-packed neutronium would have a density of about 400,000,000,000,000 grams per cubic centimeter, so that if the mass of the Sun were packed into neutronium, it would form a sphere with a radius of about 6.6 miles.

If we consider that the mass of the Milky Way Galaxy is about 135,000,000,000 times that of the Sun, then the whole of our Galaxy, converted into neutronium, would form a sphere with a radius of about 33,600 miles.

If we consider the Universe to contain a mass, 100,000,000,000 times that of our Galaxy, then the cosmic egg would have a radius of 156,000,000 miles. If the center of such a cosmic egg were made to coincide with the center of our Sun, the surface of the cosmic egg would almost coincide with the orbit of Mars. And even if the mass of the Universe were twenty thousand times as large as the mass I have cited, the cosmic egg, if it were composed of pure, well-packed neutronium, would be no larger than the orbit of Pluto.

How does the cosmic egg fit in with the well-known conservation laws?

One can easily imagine that the momentum of the cosmic egg as a whole is zero, by defining the egg as motionless. When the cosmic egg explodes and expands, the individual portions have momentum in one direction or another, but all the momenta add up to zero. In the same way, the angular momentum of the cosmic egg can be defined as zero and while the parts of the expanding universe have individual angular momenta that are not zero, the total is zero.

In short, it is tempting to try to establish a rule that for any conserved quantity, the value of that quantity in the cosmic egg is zero, or is capable of being defined as zero without logical difficulties.

Since this notion is, as far as I know, original with me—especially in the manner I intend to develop it in the course of this article—I shall throw modesty to the dogs and speak of it as "Asimov's Cosmogonic Principle."

The most economical way of expressing the principle is, "In the Beginning, there was Nothing."

For instance, how about the conservation of electric charge? Of the six particles making up the Universe, one (the proton) has a positive charge and one (the electron) has a negative charge. These cannot combine and cancel electric charge under ordinary conditions, but in forming the cosmic egg, conditions may be extreme enough to make the two combine to form neutrons. The electric charge of the cosmic egg is then zero. (In the Beginning, there was No Charge.)

In the course of the explosion and expansion of the cosmic egg, charge appears, to be sure, but in equal quantities of positive and negative so that the total remains zero.

And what about lepton number? Of the six particles making up the Universe, three are leptons. The electron and the neutrino have lepton numbers of $+1$, while the antineutrino has a lepton number of $-1$. In the formation of neutrons, all three disappear, and it is not unreasonable to suppose that the manner of the disappearance is such as to cancel out the lepton number and leave the cosmic egg with a lepton number of zero.

On the whole, one can arrange matters to show that the values of all but two of the conserved quantities known to physicists are zero in the cosmic egg, or can logically be defined as zero. The two exceptions are baryon number and energy.

Let's begin with the baryon number.

Of the six particles making up the Universe, two are baryons, the proton and the neutron. Each has a baryon number of $+1$. Since there is no particle with a baryon number of $-1$ in the list of those making up the Universe, there is no chance of cancellation of baryon number, and no chance (or so it would now appear) of a cosmic egg possessing a baryon number of zero. In the process of cosmic egg formation, the protons disappear, to be sure, but for each proton that disappears, a neutron is formed and the baryon number remains positive.

Indeed, if the cosmic egg contains the mass of 100,000,000,-000 galaxies the size of ours, then it is made up of $1.6 \times 10^{79}$ baryons and its baryon number is $+16,000,000,000,000,000,-000,000,000,000,000,000,000,000,000,000,000,000,-000,000,000,000,000,000,000$. This is a terribly long way from zero and makes hash of Asimov's Cosmogonic Principle.

There's a way out. There are particles with negative baryon numbers, even if those do not seem to occur in any but the tiniest traces in our neck of the woods. The antineutron, for instance, has a baryon number of $-1$. Well, suppose that the cosmic egg does not consist of neutrons only, but of neutrons and antineutrons, half and half. The baryon number would then be zero, as the Principle requires.

The neutron half of the cosmic egg would explode to form protons and electrons which would combine to form atoms. The antineutron half would explode to from antiprotons and antielectrons (positrons) which would combine to form antiatoms.

In short, we have now talked ourselves into supposing that the Universe is made up of equal quantities of matter and antimatter —but is it? It is absolutely inconceivable that the Universe be made up of matter and antimatter all mixed up, for if it were, the two would interact at once to produce photons. (That's exactly what happens when we, by might and main, produce a trifling quantity of antimatter in the laboratory.) A Universe composed of equal quantities of matter and antimatter, all mixed up, would actually be composed of a mass of photons, which are neither matter nor antimatter. The cosmic egg would be nothing more than compacted photons.

But the Universe is *not* made up of photons only. If, then, it is made up of equal quantities of matter and antimatter, those must be separated—effectively separated—so that they do not interact to form photons. The only separation that is separate enough would be on the galactic scale. In other words, there may be galaxies made up of matter, and other galaxies made up of antimatter. Galaxies and antigalaxies, so to speak.

We have no way of telling, so far, whether the Universe actually contains galaxies and antigalaxies. If a galaxy and an antigalaxy met, enormous quantities of energy would be formed as matter-antimatter annihilation took place. No clear-cut case of such an event has yet been detected, though there are some suspicious cases. Secondly, galaxies produce vast quantities of neutrinos as the hydrogen atoms are built up to helium in the stars they contain; while antigalaxies produce vast quantities of antineutrinos by way of the analogous process involving antimatter. When the day comes that astronomers can detect neutrinos and antineutrinos from distant galaxies, and pinpoint their sources, the galaxies and antigalaxies may be identified.

In a Universe made up of galaxies and antigalaxies, we can picture the crunching together of the cosmic egg in a new way. Neutrons and antineutrons would be formed and these would undergo mutual annihilation to form photons. We would have "photonium" in the cosmic egg, rather than neutronium. What the properties of photonium would be like, I can't imagine.

But what causes the photonium to break up into matter and antimatter in such a way that separate galaxies of each kind can be formed? Why doesn't the photonium break up into neutrons and antineutrons so well mixed that they annihilate each other at once? In short, why isn't the photonium stable? Why doesn't it remain photonium?

Well, there are theories that an antiparticle is merely a particle that is moving backward in time. If you take a film of a positron in a magnetic field, it seems to curve, let us say, leftward, rather than rightward, as an electron would under similar conditions. However, if the film is run backward, then the positron curves rightward, like an electron.

On the subatomic scale, it makes no difference whether time moves "forward" or "backward" as far as the laws of nature are concerned and consistent pictures of subatomic events can be drawn up in which particles move forward in time and antiparticles move backward.

Could it be, then, that the photonium cosmic egg, with a baryon number of zero, breaks up into two smaller eggs, one of neutronium and one of antineutronium, and that the former moves forward in time and the latter backward, so that the two are out of reach of each other before they can interact? The neutronium egg with a positive baryon number can be called a "cosmon," while the antineutronium egg with a negative baryon number can be called an "anticosmon."

We can picture the cosmon and anticosmon as both undergoing expansion and as continuing to separate along the time axis. We begin with a tiny cosmon and anticosmon, both close to the zero point on the time axis. As they move apart, they grow larger and larger and more and more separated.*

For the moment let's concentrate on the cosmon (our Universe). As it expands, the various forms of energy are spread out within it more and more evenly. We express this fact by saying that entropy increases and, indeed, entropy has sometimes been called "time's arrow." If entropy increases, you know time is moving forward.

But when the cosmon begins to contract, all the atomic and subatomic processes that took place during expansion begin to reverse. Entropy then begins to decrease and time begins to run backward.

In other words the cosmon moves forward in time when it is expanding, and backward when it is contracting. The anticosmon (behaving symmetrically) moves backward in time when it is expanding, and forward in time when it is contracting. Each does this over and over again.

Instead of an oscillating Universe, we have an oscillating double-Universe, the two oscillations being exactly in phase, and both Universes coming together to form a combined cosmic egg of photonium.

---

* Since this essay first appeared in print, I have discovered that F. R. Stannard of University College, London, is speculating on the existence of such a "negative-time" Universe on a more rigorous basis than any I can handle.

But if this picture takes care of baryon number, it does not take care of energy. The law of conservation of energy is the most fundamental generalization we know and no matter how I have sliced things so far, the Universe, cosmon and anticosmon combined, is made up of energy.

If the cosmon consists of $1.6 \times 10^{79}$ neutrons and their descendant particles, and the anticosmon consists of $1.6 \times 10^{79}$ antineutrons and their descendant particles, then the total energy content of the photonium cosmic egg formed by the coming together of the cosmon and anticosmon must be something like $4.8 \times 10^{76}$ ergs, and that must always exist, at all stages of the cosmon-anticosmon separation, expansion, contraction, and coalescence.

That is the final hurdle for Asimov's Cosmogonic Principle, for in the photonium cosmic egg all conserved quantities, *except* energy, can be set equal to zero.

How, then, can one set the energy equal to zero as well? To do so, one must postulate something we might call negative-energy.

There is no such thing *as far as we know*. It has never been observed. Nevertheless, the Principle makes its existence necessary.

In a Universe consisting only of negative-energy, all the manifestations would be broadly identical with those in our own Universe consisting of ordinary energy. However, if a sample of ordinary energy and of negative-energy were brought together they would cancel each other and produce Nothing.

There are familiar cases of partial cancellation of physical properties. Two billiard balls moving in opposite directions at equal speeds, and coated with glue to make them stick on collision, will, if they collide head-on, come to a dead halt. Momentum will have been canceled out (but the energy of motion of the billiard balls will be converted to heat). Two sound beams, or light beams, exactly out of phase, will combine to form silence, or darkness (but the energy content of the wave forms will be converted into heat).

In all these partial cancellations, the energy—most fundamental of all—always remains. Well, in the case of the combination of energy and negative-energy, cancellation will be complete. There will be left *Nothing!*

Negative-energy is made up of negative-photons, which can break down to form negative-neutrons and negative-antineutrons. The negative-neutrons can break down to form negative-matter which can be built up to negative-stars and negative-galaxies, forming a negative-cosmon. Negative-antineutrons can break down to form negative-antimatter which will build up to a negative-anticosmon.

Suppose a cosmon and anticosmon contract and combine to form a photonium cosmic egg. A negative-cosmon and a negative-anticosmon can contract to form an antiphotonium cosmic egg. The two cosmic eggs, photonium and antiphotonium can then combine to form Nothing!

We are then left with no cosmic egg at all! We are left with Nothing!

In the beginning was Nothing and this Nothing formed a photonium cosmic egg and an antiphotonium cosmic egg. The photonium cosmic egg behaved as already described, forming a cosmon moving forward in time and an anticosmon moving backward in time. The antiphotonium cosmic egg must behave analogously, forming a negative-cosmon moving forward in time and a negative-anticosmon moving backward in time.

But if the cosmon and negative-cosmon are both moving forward in time why don't they combine and cancel out to Nothing? It seems to me they must remain separate and this separation may come about through gravitational repulsion. So far, we know of gravitational attraction only, and there is no such thing (as far as we know) as gravitational repulsion. If, however, there is negative-energy, and if negative-matter is formed from it, perhaps a gravitational repulsion can also exist and be expressed between matter and negative-matter.

As the cosmon and negative-cosmon expand, gravitational repulsion drives them steadily apart, perhaps, along the space axis (see Figure 1), while both move together up the time axis. Similarly, the anticosmon and negative-anticosmon drive steadily apart along the space axis as they move downward along the time axis.

As Figure 1 shows, the result is rather like a four-leaf clover (which is the significance of the title of this chapter, in case you've been wondering all along).

Once the various Universes pass their expansion peak and begin to contract again, it is possible that not only time is reversed, but the gravitational effect as well. There are theories advanced by important physicists to the effect that gravitational force may be weakening with time and could it be, therefore, that it reaches zero at expansion peak and that during contraction matter repels matter and negative-matter repels negative-matter, while matter attracts negative-matter?

You might object at once by asking how the cosmon, for instance, will contract, if all its parts experience a mutual repulsion. To which I reply, why not? Right now the cosmon is expanding even though all its parts experience a mutual attraction. Perhaps the cosmon and its sister Universes are so arranged that the grand expansion or contraction is always in opposition to the force of gravity. The force of gravity is incredibly weak and it may be its fate always to be overborne by other forces and effects.

However, in the process of contraction, the overall gravitational attraction between cosmon and negative-cosmon on the one hand, and between anticosmon and negative-anticosmon on the other, may bring them together along the space axis just as time reversal brings them together along the time axis.

When cosmon, anticosmon, negative-cosmon, and negative-anticosmon all come together, they produce—Nothing.

In the Beginning, there is Nothing.

In the End, there is Nothing.

But if we begin with Nothing, why doesn't it stay Nothing?

Why should it? We can say that $0 + 0 = 0$, and that $+1 + (-1) = 0$. Both $0 + 0$ and $+1 + (-1)$ are equivalent ways of saying "zero" and why should one be any more "real" or "natural" than the other? The situation can slide from Nothing to Four-Leaf Clover without difficulty, for no essential has been changed by that transition.

But why should the shift come at one time rather than another? The mere fact that it comes at a particular time means that something has made it shift.

Indeed? What do you mean by time? Time and space only exist in connection with the expansion and contraction of the leaves of the Four-Leaf Clover. When the leaves don't exist, neither does time nor space.

In the Beginning, there is Nothing—not even time or space.

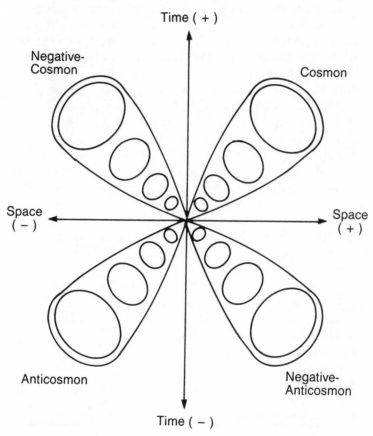

Figure 1 — the Four-Leaf Clover

The Four-Leaf Clover comes into existence at no particular time and in no particular place. When it is in existence, time and space exist in a cycle of expansion and contraction that takes eighty billion years. There is then a timeless, spaceless interval and again an expansion and contraction. Since there is nothing we can do with a timeless, spaceless interval, we can eliminate it and consider the cycles of expansion and contraction to be following immediately upon one another. We then have an oscillating quadruple-Universe, an oscillating Four-Leaf Clover.

And who says only one need exist? There are no limits, no bounds, no ends, no edges to Nothingness. There may therefore be a infinite number of oscillating Four-Leaf Clovers, separated by something that is neither time nor space.

And here the mind boggles. I have gone as far as I care to, and I leave it to the Ardent Reader to carry matters further. For myself, enough (to coin a phrase) is enough.

## AFTERWORD

This essay is rather more out of date than most of the essays I have written. Cosmogony (the study of the origin of the Universe) has advanced greatly in the past couple of decades—and I foresaw virtually none of that advance.

However, in one respect, I grasped something early on, and that is why I include the essay in this book.

I had gotten tired of hearing people ask, "Well, if the Universe started as a cosmic egg, where did the cosmic egg come from?" Clearly, they thought I could not answer that without falling back on theology.

So you'll find in the foregoing essay something I called "Asimov's Cosmogonic Principle," which I presented as: "In the Beginning, there was Nothing."

And in the new theories of the "inflationary Universe," advanced a decade later by real theoretical physicists, the Universe does indeed come into being out of Nothing. I admit that I allowed the Universe to arise out of Nothing by supposing the existence of "negative-energy," whereas the inflationary-Universe people had it happen as a result of a quantum fluctuation, but that's a detail.

The important thing is that you start with Nothing—and I got to that notion first.

# 9

# Twelve Point Three
# Six Nine

Once in junior high school, my English teacher gave the class the assignment of reading and pondering Leigh Hunt's poem "Abou ben Adhem." Perhaps you remember it.

Abou ben Adhem awoke one night from a deep dream of peace and found an angel making a list of the names of those who loved God. Ben Adhem naturally wanted to know if he was included and was told he wasn't. Humbly he asked to be included as one who loved his fellow men, at least.

The next night the angel reappeared "And show'd the names whom love of God had bless'd/And lo! Ben Adhem's name led all the rest."

I knew the poem and had a pretty good notion as to the course of the class discussion planned for the next day by the teacher. There would be little homilies about how to love God meant to love mankind and vice versa. I agreed with that, but thought it would be rather dull to spend time on so self-evident a proposition. Could not some alternate meaning be wrenched out of the miserably unsubtle poem? I could find none.

The next day, our English teacher, with a kindly smile, asked, "Now, class, who will volunteer to tell me why Abou ben Adhem's name led all the rest?"

Blinding inspiration struck me. I raised my hand violently and when the teacher nodded at me, I said, with a beatific smile, "Alphabetical order, sir!"

I didn't really expect him to be grateful for this new light I was shedding on Leigh Hunt's poem, so I wasn't surprised when he pointed his thumb quietly at the door. I left (knowing the way, for I had been ejected for obstreperous behavior on several previous occasions) and the class discussion went on without me.

But, as I discovered afterward, Abou ben Adhem had been effectively punctured and the teacher had gone on to discuss other matters, so I suppose I won out.

If I get weary of the lack of subtlety in "Abou ben Adhem" you can imagine how desperate I get at those who maintain the entire Universe to be equally unsubtle.

Naturally I get most desperate when the unsubtlety is of a sort to which I feel myself to be (in secret) deeply attracted. For instance, there are those who, having noted some simple and hackneyed relationships between numbers or between geometrical figures, promptly suppose that the structure of the Universe is designed merely to show off those relationships. (And, to my self-disgust, I always find this sort of thing interesting.)

Mystics have been guilty of such simple-mindedness, I am sure, in every society complicated enough to have invented arithmetic, but the best early examples known today are to be found among the Greeks.

For instance, Pythagoras of Samos, about 525 B.C., plucked taut strings and listened to the notes that were produced. He observed that pleasant-sounding combinations of notes were heard when strings were of lengths that bore a simple arithmetical ratio to one other: 1 to 2 or 3 to 4 to 5. It was that, perhaps, which led him and his followers to believe that the physical world was governed by numerical relationships, and simple numerical relationships at that.

It is true, of course, that numerical relationships are of importance in the Universe, but they are not always simple by any means. For instance, a fact of apparently fundamental importance is the ratio of the mass of the proton to the electron—which is 1836.11. Why 1836.11? No one knows.

But we can't blame the Pythagoreans for their lack of knowledge of modern physics. Let us rather consider with astonishment a pupil of Pythagoras by the name of Philolaus of Tarentum. As far as we know, he was the first man in history (about 480 B.C.) to suggest that the Earth moved through space.

Let's try to trace his reasoning. As the Greeks could see, the starry heavens revolved about the Earth. However, seven particular heavenly objects—the Sun, the Moon, Mercury, Venus, Mars, Jupiter, and Saturn—moved independently of the fixed stars and of each other. One might suppose, therefore, that there were eight concentric (and transparent) spheres in the heaven, revolving about the Earth. The innermost contained the Moon affixed to itself, the next Mercury, then Venus, then the Sun, then Mars, Jupiter, Saturn. The eighth and outermost contained the host of stars.

Philolaus was not content with this arrangement. He suggested that the eight spheres did not move about the Earth but about some "central fire." This central fire was invisible, but its reflection could be seen as the Sun. Furthermore, the Earth itself was also fixed in a sphere that revolved about the central fire. And, in addition, there was still *another* body, the "counter-Earth," which we never saw because it stayed always on the side of the Sun opposite ourselves, and that counter-Earth was in still another sphere that revolved about the central fire.

So a total of ten revolving spheres are allowed for in Philolaus' system: the eight ordinary ones, plus a ninth for the Earth, and a tenth for the counter-Earth.

However did Philolaus arrive at that? To be sure, two centuries after his time, Aristarchus of Samos also suggested the Earth moved—but he insisted it moved around the Sun. This was considered absurd at the time, but at least Aristarchus made use of bodies perceptible to the senses. Why did Philolaus invent an invisible central fire and an invisible counter-Earth?

The probable answer rests with the *number* of spheres. If the Earth revolved about the Sun, you would have to add a sphere for the Earth, but subtract one for the now stationary Sun and the total would still be eight. If you kept both Earth and Sun moving about an invisible center and added a counter-Earth, you would have ten.

And why ten spheres? Well, the Pythagoreans thought ten was a particularly satisfactory number because $1 + 2 + 3 + 4 = 10$, something which lent itself to involved reasoning that ended in ten as a perfect number. If, then, we argue that the Universe has to be perfect and that its notion of perfection had to agree with that of the Pythagoreans, and if it were further granted that the Universe had no reason for existence but to exhibit that perfection—then the total number of spheres has to be ten (even though two of the spheres have to be kept secret for some arcane reason).

Unfortunately the trouble with all such irrefutable arguments based on the mystical properties of numbers is that no two people can ever quite bring themselves to believe in the same mystique. The Pythagorean notion went out of the window and astronomers contented themselves with eight spheres. Indeed, since the starry sphere was dismissed as mere background, the magic number became seven.

Arguments concerning the structure of the Universe, based on simple arithmetic (and worse) did not die out with the Greeks, by any means.

In 1610 Galileo, using the telescope, discovered that Jupiter had four lesser bodies circling it. This meant that there were eleven bodies (excluding the fixed stars themselves) that circled the Earth according to the old Greek system—or eleven bodies circling the Sun, according to the new-fangled Copernican system.

Great was the opposition to this new discovery, and the arguments against it by one adversary will live forever in the history of human folly.

It was not necessary, explained the learned scholar, to look through the telescope. The new bodies could not be there, since there could only be seven bodies circling the Earth (or Sun) and no more. If the additional bodies were seen, it had to be because of a defect in the telescope, because the new bodies *could not* be there.

And how could one be sure they could not be there? Easy! As there are seven openings in the head—two eyes, two ears, two nostrils, and a mouth—so there must be seven planetary bodies in the heavens.

Thus, it seemed, it was necessary to so order the entire Universe as to make some sort of permanent record in the heavens as to the number of openings in the human head. It was as though God needed crib notes that would enable him to keep the figure in mind so that he wouldn't create Man with the wrong number of openings. (I'm sorry if that sounds blasphemous, for I don't mean it to be so. The blasphemy is on the part of those men, past and present, who try to make it appear that God is a kindergarten infant, playing with number blocks.)

Such folly dies hard. In fact, it never dies.

Astronomers, having accepted the Copernican notion of bodies circling the Sun rather than the Earth, now recognized two classes of bodies in the Solar system.

There were bodies that revolved directly about the Sun; these were the planets and in 1655, six were recognized—Mercury, Venus, Earth, Mars, Jupiter, and Saturn. Then, there were bodies that revolved not about the Sun directly, but about one of the planets. These were the satellites and there were five of them recognized at the time: our own Moon and the four satellites of Jupiter, which Galileo had discovered (Io, Europa, Ganymede, and Callisto).

But in 1655 the Dutch astronomer Christiaan Huygens discovered a satellite of Saturn which he named Titan. That meant the Solar system consisted of six planets and six satellites. Huygens was a first-class scientist and a great figure in the history of astronomy and physics, but he wasn't proof against the symmetry of six and six. He announced that the total was complete. No more bodies remained to be found.

Alas, in 1671 the Italian-French astronomer Giovanni D. Cassini discovered another satellite of Saturn and spoiled the symmetry. Huygens lived to see it, too. Indeed, he lived to see Cassini discover three more satellites of Saturn.

Then we have Johann Kepler, who was not content with merely working out the number of heavenly bodies on the basis of simple arithmetic. He went a step further and tried to work out the relationships among the distances of those bodies from the Sun by interconnection with simple geometry.

There are five and only five regular solids (solids with all faces equal and all angles equal—as is true, for instance, of the cube, the most familiar of the five).

Why not reason as follows, then? The regular solids are perfect and so is the Universe. There are just five regular solids and, since there are six planets, there are just five interplanetary gaps.

Kepler therefore attempted to nest the five regular solids in such a way that the six planets moved along the various boundaries in the proper relationship of distances. Kepler spent a lot of time trying to adjust his solids and failed. (The acid test, that makes Kepler a great deal more than a crackpot, is that, having failed, he promptly dropped the notion.)

During the last week of 1966, however, I discovered something about Kepler I had not known before.

I was attending a meeting of the American Association for the Advancement of Science and was listening to papers on the history of astronomy. One particularly interesting paper included the statement that Kepler had felt that there ought to be just 360 days in a year. The Earth was rotating faster than it should have been, which was what made the number of days in the year 365¼. (If the day were 24 hours and 21 minutes long, there would be just 360 days in the year.)

This too-fast rotation of the Earth, in Kepler's view, somehow carried over to the Moon, forcing it to revolve a bit too quickly about the Earth. Obviously the Moon should be revolving about the Earth in just 1/12 of a year; that is, in about 30⅖ days. Instead, it revolved in only about 29½ days.

If the Earth revolved about the Sun in 360 days of 24⅓ hours apiece (naturally, the hours and its subdivisions would be slightly lengthened to make just 24 hours to the slightly longer day), how convenient that would be. After all, 360 is such a pleasant number, being exactly divisible by 2, 3, 4, 5, 6, 8, 9, 10, 12, 15, 18, 20, 24, 30, 36, 40, 45, 60, 72, 90, 120, and 180. No other number approximating its size is evenly divisible in so many different ways.

And if each lunar month were equal to 30 days of a little over 24 hours each, there would be exactly 12 lunar months in a year. The number 12 is evenly divisible by 2, 3, 4, and 6; and 30 by 2, 3, 5, 6, 10, and 15.

Nor is it just a matter of tricks of numbers. With 30 days to the lunar month and 12 lunar months to the year, a beautifully simple calendar could be devised.

Instead, what do we have? About 29½ days to a lunar month, about 365¼ days to a year, and about 12⅜ lunar months to the year. And the result of this farrago of fractions? Nearly five thousand years of fiddling with calendars that has ended with one that is *still* inconvenient.

My thoughts might have ended there, but the lecturer at the AAAS meeting gave the number of lunar months in the year in decimal form rather than fractions. He said, "Instead of 12 lunar months to a year, there are 12.369."*

My eyebrows raised in astonishment at once. Indeed? Are there really 12.369 lunar months in a year? My mind began fitting notions together and at the conclusion of the lecture I raised my hand to ask a question. I wanted to know if Kepler had tried to draw a certain simple deduction from that figure. No, said the lecturer, it sounds like something Kepler might have done, but he didn't.

Excellent! Excellent! That left me free to indulge in a little mysticism of my own. After all, every one knows I am in love with figures, and I could easily design the Universe in order to show off first-grade arithmetic. What's more, I happen to be interested in the Bible, so why not show that the design of the Universe is connected with certain elementary statistics involving the Bible?

(I am not without precedent here. Isaac Newton was an indefatigable biblical student who produced nothing worthy of note; and the Scottish mathematician John Napier, who first worked

---

* Actually, this is wrong, I think. According to the best figures I can find, the number of lunar months in a year is closer to 12.368. It is 12.36827, to be exact. But let's not spoil my essay.

out logarithms, also worked out a completely worthless system for interpreting the Book of Revelation.)

Let me, therefore, go along with Kepler. Let us suppose that the whole purpose of the rate of Earth's rotation about its axis, the Moon's revolution about the Earth, and the revolution of the Earth/Moon system about the Sun, is to present mankind with pretty numbers and a symmetrical calendar.

What, then, went wrong? Surely God knew what he was doing and would not make a careless mistake. If the year were more than 360 days long there would have to be a reason for it; an exact reason. The error would be no error but would be something designed to instruct mankind in the simple-minded manner that mystics seem to like to consider characteristic of God.

There are 365¼ days in a year so that the excess over 360 (the "right" number) is 5¼ or, in decimal form, 5.25. You must admit now that 5.25 is an interesting number since 25 is the square of 5.

Let's reason like a mystic. Can 5.25 be a coincidence? Of course not. It must have meaning and that meaning must be in the Bible. (After all, God is the center about which the Bible revolves as the Sun is the center about which the Earth revolves. What is more natural than to find in the revolving Bible the reasons for the details of the revolving Earth.)

The Old Testament, according to tradition, is divided into three parts: the Law, the Prophets, and the Writings. All are holy and inspired, but the Law is the most sacred portion and that is made up of the first five books of the Bible: Genesis, Exodus, Leviticus, Numbers, and Deuteronomy.

Why, then, are there five days beyond the "proper" 360? Surely in order to mark the five books of the Law in the very motions of the Earth. And why the extra quarter day beyond the five? Why, to make the excess not merely 5 but 5.25. By squaring the 5 and emphasizing it in that fashion, the Law is demonstrated to be not only holy, but particularly holy.

Of course, there is a catch. The length of the year is not really precisely 365.25 days. It is a bit short of that, and is 365.2422 days long. (To be even more precise it is 365.242197 days long, but 365.2422 is close enough, surely.)

Does that mean that the whole scheme falls to the ground? If you think so, you don't know how the mind of a mystic works. The Bible is so large and complex a book that almost any conceivable number can be made to have a biblical significance. The only limit is the ingenuity of the human mind.

Let's, for instance, take a look at 365.2422. The excess over the "proper" 360 is 5.2422. The figures to the right of the decimal point can be broken up into 24 and 22 and the average is 23. What, then, is the significance of the 23?

We have settled that the 5 represents the five books of the Law. That leaves the Prophets and the Writings. How many books are contained in those? The answer is 34.†

That doesn't seem to get us anywhere—but wait. Twelve of the books are relatively short prophetic works: Hosea, Joel, Amos, Obadiah, Jonah, Micah, Nahum, Habakkuk, Zephaniah, Haggai, Zechariah, and Malachi. For convenience, in ancient times, these were often included in a single roll which was referred to as the Book of the Twelve.

Thus, in the apocryphal book of Ecclesiasticus (accepted as canonical by the Catholics) the author—writing about 180 B.C.—lists the great men of biblical history. After mentioning the major prophets individually, he lumps the minor prophets together:

> Ecclesiasticus 49:10. And of the twelve prophets let the memorial be blessed . . .

Well, then, if the twelve minor prophets be included as a single book—as there is ample precedent for doing—how many books are there in the Prophets and Writings together by the Jewish/Protestant count? Why, 23.

We can therefore say that of the number of days in the year (365.2422), 360 days represent the "correct" figure, 5 days represent the Law, and 0.2422 represent the Prophets and the Writ-

† At least according to Jews and Protestants. The Roman Catholic version of the Bible includes eight additional books considered apocryphal by Jews and Protestants.

ings. The days of the year thus become a memorial to the Old Testament.

That takes us to the number of lunar months in the year, which is 12.369, the number that first attracted my attention.

If the days in the year represent the Old Testament, then surely the lunar months in the year must represent the New Testament. Any mystic will tell you that this is self-evident.

Well, then, what can we say would be a central difference between the Old Testament and the New Testament? We might try this: In the Old Testament, God is treated as a single entity while in the New Testament, He is revealed as a Trinity. Consequently if this is so, and if the number of lunar months in a year represents the New Testament, that number should somehow be related to the number 3.

And if we look at 12.369, we see that it is neatly divisible by 3. Hurrah! We are on the right track, as any fool can plainly see (provided he *is* a fool, of course).

Let us, then, divide 12.369 by 3, and we come out with 4.123. Surely that is a highly significant number, consisting, as it does, of the first four integers.

And what connection do the first four integers have with the New Testament? Why the answer is obvious and springs to the mind at once.

The four gospels, of course! The four separate biographies of Jesus by Matthew, Mark, Luke, and John.

It so happens that Gospels 1, 2, and 3—Matthew, Mark, and Luke—give essentially the same view of Jesus. Many of the incidents found in one are found in the others and the general trend of events is virtually identical in all. These are the "synoptic Gospels," the word "synoptic" meaning "with one eye." Gospels 1, 2, and 3 all see Jesus with the same eye, so to speak.

Gospel 4, that of John, is quite different from the other three; differing, in fact, on almost every point, even quite basic ones.

Therefore, if we are going to have the number of lunar months in the year signify the Gospels, would it not be right to group 1, 2, and 3 together and keep 4 separate? And is this not precisely what is done in a number like 4.123?

If you had doubts before, would you not admit we were on the right track now?

We can say then that of the number of lunar months in a year, 12.369, the 12 represents the Gospel of John (4 times 3, for the Trinity) and the 0.369 represent the Synoptic Gospels (123 times 3).

But why is the Fourth Gospel first? Why is a third of the number of lunar months in a year 4.123, rather than 123.4?

This is a good and legitimate question and I have an answer. If the central fact of the New Testament is the Trinity, we must ask how the matter of the Trinity is handled in the various Gospels.

The first evidence of the existence of all three aspects of God together is at the time of Jesus' baptism by John the Baptist (who, of course, is *not* the John who wrote the Fourth Gospel). In Mark, the oldest of the Gospels, the incident at the baptism is described as follows:

> Mark 1:10. And . . . he [Jesus] saw the heavens opened, and the Spirit like a dove descending upon him:
>
> Mark 1:11. And there came a voice from heaven, saying, Thou art my beloved Son, in whom I am well pleased.

Here Father, Son, and Holy Spirit are all present at once. Nothing in this account, however, would make us necessarily think that this manifestation was apparent to anyone outside the Trinity. There is nothing to make us suppose, for instance, (if Mark only is considered) that John the Baptist, who was present at that moment, was also aware of the descent of the Spirit, or heard the voice from heaven.

Similar accounts are given in Matthew 3:16–17, and in Luke 3:22. Neither in Matthew nor in Luke is it stated that anyone outside the Trinity was aware of what was happening.

In John's Gospel, however, the Fourth, the account of the descent of the Spirit is placed in the mouth of John the Baptist.

> John 1:32. And John bare record, saying, I saw the Spirit descending from heaven like a dove, and it abode upon him.

Since, in Gospel 4, the first manifestation of the Trinity is described as clearly apparent to man, something that is not so in

Gospels 1, 2, and 3, then obviously the number *ought* to be 4.123, rather than 123.4.

What more can anyone want?

Now let me emphasize something I hope has been quite apparent to everyone. I am merely playing with numbers. What I have presented here in connection with the days and months in the year has been made up out of my head, and I am no more serious about it than I was, once long ago, about the alphabeticity of Abou ben Adhem.

And yet I would not be in the least surprised to find that some people were tempted to think there was something to all this nonsense. They might wonder if I had accidentally stumbled on a great truth without knowing it, even while I was imagining myself to be doing nothing more than playing silly games.

And I suppose that some people (maybe even the same people) would say: "Hey, I'll bet Abou ben Adhem's name led all the rest because the list *was* in alphabetical order."

## AFTERWORD

Because I am interested in the Bible and in numbers—and in crackpot theories as well (within limits)—I have read occasional articles and books in which the Bible is interpreted in all sorts of ways by the remarkably ingenious use of numbers.

I always say to anyone who is impressed by this sort of thing that given sufficient thought and time, the proper concatenation of numbers and any sufficiently complex piece of writing can be made to prove anything. (You ought to try to follow the mathematical reasoning of those who think that Shakespeare's plays are a vast cryptogram demonstrating the real author to be someone else. You would surely be amazed, provided your brain didn't turn to mush, first.)

In any case, I always suspected that given just a *little* time, I could think up something as silly as anything produced by the painful labors of the poor simps who take that sort of thing seriously. The final portion of the foregoing essay is an example of what I mean.

# 10

## Knock Plastic!

One of my favorite stories (undoubtedly apocryphal, else why would I remember it?) concerns the horseshoe that hung on the wall over the desk of Professor Niels Bohr.

A visitor stared at it with astonishment and finally could not help exclaiming, "Professor Bohr, you are one of the world's great scientists. Surely you cannot believe that object will bring you good luck?"

"Why, no," replied Bohr, smiling, "of course not. I wouldn't believe such nonsense for a moment. It's just that I've been informed it will bring me good luck whether I believe it will or not."

And I too have an amiable weakness—I am an indefatigable knocker of wood. If I make any statement which strikes me as too smug or self-satisfied, or in any way too boastful of good fortune, I look feverishly about for wood to knock.

Of course, I don't for one moment really believe that knocking wood will keep off the jealous demons who lie in wait for the unwary soul who boasts of his good luck without the proper propitiation of the spirits and demons on whom good and bad luck depend. Still—after all—you know—come to think of it—what can you lose?

I have been growing a little uneasy, in consequence, over the way in which natural wood is used less and less in ordinary construction, and is therefore harder and harder to find in an emergency. I might, in fact, have been heading for a severe nervous breakdown, had I not heard a casual remark made by a friend.

He said, some time ago, "Things are going very well for me lately." With that, he knocked on the tabletop and calmly said, "Knock plastic!"

Heavens! Talk about blinding flashes of illumination. Of course! In the modern world, the spirits will grow modern too. The old dryads, who inhabited trees and made sacred groves sacred, giving rise to the modern notion of knocking wood,* must be largely unemployed now that more than half the world's forests have been ground up into toothpicks and newsprint. Undoubtedly they now make their homes in vats of polymerizing plastic and respond eagerly to the cry of "Knock plastic!" I recommend it to one and all.

But knocking wood is only one example of a class of notions, so comforting and so productive of feelings of security, that men will seize upon them on the slightest provocation or on none at all.

Any piece of evidence tending to support such a "Security Belief," however frail and nonsensical it might be, is grabbed and hugged close to the bosom. Every piece of evidence tending to break down a Security Belief, however strong and logical that evidence might be, is pushed away. (Indeed, if the evidence against a Security Belief is strong enough, those presenting the evidence might well be in danger of violence.)

It is very important, therefore, in weighing the merits of any

---

* Some people say that knocking wood is symbolic of touching the True Cross, but I don't believe that at all. I'm sure the habit must antedate Christianity.

widely held opinion, to consider whether it can be viewed as a Security Belief. If it is, then its popularity means nothing; it must be viewed with considerable suspicion.

It might, of course, be that the view is accurate. For instance, it is a comforting thought to Americans that the United States is the richest and most powerful nation in the world. But in all truth, it *is,* and this particular Security Belief (for Americans) is justified.

Nevertheless, the Universe is an insecure place, indeed, and on general principles Security Beliefs are much more likely to be false than true.

For instance, a poll of the heavy smokers of the world would probably show that almost all of them are firmly convinced that the arguments linking smoking with lung cancer are not conclusive. The same heavy majority would exist if members of the tobacco industry were polled. Why not? The opposite belief would leave them too medically insecure, or economically insecure, for comfort.

Then, too, when I was young, we kids had the firm belief that if one dropped a piece of candy into the incredible filth of the city streets, one need only touch the candy to the lips and then wave it up to the sky ("kissing it to God") to make it perfectly pure and sanitary. We believed this despite all strictures on germs, because if we didn't believe it, that piece of candy would go uneaten by ourselves, and someone else, who did believe it, would get to eat it.

Naturally, anyone can make up the necessary evidence in favor of a Security Belief. "My grandfather smoked a pack a day for seventy years and when he died his lungs were the last to go." Or "Jerry kissed candy to God yesterday and today he won the forty-yard dash."

If Grandfather had died of lung cancer at thirty-six, or if Jerry had come down with cholera—no problem, you cite other instances.

But let's not sink to special cases. I have come up with six very broad Security Beliefs that, I think, blanket the field—although the Gentle Reader is welcome to add a seventh, if he can think of one.

Security Belief No. 1: *There exist supernatural forces that can be cajoled or forced into protecting mankind.*

Here is the essence of superstition.

When a primitive hunting society is faced with the fact that game is sometimes plentiful and sometimes not, and when a primitive agricultural society watches drought come one year and floods the next, it seems only natural to assume—in default of anything better—that some more-than-human force is arranging things in this way.

Since nature is capricious, it would seem that the various gods, spirits, demons (whatever you wish to call them) are themselves capricious. In one way or another they must be induced or made to subordinate their wild impulses to the needs of humanity.

Who says this is easy? Obviously, it calls for all the skill of the wisest and most experienced men of the society. So there develops a specialized class of spirit manipulators—a priesthood, to use that term in its broadest sense.

It is fair enough to call spirit manipulation "magic." The word comes from "magi," the name given to the priestly caste of Zoroastrian Persia.

The popularity of this Security Belief is almost total. A certain Influential Personage in science fiction, who is much given to adopting these Security Beliefs, and then pretending he is a member of a persecuted minority, once wrote to me: "Every society but ours has believed in magic. Why should we be so arrogant as to think that everyone but ourselves is wrong?"

My answer at the time was: "Every society but ours has believed the Sun revolved about the Earth. Do you want to settle the matter by majority vote?"

Actually the situation is worse than even the Influential Personage maintains. Every society, *including our own,* believes in magic. Nor do I restrict the belief only to the naïve and uneducated of our culture. The most rational elements of our society, the well educated, the scientists, retain scraps of belief in magic.

When a horseshoe hangs over Bohr's desk (assuming one really did), that is a magical warding-off of misfortune through the power of "cold iron" over a spirit world stuck in the Bronze Age. When I knock on wood (or plastic) I too engage in spirit manipulation.

But can we argue, as the Influential Personage does, that there must be something to magic since so many people believe in it?

No, of course not. It is too tempting to believe. What can be easier than to believe that one can avoid misfortune by so simple a device as knocking on wood? If it's wrong, you lose nothing. If it's right, you gain so much. One would need to be woodenly austere indeed to refuse the odds.

Still, if magic doesn't work, won't people recognize that eventually and abandon it?

But who says magic doesn't work? Of course it works—in the estimation of those who believe.

Suppose you knock on wood and misfortune doesn't follow. *See?* Of course, you might go back in time and *not* knock on wood and find out that misfortune doesn't follow, anyway—but how can you arrange a control like that?

Or suppose you see a pin and pick it up on ten successive days, and on nine of those days nothing much happened one way or the other, but on the tenth, you get good news in the mail. It is the work of a moment to remember that tenth day and forget the other nine—and what better proof do you want anyway?

Or what if you carefully light two on a match and three minutes later fall and break your leg. Surely you can argue that if you had lit that third cigarette, you would have broken your neck, not your leg.

You can't lose! If you want to believe, you can believe!

Indeed, magic can work in actual fact. A tightrope walker, having surreptitiously rubbed the rabbit's foot under his belt, can advance with such self-confidence as to perform perfectly. An actor, stepping out on stage just after someone has whistled in his dressing room, can be so nervous that he will muff his lines. In other words, even if magic doesn't work, belief in magic does.

But then, how do scientists go about disproving the usefulness of magic? They don't! It's an impossibility. Few, if any, believers would accept the disproof anyway.

What scientists do is to work on the *assumption* that Security Belief No. 1 is false. They take into account no capricious forces in their analysis of the Universe. They set up a minimum number of generalizations (miscalled "natural laws") and assume that nothing happens or can be made to happen that is outside those natural laws. Advancing knowledge may make it necessary to modify the generalizations now and then, but always they remain noncapricious.

Ironically enough, scientists themselves become a new priest-hood. Some Security Believers see in the scientist the new magus. It is the scientist, now, who can manipulate the Universe, by mysterious rites understood by him only, so as to insure the safety of man under all circumstances. This belief, in my opinion, is as ill-founded as the earlier one.

Again, a Security Belief can be modified to give it a scientific tang. Thus, where once we had angels and spirits descending to Earth to interfere in our affairs and mete out justice, we now have advanced beings in flying saucers doing so (according to some). In fact, part of the popularity of the whole flying saucer mystique is, in my opinion, the ease with which the extraterrestrials can be looked upon as a new scientific version of angels.

Security Belief No. 2: *There is no such thing, really, as death.*

Man, as far as we know, is the only species capable of foreseeing the inevitability of death. An individual man or woman knows, for certain, as no other creature can, that someday he or she must die.

This is an absolutely shattering piece of knowledge and one can't help but wonder how much it, by itself, affects human behavior, making it fundamentally different from the behavior of other animals.

Or perhaps the effect is less than we might expect, since men so universally and so resolutely refuse to think of it. How many individuals live as though they expect to keep on going forever? Almost every one of us, I think.

A comparatively sensible way of denying death is to suppose that it is a family that is the real living entity and that the individual does not truly die while the family lives. This is one of the bases of ancestor worship, since the ancestor lives as long as he has a descendant to worship him.

Under these circumstances, naturally, the lack of children (especially sons, for in most tribal societies women didn't count) was a supreme disaster. It was so in early Israelite society, for instance, as the Bible tells us. Definite rules are given in the Bible that oblige men to take, as wives, the widows of their childless brothers, in order to give those wives sons who might be counted as descendants of the dead man.

The crime of Onan ("onanism") is not what you probably think it is, but was his refusal to perform this service for his dead brother (see Genesis 38:7–10).

A more literal denial of death is also very popular. Almost every society we know of has some notion of an "afterlife." There is someplace where an immortal residue of each human body can go. The shade can live a gray and dismal existence in a place like Hades or Sheol, but he lives.

Under more imaginative conditions, the afterlife, or a portion of it, can become an abode of bliss while another portion can become an abode of torment. Then, the notion of immortality can be linked with the notion of reward and punishment. There is a Security Belief angle to this too, since it increases one's security in the midst of poverty and misery to know you'll live like a god in Heaven, while that rich fellow over there is going straight to Hell, ha, ha, and good for him.

Failing an afterlife in some place beyond Earth, you can have one on Earth itself by arranging a belief in reincarnation or in transmigration of souls.

While reincarnation is no part of the dominant religious beliefs in the Western world, such are its Security Belief values that any evidence in its favor is delightedly accepted. When, in the 1950s, a rather silly book entitled *The Search for Bridey Murphy* appeared and seemed to indicate the actual existence of reincarnation, it became a best seller at once. There was nothing to it, to be sure.

And, of course, the whole doctrine of spiritualism, the entire battery of mediums and table-rappings and ectoplasm and ghosts and poltergeists and a million other things are all based on the firm insistence of mankind that death does not take place; that something persists; that the conscious personality is somehow immortal.

Is there any use then in trying to debunk spiritualism? It can't be done. No matter how many mediums are shown to be fakes, the ardent believer will believe the next medium he encounters.

He may do even better. He may denounce the proof of fakedom as itself a fraud and continue to have faith in the fake, however transparent.

Science proceeds on the assumption that Security Belief No. 2 is false also.

Yet scientists are human too, and individuals among them (as distinct from Science in the abstract) long for security. Sir Oliver J. Lodge, a scientist of considerable reputation, depressed by the death of a son in World War I, tried to reach him through spiritualism and became a devotee of "psychic research."

My friend, the Influential Personage, has often cited Lodge and men like him as evidence of the value of psychic research. "If you believe Lodge's observations on the electron, why don't you believe his observations on spirits?"

The answer is, of course, that Lodge has no security to gain from an electron but does from spirits. —And scientists are human too.

Security Belief No. 3: *There is some purpose to the Universe.*

After all, if you're going to have a whole battery of spirits and demons running the Universe, you can't really have them doing it all for nothing.

The Zoroastrians of Persia worked out a delightfully complicated scheme of the Universe. They imagined the whole of existence to be engaged in a cosmic war. Ahura Mazda, leading countless spirits under the banner of Light and Good, encountered an equally powerful army under Ahriman fighting for Darkness and Evil. The forces were almost evenly matched and individual men could feel that with them lay the balance of power. If they strove to be good they were contributing to the "right side" in the most colossal conflict ever imagined.

Some of these notions crept into Judaism and Christianity, and we have the war of God versus the Devil. In the Judeo-Christian view, however, there is no question as to who will win. God must and will win. It makes things less exciting.

This Security Belief is also assumed to be false by Science. Science does not merely ignore the possibility of a cosmic war, when it tries to work out the origins and ultimate fate of the

Universe; it ignores the possibility of any deliberate purpose anywhere.

The most basic generalizations of science (the laws of thermo-dynamics, for instance, or quantum theory) assume random movement of particles, random collisions, random energy trans-fers, and so on. From considerations of probability one can assume that with many particles and over long periods of time, certain events are reasonably sure to take place, but concerning individual particles and over short periods of time, nothing can be predicted.

Possibly, no scientific view is so unpopular with nonscientists as this one. It seems to make everything so "meaningless."

But does it? Is it absolutely necessary to have the entire Uni-verse or all of life meaningful. Can we not consider that what is meaningless in one context is meaningful in another; that a book in Chinese which is meaningless to me is meaningful to a China-man? And can we not consider that each of us can so arrange his own particular life so as to make it meaningful to himself and to those he influences? And in that case does not all of life and all the Universe come to have meaning *to him?*

Surely it is those who find their own lives essentially meaning-less who most strive to impose meaning on the Universe as a way of making up for the personal lack.

Security Belief No. 4: *Individuals have special powers that will enable them to get something for nothing.*

"Wishing will make it so" is a line from a popular song and oh, how many people believe it. It is much easier to wish, hope, and pray, than to take the trouble to *do* something.

I once wrote a book in which a passage contained a description of the dangers of the population explosion and of the necessity for birth control. A reviewer who looked over that passage wrote in the margin, "I'd say this was God's problem, wouldn't you?"

It was like taking candy from a baby to write under that in clear print: "God helps those who help themselves."

But think of the popularity of stories in which characters get three wishes, or the power to turn everything they touch into gold, or are given a spear that will always find the mark, or a gem that will discolor in the presence of danger.

And just imagine if we had amazing powers all the time and didn't know it—telepathy, for instance. How eager we are to have it. (Who hasn't experienced a coincidence and at once cried out "Telepathy!") How ready we are to believe in advanced cases elsewhere since that will improve the possibilities of ourselves possessing the power if we practiced hard enough.

Some wild powers represent the ability to foresee the future—clairvoyance. Or else one gains the knowledge to calculate the future by means of astrology, numerology, palmistry, tea leaves, or a thousand other hoary frauds.

Here we come close to Security Belief No. 1. If we foresee the future, we might change it by appropriate action and this is nearly the equivalent of spirit manipulation.

In a way, Science has fulfilled the fairy tales. The jet plane goes far faster and farther than the flying horse and the seven-league boots of the fable-writers of yore. We have rockets which seek out their targets, like Thor's Hammer, and do far more damage. We have, not gems, but badges that discolor in the presence of too much accumulated radiation.

But these do not represent "something for nothing." They are not awarded through supernatural agency and don't act capriciously. They are the hard-earned products of the generalizations concerning the Universe built up by a Science that denies most or all of the Security Beliefs.

Security Belief No. 5: *You are better than the next fellow.*

This is a very tempting belief, but it is often a dangerous one. You tell this to that big bruiser facing you and he's liable to break your neck. So you appoint a surrogate: Your father is better than his father; your college is better than his college; your accent is better than his accent; your cultural group is better than his cultural group.

Naturally this fades off into racism and it is not at all surprising that the more lowly the social, economic, or personal position of an individual, the more likely he is to fall prey to the racist temptation.

It is not surprising that even scientists as individuals have trouble with this one. They can rationalize and say that it must surely be possible to divide mankind into categories in such a way that some categories are superior to others in some ways. Some groups are taller than other groups, for instance, as a matter of genetic inheritance. Might it not be that some groups are, by birth and nature, more intelligent or more honest than others?

A certain Nobel Prize winner demanded, some time ago, that scientists stop ducking the issue; that they set about determining whether slum-dwellers (English translation: Negroes) are not actually "inferior" to non-slum-dwellers and whether attempts to help them were not therefore futile.

I was asked by a certain newspaper to write my views about this, but I said I had better tell them, in advance, what my views were going to be, and save myself the trouble of writing an article they wouldn't print.

I said that, in the first place, it was very likely that those who were most enthusiastic for such an investigation were quite confident that they had set up measurement standards by which the slum-dwellers would indeed prove to be "inferior." This would then relieve the superior non-slum-dwellers of responsibility toward the slum-dwellers and of any guilt feelings they might possess.

If I were wrong, I went on to say, then I felt the investigators should be as eager to find a superior minority as an inferior one. For instance, I strongly suspected that by the measurement standards prevailing in our society, it would turn out that Unitarians and Episcopalians would have a higher average IQ and a higher performance record than other religious groups.

If this proved to be so, I suggested, Unitarians and Episcopalians ought to wear some distinctive badge, be ushered to the front of the bus, be given the best seats at the theaters, be allowed to use the cleaner rest rooms and so on.

So the newspaper said, "Forget it!" and it's just as well. No one wants to search out superiors to one's self—only inferiors.

Security Belief No. 6: *If anything goes wrong, it's not one's own fault.*

Virtually everyone has a slight touch of paranoia. With a little practice, this can easily lead one into accepting one of the conspiracy theories of history.

How comforting it is to know that if you're failing in business, it's the unfair crooked tactics of the Bulgarian who owns the store down the block; if you've got a pain, it's because of the conspiracy of Nigerian doctors all about you; if you tripped when you turned to look at a girl, it was some rotten Ceylonese who put that crack in the sidewalk there.

And it is here at last that scientists are touched most closely— for this Security Belief can turn directly against them for standing out against Security Beliefs in general.

When the Security Believers are stung by the explosion of the hoaxes and follies that deceive them, what is their last, best defense? Why, that there is a conspiracy of scientists against them.

I am myself constantly being accused of participating in such a conspiracy. In today's mail, for instance, I got a most violent and indignant letter, from which I will quote only a couple of mild sentences:

"Not only are we [the public] being played for fools by politicians . . . but now these tactics have spread to science as well. If your purpose is deceiving others for whatever intention, let this tell you that you are not one hundred percent successful."

I read the letter carefully through and it seemed that he had read some magazine article which had rebutted one of his pet beliefs. He was instantly sure, therefore, not that he himself might be wrong, but that scientists were in a conspiracy against him and were under orders from NASA to lie to him.

The trouble was that he was referring to some article which had been written by someone else, not me—and I didn't know what on earth he was talking about.

However, I am positive that the forces of Rationality will rise triumphant over the onslaughts of Security Believers despite everything. (Knock plastic!)


AFTERWORD

I have lost count of how many articles I have written in which I have waxed merrily sarcastic over the irrationalities that have such a hold on most people. I am fortunate that I live in a society where being punished by torture and execution for the crime of telling the truth is considered in bad taste, or I would be in deep trouble.

Usually, even in our own permissive society, I have a tendency to pull my punches just a bit, out of a natural desire to avoid stirring up people to too great an extent, and getting too many letters filled with obscene vituperation.

When I am writing this series of essays, however, I am convinced I am addressing an audience that is particularly enlightened, and that they will let me have my say, without foaming at the mouth, even if they don't agree with me.

That makes it possible for me to write essays such as the foregoing one, and this does wonders for my psychological balance and helps keep me the sunny, ebullient person I am.

# II

## Uncertain, Coy, and Hard to Please

What with one thing and another, I have read a good deal of Shakespeare and I've noticed a great many things, including the following: Shakespeare's romantic heroines are usually much superior to his heroes in intelligence, character, and moral strength.

Juliet takes strenuous and dangerous action where Romeo merely throws himself on the ground and weeps *(Romeo and Juliet)*; Portia plays a difficult and active role where Bassanio can only stand on the sidelines and wring his hands *(Merchant of Venice)*; Benedick is a quick-witted fellow but he isn't a match for Beatrice *(Much Ado About Nothing)*. Nor is Biron a match for Rosaline *(Love's Labour's Lost)* or Orlando a match for Rosalind *(As You Like It)*. In some cases, it isn't even close. Julia is infinitely superior in every way to Proteus *(Two Gentlemen of Verona)* and Helena to Bertram *(All's Well That Ends Well)*.

The only play in which Shakespeare seems to fall prey to male chauvinism is *The Taming of the Shrew* and a good case can be made out for something more subtle than merely a strong man beating down a strong woman—but I won't bother you about that here.

Yet, despite all this, I never hear of anyone objecting to Shakespeare on the ground that he presents women inaccurately. I have never heard anyone say, "Shakespeare is all right but he doesn't understand women." On the contrary, I hear nothing but praise for his heroines.

How is it, then, that Shakespeare—who, by common consent, has caught the human race at its truest and most naked under the probing and impersonal light of his genius—tells us women are, if anything, the superior of men in all that counts, and yet so many of us nevertheless remain certain that women are inferior to men. I say "us" without qualification because women, by and large, accept their own inferiority.

You may wonder why this matter concerns me. Well, it concerns me (to put it most simply) because everything concerns me. It concerns me as a science fiction writer, especially, because science fiction involves future societies, and these, I hope, will be more rational in their treatment of 51 percent of the human race than our present society is.

It is my belief that future societies *will* be more rational in this respect, and I want to explain my reasons for this belief. I would like to speculate about Woman in the future, in the light of what has happened to Woman in the past and what is happening to Woman in the present.

To begin with, let's admit there are certain ineradicable physiological differences between men and women. (First one to yell "Vive la différence!" leaves the room.)

But are there any differences that are primarily nonphysiological? Are there intellectual, temperamental, emotional differences that you are *sure* of and that will serve to distinguish women from men in a broad, general way? I mean differences that will hold for all cultures, as the physiological differences do, and differences that are not the result of early training.

For instance, I am not impressed by the "Women are more refined" bit, since we all know that mothers begin very early in the game to slap little hands and say, "No, no, no, nice little girls don't do that."

I, myself, take the rigid position that we can never be sure about cultural influences and that the only safe distinctions we can make between the sexes are the physiological ones. Of these, I recognize two:

1. Most men are physically larger and physically stronger than most women.
2. Women get pregnant, bear babies, and suckle them. Men don't.

What can we deduce from these two differences *alone?* It seems to me that this is enough to put women at a clear disadvantage with respect to men in a primitive hunting society, which is all there was prior to, say, 10,000 B.C.

Women, after all, would be not quite as capable at the rougher aspects of hunting and would be further handicapped by a certain ungainliness during pregnancy and certain distractions while taking care of infants. In a catch-as-catch-can jostle for food, she would come up at the rear every time.

It would be convenient for a woman to have some man see to it that she was thrown a haunch after the hunting was over and then see to it, further, that some other man didn't take it away from her. A primitive hunter would scarcely do this out of humanitarian philosophy; he would have to be bribed into it. I suppose you're all ahead of me in guessing that the obvious bribe is sex.

I visualize a Stone Age treaty of mutual assistance between Man and Woman—sex for food—and as a result of this kind of togetherness, children are reared and the generations continue.*

I don't see that any of the nobler passions can possibly have had anything to do with this. I doubt that anything we would recognize as "love" was present in the Stone Age, for romantic

* After this article appeared, an anthropologist named Charlotte O. Kursh wrote me a long and fascinating letter that made it quite clear that I had dreadfully oversimplified the situation described here, that hunting was not the only food-source, and that questions of status were even more important than sex. Once one substituted "status-for-food" for "sex-for-food" she found she tended to agree with what followed. So, with this warning to take my anthropology with a grain of salt, let's continue.

love seems to have been a rather late invention and to be anything but widespread even today. (I once read that the Hollywood notion of romantic love was invented by the medieval Arabs and was spread to our own Western society by the Provençal troubadours.)

As for the concern of a father for his children, forget it. There seem definite indications that men did not really understand the connection between sexual intercourse and children until nearly historic times. Mother love may have its basis in physiology (the pleasure of suckling, for instance) but I strongly suspect that father love, however real it may be, is cultural in origin.

Although the arrangement of sex for food seems a pretty reasonable *quid pro quo*, it isn't. It is a terribly unfair arrangement because one side can break the agreement with impunity and the other cannot. If a woman punishes by withholding sex and a man by withholding food, which side will win out? *Lysistrata* to the contrary, a week without sex is a lot easier than a week without food. Furthermore, a man who tires of this mutual strike can take what he wants by force; a woman can't.

It seems to me, then, that for definite physiological reasons, the original association of men and women was a strictly unequal one, with man in the role of master and woman in the role of slave.

This is not to say that a clever woman, even in Stone Age times, might not have managed to wheedle and cajole a man into letting her have her own way. And we all know that this is certainly true nowadays, but wheedling and cajolery are slave weapons. If you, Proud Reader, are a man and don't see this, I would suggest you try to wheedle and cajole your boss into giving you a raise, or wheedle and cajole a friend into letting you have your way, and see what happens to your self-respect.

In any master-slave relationship, the master does only that portion of the work that he likes to do or that the slave cannot do; all else is reserved for the slave. It is indeed frozen into the slaves' duties not only by custom but by stern social law which defines slaves' work as unfit for free men to do.

Suppose we divide work into "big-muscle" and "little-muscle." Men would do the "big-muscle" work because he would have to and the women would then do the "little-muscle" work. Let's face it; this is usually (not always) a good deal for men because there is far more "little-muscle" work to do. ("Men work from sun to sun; women's work is never done," the old saying goes.)

Sometimes, in fact, there is no "big-muscle" work to do at all. In that case the Indian brave sits around and watches the squaw work—a situation that is true for many non-Indian braves who sit and watch their non-Indian squaws work.† Their excuse is, of course, that as proud and gorgeous males they can scarcely be expected to do "women's work."

The social apparatus of man-master and woman-slave was carried right into the most admired cultures of antiquity and was never questioned there. To the Athenians of the Golden Age, women were inferior creatures, only dubiously superior to domestic animals, and with nothing in the way of human rights. To the cultivated Athenian, it seemed virtually self-evident that male homosexuality was the highest form of love, since that was the only way in which a human being (male, that is) could love an equal. Of course, if he wanted children, he had to turn to a woman, but so what; if he wanted transportation, he turned to his horse.

As for that other great culture of the past, the Hebrew, it is quite obvious that the Bible accepts male superiority as a matter of course. It is not even a subject for discussion at any point.

In fact, by introducing the story of Adam and Eve, it has done more for woman's misery than any other book in history. The tale has enabled dozens of generations of men to blame everything on women. It has made it possible for a great many holy men of the past to speak of women in terms that a miserable sinner like myself would hesitate to use in referring to mad dogs.

In the ten commandments themselves, women are casually lumped with other forms of property, animate and inanimate. It says, in Exodus 20:17: "Thou shalt not covet thy neighbour's house, thou shalt not covet thy neighbour's wife, nor his man-

---

† Of course, if they are too chivalrous to watch a woman do all the work, they can always close their eyes. That will even give them a chance to sleep.

servant, nor his maidservant, nor his ox, nor his ass, nor any thing that is thy neighbour's."

Nor is the New Testament any better. There are a number of quotations I can choose from, but I will give you this one from Ephesians 5:22–24: "Wives, submit yourselves unto your own husbands, as unto the Lord. For the husband is the head of the wife, even as Christ is the head of the church: and he is the saviour of the body. Therefore as the church is subject unto Christ, so let the wives be to their own husbands in every thing."

This seems to me to aspire to a change in the social arrangement of man/woman from master/slave to God/creature.

I don't deny that there are many passages in both the Old and New Testaments that praise and dignify womankind. (For example, there is the Book of Ruth.) The trouble is, though, that in the social history of our species, those passages of the Bible which taught feminine wickedness and inferiority were by far the more influential. To the self-interest that led men to tighten the chains about women was added the most formidable of religious injunctions.

The situation has not utterly changed in its essence, even now. Women have attained a certain equality before the law—but only in our own century, even here in the United States. Think how shameful it is that no woman, however intelligent and educated, could vote in a national election until 1920—despite the fact that the vote was freely granted to every drunkard and moron, provided only that he happened to be male.

Yet even so—though women can vote, and hold property, and even own their own bodies—all the social apparatus of inferiority remains.

Any man can tell you that a woman is intuitive rather than logical, emotional rather than reasonable, finicky rather than creative, refined rather than vigorous. They don't understand politics, can't add a column of figures, drive cars poorly, shriek with terror at mice, and so on and so on and so on.

Because women are all these things how can they be allowed an equal share with men in the important tasks of running industry, government, society?

Such an attitude is self-fulfilling, too.

We begin by teaching a young man that he is superior to young women, and this is comforting for him. He is automatically in the top half of the human race, whatever his shortcomings may be. Anything that tends to disturb this notion threatens not only his personal self-respect but his very virility.

This means that if a woman happens to be more intelligent than a particular man in whom she is (for some arcane reason) interested, she must never, for her very life, reveal the fact. No sexual attraction can then overcome the mortal injury he receives in the very seat and core of his masculine pride, and she loses him.

On the other hand, there is something infinitely relieving to a man in the sight of a woman who is, manifestly, inferior to himself. It is for that reason that a silly woman seems "cute." The more pronouncedly male-chauvinistic a society the more highly valued is silliness in a woman.

Through long centuries, women have had to interest men somehow, if they were to achieve any economic security and social status at all, and so those who were not stupid and silly by nature had to carefully cultivate such stupidity and silliness until it came natural and they forgot they ever were intelligent.

It is my feeling that all the emotional and temperamental distinctions between men and women are of cultural origin, and that they serve the important function of maintaining the man/woman master/slave arrangement.

It seems to me that any clear look at social history shows this— and shows, moreover, that the feminine "temperament" jumps through hoops whenever that is necessary to suit man's convenience.

What was ever more feminine than Victorian womanhood, with its delicacy and modesty, its blushes and catchings of breath, its incredible refinement and its constant need for the smelling salts to overcome a deplorable tendency to faint? Was there ever a sillier toy than the stereotype of the Victorian woman; was there ever a greater insult to the dignity of *Homo sapiens?*

But you can see why the Victorian woman (or a rough approximation of her) had to exist in the late nineteenth century. It was a time when among the upper classes, there was no "little-muscle" work for her to do since servants did it. The alternative was to let her use her spare time in joining men in their work, or to have her do nothing. Firmly, men had her do nothing (except for such make-work nothings as embroidery and hack piano-playing). Women were even encouraged to wear clothes that hampered their physical movements to the point where they could scarcely walk or breathe.

What was left to them, then, but a kind of ferocious boredom that brought out the worst aspects of the human temperament, and made them so unfit an object even for sex, that they were carefully taught that sex was dirty and evil so that their husbands could go elsewhere for their pleasures.

But in this very same era, no one ever thought of applying the same toy-dog characteristics to the women of the lower classes. There was plenty of "little-muscle" work for them to do and since they had no time for fainting and refinement, the feminine temperament made the necessary adjustment and they did without either fainting or refinement.

The pioneer women of the American West not only cleaned house, cooked, and bore baby after baby, but they grabbed up rifles to fight off Indians when necessary. I strongly suspect they were also hitched to the plow on such occasions as the horse needed a rest, or the tractor was being polished. And this was in Victorian times.

We see it all about us even now. It's an article of faith that women just aren't any good at even the simplest arithmetic. You know how those cute little dears can't balance a checkbook. When I was a kid, all bank tellers were male for that very reason. But then it got hard to hire male bank tellers. Now 90 percent of them are female and apparently they can add up figures and balance checkbooks after all.

There was a time all nurses were males because everyone knew that women were simply too delicate and refined for such work. When the economic necessities made it important to hire females as nurses, it turned out they weren't all that delicate and refined after all. (Now nursing is "woman's work" that a proud man wouldn't do.)

Doctors and engineers are almost always men—until some sort of social or economic crunch comes—and then the female temperament makes the necessary change and, as in the Soviet Union, women become doctors and engineers in great numbers.

What it amounts to is best expressed in a well-known verse by Sir Walter Scott:

> O woman! in our hours of ease,
> Uncertain, coy, and hard to please,
> . . .
> When pain and anguish wring the brow,
> A ministering angel thou!

Most women seem to think this is a very touching and wonderful tribute to them, but I think that it is a rather bald exhibition of the fact that when man is relaxing he wants a toy and when he is in trouble he wants a slave and woman is on instant call for either role.

What if pain and anguish wring *her* brow? Who's *her* ministering angel? Why, another woman who is hired for the occasion.

But let's not slip to the other extreme either. During the fight for women's votes, the male chauvinists said that this would wreck the nation since women had no feeling for politics and would merely be manipulated by their menfolks (or by their priests, or by any political quack with a scalpful of curls and a mouthful of teeth).

Feminists, on the other hand, said that when women brought their gentleness and refinement and honesty to the polling booth, all graft, corruption, and war would be brought to an end.

You know what happened when women got the vote? *Nothing.* It turned out that women were no stupider than men—and no wiser, either.

What of the future? Will women gain true equality?

Not if basic conditions continue as they have ever since *Homo sapiens* became a species. Men won't voluntarily give up their advantage. Masters never do. Sometimes they are forced to do so by violent revolution of one sort or another. Sometimes they are forced to do so by their wise foresight of a coming violent revolution.

An *individual* may give up an advantage out of a mere sense of decency, but such are always in the minority and a group as a whole never does.

Indeed, in the present case, the strongest proponents of the status quo are the women themselves (at least most of them). They have played the role so long they would feel chills about the wrists and ankles if the chains were struck off. And they have grown so used to the petty rewards (the tipped hat, the offered elbow, the smirk and leer, and, most of all, the freedom to be silly) that they won't exchange them for freedom. Who is hardest on the independent-minded woman who defies the slave-conventions? Other women, of course, playing the fink on behalf of men.

Yet things will change even so, because the basic conditions that underlie woman's historic position are changing.

What was the first essential difference between men and women?

1. Most men are physically larger and physically stronger than most women.

So? What of that today. Rape is a crime and so is physical mayhem even when only directed against women. That doesn't stop such practices altogether, but it does keep them from being the universal masculine game they once were.

And does it matter that men are larger and stronger, in the economic sense? Is a woman too small and weak to earn a living? Does she have to crawl into the protecting neck-clutch of a male, however stupid or distasteful he may be, for the equivalent of the haunch of the kill?

Nonsense! "Big-muscle" jobs are steadily disappearing and only "little-muscle" jobs are left. We don't dig ditches any more, we push buttons and let machines dig ditches. The world is being computerized and there is nothing a man can do in the way of pushing paper, sorting cards, and twiddling contacts, that a woman can't do just as well.

In fact, littleness may be at a premium. Smaller and slenderer fingers may be just what is wanted.

More and more, women will learn they need only offer sex for sex and love for love, and nevermore sex for food. I can think of nothing that will dignify sex more than this change, or more quickly do away with the degrading master/slave existence of "the double standard."

But how about the second difference:

2. Women get pregnant, bear babies, and suckle them. Men don't.

I frequently hear tell that women have a "nest-building" instinct, that they really *want* to take care of a man and immolate themselves for his sake. Maybe so, under conditions as they used to be. But how about now?

With the population explosion becoming more and more of a cliff-hanger for all mankind, we will, before the end of the century, have evolved a new attitude toward babies or our culture will die.

It will become perfectly all right for a woman not to have babies. The stifling social pressure to become a "wife and mother" will lift and that will mean even more than the lifting of the economic pressure. Thanks to the pill, the burden of babies can be lifted without the abandonment of sex.

This doesn't mean women *won't* have babies; it means merely they won't *have* to have babies.

In fact, I feel that female slavery and the population explosion go hand in hand. Keep a woman in subjection and the only way a man will feel safe is to keep her "barefoot and pregnant." If she has nothing to do except undignified and repetitive labor, a woman will want baby after baby as the only escape to something else.

On the other hand, make women truly free and the population explosion will stop of its own accord. Few women would want to sacrifice their freedom for the sake of numerous babies. And don't say "No" too quickly; feminine freedom has never been truly tried, but it must be significant that the birth rate is highest where the social position of women is lowest.

In the twenty-first century, then, I predict that women will be completely free for the first time in the history of the species.

Nor am I afraid of the counter-prediction that all things go in cycles and that the clearly visible trend toward feminine emancipation will give way to a swing back to a kind of neo-Victorianism.

Effects can be cyclic, yes—but only if causes are cyclic, and the basic causes here are non-cyclic, barring world-wide thermonuclear war.

In order for the pendulum to swing back toward feminine slavery, there would have to be an increase in "big-muscle jobs" that only men could do. Women must begin once more to fear starvation without a man to work for them. Well, do you think the present trend toward computerization and social security will reverse itself short of global catastrophe? Honestly?

In order for the pendulum to swing back, there would have to be a continuation of the desire for large families and lots of children. There's no other way of keeping women contented with her slavery on a large scale (or too busy to think about it, which amounts to the same thing). Given our present population explosion and the situation as it will be by 2000, do you honestly expect women to be put to work breeding baby after baby?

So the trend toward woman's freedom is irreversible.

There's the beginning of it right now and it is well established. Do you think that the present era of increasing sexual permissiveness (almost everywhere in the world) is just a temporary breakdown in our moral fiber and that a little government action will restore the stern virtues of our ancestors?

Don't you believe it. Sex has been divorced from babies, and it will continue to be so, since sex can't possibly be suppressed and babies can't possibly be encouraged. Vote for whom you please but the "sexual revolution" will continue.

Or take even something so apparently trivial as the new fad of hairiness in man. (I've just grown a pair of absolutely magnificent sideburns myself.) Sure, it will change in details, but what it really stands for is the breakdown of trivial distinctions between the sexes.

It is indeed this which disturbs the conventional. Over and over, I hear them complain that some particular long-haired boy looks just like a girl. And then they say, "You can't tell them apart any more!"

This always makes me wonder why it is so important to tell a boy from a girl at a glance, unless one has some personal object in view where the sex makes a difference. You can't tell at a glance whether a particular person is Catholic, Protestant, or Jew; whether he/she is a piano player or a poker player, an engineer or an artist, intelligent or stupid.

After all, if it were *really* important to tell the sexes apart at the distance of several blocks with one quick glance, why not make use of Nature's distinction? That is *not* long hair since both sexes in all cultures grow hair of approximately equal length. On the other hand, men always have more facial hair than women; the difference is sometimes extreme. (My wife, poor thing, couldn't grow sideburns even if she tried.)

Well, then, should all men grow beards? Yet the very same conventional people who object to long hair on a man, also object to beards. *Any* change unsettles them, so when change becomes necessary, conventional people must be ignored.

But *why* this fetish of short hair for men and long hair for women, or, for that matter, pants for men and skirts for women, shirts for men and blouses for women? Why a set of artificial distinctions to exaggerate the natural ones? Why the sense of disturbance when the distinctions are blurred?

Can it be that the loud and gaudy distinction of dress and hair between the two sexes is another sign of the master-slave relationship? No master wants to be mistaken for a slave at any distance, or have a slave mistaken for a master, either. In slave societies, slaves are always carefully distinguished (by a pigtail when the Manchus ruled China, by a yellow Star of David when the Nazis ruled Germany, and so on). We ourselves tend to forget this since our most conspicuous non-female slaves had a distinctive skin color and required very little else to mark them.

In the society of sexual equality that is coming, then, there will be a blurring of artificial distinctions between the sexes, a blurring that is already on the way. But so what? A particular boy will know who his particular girl is and vice versa, and if someone else is not part of the relationship what does he/she care which is which?

I say we can't beat the trend and we should therefore join it. I say it may even be the most wonderful thing that has ever happened to mankind.

I think the Greeks *were* right in a way and that it *is* much better to love an equal. And if that be so, why not hasten the time when we heterosexuals can have love at its best?

## AFTERWORD

I'm proud of the foregoing essay. In 1969, it was still early days for the feminist movement. Betty Friedan's book *The Feminine Mystique,* which was a chief factor in moving it into high gear, had only been published in 1963. But, then, I didn't have to wait for that. I have always been for the downtrodden, regardless of race or sex.

I was pleased, then, to get a letter from a woman who said she had read the essay with the deepest suspicion, waiting for me to begin to qualify my beliefs; and was astonished that I never did.

To be sure, such is my admiration for women that, in my time, I have frequently been accused of treating them as sex objects, but I always say, with a hurt quaver in my voice, "Well, let them treat me as a sex object, too, and then we'll have sexual equality."

Incidentally, I have never received any letter objecting to my writing my science essays on subjects far removed from science, as in the case of this one—but then, sociology is considered a science, too, isn't it?

# 12

# The Luxon Wall

You wouldn't think my science essays would get a mention in *Time*, would you?* Well, they did, and the particular article that was mentioned was one that dealt with the impossibility of attaining or surpassing the velocity of light. After the article was published, there came to be a great deal of talk about faster-than-light particles and suddenly I sounded like a fuddy-duddy left flat-footed by the advance of physics past the bounds I had mistakenly thought fixed.

At least that's the way *Time* made me sound. To make it even worse, they cited my good old friend Arthur C. Clarke,† and his rebuttal entitled "Possible, That's All" in a way that sounded as though they thought Arthur more forward-looking than myself.

Fortunately, I am a tolerant man who is not disturbed by such things and I shrugged it off. When I next met Arthur, we were

---

* Come to think of it, why not?
† He's three years older than I am. I thought I'd just casually mention that.

still the best of friends if you don't count the kick in the shin I gave him.

Anyway, I am *not* a fuddy-duddy and I am now going to explain the situation in greater detail in order to prove it.

Let's begin with an equation that was first worked out by the Dutch physicist Hendrik Antoon Lorentz in the 1890s. Lorentz thought it applied specifically to electrically charged bodies but Einstein later incorporated it into his Special Theory of Relativity, showing that it applied to all bodies, whether they carried an electric charge or not.

I will not present the Lorentz equation in its usual form but will make a small change for purposes that will eventually become clear. My version of the equation, then, is as follows:

$$m = k/\sqrt{1 - (v/c)^2} \qquad \text{(Equation 1)}$$

In Equation 1, $m$ represents the mass of the body under discussion, $v$ is the velocity with which it is moving with respect to the observer, $c$ is the velocity of light in a vacuum, and $k$ is some value that is constant for the body in question.

Suppose, next, that the body is moving at one-tenth the velocity of light. That means $v = 0.1c$. In that case, the denominator of the fraction on the right-hand side of Equation 1 becomes $\sqrt{1 - (0.1c/c^2)} = \sqrt{1 - 0.1^2} = \sqrt{1 - 0.01} = \sqrt{0.99} = 0.995$. Equation 1 therefore becomes $m = k/0.995 = 1.005k$

We can make the same sort of evaluation for the case of the same body at gradually increasing velocities, say at velocities equal to $0.2c$, $0.3c$, $0.4c$ and so on. I won't bore you with the calculations but the results come out as follows:

| Velocity | Mass |
|----------|----------|
| $0.1c$ | $1.005k$ |
| $0.2c$ | $1.03k$ |
| $0.3c$ | $1.05k$ |
| $0.4c$ | $1.09k$ |
| $0.5c$ | $1.15k$ |
| $0.6c$ | $1.24k$ |
| $0.7c$ | $1.41k$ |

$$0.8c \qquad 1.67k$$
$$0.9c \qquad 2.29k$$

As you see, the Lorentz equation, if correct, would indicate that the mass of any object increases steadily (and, indeed, more and more rapidly) as its velocity increases. When this was first suggested, it seemed utterly against common sense because no such change in mass had ever been detected.

The reason for the nondetection, however, lay in the fact that the value of $c$ was so huge by ordinary standards—186,281 miles per second. At a velocity of only one tenth the speed of light, the mass of an object has increased to one half of one percent more than its mass at, say, sixty miles per hour, and this increase would be easily detectable in principle. However, a velocity of "only" one tenth the speed of light $(0.1c)$ is still 18,628 miles per second or over 67 million miles per hour. In other words, to get measurable changes in mass, velocities must be attained which were completely outside the range of experience of the scientists of the 1890s.

A few years later, however, subatomic particles were detected speeding out of radioactive atomic nuclei and their velocities were sometimes considerable fractions of the velocity of light. Their masses could be measured quite accurately at different velocities and the Lorentz equation was found to hold with great precision. In fact, down to this moment, no violation of the Lorentz equation has ever been discovered for any body at any measured velocity.

We must, therefore, accept the Lorentz equation as a true representation of that facet of the Universe which it describes— at least until further notice.

Now, accepting the Lorentz equation, let's ask ourselves some questions. First, what does $k$ represent?

To answer that, let's consider a body (any body that possesses mass) that is at rest relative to the observer. In that case, its velocity is zero and since $v = 0$, then $v/c = 0$ and $(v/c)^2 = 0$. What's more, $\sqrt{1 - (v/c)^2}$ is then $\sqrt{1 - 0}$ or $\sqrt{1}$ or 1.

This means that for a body at rest relative to the observer, the Lorentz equation becomes $m = k/1 = k$. We conclude then that

$k$ represents the mass of a body that is at rest relative to the observer. This is usually called the "rest-mass" and is symbolized as $m_0$. To write the Lorentz equation in the form it is usually seen, then, we have:

$$m = m_0 / \sqrt{1 - (v/c)^2} \qquad \text{(Equation 2)}$$

The next question is what happens if an object moves at velocities higher than the highest velocity given in the small table presented earlier in the article. Suppose the object moved at a velocity of $1.0c$ relative to an observer; in other words, if it moved at the velocity of light.

In that case the denominator of the Lorentz equation becomes $\sqrt{1 - (1.0c)^2} = \sqrt{1 - 1^2} = \sqrt{1 - 1} = \sqrt{0} = 0$. For a body moving at the speed of light, the Lorentz equation becomes $m = m_0/0$ and if there is one thing we are not allowed to do in mathematics, it is to divide by zero. Mathematically, the Lorentz equation becomes meaningless for a body possessing mass that is moving at the velocity of light.

Well, then, let's sneak up on the velocity of light and not try to land right on it with a bang.

As one increases the value of $v$, in Equation 2, past $0.9c$, while keeping it always *less* than $1.0c$, the value of the denominator steadily approaches zero and, as it does so, the value of $m$ gets larger without limit. This is true no matter what the value of $m_0$ so long as that value is greater than zero. (Try it for yourself, calculating $m$ for values of $v$ equal to $0.99c$, $0.999c$, $0.9999c$ and so on for as long as you have patience.)

In mathematical language, we would say that in any fraction $c = a/b$, where $a$ is greater than 0, then, as $b$ approaches zero, $c$ increases without limit. A shorthand way of saying this, and one that is frowned upon by strict mathematicians, is $a/0 = \infty$, where $\infty$ represents increase without limit or "infinity."

So we can say, then, that for any object possessing mass (however little) that mass approaches infinite values as its velocity approaches the velocity of light relative to the observer.

This means that the body cannot actually attain the velocity of light (though it can fall only infinitesimally short of that value) and certainly cannot surpass it. You can show this by either of two lines of argument.

The only way we know of by which an ordinary mass-possessing object can be made to go at a greater velocity than it already possesses is to apply a force and therefore produce an acceleration. The greater the mass, however, the smaller the acceleration produced by a given force and, therefore, as the mass approaches infinite values the acceleration which it can attain when subjected to any force, however great, approaches zero. Consequently, the object cannot be made to go faster than the velocity at which its mass becomes infinite.

The second line of argument is as follows. A moving body possesses kinetic energy which we may set equal to $mv^2/2$, where $m$ is its mass and $v$ is its velocity. If a force is applied to the body so that its kinetic energy is increased, that energy may be increased because $v$ is increased, or because $m$ is increased, or because both $v$ and $m$ are increased. At ordinary, everyday velocities, all the measurable increase goes into velocity, so we assume (wrongly) that mass remains constant under all conditions.

Actually, though, both velocity and mass are increased as the result of an applied force, but the mass so slightly at ordinary velocities as to make the change immeasurable. As the velocity relative to the observer increases, however, a larger and larger fraction of the added energy produced by an applied force goes into increasing the mass and a smaller and smaller fraction into increasing the velocity. By the time the velocity is very close to that of light, virtually all the energy increase appears in the form of an increase in mass; virtually none in the form of an increase in velocity. The change in emphasis is such that the final velocity can never attain, let alone exceed, the velocity of light.

And don't ask why. That's the way the Universe is constructed.

I hope you notice, though, that when I was discussing the fact that mass becomes infinite at the speed of light I was forced by the mathematical facts of life to say, "This is true no matter what the value of $m_0$ so long as that value is greater than zero."

Of course, all the particles that build up ourselves and our devices—protons, electrons, neutrons, mesons, hyperons, etc. etc.—have rest masses greater than zero so that the restriction doesn't seem very restrictive. In fact, people generally say, "It is impossible to attain or surpass the velocity of light," without specifying that they mean for objects possessing rest mass greater than zero because that seems to include virtually everything anyway.

I neglected to make the restriction myself in "Impossible, That's All," which is what left me open to the fuddy-duddy implication. If we *include* the restriction, then everything I said in the article is perfectly valid.

Now let's go on and consider bodies with $m_0$ not greater than zero.

Consider a photon, for instance, a "particle" of electromagnetic radiation—visible light, microwaves, gamma rays, etc.

What do we know about photons? In the first place, a photon always possesses finite energy so that its energy content is somewhere between 0 and $\infty$. Energy, as Einstein showed, is equivalent to mass according to a relationship which he expressed as $e = mc^2$. This means that any photon can be assigned a mass value which can be calculated by this equation and which will also fall somewhere between 0 and $\infty$.

Another thing we know about photons is that they move (relative to any observer) at the velocity of light. Indeed, light has that velocity because it is made up of photons.

Now that we know these two things, let us convert Equation 2 into another but equivalent form:

$$m\sqrt{1 - (v/c)^2} = m_0 \qquad \text{(Equation 3)}$$

For a photon, $v = c$, and by now you should see at once that this means that, for a photon, Equation 3 becomes:

$$m(0) = m_0 \qquad \text{(Equation 4)}$$

If a photon were an ordinary mass-possessing object and were traveling at the velocity of light, its mass ($m$) would be infinite. Equation 4 would then become $\infty \times 0 = m_0$ and such an equation is not permitted in mathematics.

A photon, however, can be assigned a value for $m$ which is between 0 and $\infty$, even though it is traveling at the velocity of light, and for *any* value between 0 and $\infty$ assigned to $m$, the value of $m_0$ in Equation 4 turns out to equal 0.

This means that for photons, then, the rest mass ($m_0$) equals zero. If the rest mass is zero, in other words, an object *can* move at the velocity of light.

(This should dispose of the perennial question I am asked by correspondents who think they have discovered a flaw in Einstein's logic and say: "If anything moving at the velocity of light has infinite mass, how come photons don't have infinite mass?" The answer is that a distinction must be made between particles with a rest mass of 0 and particles with a rest mass greater than 0. But don't worry. Correspondents will continue to ask the question no matter how often I explain.)

But let's go farther. Suppose a photon traveled at a velocity *less* than that of light. In that case the quantity under the square root sign in Equation 3 would be greater than zero and this would be multiplied by $m$ which itself possesses a value greater than zero. If two values, each greater than zero, are multiplied, then the product (in this case, $m_0$) must be greater than zero.

This means that if a photon traveled at less than the velocity of light (no matter how infinitesimally less), it would no longer have a rest mass equal to zero. The same would be true if it traveled at more than the velocity of light, no matter how infinitesimally more. (Funny things happen to the equation at velocities greater than light as we shall soon see, but one thing that the funniness cannot obscure is that the rest mass would no longer be equal to zero.)

Physicists insist that a rest mass must be constant for any given body, since all the phenomena they measure make sense only if this is so. In order for a photon's rest mass to remain constant, then (that is, for it to remain always zero) the photon must *always* move at the velocity of light, not a hair less and not a hair more provided it is moving through a vacuum.

When a photon is formed, it *instantly,* with no measurable time lapse, begins moving away from the point of origin at 186,281 miles per second. This may sound paradoxical because it implies an infinite rate of acceleration and therefore an infinite force but stop—

Newton's second law, connecting force, mass and acceleration, applies only to bodies with a rest mass greater than zero. It does *not* apply to bodies with a rest mass equal to zero.

Thus, if energy is poured into an ordinary body under ordinary circumstances, its velocity increases; if energy is subtracted, its velocity decreases. If energy is poured into a photon, its frequency (and mass) increases but its velocity remains unchanged; if energy is subtracted, its frequency (and mass) decreases but its velocity remains unchanged.

But if all this is so, it seems to make poor logic to speak of "rest mass" in connection with photons, for that implies the mass a photon would have if it were at rest—and a photon never can be at rest.

An alternate term has been suggested by O.-M. Bilaniuk and E. C. G. Sudarshan.‡ This is "proper-mass." The proper mass of an object would be a constant mass value that is inherent in the body and is not dependent on velocity. In the case of ordinary bodies, this inherent mass is equal to that which can be measured when the body is at rest. In the case of photons, it can be worked out by deduction, rather than by direct measurement.

A photon is not the only body that can and *must* travel at the velocity of light. Any body with a proper mass of zero can and must do so. In addition to photons, there are no less than five different kinds of particles that are thought to have a proper mass of zero.

One of these is the hypothetical graviton, which carries the gravitational force and which, in 1969, may have finally been detected.

The other four are the various neutrinos: 1) the neutrino itself, 2) the antineutrino, 3) the muon-neutrino, and 4) the muon-antineutrino.

The graviton and all the neutrinos can and must travel at the velocity of light. Bilaniuk and Sudarshan suggest that all these velocity-of-light particles be lumped together as "luxons" (from the Latin word for "light").

All particles with a proper mass greater than zero, which therefore cannot attain the velocity of light and must always and forever travel at lesser velocities, they lump together as "tardy-

‡ In an article entitled "Particles Beyond the Light Barrier," *Physics Today*, May 1969, for those of you who wish I would give a reference now and then.

ons." They further suggest that tardyons be said to travel always at "subluminal" ("slower-than-light") velocities.

But now what if we think of the unthinkable and consider particles at "superluminal" ("faster-than-light") velocities? This was done for the first time with strict adherence to relativistic principles (as opposed to mere science-fictional speculation) by Bilaniuk, Deshpande and Sudarshan in 1962, and such work hit the headlines at last when Gerald Feinberg published a similar discussion in 1967. (It was Feinberg's work which inspired the discussion in *Time.*)

Suppose a particle traveled at a velocity of $2c$; that is, at twice the velocity of light. In that case, $v/c$ would become $2c/c$ or 2 and $(v/c)^2$ would be 4. The term $\sqrt{1 - (v/c)^2}$ would become $\sqrt{1 - 4}$ or $\sqrt{-3}$ or $\sqrt{3}\sqrt{-1}$.

Since it is usual to express $\sqrt{-1}$ as $i$ and since $\sqrt{3}$ is approximately 1.73, we can say that for a particle traveling at the velocity twice that of light, Equation 3 becomes:

$$1.73mi = m_0 \qquad \text{(Equation 5)}$$

Any expression that contains $i$ (that is $\sqrt{-1}$) is said to be imaginary, a poor name but one that is ineradicable.

It turns out, as you can see for yourself if you try a few random examples that for any object traveling at superluminal velocities, the proper mass is imaginary.

An imaginary mass has no physical significance in our own subluminal Universe, so it has long been customary to dismiss superluminal velocities at once, and say that faster-than-light particles are impossible because there can be no such thing as an imaginary mass. I've said it myself in my time.

But is an imaginary mass truly without meaning? Or is a mass represented by $mi$ merely a mathematical way of expressing a set of rules not like the rules we are accustomed to, but rules that *still* obey the dictates of Einstein's special relativity?

Thus, in the case of games such as baseball, football, basketball, soccer, hockey and so on and so on, the contestant or contestants who make the higher score win. Yet can one say from this that a game in which the lower score wins is unthinkable? How about golf? The essential point in any game of skill is that the contestant who achieves the more difficult task wins—the more difficult task usually involving a higher score, but in golf involving a lower score.

In the same way, in order to obey special relativity, an object with an imaginary rest mass must behave in ways which seem paradoxical to those of us who are used to the behavior of objects with real rest masses.

For instance, it can be shown that if an object with an imaginary rest mass increases in energy, its velocity *decreases;* if it decreases in energy, its velocity *increases.* In other words, an object with an imaginary rest mass will slow down when a force is applied and speed up when resistance is encountered.

Furthermore, as such particles add energy and slow down, they can never quite slow down to the velocity of light. At the velocity of light their mass becomes infinite. As their energy decreases to zero, however, their velocity increases without limit. A body with imaginary rest mass, which possesses zero energy, would have infinite velocity. Such particles move always faster than light and Feinberg has suggested they be termed "tachyons" from a Greek word meaning "fast."

Well, then, the tardyon Universe is subluminal, with possible velocities ranging from 0 for zero energy to $c$ for infinite energy. The tachyon Universe is superluminal, with possible velocities ranging from $c$ for infinite energy to $\infty$ for zero energy. Between the two Universes is the luxon Universe, with possible velocities confined to $c$, and never either less or more, at any energy.

We might view the total Universe as divided into two compartments by an unbreachable wall. We have the tardyon Universe on one side, the tachyon Universe on the other side, and between them, the infinitely thin but infinitely rigid luxon wall.

In the tardyon Universe most objects have little kinetic energy. Those objects that have great velocities (like a cosmic-ray particle) have very little mass. Those objects with great masses (like a star) have very little velocity.

The same is very likely true in the tachyon Universe. Objects with relatively slow velocities (just slightly more than light) and therefore great energies must have very little mass and be not too different from our cosmic-ray particles. Objects with great masses would have very little kinetic energy and therefore enormous velocities. A tachyon star might be moving at trillions of times the velocity of light, for instance. But that would mean that the mass of the star would be distributed over vast distances through tiny time intervals so that very little of it would be present in any one place at any one time, so to speak.

The two universes can impinge and become detectable, one to the other, at only one place—the luxon wall at which they meet. (Both universes hold photons, neutrinos and gravitons in common.)

If a tachyon is energetic enough and therefore moving slowly enough, it might have sufficient energy and hang around long enough to give off a detectable burst of photons. Scientists are watching for those bursts, but the chance of happening to have an instrument in just the precise place where one of those (possibly very infrequent) bursts appears for a billionth of a second or less is not very great.

Of course, we might wonder whether there might not be some possibility of breaching the luxon wall by some means less direct than accelerating past it—which is impossible (that's all). Can one turn tardyons into tachyons somehow (possibly by way of photons) so that suddenly one finds one's self transferred from one side of the wall to the other without ever having gone through it? (Just as one can combine tardyons to produce photons and suddenly have objects moving at the velocity of light without having been accelerated to it.)

The conversion to tachyons would be equivalent to the entry into "hyperspace," a concept dear to science fiction writers. Once in the tachyon Universe, a spaceship with the energy necessary to go only a tiny fraction of the velocity of light would find itself going (with the same energy) at very many times the velocity of light. It could get to a distant galaxy in, say, three seconds, then turn back automatically to tardyons and be in our own Universe again. That would be equivalent to the interstellar "jump" that I am always talking about in my own novels.

In connection with that, though, I have an idea which, as far as I know, is completely original with me. It is not based on any consideration of physical law but is purely intuitive and arises only because I am convinced that the overriding characteristic of the Universe is its symmetry and that its overriding principle is the horrid doctrine of "You can't win!"

I think that each Universe sees itself as the tardyon Universe and the other as the tachyon Universe, so that to an observer from neither (perched on top of the luxon wall, so to speak) it would appear that the luxon wall separates identical twins, really.

If we managed to transfer a spaceship into the tachyon Universe, we would find ourselves (I intuitively feel) still going at subluminal velocities by our new measurements and looking back at the Universe we had just left as superluminal.

And if so, then whatever we do, *whatever* we do, tachyons and all, attaining or surpassing the velocity of light will remain impossible, that's all.


AFTERWORD

The foregoing essay is one I feel a certain chagrin over. I explained in the introduction that I wrote it primarily because my good pal and buddy, Arthur Clarke, had made me appear to be a conservative fuddy-duddy. Well, I should not have reacted as I did. I should not have let myself be stampeded into writing an article on tachyons just to prove that I was, too, a "with-it" live wire.

I should have stuck to my feeling that tachyons were a mathematical myth and had no physical reality. After all, in the twenty years since the possibility of their existence was first put forward, no evidence at all that would translate the possibility into an actuality has showed up. What's worse is that their existence would upset the principle of causality, and few scientists are willing to concede that tachyons are possible even in theory.

However, I managed to salvage one thing. I ended with my guess that if there are two universes, a tardyon and a tachyon, then *whichever* of these you actually inhabited would seem to be the tardyon. It would always be the *other* one which would seem to allow faster-than-light travel. I received a surprised letter from the inventor of the tachyon theory to tell me that, indeed, my intuition was correct and that's the way it was.

# 13

# Pompey and Circumstance

Rationalists have a hard time of it, because the popular view is that they are committed to "explaining" everything.

This is not so. Rationalists maintain that the proper way of arriving at an explanation is through reason—but there is no guarantee that some particular phenomenon can be explained in that fashion at some given moment in history or from some given quantity of observation.*

Yet how often I (or any rationalist) am presented with something odd and am challenged, "How do you explain that?" The implication is that if I don't explain it instantly to the satisfaction of the individual posing the question, then the entire structure of science may be considered to be demolished.

But things happen to me, too. One day in April 1967, my car broke down and had to be towed to a garage. In seventeen years

---

* It is the mystics, really, who are committed to explaining *everything,* for they need nothing but imagination and words—*any* words, chosen at random.

of driving various cars, that was the first time I ever had to endure the humiliation of being towed.

When do you suppose the second time was? —Two hours later, on the same day, for a completely different reason.

Seventeen years without a tow, and then two tows on the same day! And how do you explain *that*, Dr. Asimov? (Gremlins? A vengeful Deity? An extraterrestrial conspiracy?)

On the second occasion, I did indeed loudly advance all three theories to my unruffled garageman. *His* theory (he was also a rationalist) was that my car was old enough to be falling apart. So I bought a new car.

Let's look at it this way! To every single person on Earth, a large number of events, great, small, and insignificant, happen each day. Every one of those events has some probability of occurrence, though we can't always decide the exact probability in each case. On the average, though, we might imagine that one out of every thousand events has an only one-in-a-thousand chance of happening; one out of every million events has an only one-in-a-million change of happening; and so on.

This means that every one of us is constantly experiencing some pretty low-probability events. That is the normal result of chance. If any of us went an appreciable length of time with nothing unusual happening, that would be *very* unusual.

And suppose we don't restrict ourselves to one person, but consider, instead, all the lives that have ever been lived. The number of events then increases by a factor of some sixty billion and we can assume that sometime, to someone, something will happen that is sixty billion times as improbable as anything happening to some other particular man. Even such an event requires no explanation. It is part of our normal universe going along its business in a normal way.

Examples? We've all heard very odd coincidences that have happened to someone's second cousin, odd things that represent such an unusual concatenation of circumstance that surely we *must* admit the existence of telepathy or flying saucers or Satan or *something*.

Let me offer something, too. Not something that happened to my second cousin, but to a notable figure of the past whose life is quite well documented. Something very unusual happened to him, which in all my various and miscellaneous reading of history I have never seen specifically pointed out. I will, therefore, stress it to you as something more unusual and amazing than anything I have ever come across, and even so, it *still* doesn't shake my belief in the supremacy of the rational view of the universe. Here goes—

The man in question was Gnaeus Pompeius, who is better known to English-speaking individuals as Pompey.

Pompey was born in 106 B.C. and the first forty-two years of his life were characterized by uniform good fortune. Oh, I dare say he stubbed his toe now and then and got attacks of indigestion at inconvenient times and lost money on the gladiatorial contests— but in the major aspects of life, he remained always on the winning side.

Pompey was born at a time when Rome was torn by civil war and social turmoil. The Italian allies, who were not Roman citizens, rose in rebellion against a Roman aristocracy who wouldn't extend the franchise. The lower classes, who were feeling the pinch of a tightening economy, now that Rome had completed the looting of most of the Mediterranean area, were struggling against the senators, who had kept most of the loot.

When Pompey was in his teens, his father was trying to walk the tightrope. The elder Pompey had been a general who had served as consul in 89 B.C., and had defeated the Italian noncitizens and celebrated a triumph. But he was not an aristocrat by birth and he tried to make a deal with the radicals. This might have gotten him in real trouble, for he had worked himself into a spot where neither side trusted him, but in 87 B.C. he died in the course of an epidemic that swept his army.

That left young Pompey as a fatherless nineteen-year-old who had inherited enemies on both sides of the civil war.

He had to choose and he had to choose carefully. The radicals were in control of Rome, but off in Asia Minor, fighting a war against Rome's enemies, was the reactionary general Lucius Cornelius Sulla.

Pompey, uncertain as to which side would win, lay low and out of sight. When he heard that Sulla was returning, victorious, from Asia Minor, he made his decision. He chose Sulla as probable victor. At once, he scrabbled together an army from among those soldiers who had fought for his father, loudly proclaimed himself on Sulla's side, and took the field against the radicals. There was his first stroke of fortune. He had backed the right man. Sulla arrived in Italy in 83 B.C. and began winning at once. By 82 B.C. he had wiped out the last opposition in Italy and at once made himself dictator. For three years he was absolute ruler of Rome. He reorganized the government and placed the senatorial aristocrats firmly in control.

Pompey benefited, for Sulla was properly grateful to him. Sulla sent Pompey to Sicily, then to Africa, to wipe out the disorganized forces that still clung to the radical side there, and this was done without trouble.

The victories were cheap and Pompey's troops were so pleased that they acclaimed Pompey as "the Great," so that he became Gnaeus Pompeius Magnus—the only Roman to bear this utterly un-Roman cognomen. Later accounts say that he received this name because of a striking physical resemblance between himself and Alexander the Great, but such a resemblance could have existed only in Pompey's own imagination.

Sulla ordered Pompey to disband his army after his African victories but Pompey refused to do so, preferring to stay surrounded by his loyal men. Ordinarily, one did not lightly cross Sulla, who had no compunctions whatever about ordering a few dozen executions before breakfast. Pompey, however, proceeded to marry Sulla's daughter. Apparently, this won Sulla over to the point of not only accepting the title of "the Great" for the young man, but also to the point of allowing him to celebrate a triumph in 79 B.C. even though he was below the minimum age at which triumphs were permitted.

Almost immediately thereafter, Sulla resigned the dictatorship, feeling his work was done, but Pompey's career never as much as stumbled. He now had a considerable reputation (based on his easy victories). What's more, he was greedy for further easy victories.

For instance, after Sulla's death, a Roman general, Marcus Aemilius Lepidus, turned against Sulla's policies. The reactionary Senate at once sent an army against him. The senatorial army was led by Quintus Catulus, with Pompey as second-in-command. Until then, Pompey had supported Lepidus, but again he guessed the winning side in time. Catulus easily defeated Lepidus, and Pompey managed to get most of the credit.

There was trouble in Spain at this time, for it was the last stronghold of radicalism. In Spain, a radical general, Quintus Sertorius, maintained himself. Under him, Spain was virtually independent of Rome and was blessed with an enlightened government, for Sertorius was an efficient and liberal administrator. He treated the native Spaniards well, set up a Senate into which they were admitted, and established schools where their young men were trained in Roman style.

Naturally, the Spaniards, who for some centuries had had a reputation as fierce and resolute warriors, fought heart and soul on the side of Sertorius. When Sulla sent Roman armies into Spain, they were defeated.

So, in 77 B.C., Pompey, all in a glow over Catulus' easy victory over Lepidus, offered to go to Spain to take care of Sertorius. The Senate was willing and off to Spain marched Pompey and his army. On his way through Gaul, he found the dispirited remnants of Lepidus' old army. Lepidus himself was dead by now but what was left of his men were under Marcus Brutus (whose son would, one day, be a famous assassin).

There was no trouble in handling the broken army and Pompey offered Brutus his life if he would surrender. Brutus surrendered and Pompey promptly had him executed. One more easy victory, topped by treachery, and Pompey's reputation increased.

On to Spain went Pompey. In Spain, a sturdy old Roman general, Metellus Pius, was unsuccessfully trying to cope with Sertorius. Vaingloriously, Pompey advanced on his own to take over the job—and Sertorius, who was the first good general Pompey had yet encountered, promptly gave the young man a first-class drubbing. Pompey's reputation might have withered then and there, but just in time, Metellus approached with reinforcements and Sertorius had to withdraw. At once, Pompey called it a victory, and, of course, got the credit for it. His luck held.

For five years, Pompey remained in Spain, trying to handle Sertorius, and for five years he failed. And then he had a stroke of luck, the luck that never failed Pompey, for Sertorius was assassinated. With Sertorius gone, the resistance movement in Spain collapsed. Pompey could at once win another of his easy victories and could then return to Rome in 71 B.C., claiming to have cleaned up the Spanish mess.

But couldn't Rome have seen it took him five years?

No, Rome couldn't, for all the time Pompey had been in Spain, Italy itself had been going through a terrible time and there had been no chance of keeping an eye on Spain.

A band of gladiators, under Spartacus, had revolted. Many dispossessed flocked to Spartacus' side and for two years, Spartacus (a skillful fighter) destroyed every Roman army sent out against him and struck terror into the heart of every aristocrat. At the height of his power he had 90,000 men under his command and controlled almost all of southern Italy.

In 72 B.C., Spartacus fought his way northward to the Alps, intending to leave Italy and gain permanent freedom in the barbarian regions to the north. His men, however, misled by their initial victories, preferred to remain in Italy in reach of more loot. Spartacus turned south again.

The senators now placed an army under Marcus Licinius Crassus, Rome's richest and most crooked businessman. In two battles, Crassus managed to defeat the gladiatorial army and in the second one, Spartacus was killed. Then, just as Crassus had finished the hard work, Pompey returned with his Spanish army and hastily swept up the demoralized remnants. He immediately represented himself, successfully, as the man who had cleaned up the gladiatorial mess after having taken care of Spain. The result was that Pompey was allowed to celebrate a triumph, but poor Crassus wasn't.

The Senate, though, was growing nervous. They were not sure they trusted Pompey. He had won too many victories and was becoming entirely too popular.

Nor did they like Crassus (no one did). For all his wealth, Crassus was not a member of the aristocratic families and he grew angry at being snubbed by the socially superior Senate. Crassus began to court favor with the people with well-placed philanthropies. He also began to court Pompey.

Pompey always responded to courting and, besides, had an

unfailing nose for the winning side. He and Crassus ran for the consulate in 70 B.C. (two consuls were elected each year), and they won. Once consul, Crassus began to undo Sulla's reforms of a decade earlier in order to weaken the hold of the senatorial aristocracy on the government. Pompey, who had been heart and soul with Sulla when that had been the politic thing to do, turned about and went along with Crassus, though not always happily.

But Rome was still in trouble. The West had been entirely pacified, but there was mischief at sea. Roman conquests had broken down the older stable governments in the East without having, as yet, established anything quite as stable in their place. The result was that piracy was rife throughout the eastern Mediterranean. It was a rare ship that could get through safely and, in particular, the grain supply to Rome itself had become so precarious that the price of food skyrocketed.

Roman attempts to clear out the pirates failed, partly because the generals sent to do the job were never given enough power. In 67 B.C., Pompey maneuvered to have himself appointed to the task—but under favorable conditions. The Senate, in a panic over the food supply, leaped at the bait.

Pompey was given dictatorial powers over the entire Mediterranean coast to a distance of fifty miles inland for three years and was told to use that time and the entire Roman fleet to destroy the pirates. So great was Roman confidence in Pompey that food prices fell as soon as news of his appointment was made public.

Pompey was lucky enough to have what no previous Roman had—adequate forces and adequate power. Nevertheless one must admit that he did well. In three *months,* not three years, he scoured the Mediterranean clear of piracy.

If he had been popular before, he was Rome's hero now.

The only place where Rome still faced trouble was in eastern Asia Minor, where the kingdom of Pontus had been fighting Rome with varying success for over twenty years. It had been against Pontus that Sulla had won victories in the East, yet Pontus kept fighting on. Now a Roman general, Lucius Licinius Lucullus, had almost finished the job, but he was a hard-driving martinet, hated by his soldiers.

When Lucullus' army began to mutiny in 66 B.C., just when

one more drive would finish Pontus, he was recalled and good old Pompey was sent eastward to replace him. Pompey's reputation preceded him; Lucullus' men cheered him madly and for him did what they wouldn't do for Lucullus. They marched against Pontus and beat it. Pompey supplied the one last push and, as always, demanded and accepted credit for the whole thing.

All of Asia Minor was now either Roman outright or was under the control of Roman puppet governments. Pompey therefore decided to clean up the East altogether. He marched southward and around Antioch found the last remnant of the Seleucid Empire, established after the death of Alexander the Great two and a half centuries before. It was now ruled by a nonentity called Antiochus XIII. Pompey deposed him, and annexed the empire to Rome as the province of Syria.

Still further south was the kingdom of Judea. It had been independent for less than a century, under the rule of a line of kings of the Maccabean family. Two of the Maccabeans were now fighting over the throne and one appealed to Pompey.

Pompey at once marched into Judea and laid siege to Jerusalem. Ordinarily, Jerusalem was a hard nut to crack, for it was built on a rocky prominence with a reliable water supply; it had good walls; and it was usually defended with fanatic vigor.

Pompey, however, noticed that every seven days things were quiet. Someone explained to him that on the Sabbath, the Jews wouldn't fight unless attacked and even then fought without real conviction. It must have taken quite a while to convince Pompey of such a ridiculous thing but, once convinced, he used a few Sabbaths to bring up his siege machinery without interference, and finally attacked on another Sabbath. No problem.

Pompey ended the Maccabean kingdom and annexed Judea to Rome while allowing the Jews to keep their religious freedom, their Temple, their high-priests, and their peculiar, but useful, Sabbath.

Pompey was forty-two years old at this time, and success had smiled at him without interruption. I now skip a single small event in Pompey's life and represent it by a line of asterisks: one apparently unimportant circumstance.

\* \* \* \* \* \* \* \* \* \*

Pompey returned to Italy in 61 B.C. absolutely on top of the world, boasting (with considerable exaggeration) that what he had found as the eastern border of the realm he had left at its center. He received the most magnificent triumph Rome had ever seen up to that time.

The Senate was in terror lest Pompey make himself a dictator and turn to the radicals. This Pompey did not do. Once, twenty years before, when he had an army, he kept that army even at the risk of Sulla's displeasure. Now, something impelled him to give up his army, disband it, and assume a role as a private citizen. Perhaps he was convinced that he had reached a point where the sheer magic of his name would allow him to dominate the republic.

At last, though, his nose for the right action failed him. And once having failed him, it failed him forever after.

To begin with, Pompey asked the Senate to approve everything he had done in the East, his victories, his treaties, his depositions of kings, his establishment of provinces. He also asked the Senate to distribute land to his soldiers, for he himself had promised them land. He was sure that he had but to ask and he would be given.

Not at all. Pompey was now a man without an army and the Senate insisted on considering each individual act separately and nit-pickingly. As for land grants, that was rejected.

What's more, Pompey found that he had no one on his side within the government. All his vast popularity suddenly seemed to count for nothing as all parties turned against him for no discernible reason. What's more, Pompey could do nothing about it. Something had happened, and he was no longer the clever, golden-boy Pompey he had been before 64 B.C. Now he was uncertain, vacillating, and weak.

Even Crassus was no longer his friend. Crassus had found someone else: a handsome, charming individual with a silver tongue and a genius for intrigue—a man named Julius Caesar. Caesar was a playboy aristocrat but Crassus paid off the young man's enormous debts and Caesar served him well in return.

While Pompey was struggling with the Senate, Caesar was off

in Spain, winning some small victories against rebellious tribes and gathering enough ill-gotten wealth (as Roman generals usually did) to pay off Crassus and make himself independent. When he returned to Italy and found Pompey furious with the Senate, he arranged a kind of treaty of alliance between himself, Crassus, and Pompey—the "First Triumvirate."

But it was Caesar and not Pompey who profited from this. It was Caesar who used the alliance to get himself elected consul in 59 B.C. Once consul, Caesar controlled the Senate with almost contemptuous ease, driving the other consul, a reactionary, into house arrest.

One thing Caesar did was to force the aristocrats of the Senate to grant all of Pompey's demands. Pompey got the ratification of all of his acts and he got the land for his soldiers—and yet he did not profit from this. Indeed, he suffered humiliation, for it was quite clear that he was standing, hat in hand, while Caesar graciously bestowed largesse on him.

Yet Pompey could do nothing, for he had married Julia, Caesar's daughter. She was beautiful and winning and Pompey was crazy about her. While he had her, he could do nothing to cross Caesar.

Caesar was running everything now. In 58 B.C., he suggested that he, Pompey, and Crassus each have a province in which they could win military victories. Pompey was to have Spain; Crassus was to have Syria; and Caesar was to have southern Gaul, which was then in Roman hands. Each was to be in charge for five years.

Pompey was delighted. In Syria, Crassus would have to face the redoubtable Parthian kingdom, and in Gaul, Caesar would have to face the fierce-fighting barbarians of the North. With luck, both would end in disaster, since neither was a trained military man. As for Pompey, since Spain was quiet, he could stay in Italy and control the government. Who could ask for more?

It might almost seem that if Pompey reasoned this way, his old nose for victory had returned. By 53 B.C., Crassus' army was destroyed by the Parthians east of Syria and Crassus himself was killed.

But Caesar? No, Pompey's luck had *not* returned. To the astonishment of everyone in Rome, Caesar, who, until then, had seemed to be nothing but a playboy and intriguer, turned out, in middle age (he was forty-four when he went to Gaul), to be a first-class military genius. He spent five years fighting the Gauls, annexing the vast territory they inhabited, conducting successful forays into Germany and Britain. He wrote up his adventures in his *Commentaries* for the Roman reading public, and suddenly Rome had a new military hero. —And Pompey, sitting in Italy, doing nothing, was nearly dead of frustration and envy.

In 54 B.C., though, Julia died, and Pompey was no longer held back in his animus against Caesar. The senatorial aristocrats, now far more afraid of Caesar than of Pompey, flattered the latter, who promptly joined them and married a new wife, the daughter of one of the leading senators.

When Caesar returned from Gaul in 50 B.C., the Senate ordered him to disband his armies and enter Italy alone. It was clear that if Caesar did so, he would be arrested and probably executed. What, then, if he defied the Senate and brought his army with him?

"Fear not," said Pompey, confidently, "I have but to stamp my foot upon the ground and legions will rise up to support us."

In 49 B.C., Caesar crossed the Rubicon River, which represented the boundary of Italy, and did so with his army. Pompey promptly stamped his foot—and nothing happened. Indeed, those soldiers stationed in Italy began to flock to Caesar's standards. Pompey and his senatorial allies were forced to flee, in humiliation, to Greece.

Grimly, Caesar and his army followed them.

In Greece, Pompey managed to collect a sizable army. Caesar, on the other hand, could only bring so many men across the sea and so Pompey now had the edge. He might have taken advantage of his superior numbers to cut Caesar off from his base and then stalk him carefully, without risking battle, and slowly wear him down and starve him out.

Against this was the fact that the humiliated Pompey, still dreaming of the old days, was dying to defeat Caesar in open battle and show him the worth of a *real* general. Worse yet, the senatorial party insisted on a battle. So Pompey let himself be talked into one; after all, he outnumbered Caesar two to one.

The battle was fought at Pharsalus in Thessaly on June 29, 48 B.C.

Pompey was counting on his cavalry in particular, a cavalry consisting of gallant young Roman aristocrats. Sure enough, at the start of the battle, Pompey's cavalry charged round the flank of Caesar's army and might well have wreaked havoc from the rear and cost Caesar the battle. Caesar, however, had foreseen this and had placed some picked men to meet the cavalry, with instructions not to throw their lances but to use them to poke directly at the faces of the horsemen. He felt that the aristocrats would not stand up to the danger of being disfigured and he was right. The cavalry broke.

With Pompey's cavalry out, Caesar's hardened infantry broke through the more numerous but much softer Pompeian line and Pompey, unused to handling armies in trouble, fled. In one blow, his entire military reputation was destroyed and it was quite clear that it was Caesar, not Pompey, who was the real general.

Pompey fled to the one Mediterranean land that was not yet entirely under Roman control—Egypt. But Egypt was in the midst of a civil war at the time. The boy-king, thirteen-year-old Ptolemy XII, was fighting against his older sister, Cleopatra, and the approach of Pompey created a problem. The politicians supporting young Ptolemy dared not turn Pompey away and earn the undying enmity of a Roman general who might yet win out. On the other hand, they dared not give him refuge and risk having Caesar support Cleopatra in revenge.

So they let Pompey land—and assassinated him.

And that was the end of Pompey, at the age of fifty-six.

Up to the age of forty-two he had been uniformly successful; nothing he tried to do failed. After the age of forty-two he had been uniformly unsuccessful; nothing he tried to do succeeded.

What happened at the age of forty-two? What circumstance took place in the interval represented earlier in the article by the line of asterisks that might "explain" this. Well, let's go back and fill in that line of asterisks.

\* \* \* \* \* \* \* \* \* \*

We are back in 64 B.C.

Pompey is in Jerusalem, curious about the queer religion of the Jews. What odd things do they do besides celebrate a Sabbath? He began collecting information.

There was the Temple, for instance. It was rather small and unimpressive by Roman standards but was venerated without limit by the Jews and differed from all other temples in the world by having no statue of a god or goddess inside. It seemed the Jews worshiped an invisible god.

"Really?" said the amused Pompey.

Actually, he was told, there was an innermost chamber in the Temple, the Holy of Holies, behind a veil. No one could ever go beyond the veil but the high priest, and he could only do so on the Day of Atonement. Some people said that the Jews secretly worshiped an ass's head there, but of course, the Jews themselves maintained that only the invisible presence of God was in that chamber.

Pompey, unimpressed by superstition, decided there was only one way of finding out. He would look inside this secret chamber.

The high priest was shocked, the Jews broke into agonized cries of dismay, but Pompey was adamant. He was curious and he had his army all around him. Who could stop him? So he entered the Holy of Holies.

The Jews were undoubtedly certain that he would be struck by lightning or otherwise destroyed by an offended God, but he wasn't.

He came out again in perfect health. He had found nothing, apparently, and nothing had happened to him, *apparently.*†

## AFTERWORD

I *love* the foregoing essay. In the first place, it made it possible for me to make the title a piece of outrageous wordplay, and there is nothing that gives me greater pleasure than outrageous wordplay. Well, almost nothing.

---

† In case you think I'm turning mystical myself, please reread the introduction to this chapter.

Secondly, it gave me a chance to indulge in my penchant for writing on historical subjects. After all I have written over a dozen history books, and many of my books on science have their historical aspects.

And finally, it let me pamper my penchant for discovering odd coincidences in history—and for insisting that they are only coincidences and must not be used as an excuse to search out some silly mystical piece of causation. And Pompey's sudden turnaround is the most beautiful example of coincidence I have ever come across.

# 14

# Lost in Non-Translation

At the Noreascon (the 29th World Science Fiction Convention), which was held in Boston on the Labor Day weekend of 1971, I sat on the dais, of course, since, as the Bob Hope of science fiction, it is my perennial duty to hand out the Hugos. On my left was my daughter, Robyn, sixteen, blond, blue-eyed, shapely, and beautiful. (No, that last adjective is not a father's proud partiality. Ask anyone.)

My old friend Clifford D. Simak was guest of honor, and he began his talk by introducing, with thoroughly justified pride, his two children, who were in the audience. A look of alarm instantly crossed Robyn's face.

"Daddy," she whispered urgently, knowing full well my capacity for inflicting embarrassment, "are you planning to introduce *me?*"

"Would that bother you, Robyn?" I asked.

"Yes, it would."

"Then I won't," I said, and patted her hand reassuringly.

She thought a while. Then she said, "Of course, Daddy, if you have the urge to refer, in a casual sort of way, to your beautiful daughter, that would be all right."

So you can bet I did just that, while she allowed her eyes to drop in a charmingly modest way.

But I couldn't help but think of the blond, blue-eyed stereotype of Nordic beauty that has filled Western literature ever since the blond, blue-eyed Germanic tribes took over the western portions of the Roman Empire, fifteen centuries ago, and set themselves up as an aristocracy.

. . . And of the manner in which that has been used to subvert one of the clearest and most important lessons in the Bible—a subversion that contributes its little bit to the serious crisis that today faces the world, and the United States in particular.

In line with my penchant for beginning at the beginning, come back with me to the sixth century B.C. A party of Jews have returned from Babylonian Exile to rebuild the Temple at Jerusalem, which Nebuchadrezzar had destroyed seventy years before.

During the Exile, under the guidance of the prophet Ezekiel the Jews had firmly held to their national identity by modifying, complicating, and idealizing their worship of Yahweh into a form that was directly ancestral to the Judaism of today. (In fact Ezekiel is sometimes called "the father of Judaism.")

This meant that when the exiles returned to Jerusalem, they faced a religious problem. There were people who, all through the period of the Exile, had been living in what had once been Judah, and who worshiped Yahweh in what they considered the correct, time-honored ritual. Because their chief city (with Jerusalem destroyed) was Samaria, the returning Jews called them Samaritans.

The Samaritans rejected the newfangled modifications of the returning Jews, and the Jews abhorred the old-fashioned beliefs of the Samaritans. Between them arose an undying hostility, the kind that is exacerbated because the differences in belief are comparatively small.

In addition, there were, of course, also living in the land, those who worshiped other gods altogether—Ammonites, Edomites, Philistines, and so on.

The pressures on the returning band of Jews were not primarily military, for the entire area was under the more or less beneficent rule of the Persian Empire, but it was social, and perhaps even stronger for that. To maintain a strict ritual in the face of overwhelming numbers of non-believers is difficult, and the tendency to relax that ritual was almost irresistible. Then, too, young male returnees were attracted to the women at hand and there were intermarriages. Naturally, to humor the wife, ritual was further relaxed.

But then, possibly as late as about 400 B.C., a full century after the Second Temple had been built, Ezra arrived in Jerusalem. He was a scholar of the Mosaic law, which had been edited and put into final form in the course of the Exile. He was horrified at the backsliding and put through a tub-thumping revival. He called the people together, led them in chanting the law and expounding upon it, raised their religious fervor, and called for confession of sins and renewal of faith.

One thing he demanded most rigorously was the abandonment of all non-Jewish wives and their children. Only so could the holiness of strict Judaism be maintained, in his view. To quote the Bible (and I will use the recent New English Bible for the purpose):

"Ezra the priest stood up and said, 'You have committed an offence in marrying foreign wives and have added to Israel's guilt. Make your confession now to the Lord the God of your fathers and do his will, and separate yourselves from the foreign population and from your foreign wives.' Then all the assembled people shouted in reply, 'Yes; we must do what you say. . . .'" (Ezra 10:10–12)

From that time on, the Jews as a whole began to practice an exclusivism, a voluntary separation from others, a multiplication of peculiar customs that further emphasized their separateness; and all of this helped them maintain their identity through all the miseries and catastrophes that were to come, through all the crises, and through exiles and persecutions that fragmented them over the face of the Earth.

The exclusivism, to be sure, also served to make them socially indigestible and imparted to them a high social visibility that helped give rise to conditions that made exiles and persecutions more likely.

Not everyone among the Jews adhered to this policy of exclusivism. There were some who believed that all men were equal in the sight of God and that no one should be excluded from the community on the basis of group identity alone.

And one who believed this (but who is forever nameless) attempted to present this case in the form of a short piece of historical fiction. In this fourth-century-B.C. tale the heroine was Ruth, a Moabite woman. (The tale was presented as having taken place in the time of the judges, so the traditional view was that it was written by the prophet Samuel in the eleventh century B.C. No modern student of the Bible believes this.)

Why a Moabite woman, by the way?

It seems that the Jews, returning from Exile, had traditions concerning their initial arrival at the borders of Canaan under first Moses, then Joshua, nearly a thousand years before. At that time, the small nation of Moab, which lay east of the lower course of the Jordan and of the Dead Sea, understandably alarmed at the incursion of tough desert raiders, took steps to oppose them. Not only did they prevent the Israelites from passing through their territory, but, tradition had it, they called in a seer, Balaam, and asked him to use his magical abilities to bring misfortune and destruction upon the invaders.

That failed, and Balaam, on departing, was supposed to have advised the king of Moab to let the Moabite girls lure the desert raiders into liaisons, which might subvert their stern dedication to their task. The Bible records the following:

"When the Israelites were in Shittim, the people began to have intercourse with Moabite women, who invited them to the sacrifices offered to their gods; and they ate the sacrificial food and prostrated themselves before the gods of Moab. The Israelites joined in the worship of the Baal of Peor, and the Lord was angry with them." (Numbers 25:1–3)

As a result of this, "Moabite women" became the quintessence of the type of outside influence that by sexual attraction tried to subvert pious Jews. Indeed Moab and the neighboring kingdom to the north, Ammon, were singled out in the Mosaic code:

"No Ammonite or Moabite, even down to the tenth generation, shall become a member of the assembly of the Lord . . . because they did not meet you with food and water on your way out of Egypt, and because they hired Balaam . . . to revile you. . . . You shall never seek their welfare or their good all your life long." (Deuteronomy 23:3–4, 6)

And yet there were times in later history when there was friendship between Moab and at least some men of Israel, possibly because they were brought together by some common enemy.

For instance, shortly before 1000 B.C. Israel was ruled by Saul. He had held off the Philistines, conquered the Amalekites, and brought Israel to its greatest pitch of power to that point. Moab naturally feared his expansionist policies and so befriended anyone rebelling against Saul. Such a rebel was the Judean warrior David of Bethlehem. When David was pressed hard by Saul and had retired to a fortified stronghold, he used Moab as a refuge for his family.

"David . . . said to the king of Moab, 'Let my father and mother come and take shelter with you until I know what God will do for me.' So he left them at the court of the king of Moab, and they stayed there as long as David was in his stronghold." (1 Samuel 22:3–4)

As it happened, David eventually won out, became king first of Judah, then of all Israel, and established an empire that took in the entire east coast of the Mediterranean, from Egypt to the Euphrates, with the Phoenician cities independent but in alliance with him. Later, Jews always looked back to the time of David and of his son Solomon as a golden age, and David's position in Jewish legend and thought was unassailable. David founded a dynasty that ruled over Judah for four centuries, and the Jews never stopped believing that some descendant of David would yet return to rule over them again in some idealized future time.

Yet, on the basis of the verses describing David's use of Moab as a refuge for his family, there may have arisen a tale to the effect that there was a Moabite strain in David's ancestry. Apparently, the author of the Book of Ruth determined to make use of this tale to point up the doctrine of non-exclusivism by using the supremely hated Moabite woman as his heroine.

The Book of Ruth tells of a Judean family of Bethlehem—a

man, his wife, and two sons—who are driven by famine to Moab. There the two sons marry Moabite girls, but after a space of time all three men die, leaving the three women—Naomi, the mother-in-law, and Ruth and Orpah, the two daughters-in-law—as survivors.

Those were times when women were chattels and when unmarried women, without a man to own them and care for them, could subsist only on charity. (Hence the frequent biblical injunction to care for widows and orphans.)

Naomi determined to return to Bethlehem, where kinsmen might possibly care for her, but urged Ruth and Orpah to remain in Moab. She does not say, but we might plausibly suppose she is thinking, that Moabite girls would have a rough time of it in Moab-hating Judah.

Orpah remains in Moab, but Ruth refuses to leave Naomi, saying, "Do not urge me to go back and desert you. . . . Where you go, I will go, and where you stay, I will stay. Your people shall be my people, and your God my God. Where you die I will die, and there I will be buried. I swear a solemn oath before the Lord your God: nothing but death shall divide us." (Ruth 1:16–17)

Once in Bethlehem, the two were faced with the direst poverty and Ruth volunteered to support herself and her mother-in-law by gleaning in the fields. It was harvesttime and it was customary to allow any stalks of grain that fell to the ground in the process of gathering to remain there to be collected by the poor. This gleaning was a kind of welfare program for those in need. It was, however, backbreaking work, and any young woman, particularly a Moabite, who engaged in it, underwent certain obvious risks at the hands of the lusty young reapers. Ruth's offer was simply heroic.

As it happened, Ruth gleaned in the lands of a rich Judean farmer named Boaz, who coming to oversee the work, noticed her working tirelessly. He asked after her, and his reapers answered, "She is a Moabite girl . . . who has just come back with Naomi from the Moabite country." (Ruth 2:6)

Boaz speaks kindly to her and Ruth says, "Why are you so kind as to take notice of me when I am only a foreigner?" (Ruth 2:10) Boaz explains that he has heard how she has forsaken her own land for love of Naomi and how hard she must work to take care of her.

As it turned out, Boaz was a relative of Naomi's dead husband, which must be one reason why he was touched by Ruth's love and fidelity. Naomi, on hearing the story, had an idea. In those days, if a widow was left childless, she had the right to expect her dead husband's brother to marry her and offer her his protection. If the dead husband had no brother, some other relative would fulfill the task.

Naomi was past the age of childbearing, so she could not qualify for marriage, which in those days centered about children; but what about Ruth? To be sure, Ruth was a Moabite woman and it might well be that no Judean would marry her, but Boaz had proven kind. Naomi therefore instructed Ruth how to approach Boaz at night and, without crudely seductive intent, appeal for his protection.

Boaz, touched by Ruth's modesty and helplessness, promised to do his duty, but pointed out that there was a kinsman closer than he and that, by right, this other kinsman had to have his chance first.

The very next day, Boaz approached the other kinsman and suggested that he buy some property in Naomi's charge and, along with it, take over another responsibility. Boaz said, "On the day when you acquire the field from Naomi, you also acquire Ruth the Moabitess, the dead man's wife. . . ." (Ruth 4:5)

Perhaps Boaz carefully stressed the adjectival phrase "the Moabitess," for the other kinsman drew back at once. Boaz therefore married Ruth, who in time bore him a son. The proud and happy Naomi held the child in her bosom and her women friends said to her, "The child will give you new life and cherish you in your old age; for your daughter-in-law who loves you, who has proved better to you than seven sons, has borne him." (Ruth 4:15)

This verdict of Judean women on Ruth, a woman of the hated land of Moab, in a society that valued sons infinitely more than daughters, a verdict that she "has proved better to you than seven sons" is the author's moral—that there are nobility and virtue in all groups and that none must be excluded from consideration in advance simply because of their group identification.

And then, to clinch the argument for any Judean so nationalis-
tic as to be impervious to mere idealism, the story concludes:
"Her neighbors gave him a name: 'Naomi has a son,' they said;
'we will call him Obed.' He was the father of Jesse, the father of
David." (Ruth 4:17)

Where would Israel have been, then, if there had been an Ezra
present then to forbid the marriage of Boaz with a "foreign
wife"?

Where does that leave us? That the Book of Ruth is a pleasant
story, no one will deny. It is almost always referred to as a
"delightful idyl" or words to that effect. That Ruth is a most
successful characterization of a sweet and virtuous woman is
beyond dispute.

In fact everyone is so in love with the story and with Ruth that
the whole point is lost. It is, by right, a tale of tolerance for the
despised, of love for the hated, of the reward that comes of
brotherhood. By mixing the genes of mankind, by forming the
hybrid, great men will come.

The Jews included the Book of Ruth in the canon partly because it is so wonderfully told a tale but mostly (I suspect) because it gives the lineage of the great David, a lineage that is *not*
given beyond David's father, Jesse, in the soberly historic books
of the Bible that anteceded Ruth. But the Jews remained, by and
large, exclusivistic and did not learn the lesson of universalism
preached by the Book of Ruth.

Nor have people taken its lesson to heart since. Why should
they, since every effort is made to wipe out that lesson? The story
of Ruth has been retold any number of times, from children's
tales to serious novels. Even movies have been made of it. Ruth
herself must have been pictured in hundreds of illustrations.
And in every illustration I have ever seen, she is presented as
blond, blue-eyed, shapely, and beautiful—the perfect Nordic
stereotype I referred to at the beginning of the article.

For goodness' sake, why shouldn't Boaz have fallen in love
with her? What great credit was there in marrying her? If a girl
like that had fallen at your feet and asked you humbly to do your
duty by her and kindly marry her, you would probably have done
it like a shot.

Of course she was a Moabite woman, but so what? What does

the word "Moabite" mean to you? Does it arouse any violent reaction? Are there many Moabites among your acquaintances? Have your children been chased by a bunch of lousy Moabites lately? Have they been reducing property values in your neighborhood? When was the last time you heard someone say, "Got to get those rotten Moabites out of here. They just fill up the welfare rolls."

In fact, judging by the way Ruth is drawn, Moabites are English aristocrats and their presence would raise property values.

The trouble is that the one word that is *not translated* in the Book of Ruth is the key word "Moabite," and as long as it is not translated, the point is lost; it is lost in non-translation.

The word Moabite really means "someone of a group that receives from us and deserves from us nothing but hatred and contempt." How should this word be translated into a single word that means the same thing to, say, many modern Greeks? . . . Why, "Turk." And to many modern Turks? . . . Why, "Greek." And to many modern white Americans? . . . Why, "Black."

To get the proper flavor of the Book of Ruth, suppose we think of Ruth not as a Moabite woman but as a Black woman.

Reread the story of Ruth and translate Moabite to Black every time you see it. Naomi (imagine) is coming back to the United States with her two Black daughters-in-law. No wonder she urges them not to come with her. It *is* a marvel that Ruth so loved her mother-in-law that she was willing to face a society that hated her unreasoningly and to take the risk of gleaning in the face of leering reapers who could not possibly suppose they need treat her with any consideration whatever.

And when Boaz asked who she was, don't read the answer as "She is a Moabite girl," but as "She is a Black girl." More likely, in fact, the reapers might have said to Boaz something that was the equivalent of (if you'll excuse the language), "She is a nigger girl."

Think of it that way and you find the whole point is found in translation and only in translation. Boaz' action in being willing to marry Ruth because she was virtuous (and not because she was a Nordic beauty) takes on a kind of nobility. The neighbors' decision that she was better to Naomi than seven sons becomes something that could have been forced out of them only by overwhelming evidence to that effect. And the final stroke that out of this miscegenation was born none other than the great David is rather breath-taking.

We get something similar in the New Testament. On one occasion a student of the law asks Jesus what must be done to gain eternal life, and answers his own question by saying, "Love the Lord your God with all your heart, with all your soul, with all your strength, and with all your mind; and your neighbour as yourself." (Luke 10:27)

These admonitions are taken from the Old Testament, of course. That last bit about your neighbor comes from a verse that says, "You shall not seek revenge, or cherish anger towards your kinsfolk; you shall love your neighbour as a man like yourself." (Leviticus 19:18)

(The New English Bible translations sounds better to me here than the King James's: "Thou shalt love thy neighbour as thyself." Where is the saint who can truly feel another's pain or ecstasy precisely as he feels his own? We must not ask too much. But if we simply grant that someone else is "a man like yourself," then he can be treated with decency at least. It is when we refuse to grant even this and talk of another as our inferior that contempt and cruelty come to seem natural, and even laudable.)

Jesus approves the lawyer's saying, and the lawyer promptly asks, "And who is my neighbour?" (Luke 10:29) After all, the verse in Leviticus first speaks of refraining from revenge and anger toward *kinsfolk;* might not, then, the concept of "neighbour" be restricted to kinsfolk, to one's own kind, only?

In response, Jesus replies with perhaps the greatest of the parables—of a traveler who fell in with robbers, who was mugged and robbed and left half dead by the road. Jesus goes on, "It so happened that a priest was going down by the same road; but when he saw him, he went past on the other side. So too a Levite came to the place, and when he saw him went past on the other side. But a Samaritan who was making the journey came upon him, and when he saw him was moved to pity. He went up and bandaged his wounds, bathing them with oil and wine. Then he lifted him on to his own beast, brought him to an inn, and looked after him there." (Luke 10:31–34)

Then Jesus asks who the traveler's neighbor was, and the lawyer is forced to say, "The one who showed him kindness." (Luke 10:37)

This is known as the Parable of the Good Samaritan, even though nowhere in the parable is the rescuer called a *good* Samaritan, merely a Samaritan.

The force of the parable is entirely vitiated by the common phrase "good" Samaritan, for that has cast a false light on who the Samaritans were. In a free-association test, say "Samaritan" and probably every person being tested will answer, "Good." It has become so imprinted in all our brains that Samaritans are good that we take it for granted that a Samaritan would act like that and wonder why Jesus is making a point of it.

We forget who the Samaritans were, in the time of Jesus!

To the Jews, they were *not* good. They were hated, despised, contemptible heretics with whom no good Jew would have anything to do. Again, the whole point is lost through non-translation.

Suppose, instead, that it is a white traveler in Mississippi who has been mugged and left half dead. And suppose it was a minister and a deacon who passed by and refused to "become involved." And suppose it was a Black sharecropper who stopped and took care of the man.

*Now* ask yourself: Who was the neighbor whom you must love as though he were a man like yourself if you are to be saved?

The Parable of the Good Samaritan clearly teaches that there is nothing parochial in the concept "neighbor," that you cannot confine your decency to your own group and your own kind. All mankind, right down to those you most despise, are your neighbors.

Well, then, we have in the Bible two examples—in the Book of Ruth and in the Parable of the Good Samaritan—of teachings that are lost in non-translation, yet are terribly applicable to us today.

The whole world over, there are confrontations between sections of mankind defined by race, nationality, economic philosophy, religion, or language as belonging to different groups, so that one is not "neighbor" to the other.

These more or less arbitrary differences among peoples who are members of a single biological species are terribly dangerous and nowhere more so than here in the United States, where the most perilous confrontation (I need not tell you) is between White and Black.

Next to the population problem generally, mankind faces no danger greater than this confrontation, particularly in the United States.

It seems to me that more and more, each year, both Whites and Blacks are turning, in anger and hatred, to violence. I see no reasonable end to the steady escalation but an actual civil war.

In such a civil war, the Whites, with a preponderance of numbers and an even greater preponderance of organized power would, in all likelihood, "win." They would do so, however, at an enormous material cost and, I suspect, at a fatal spiritual one.

And why? Is it so hard to recognize that we are all neighbors, after all? Can we, on both sides—on *both* sides—find no way of accepting the biblical lesson?

Or if quoting the Bible sounds too mealymouthed and if repeating the words of Jesus seems too pietistic, let's put it another way, a practical way:

Is the privilege of feeling hatred so luxurious a sensation that it is worth the material and spiritual hell of a White-Black civil war?

If the answer is really "Yes," then one can only despair.

## AFTERWORD

It is embarrassing these days to take up themes such as the siblinghood of humanity (clumsier, but more suitable, than the sexist phrase "the brotherhood of man").

After all, in the 1980s, it was discovered that one can win elections by denouncing people who are tainted by the "l-word" (i.e., "liberalism," if you don't mind my using bad language). It turns out that you become suspect, and an object of contempt, if you show sympathy for the poor, the needy, the downtrodden, the miserable.

I've tried to tell myself to change. I've said to myself, "Be a solid citizen. Sympathize with the rich and greedy. Admire the yuppistical and selfish. Rub shoulders with the inside traders on Wall Street and the influence-peddlers in Washington. Shake hands with those who dip into the public funds quietly while being very patriotic out loud."

The trouble is, I can't. I don't know how. I remain an l-word. I published the foregoing essay in 1972, in the deep sludge of the Nixon era, and I reprint it now.

# 15

## The Ancient and the Ultimate

About three weeks ago (as I write this) I attended a seminar in upstate New York, one that dealt with communications and society. The role assigned was a small one, but I spent four full days there, so I had a chance to hear all the goings-on.*

The very first night I was there I heard a particularly good lecture by an extraordinarily intelligent and charming gentleman who was involved in the field of TV cassettes. He made out an attractive and, to my way of thinking, irrefutable case in favor of the cassettes as representing the communications wave of the future—or, anyway, one of the waves.

He pointed out that for the commercial programs intended to support the fearfully expensive TV stations and the frightfully avid advertisers, audiences in the tens of millions were an absolute necessity.

As we all know, the only things that have a chance of pleasing

---

* Lest you think I was violating my principles by taking a vacation, I might as well tell you that I brought my hand typewriter with me, and used it, too.

twenty-five to fifty million different people are those that carefully avoid giving any occasion for offense. Anything that will add spice or flavor will offend someone and lose.

So it's the unflavored pap that survives, not because it pleases, but because it gives no occasion for displeasing. (Well, some people, you and I, for instance, are displeased, but when advertising magnates add up the total number of you and me and others like us, the final sum sends them into fits of scornful laughter.)

Cassettes, however, that please specialized tastes are selling content only, and don't have to mask it with a spurious and costly polish or the presence of a high-priced entertainment star. Present a cassette on chess strategy with chessmen symbols moving on a chessboard, and nothing else is needed to sell $x$ number of cassettes to $x$ number of chess enthusiasts. If enough is charged per cassette to cover the expense of making the tape (plus an honest profit) and if the expected number of sales are made, then all is well. There may be unexpected flops, but there may be unexpected best sellers too.

In short, the television-cassette business will rather resemble the book-publishing business.

The speaker made this point perfectly clear, and when he said, "The manuscript of the future will not be a badly typed sheaf of papers but a neatly photographed sequence of images," I could not help but fidget.

Maybe the fidgeting made me conspicuous as I sat there in the front row, for the speaker then added, "And men like Isaac Asimov will find themselves outmoded and replaced."

Naturally I jumped—and everybody laughed cheerfully at the thought of my being outmoded and replaced.

Two days later, the speaker scheduled for that evening made a trans-Atlantic call to say he was unavoidably detained in London, so the charming lady who was running the seminar came to me and asked me sweetly if I would fill in.

Naturally I said I hadn't prepared anything, and naturally she said that it was well known that I needed no preparation to give a terrific talk, and naturally I melted at the first sign of flattery, and naturally I got up that evening, and naturally I gave a terrific talk.† It was all very natural.

I can't possibly tell you exactly what I said, because, like all my talks, it was off the cuff, but, as I recall, the essence was something like this:

The speaker of two days before having spoken of TV cassettes and having given a fascinating and quite brilliant picture of a future in which cassettes and satellites dominated the communications picture, I was now going to make use of my science-fiction expertise to look still further ahead and see how cassettes could be further improved and refined, and made still more sophisticated.

In the first place, the cassettes, as demonstrated by the speaker, needed a rather bulky and expensive piece of apparatus to decode the tape, to place images on a television screen, and to put the accompanying sound on a speaker.

Obviously we would expect this auxiliary equipment to be made smaller, lighter, and more mobile. Ultimately we would expect it to disappear altogether and become part of the cassette itself.

Secondly, energy is required to convert the information contained in the cassette into image and sound, and this places a strain on the environment. (All use of energy does that, and while we can't avoid using energy, there is no value in using more than we must.)

Consequently we can expect the amount of energy required to translate the cassette to decrease. Ultimately we would expect it to reach a value of zero and disappear.

Therefore we can imagine a cassette that is completely mobile and self-contained. Though it requires energy in its formation, it requires no energy and no special equipment for its use thereafter. It needn't be plugged into the wall; it needs no battery replacements; it can be carried with you wherever you feel most comfortable about viewing it: in bed, in the bathroom, in a tree, in the attic.

A cassette as ordinarily viewed makes sounds, of course, and

† Well, everybody said so.

casts light. Naturally it should make itself plain to you in both image and sound, but for it to obtrude on the attention of others, who may not be interested, is a flaw. Ideally, the self-contained mobile cassette should be seen and heard only by you.

No matter how sophisticated the cassettes now on the market, or those visualized for the immediate future, they do require controls. There is an on-off knob or switch, and others to regulate color, volume, brightness, contrast, and all that sort of thing. In my vision, I want to make such controls operated, as far as possible, by the will.

I foresee a cassette in which the tape stops as soon as you remove your eye. It remains stopped till you bring your eye back, at which point it begins to move again immediately. I foresee a cassette that plays its tape quickly or slowly, forward or backward, by skips, or with repetitions, entirely at will.

You'll have to admit that such a cassette would be a perfect futuristic dream: self-contained, mobile, non-energy-consuming, perfectly private, and largely under the control of the will.

Ah, but dreams are cheap, so let's get practical. Can such a cassette possibly exist? To this, my answer is, Yes, of course.

The next question is: How many years will we have to wait for such a deliriously perfect cassette?

I have that answer too, and quite a definite one. We will have it in minus five thousand years—because what I have been describing (as perhaps you have guessed) is the book!

Am I cheating? Does it seem to you, O Gentle Reader, that the book is *not* the ultimately refined cassette, for it presents words only, and no image, that words without images are somehow one-dimensional and divorced from reality, that we cannot expect to get information by words alone concerning a universe that exists in images?

Well, let's consider that. Is the image more important than the word?

Certainly if we consider man's purely physical activities, the sense of sight is by far the most important way in which he gathers information concerning the universe. Given my choice of running across rough country with my eyes blindfolded and my hearing sharp, or with my eyes open and my hearing out of action, I would certainly use my eyes. In fact, with my eyes closed I would move at all only with the greatest caution.

*But* at some early stage in man's development he invented speech. He learned how to modulate his expired breath and how to use different modulations of sound to serve as agreed-upon symbols of material objects and actions and—far more important—of abstractions.

Eventually he learned to encode modulated sounds into markings that could be seen by the eye and translated into the corresponding sound in the brain. A book, I need not tell you, is a device that contains what we might call "stored speech."

It is speech that represents the most fundamental distinction between man and all other animals (except possibly the dolphin, which may conceivably have speech but has never worked out a system for storing it).

Not only do speech and the potential capacity to store speech differentiate man from all other species of life who have lived now or in the past, but it is something all men have in common. All known groups of human beings, however "primitive" they may be, can and do speak, and can and do have a language. Some "primitive" peoples have very complex and sophisticated languages, I understand.

What's more, all human beings who are even nearly normal in mentality learn to speak at an early age.

With speech the universal attribute of mankind, it becomes true that more information reaches us—as *social* animals— through speech than through images.

The comparison isn't even close. Speech and its stored forms (the written or printed word) are so overwhelmingly a source of the information we get, that without them we are helpless.

To see what I mean, let's consider a television program, since that ordinarily involves both speech and image, and let's ask ourselves what happens if we do without the one or the other.

Suppose you darken the picture and allow the sound to remain. Won't you still get a pretty good notion of what's going on? There may be spots rich in action and poor in sound and may leave you frustrated by dark silence, but if it were anticipated that you would not see the image, a few lines could be added and you would miss nothing.

Indeed radio got by on sound alone. It used speech and "sound effects." This meant that there were occasional moments when the dialogue was artificial to make up for the lack of image: "There comes Harry now. Oh, he doesn't see the banana. Oh, he's stepping on the banana. There he goes." By and large, though, you could get along. I doubt that anyone listening to radio seriously missed the absence of image.

Back to the TV tube, however. Now turn off the sound and allow the vision to remain untouched—in perfect focus and full color. What do you get out of it? Very little. Not all the play of emotion on the face, not all the impassioned gestures, not all the tricks of the camera as it focuses here and there are going to give you more than the haziest notion of what is going on.

Corresponding to radio, which is only speech and miscellaneous sound, there were the silent movies, which were only images. In the absence of sound and speech, the actors in the silent films had to "emote." Oh, the flashing eyes; oh, the hands at the throat, in the air, raised to heaven; oh, the fingers pointing trustingly to heaven, firmly to the floor, angrily to the door; oh, the camera moving in to show the banana skin on the floor, the ace in the sleeve, the fly on the nose. And with every extreme of inventiveness of visualization in its most exaggerated form, what did we have every fifteen seconds? An utter halt to the action, while words flashed on the screen.

This is not to say that one cannot communicate after a fashion by vision alone—by the use of pictorial images. A clever pantomimist like Marcel Marceau or Charlie Chaplin or Red Skelton can do wonders—but the very reason we watch them and applaud is that they communicate so much with so poor a medium as pictorialization.

As a matter of fact, we amuse ourselves by playing charades and trying to have someone guess some simple phrase we "act out." It wouldn't be a successful game if it didn't require much ingenuity, and, even so, practitioners of the game work up sets of signals and devices that (whether they know it or not) take advantage of the mechanics of speech.

They divide words into syllables, they indicate whether a word is short or long, they use synonyms and "sounds like." In all this, they are using visual images to *speak*. Without using any trick that involves any of the properties of speech, but simply by gesture and action alone, can you get across as simple a sentence as, "Yesterday the sunset was beautiful in rose and green"?

Of course a movie camera can photograph a beautiful sunset and you can point to that. This involves a great investment of technology, however, and I'm not sure that it will tell you that the sunset was like that *yesterday* (unless the film plays tricks with calendars—which represent a form of speech).

Or consider this: Shakespeare's plays were written to be acted. The image was of the essence. To get the full flavor, you must see the actors and what they are doing. How much do you miss if you go to *Hamlet* and close your eyes and merely listen? How much do you miss if you plug your ears and merely look?

Having made clear my belief that a book, which consists of words but no images, loses very little by its lack of images and has therefore every right to be considered an extremely sophisticated example of a television cassette, let me change my ground and use an even better argument.

Far from lacking the image, a book *does* have images, and what's more, far better images, because personal, than any that can possibly be presented to you on television.

When you are reading an interesting book, are there no images in your mind? Do you not see all that is going on, in your mind's eye?

Those images are *yours.* They belong to you and to you alone, and they are infinitely better for you than those wished on you by others.

I saw Gene Kelly in *The Three Musketeers* once (the only version I ever saw that was reasonably faithful to the book). The sword fight between D'Artagnan, Athos, Porthos, and Aramis on one side and the five men of the Cardinal's Guard on the other, which occurs near the beginning of the picture, was absolutely beautiful. It was a dance of course, and I reveled in it. . . . But Gene Kelly, however talented a dancer he might be, does not happen to fit the picture of D'Artagnan that I have in my mind's eye, and I was unhappy all through the picture because it did violence to "my" *The Three Musketeers.*

This is not to say that sometimes an actor might not just

happen to match your own vision. Sherlock Holmes in my mind just happens to be Basil Rathbone. In *your* mind, however, Sherlock Holmes might *not* be Basil Rathbone; he might be Dustin Hoffman, for all I know. Why should all our millions of Sherlock Holmes's have to be fitted into a single Basil Rathbone?

You see, then, why a television program, however excellent, can never give as much pleasure, be as absorbing, fill so important a niche in the life of the imagination, as a book can. To the television program we need only bring an empty mind and sit torpidly while the display of sound and image fills us, requiring nothing of our imagination. If others are watching, they are filled to the brim in precisely the same way, all of them, and with precisely the same sounding images.

The book, on the other hand, demands co-operation from the reader. It insists he take part in the process.

In doing so, it offers an interrelationship that is made to order by the reader himself for the reader himself—one that most neatly fits his own peculiarities and idiosyncracies.

When you read a book, you create your own images, you create the sound of various voices, you create gestures, expressions, emotions. You create *everything* but the bare words themselves. And if you take the slightest pleasure in creation, the book has given you something the television program can't.

Furthermore, if ten thousand people read the same book at the same time, each nevertheless creates his own images, his own sound of the voice, his own gestures, expressions, emotions. It will be not one book but ten thousand books. It will not be the product of the author alone, but the product of the interaction of the author and each of the readers separately.

What, then, can replace the book?

I admit that the book may undergo changes in non-essentials. It was once handwritten; it is now printed. The technology of publishing the printed book has advanced in a hundred ways, and in the future a book may be turned out electronically from a television set in your house.

In the end, though, you will be alone with the printed word, and what can replace it?

Is all this wishful thinking? Is it just that I make my living out of books, so I don't want to accept the fact that books may be replaced? Am I just inventing ingenious arguments to console myself?

Not at all. I am certain that books will not be replaced in the future, because they have not been replaced in the past.

To be sure, many more people watch television than read books, but that is not new. Books were *always* a minority activity. Few people read books before television, and before radio, and before anything you care to name.

As I said, books are demanding, and require creative activity on the part of the reader. Not everyone, in fact darned few, are ready to give what is demanded, so they don't read, and they *won't* read. They are not lost just because the book fails them somehow; they are lost by nature.

In fact let me make the point that reading itself is difficult, inordinately difficult. It is not like talking, which every even halfway normal child learns without any program of conscious teaching. Imitation beginning at the age of one will do the trick.

Reading, on the other hand, must be carefully taught and, usually, without much luck.

The trouble is that we mislead ourselves by our own definition of literacy. We can teach almost anyone (if we try hard enough and long enough) to read traffic signs and to make out instructions and warnings on posters, and to puzzle out newspaper headlines. Provided the printed message is short and reasonably simple and the motivation to read it is great, almost everyone can read.

And if this is called literacy, then almost every American is literate. But if you then begin to wonder why so few Americans read books (the average American out of school, I understand, does not even read one complete book a year), you are being misled by your own use of the term literate.

Few people who are literate in the sense of being able to read a sign that says NO SMOKING ever become so familiar with the printed word and so at ease with the process of quickly decoding by eye the small and complicated shapes that stand for modulated sounds that they are willing to tackle any extended reading task—as for instance making their way through one thousand consecutive words.

Nor do I think it's entirely a matter of the failure of our educational system (though heaven knows it's a failure). No one expects that if one teaches every child how to play baseball, they will all be talented baseball players, or that every child taught how to play the piano will be a talented pianist. We accept in almost every field of endeavor the notion of a talent that can be encouraged and developed but cannot be created from nothing.

Well, in my view, reading is a talent too. It is a very difficult activity. Let me tell you how I discovered that.

When I was a teen-ager, I sometimes read comic magazines, and my favorite character, if you're interested, was Scrooge McDuck. In those days, comic magazines cost ten cents, but of course I read them for nothing off my father's newsstand. I used to wonder, though, how anyone would be so foolish as to pay ten cents, when by simply glancing through the magazine for two minutes at the newsstand, he could read the whole thing.

Then one day on the subway to Columbia University, I found myself hanging from a strap in a crowded car with nothing handy to read. Fortunately the teen-age girl seated in front of me was reading a comic magazine. Something is better than nothing, so I arranged myself so I could look down on the pages and read along with her. (Fortunately I can read upside down as easily as right side up.)

Then, after a few seconds, I thought, Why doesn't she turn the page?

She did, eventually. It took minutes for her to finish each double-page spread, and as I watched her eyes going from one panel to the next and her lips carefully mumbling the words, I had a flash of insight.

What she was doing was what I would be doing if I were faced with English words written phonetically in the Hebrew, Greek, or Cyrillic alphabet. Knowing the respective alphabets dimly, I would have to first recognize each letter, then sound it, then put them together, then recognize the word. Then I would have to pass on to the next word and do the same. Then, when I had done several words this way, I would have to go back and try to get them in combination.

You can bet that under those circumstances, I would do very little reading. The *only* reason I read is that when I look at a line of print I see it all as words, and at once.

And the difference between the reader and the non-reader grows steadily wider with the years. The more a reader reads, the more information he picks up, the larger his vocabulary grows, the more familiar various literary allusions become. It becomes steadily easier and more fun for him to read, while for the non-reader it becomes steadily harder and less worth while.

The result of this is that there are and *always have been* (whatever the state of supposed literacy in a particular society) both readers and non-readers, with the former making up a tiny minority, of, I guess, less than 1 percent.

I have estimated that four hundred thousand Americans have read some of my books (out of a population of two hundred million), and I am considered, and consider myself, a successful writer. If a particular book should sell two million copies in all its American editions, it would be a remarkable best seller—and all that would mean would be that 1 percent of the American population had managed to nerve themselves to buy it. Of that total, moreover, I'm willing to bet that at least half would manage to do no more than stumble through some of it in order to find the dirty parts.

Those people, those non-readers, those passive receptacles for entertainment, are terribly fickle. They will switch from one thing to another in the eternal search for some device that will give them as much as possible and ask of them as little as possible.

From minstrels to theatrical performances, from the theater to the movies, from the silents to the talkies, from black-and-white to color, from the record player to the radio and back, from the movies to television to color television to cassettes.

What does it matter?

But through it all, the faithful less-than-1-percent minority stick to the books. Only the printed word can demand as much from them, only the printed word can force creativity out of them, only the printed word can tailor itself to their needs and desires, only the printed word can give them what nothing else can.

The book may be ancient but it is also the ultimate, and readers will never be seduced away from it. They will remain a minority, but they will *remain.*

So despite what my friend said in his speech on cassettes, writers of books will never be outmoded and replaced. Writing books may be no way to get rich (oh, well, what's money!), but as a profession, it will always be there.

## AFTERWORD

In some ways, the foregoing has proved the most successful of my essays. It has been reprinted more times than any other, and selections from it have even been reprinted in bookmark form and have been distributed free of charge by libraries.

Of course, I have been told that in upholding the book, I am simply being self-serving, trying to encourage the use of that by means of which I amass my modest livelihood.

If so, I am being extremely inefficient about it. If my only concern was that of getting rich, I wouldn't try to do it by touting books in a cerebral essay. I would write steamy, sexy novels, riddled with violence and perversion. That would work much better. Or I would go to California and get into the movie-writing business, complete with tennis court and swimming pool. That would work much better, too.

The fact that I don't do these things, but continue to write my essays, here in New York, may indicate that I actually like books for their own sake, and feel they ought to be read for the sake of the reader much more than for that of the writer.

# 16

## Look Long upon a Monkey

Considering that I work so hard at establishing my chosen persona as a man who is cheerfully self-appreciative, I am sometimes absurdly sensitive to the fact that every once in a while people who don't know me take the persona for myself.

I was interviewed recently by a newspaper reporter who was an exceedingly pleasant fellow but who clearly knew very little about me. I was curious enough, therefore, to ask why he had decided to interview me.

He explained without hesitation. "My boss asked me to interview you," he said. Then he smiled a little and added, "He has strong, ambivalent feelings about you."

I said, "You mean he likes my writing but thinks I am arrogant and conceited."

"Yes," he said, clearly surprised. "How did you know?"

"Lucky guess," I said, with a sigh.

You see, it's *not* arrogance and conceit; it's cheerful self-appreciation, and anyone who knows me has no trouble seeing the difference.

Of course, I could save myself this trouble by choosing a different persona, by practicing aw-shucks modesty and learning how to dig my toe into the ground and bring the pretty pink to my cheeks at the slightest word of praise.

But no, thanks. I write on just about every subject and for every age level, and once I begin to practice a charming diffidence, I will make myself doubt my own ability to do so, and that would be ruinous.

So I'll go right along the path I have chosen and endure the ambivalent feelings that come my way, for the sake of having the self-assurance to write my wide-ranging essays—like this one on evolution.

I suspect that if man* could only have been left out of it, there would never have been any trouble about accepting biological evolution.

Anyone can see, for instance, that some animals resemble each other closely. Who can deny that a dog and a wolf resemble each other in important ways? Or a tiger and a leopard? Or a lobster and a crab? Twenty-three centuries ago the Greek philosopher Aristotle lumped different types of species together and prepared a "ladder of life," by arranging those types from the simplest plants upward to the most complex animals, with (inevitably) man at the top.

Once this was done, we moderns could say, with the clear vision of hindsight, that it was inevitable that people should come to see that one type of species had changed into another; that the more complex had developed from the less complex; that, in short, there was not only a ladder of life but a system whereby life forms climbed that ladder.

Not so! Neither Aristotle nor those who came after him for more than two thousand years moved from the ladder of life as a static concept to one that was a dynamic and evolutionary one.

The various species, it was considered, were *permanent.* There

---

* Anyone who reads these essays knows that I am a women's-libber, but I also have a love for the English language. I try to circumlocute "man" when I mean "human being" but the flow of sound suffers sometimes when I do. *Please* accept, in this article, "man" in the general, embracing "woman." (Yes, I know what I said.)

might be families and hierarchies of species, but that was the way in which life was created from the beginning. Resemblances had existed from the beginning, it was maintained, and no species grew to resemble another more—or less—with the passage of time.

My feeling is that the insistence on this constancy of species arose, at least in part, out of the uncomfortable feeling that once change was allowed, man would lose his uniqueness and become "just another animal."

Once Christianity grew dominant in the Western world, views on the constancy of species became even more rigid. Not only did Genesis 1 clearly describe the creation of the various species of life as already differentiated and in their present form, but man was created differently from all the rest. "And God said, Let us make man in our image, after our likeness . . ." (Genesis 1:26).

No other living thing was made in God's image and that placed an insuperable barrier between man and all other living things. Any view that led to the belief that the barriers between species generally were not leakproof tended to weaken that all-important barrier protecting man.

It would have been nice, of course, if all the other life forms on Earth were enormously different from man so that the insuperable barrier would be clearly reflected physically. Unfortunately, the Mediterranean world was acquainted, even in early times, with certain animals we now call "monkeys."

The various monkeys with which the ancients came in contact had faces that, in some cases, looked like those of shriveled little men. They had hands that clearly resembled human hands and they fingered things as human beings did and with a clearly lively curiosity. However, they had tails and that rather saved the day. The human being is so pronouncedly tailless and most of the animals we know are so pronouncedly tailed that that, in itself, would seem to be a symbol of that insuperable barrier between man and monkey.

There are, indeed, some animals without tails or with very short tails, such as frogs, guinea pigs, and bears, but these, even without tails, do not threaten man's status. And yet—

There is a reference to a monkey in the Bible, one for which the translators used a special word. In discussing King Solomon's trading ventures, the Bible says (1 Kings 10:22), ". . . once in three years came the navy of Tharshish, bringing gold, and silver, ivory, and apes, and peacocks."

Tharshish is often identified as Tartessus, a city on the Spanish coast just west of the Strait of Gibraltar, a flourishing trading center in Solomon's time that was destroyed by the Carthaginians in 480 B.C. In northwestern Africa across from Tartessus, there existed then (and now) a type of monkey of the macaque group. It was this macaque that was called an "ape," and in later years, when northwestern Africa became part of "Barbary" to Europeans, it came to be called "Barbary ape."

The Barbary ape is tailless and therefore more resembles man than other monkeys do. Aristotle, in his ladder of life, placed the Barbary ape at the top of the monkey group, just under man. Galen, the Greek physician of about A.D. 200, dissected apes and showed the resemblance to man to be internal as well as external.

It was the resemblance to man that made the Barbary ape amusing to the ancients, and yet annoying as well. The Roman poet Ennius is quoted as saying, "The ape, vilest of beasts, how like to us!" Was the ape really the "vilest of beasts"? Objectively, of course not. It was its resemblance to man and its threat, therefore, to man's cherished uniqueness that made it vile.

In medieval times, when the uniqueness and supremacy of man had become a cherished dogma, the existence of the ape was even more annoying. They were equated with the Devil. The Devil, after all, was a fallen and distorted angel, and as man had been created in God's image, so the ape was created in the Devil's.

Yet no amount of explanation removed the unease. The English dramatist William Congreve wrote in 1695: "I could never look long upon a monkey, without very mortifying reflections." It is not so hard to guess that those "mortifying reflections" must have been to the effect that man might be described as a large and somewhat more intelligent ape.

Modern times had made matters worse by introducing the proud image-of-God European to animals, hitherto unknown, which resembled him even more closely than the Barbary ape did.

In 1641 a description was published of an animal brought from Africa and kept in the Netherlands in a menagerie belonging to the Prince of Orange. From the description it seems to have been a chimpanzee. There were also reports of a large manlike animal in Borneo, one we now call the orangutan.

The chimpanzee and the orangutan were called "apes" because, like the Barbary ape, they lacked tails. In later years, when it was recognized that the chimpanzee and orangutan resembled monkeys less and men more, they came to be known as "anthropoid" (man-like) apes.

In 1758 the Swedish naturalist Carolus Linnaeus made the first thoroughly systematic attempt to classify all species. He was a firm believer in the permanence of species and it did not concern him that some animal species closely resembled man— that was just the way they were created.

He therefore did not hesitate to lump the various species of apes and monkey together, *with man included as well,* and call that group "Primates," from a Latin word for "first," since it included man. We still use the term.

The monkeys and apes, generally, Linnaeus put into one subgroup of Primates and called that subgroup "Simia," from the Latin word for "ape." For human beings, Linnaeus invented the subgroup "Homo," which is the Latin word for "man." Linnaeus used a double name for each species (called "binomial nomenclature," with the family name first, like Smith, John, and Smith, William), so human beings rejoiced in the name *"Homo sapiens"* (Man, wise). But Linnaeus placed another member in that group. Having read the description of the Bornean orangutan, he named it "Homo troglodytes" (Man, cave-dwelling).

"Orangutan" is from a Malay word meaning "man of the forest." The Malays, who were there on the spot, were more accurate in their description, for the orangutan is a forest dweller and not a cave dweller, but either way it cannot be considered near enough to man to warrant the Homo designation.

The French naturalist Georges de Buffon was the first, in the middle 1700s, to describe the gibbons, which represent a third kind of anthropoid ape. The various gibbons are the smallest of the anthropoids and the least like man. They are sometimes put to one side for that reason, the remaining anthropoids being called the "great apes."

As the classification of species grew more detailed, naturalists were more and more tempted to break down the barriers between them. Some species were so similar to other species that it was uncertain whether any boundary at all could be drawn between them. Besides, more and more animals showed signs of being caught in the middle of change, so to speak.

The horse, Buffon noted, had two "splints" on either side of its leg bones, which seemed to indicate that once there had been three lines of bones there and three hoofs to each leg.

Buffon argued that if hoofs and bones could degenerate, so might entire species. Perhaps God had created only certain species and that each of these had, to some extent, degenerated and formed additional species. If horses could lose some of their hoofs, why might not some of them have degenerated all the way to donkeys?

Since Buffon wished to speculate on what was, after all, the big news in man-centered natural history, he suggested that apes were degenerated men.

Buffon was the first to talk of the mutability of species. Here, however, he avoided the worst danger—that of suggesting that man-the-image-of-God had once been something else—but he did say that man could *become* something else. Even that was too much, for once the boundaries were made to leak in one direction, it would be hard to make it leakproof in the other. The pressure was placed on Buffon to recant, and recant he did.

The notion of the mutability of species did not die, however. A British physician, Erasmus Darwin, had the habit of writing long poems of indifferent quality in which he presented his ofttimes interesting scientific theories. In his last book, *Zoonomia,* published in 1796, he amplified Buffon's ideas and suggested that species underwent changes as a result of the direct influence upon them of the environment.

This notion was carried still further by the French naturalist Jean Baptiste de Lamarck, who, in 1809, published *Zoological*

*Philosophy* and was the first scientist of note to advance a theory of evolution, a thoroughgoing description of the mechanisms by which an antelope, for instance, could conceivably change, little by little over the generations, into a giraffe. (Both Darwin and Lamarck were virtually ostracized for their views by the Establishments, both scientific and non-scientific, of those days.)

Lamarck was wrong in his notion of the evolutionary mechanism, but his book made the concept of evolution well known in the scientific world and it inspired others to find a perhaps more workable mechanism.†

The man who turned the trick was the English naturalist Charles Robert Darwin (grandson of Erasmus Darwin), who spent nearly twenty years gathering data and polishing his argument. This he did, first, because he was a naturally meticulous man. Secondly, he knew the fate that awaited anyone who advanced an evolutionary theory, and he wanted to disarm the enemy by making his arguments cast-iron.

When he published his book *On the Origin of Species by Means of Natural Selection* in 1859, he carefully refrained from discussing man in it. That didn't help, of course. He was a gentle and virtuous person, as nearly a saint as any cleric in the kingdom, but if he had bitten his mother to death, he couldn't have been denounced more viciously.

Yet the evidence in favor of evolution had kept piling up. In 1847 the largest of the anthropoid apes, the gorilla, was finally brought into the light of European day, and it was the most dramatic ape of all. In size, at least, it seemed most nearly human, or even superhuman.

Then, too, in 1856 the very first fossil remnants of an organism that was clearly more advanced than any of the living anthro-

---

† Antievolutionists usually denounce evolution as "merely a theory" and cite various uncertainties in the details, uncertainties that are admitted by biologists. In this, the antievolutionists are being fuzzy-minded. That evolution has taken place is as nearly a *fact* as anything non-trivial can be. The exact details of the mechanism by which evolution proceeds, however, remain theoretical in many respects. The mechanism, however, is not the thing. Thus, very few people really understand the mechanism by which an automobile runs, but those who are uncertain of the mechanism do not argue from that that the automobile itself does not exist.

poids and as clearly more primitive than any living man was discovered in the Neander valley in Germany. This was "Neanderthal man." Not only was the evidence in favor of evolution steadily rising, but so was the evidence in favor of *human* evolution.

In 1863 the Scottish geologist Charles Lyell published *The Antiquity of Man,* which used the evidence of ancient stone tools to argue that mankind was much older than the six thousand years allotted him (and the Universe) in the Bible. He also came out strongly in favor of the Darwinian view of evolution.

And in 1871 Darwin finally carried the argument to man with his book *The Descent of Man.*

The antievolutionists remain with us, of course, to this day, ardent and firm in their cause. I get more than my share of letters from them, so that I know what their arguments are like.

They concentrate on one point, and on one point only—the descent of man. I have never once received any letter arguing emotionally that the beaver is *not* related to the rat or that the whale is *not* descended from a land mammal. I sometimes think they don't even realize that evolution applies to all species. Their only insistence is that man is not, *not,* NOT descended from or related to apes or monkeys.

Some evolutionists try to counter this by saying that Darwin never said that man is descended from monkeys; that no living primate is an ancestor of man. This, however, is a quibble. The evolutionary view is that man and the apes had some common ancestor that is not alive today but that looked like a primitive ape when it was alive. Going farther back, man's various ancestors had a distinct monkeyish appearance—to the non-zoologist at least.

As an evolutionist, I prefer to face that fact without flinching. I am perfectly prepared to maintain that man *did* descend from monkeys, as the simplest way of stating what I believe to be the fact.

And we've got to stick to monkeys in another way, too. Evolutionists may talk about the "early hominids," about "Homo erectus," the "Australopithecines," and so on. We may use that as evidence of the evolution of man and of the type of organism from which he descended.

This, I suspect, doesn't carry conviction to the antievolutionists or even bother them much. Their view seems to be that when
a bunch of infidels who call themselves scientists find a tooth
here, a thigh bone there, and a piece of skull yonder and jigsaw
them all together into a kind of ape man, that doesn't mean a
thing.

From the mail I get and from the literature I've seen, it seems
to me that the emotionalism of the antievolutionist boils itself
down to man and monkey, and nothing more.

There are two ways in which an antievolutionist, it seems to
me, can handle the man-and-monkey issue. He can stand pat on
the Bible, declare that it is divinely inspired and that it says man
was created out of the dust of the Earth by God, in the image of
God, six thousand years ago, and that's it. If that is his position,
his views are clearly non-negotiable, and there is no point in
trying to negotiate. I will discuss the weather with such a person,
but not evolution.

A second way is for the antievolutionist to attempt some rational justification for his stand; a justification that is, that does
not rest on authority, but can be tested by observation or experiment and argued logically. For instance, one might argue that
the differences between man and all other animals are so fundamental that it is unthinkable that they be bridged and that no
animal can conceivably develop into a man by the operation of
nothing more than the laws of nature—that supernatural inter-
vention is required.

An example of such an unbridgeable difference is a claim, for
instance, that man has a soul and that no animal has one, and
that a soul cannot be developed by any evolutionary procedure.
—Unfortunately, there is no way of measuring or detecting a
soul by those methods known to science. In fact, one cannot
even define a soul except by referring to some sort of mystical
authority. This falls outside observation or experiment, then.

On a less exalted plane, an antievolutionist might argue that
man has a sense of right and wrong; that he has an appreciation
of justice; that he is, in short, a moral organism while animals are
not and cannot be.

That, I think, leaves room for argument. There are animals

that act as though they love their young and that sometimes give their lives for them. There are animals that co-operate and protect each other in danger. Such behavior has survival value and it is exactly the sort of thing that evolutionists would expect to see developed bit by bit, until it reaches the level found in man.

If you were to argue that such apparently "human" behavior in animals is purely mechanical and is done without understanding, then once again we are back to argument by mere assertion. We don't know what goes on inside an animal's mind and, for that matter, it is by no means certain that our own behavior isn't as mechanical as that of animals—only a degree more complicated and versatile.

There was a time when things were easier than they are now, when comparative anatomy was in its beginnings, and when it was possible to suppose that there was some gross physiological difference that set off man from all other animals. In the seventeenth century the French philosopher René Descartes thought the pineal gland was the seat of the soul, for he accepted the then-current notion that this gland was found only in the human being and in no other organism whatever.

Alas, not so. The pineal gland is found in all vertebrates and is most highly developed in a certain primitive reptile called the tuatara. As a matter of fact, there is no portion of the physical body which the human being owns to the exclusion of all other species.

Suppose we get more subtle and consider the biochemistry of organisms. Here the differences are much less marked than in the physical shape of the body and its parts. Indeed, there is so much similarity in the biochemical workings of *all* organisms, not only if we compare men and monkeys, but if we compare men and bacteria, that if it weren't for preconceived notions and species-centered conceit, the fact of evolution would be considered self-evident.

We must get very subtle indeed and begin to study the very fine chemical structure of the all but infinitely versatile protein molecule in order to find something distinctive for each species. Then, by the tiny differences in that chemical structure, one can get a rough measure of how long ago in time two organisms may have branched away from a common ancestor.

By studying protein structure, we find no large gaps; no differences between one species and all others that is so huge as to indicate a common ancestor so long ago that in all the history of Earth there was no time for such divergence to have taken place. If such a large gap existed between one species and all the rest, then that one species would have arisen from a different globule of primordial life than that which gave birth to all the rest. It would still have evolved, still have descended from more primitive species, but it would not be related to any other Earthly life form. I repeat, however, that no such gap has been found and none is expected. *All* Earthly life is interrelated.

Certainly man is not separated from other forms of life by some large biochemical gap. Biochemically, he falls within the Primates group and is not particularly more separate than the others are. In fact, he seems quite closely related to the chimpanzee. The chimpanzee, by the protein structure test, is closer to man than to the gorilla or orangutan.

So it is from the chimpanzee, specifically, that the antievolutionist must protect us. Surely, if, in Congreve's words, we "look long upon the monkey," meaning the chimpanzee in this case, we must admit it differs from us in nothing vital but the brain. The human brain is four times the size of the chimpanzee brain!

It might seem that even this large difference in size is but a difference in degree, and one that can be easily explained by evolutionary development—especially since fossil hominids had brains intermediate in size between the chimpanzee and modern man.

The antievolutionist, however, might dismiss fossil hominids as unworthy of discussion and go on to maintain that it is not the physical size of the brain that counts, but the quality of the intelligence it mediates. It can be argued that human intelligence so far surpasses chimpanzee intelligence that any thought of a relationship between the two species is out of the question.

For instance, a chimpanzee cannot talk. Efforts to teach young chimpanzees to talk, however patient, skillful, and prolonged, have always failed. And without speech, the chimpanzee remains nothing but an animal; intelligent for an animal, but just an animal. With speech, man climbs to the heights of Plato, Shakespeare, and Einstein.

But might it be that we are confusing communication with speech? Speech is, admittedly, the most effective and delicate form of communication ever conceived. (Our modern devices from books to television sets transmit speech in other forms, but speech still.) —But is speech all?

Human speech depends upon human ability to control rapid and delicate movements of throat, mouth, tongue, and lips, and all this seems to be under the control of a portion of the brain called "Broca's convolution." If Broca's convolution is damaged by a tumor or by a blow, a human being suffers from aphasia and can neither speak nor understand speech. —Yet such a human being retains intelligence and is able to make himself understood by gesture, for instance.

The section of the chimpanzee brain equivalent to Broca's convolution is not large enough or complex enough to make speech in the human sense possible. But what about gesture? Chimpanzees use gestures to communicate in the wild—

Back in June 1966, then, Beatrice and Allen Gardner at the University of Nevada chose a one-and-a-half-year-old female chimpanzee they named Washoe and decided to try to teach her a deaf-and-dumb language. The results amazed them and the world.

Washoe readily learned dozens of signs, using them appropriately to communicate desires and abstractions. She invented new modifications which she also used appropriately. She tried to teach the language to other chimpanzees, and she clearly enjoyed communicating.

Other chimpanzees have been similarly trained. Some have been taught to arrange and rearrange magnetized counters on a wall. In so doing, they showed themselves capable of taking grammar into account and were not fooled when their teachers deliberately created nonsense sentences.

Nor is it a matter of conditioned reflexes. Every line of evidence shows that chimpanzees know what they are doing, in the same sense that human beings know what they are doing when they talk.

To be sure, the chimpanzee language is very simple compared to man's. Man is still enormously the more intelligent. However,

Washoe's feat makes even our ability to speak differ from the chimpanzee's in degree only, not in kind.

"Look long upon a monkey." There are no valid arguments, save those resting on mystical authority, that serve to deny the cousinship of the chimpanzee to man or the evolutionary development of *Homo sapiens* from non-Homo non-sapiens.

## AFTERWORD

I have made it very much my business in this last couple of decades to support the evolutionary view of life and the Universe and to oppose the ridiculous assertions of those people who speak of "scientific creationism" as a respectable synonym (they hope) for what is really "religious mythology."

This makes me a prime target for denunciation on the part of the fundamentalists, especially since I am president of the American Humanist Association. That suits me, though. I am proud of the nature of the denunciations I receive and of the type of denunciators I attract.

One thing makes me wonder, however. I don't think fundamentalists would feel that anything I write could shake their faith in the literal truth of the biblical myth of creation. They are certain that they are firm as steel, rockbound, staunch in their creed, true to their beliefs, unshaken by the storm.

But what makes them think that I am different? Some of them send me their little tracts and pamphlets and homilies, thinking that all I need are a few primitive sentences and I'll abandon three centuries of careful, rational scientific findings just like that. Do they think they have a monopoly on firm conviction?

# 17

# Thinking About Thinking

I have just returned from a visit to Great Britain. In view of my antipathy to traveling (which has not changed), I never thought I would walk the streets of London or stand under the stones of Stonehenge, but I did. Of course, I went by ocean liner both ways, since I don't fly.

The trip was an unqualified success. The weather during the ocean crossing was calm; the ships fed me (alas) all I could eat; the British were impeccably kind to me, even though they did stare a bit at my varicolored clothes, and frequently asked me what my bolo ties were.

Particularly pleasant to me was Steve Odell, who was publicity director of Mensa, the organization of high-IQ people which more or less sponsored my visit. Steve squired me about, showed me the sights, kept me from falling into ditches and under cars, and throughout maintained what he called his "traditional British reserve."

For the most part, I managed to grasp what was said to me despite the funny way the British have of talking. One girl was occasionally incomprehensible, however, and I had to ask her to speak more slowly. She seemed amused by my failure to understand her, although I, of course, attributed it to her imperfect command of the language. "You," I pointed out, "understand *me.*"

"Of course I understand you," she said. "You speak slowly in a Yankee drool."

I had surreptitiously wiped my chin before I realized that the poor thing was trying to say "drawl."

But I suppose the most unusual part of the trip (which included three speeches, three receptions, innumerable interviews by the various media, and five hours of book-signing at five bookstores in London and Birmingham) was being made a vice-president of International Mensa.

I took it for granted that the honor was bestowed upon me for the sake of my well-known intelligence, but I thought of it during my five-day return on the *Queen Elizabeth 2* and it dawned on me that I didn't really know much about intelligence. I *assume* I am intelligent, but how can I *know*?

So I think I had better think about it—and where better than here among all my Gentle Friends and Readers?

One common belief connects intelligence with (1) the ready accumulation of items of knowledge, (2) the retention of such items, and (3) the quick recall, on demand, of such items.

The average person, faced with someone like myself (for instance) who displays all these characteristics in abundant degree is quite ready to place the label of "intelligent" upon the displayer and to do so in greater degree the more dramatic the display.

Yet surely this is wrong. One may possess all three characteristics and yet give evidence of being quite stupid; and, on the other hand, one may be quite unremarkable in these respects and yet show unmistakable signs of what would surely be considered intelligence.

During the 1950s, the nation was infested with television programs in which large sums were paid out to those who could come up with obscure items of information on demand (and under pressure). It turned out that some of the shows weren't entirely honest, but that is irrelevant.

Millions of people who watched thought that the mental calisthenics indicated intelligence.* The most remarkable contestant was a postal employee from St. Louis who, instead of applying his expertise to one category as did others, took the whole world of factual items for his province. He amply displayed his prowess and struck the nation with awe. Indeed, just before the quiz-program fad collapsed, there were plans to pit this man against all comers in a program to be entitled "Beat the Genius."

Genius? Poor man! He had barely competence enough to make a poor living and his knack of total recall was of less use to him than the ability to walk a tightrope would have been.

But not everyone equates the accumulation and ready regurgitation of names, dates, and events with intelligence. Very often, in fact, it is the lack of this very quality that is associated with intelligence. Have you never heard of the absent-minded professor?

According to one kind of popular stereotype, all professors, and all intelligent people generally, are absent-minded and couldn't remember their own names without a supreme effort. But then what makes them intelligent?

I suppose the explanation would be that a very knowledgeable person bends so much of his intellect to his own sector of knowledge that he has little brain to spare for anything else. The absent-minded professor is therefore forgiven all his failings for the sake of his prowess in his chosen field.

Yet that cannot be the whole story either, for we divide categories of knowledge into a hierarchy and reserve our admiration for some only, labeling successful jugglery in those and those only as "intelligent."

We might imagine a young man, for instance, who has an encyclopedic knowledge of the rules of baseball, its procedures, its records, its players, and its current events. He may concentrate so thoroughly on such matters that he is extremely absent-

---

* I was asked to be on one of these shows and refused, feeling that I would gain nothing by a successful display of trivial mental pyrotechnics and would suffer needless humiliation if I were human enough to muff a question.

minded with respect to mathematics, English grammar, geography, and history. He is not then forgiven his failure in some respects for the sake of his success in others; he is *stupid!* On the other hand, the mathematical wizard who cannot, even after explanation, tell a bat boy from a home run is, nonetheless, *intelligent.*

Mathematics is somehow associated with intelligence in our judgments and baseball is not, and even moderate success in grasping the former is enough for the label of intelligent, while supreme knowledge of the latter gains you nothing in that direction (though much, perhaps, in others).

So the absent-minded professor, as long as it is only his name he doesn't remember, or what day it is, or whether he has eaten lunch or has an appointment to keep (and you should hear the stories about Norbert Wiener), is still intelligent as long as he learns, remembers, and recalls a great deal about some category *associated* with intelligence.

And what categories are these?

We can eliminate every category in which excellence involves merely muscular effort or co-ordination. However admirable a great baseball player or a great swimmer, painter, sculptor, flautist, or cellist may be, however successful, famous, and beloved, excellence in these fields is, in itself, no indication of intelligence.

Rather it is in the category of theory that we find an association with intelligence. To study the technique of carpentry and write a book on the various fashions of carpentry through the ages is a sure way of demonstrating intelligence even though one could not, on any single occasion, drive a nail into a beam without smashing one's thumb.

And if we confine ourselves to the realm of thought, it is clear that we are readier to associate intelligence with some fields than with others. We are almost sure to show more respect for a historian than for a sports writer, for a philosopher than for a cartoonist, and so on.

It seems an unavoidable conclusion to me that our notions of intelligence are a direct inheritance from the days of ancient Greece, when the mechanical arts were despised as fit only for artisans and slaves, while only the "liberal" arts (from the Latin word for "free men") were respectable, because they had no practical use and were therefore fit for free men.

So nonobjective is our judgment of intelligence, that we can see its measure change before our eyes. Until fairly recently, the proper education for young gentlemen consisted very largely in the brute inculcation (through beatings, if necessary) of the great Latin writers. To know no Latin seriously disqualified anyone for enlistment in the ranks of the intelligent.

We might, of course, point out that there is a difference between "educated" and "intelligent" and that the foolish spouting of Latin marked only a fool after all—but that's just theory. In actual fact, the uneducated intelligent man is invariably downgraded and underestimated and, at best, is given credit for "native wit" or "shrewd common sense." And women, who were not educated, were shown to be unintelligent by their lack of Latin and that was the excuse for not educating them. (Of course that's circular reasoning, but circular reasoning has been used to support all the great injustices of history.)

Yet see how things change. It used to be Latin that was the mark of intelligence and now it is science, and I am the beneficiary, I know no Latin except for what my flypaper mind has managed to pick up accidentally, but I know a great deal of science—so without changing a single brain cell, I would be dumb in 1775 and terribly smart in 1975.

You might say that it isn't knowledge itself, not even the properly fashionable category of knowledge, that counts, but the *use* that is made of it. It is, you might argue, the manner in which the knowledge is displayed and handled, the wit, originality, and creativity with which it is put to use, that counts. Surely, *there* is the measure of intelligence.

And to be sure, though teaching, writing, scientific research are examples of professions often associated with intelligence, we all know there can be pretty dumb teachers, writers, and researchers. The creativity or, if you like, the intelligence can be missing and still leave behind a kind of mechanical competence.

But if creativity is what counts, that, too, only counts in approved and fashionable areas. A musician, unlearned, uneducated, unable to read music perhaps, may be able to put together notes and tempos in such a way as to create, brilliantly, a whole new school of music. Yet that in itself will not earn him the accolade of "intelligent." He is merely one of those unaccountable "creative geniuses" with a "gift from God." Since he doesn't know how he does it, and cannot explain it after he's done it,† how can he be considered intelligent?

The critic who, after the fact, studies the music, and finally, with an effort, decides it is not merely an unpleasant noise by the old rules, but is a great accomplishment by certain new rules— why *he* is intelligent. (But how many critics would you exchange for one Louis Armstrong?)

But in that case, why is the brilliant scientific genius considered intelligent? Do you suppose he knows how his theories come to him or can explain to you how it all happened? Can the great writer explain how he writes so that you can do as he does?

I am not, myself, a great writer by any standard I respect, but I have my points and I have this value for the present occasion— that I am one person, generally accepted as intelligent, whom I can view from within.

Well, my clearest and most visible claim to intelligence is the nature of my writing—the fact that I write a great many books in a great many fields in complex yet clear prose, displaying great mastery of much knowledge in doing so.

So what?

No one ever taught me to write. I had worked out the basic art of writing when I was eleven. And I can certainly never explain what that basic art is to anyone else.

I dare say that some critic, who knows far more of literary theory than I do (or than I would ever care to), might, if he chose, analyze my work and explain what I do and why, far better than I ever could. Would that make him more intelligent than I am? I suspect it might, to many people.

In short, I don't know of any way of defining intelligence that does not depend on the subjective and the fashionable.

---

† The great trumpeter Louis Armstrong, on being asked to explain something about jazz, is reported to have said (translated into conventional English), "If you've got to ask, you aren't ever going to know." —These are words fit to be inscribed on jade in letters of gold.

Now, then, we come to the matter of intelligence-testing, the determination of the "intelligence quotient" or "IQ."

If, as I maintain and firmly believe, there is no objective definition of intelligence, and what we call intelligence is only a creation of cultural fashion and subjective prejudice, what the devil is it we test when we make use of an intelligence test?

I hate to knock the intelligence test, because I am a beneficiary of it. I routinely end up on the far side of 160 when I am tested and even then I am invariably underestimated because it almost always takes me less time to do a test than the time allotted.

In fact, out of curiosity, I got a paperback book containing a sizable number of different tests designed to measure one's IQ. Each test had a half-hour time limit. I worked on each one as honestly as I could, answering some questions instantly, some after a bit of thought, some by guesswork, and some not at all. — And naturally, I got some answers wrong.

When I was done, I worked out the results according to directions and it turned out I had an IQ of 135. —But wait! I had not accepted the half-hour limit offered me, but broke off each section of the test at the fifteen-minute mark and went on to the rest. I therefore doubled the score and decided I have an IQ of 270. (I'm sure that the doubling is unjustified, but the figure of 270 pleases my sense of cheerful self-appreciation, so I intend to insist on it.)

But however much all this soothes my vanity, and however much I appreciate being vice-president of Mensa, an organization which bases admission to its membership on IQ, I must, in all honesty, maintain that it means nothing.

What, after all, does such an intelligence test measure but those skills that are associated with intelligence by the individuals designing the test? And those individuals are subject to the cultural pressures and prejudices that force a subjective definition of intelligence.

Thus, important parts of any intelligence test measure the size of one's vocabulary, but the words one must define are just those words one is apt to find in reading approved works of literature. No one asks for the definition of "two-bagger" or "snake eyes" or "riff," for the simple reason that those who design the tests don't know these terms or are rather ashamed of themselves if they do.

This is similarly true of tests of mathematical knowledge, of logic, of shape-visualization, and of all the rest. You are tested in what is culturally fashionable—in what educated men consider to be the criteria of intelligence—i.e., of minds like their own.

The whole thing is a self-perpetuating device. Men in intellectual control of a dominating section of society define themselves as intelligent, then design tests that are a series of clever little doors that can let through only minds like their own, thus giving them more evidence of "intelligence" and more examples of "intelligent people" and therefore more reason to devise additional tests of the same kind. More circular reasoning!

And once someone is stamped with the label "Intelligent" on the basis of such tests and such criteria, any demonstration of stupidity no longer counts. It is the label that matters, not the fact. I don't like to libel others, so I will merely give you two examples of clear stupidity which I myself perpetrated (though I can give you two hundred, if you like)—

1) On a certain Sunday, something went wrong with my car and I was helpless. Fortunately, my younger brother, Stan, lived nearby and since he is notoriously goodhearted, I called him. He came out at once, absorbed the situation, and began to use the yellow pages and the telephone to try to reach a service station, while I stood by with my lower jaw hanging loose. Finally, after a period of strenuous futility, Stan said to me with just a touch of annoyance, "With all your intelligence, Isaac, how is it you lack the brains to join the AAA?" Whereupon, I said, "Oh, I belong to the AAA," and produced the card. He gave me a long, strange look and called the AAA. I was on my wheels in half an hour.

2) Sitting in Ben Bova's room at a recent science fiction convention, I was waiting, rather impatiently, for my wife to join us. Finally, there was a ring at the door. I sprang to my feet with an excited "Here's Janet!" flung open a door, and dashed into the closet—when Ben opened the room door and let her in.

Stan and Ben love to tell these stories about me and they're harmless. Because I have the label "intelligent," what would surely be evidence of stupidity is converted into lovable eccentricity.

This brings us to a serious point. There has been talk in recent years of racial differences in IQ. Men like William B. Shockley, who has a Nobel Prize (in physics), point out that measurements show the average IQ of Blacks to be substantially lower than that of Whites, and this has created quite a stir.

Many people who, for one reason or another, have already concluded that Blacks are "inferior" are delighted to have "scientific" reason to suppose that the undesirable position in which Blacks find themselves is their own fault after all.

Shockley, of course, denies racial prejudice (sincerely, I'm sure) and points out that we can't deal intelligently with racial problems if, out of political motives, we ignore an undoubted scientific finding; that we ought to investigate the matter carefully and study the intellectual inequality of man. Nor is it just a matter of Blacks versus Whites; apparently some groups of Whites score less well than do other groups of Whites, and so on.

Yet to my mind the whole hip-hurrah is a colossal fraud. Since intelligence is (as I believe) a matter of subjective definition and since the dominant intellectuals of the dominant sector of society have naturally defined it in a self-serving manner, what is it we say when we say that Blacks have a lower average IQ than Whites have? What we are saying is that the Black subculture is substantially different from the dominant White subculture and that the Black values are sufficiently different from dominant White values to make Blacks do less well on the carefully designed intelligence tests produced by the Whites.

In order for Blacks, on the whole, to do as well as Whites, they must abandon their own subculture for the White and produce a closer fit to the IQ-testing situation. This they may not want to do; and even if they want to, conditions are such that it is not made easy for them to fulfill that desire.

To put it as succinctly as possible: Blacks in America have had a subculture created for them, chiefly by White action, and have been kept in it chiefly by White action. The values of that subculture are defined as inferior to those of the dominant culture, so that the Black IQ is arranged to be lower; and the lower IQ is then used as an excuse for the continuation of the very conditions that produced it. Circular reasoning? Of course.

But then, I don't want to be an intellectual tyrant and insist that what I speak must be the truth.

Let us say that I am wrong; that there *is* an objective definition of intelligence, that it *can* be measured accurately, and that Blacks *do* have lower IQ ratings than Whites do, on the average, not because of any cultural differences but because of some innate, biologically based intellectual inferiority. Now what? How should Whites treat Blacks?

That's a hard question to answer, but perhaps we can get some good out of supposing the reverse. What if we test Blacks and find out, more or less to our astonishment, that they end up showing a *higher* IQ than do Whites, on the average?

How should we *then* treat them? Should we give them a double vote? Give them preferential treatment in jobs, particularly in the government? Let them have the best seats in the bus and theater? Give them cleaner restrooms than Whites have, and a higher average pay scale.

I am *quite* certain that the answer would be a decided, forceful, and profane negative for each of these propositions and any like them. I suspect that if it were reported that Blacks had higher IQ ratings than Whites do, most Whites would at once maintain, with considerable heat, that IQ could not be measured accurately and that it was of no significance if it could be, that a person was a person regardless of book learning, fancy education, big words, and fol-de-rol, that plain ordinary horsesense was all anyone needed, that all men were equal in the good old United States, and those damned pinko professors and their IQ tests could just shove it—

Well, if we're going to ignore IQ when *we* are on the low end of the scale, why should we pay such pious attention to it when *they* are?

But hold on. I may be wrong again. How do I know how the dominants would react to a high-IQ minority? After all, we *do* respect intellectuals and professors to a certain extent, don't we? Then, too, we're talking about oppressed minorities, and a high-IQ minority wouldn't be oppressed in the first place, so the artificial situation I set up by pretending the Blacks scored high is just a straw man, and knocking it down has no value.

Really? Let's consider the Jews, who, for some two millennia, have been kicked around whenever Gentiles found life growing dull. Is this because Jews, as a group, are low-IQ? —You know, I *never* heard that maintained by anyone, however anti-Semitic.

I do not, myself, consider Jews, as a group, to be markedly high-IQ. The number of stupid Jews I have met in the course of a lifetime is enormous. That, however, is not the opinion of the anti-Semite, whose stereotype of the Jews involves their possession of a gigantic and dangerous intelligence. Although they may make up less than half a percent of a nation's population, they are forever on the point of "taking over."

But then, shouldn't they, if they are high-IQ? Oh, no, for that intelligence is merely "shrewdness," or "low cunning," or "devious slyness," and what really counts is that they lack the Christian, or the Nordic, or the Teutonic, or the what-have-you virtues of other sorts.

In short, if you are on the receiving end of the game-of-power, any excuse will do to keep you there. If you are seen as low-IQ, you are despised and kept there because of that. If you are seen as high-IQ, you are feared and kept there because of that.

Whatever significance IQ may have, then, it is, at present, being made a game for bigots.

Let me end, then, by giving you my own view. Each of us is part of any number of groups corresponding to any number of ways of subdividing mankind. In each of these ways, a given individual may be superior to others in the group, or inferior, or either, or both, depending on definition and on circumstance.

Because of this, "superior" and "inferior" have no useful meaning. What *does* exist, objectively, is "different." Each of us is different. I am different, and you are different, and you, and you, and you—

It is this difference that is the glory of *Homo sapiens* and the best possible salvation, because what some cannot do, others can, and where some cannot flourish, others can, through a wide range of conditions. I think we should value these differences as mankind's chief asset, as a species, and try never to use them to make our lives miserable, as individuals.

# AFTERWORD

In my afterword to the essay "The Ancient and the Ultimate," I pointed out that my defense of books and of literacy might be deemed self-serving.

It is a pleasure, then, to point out that in the foregoing essay I am obviously being anything but self-serving. I have been the lifelong beneficiary of the IQ system, scoring high in every one I have ever taken, and having my mentality described in all sorts of flattering ways even when it is not I who am doing the describing.

And yet I have always derided the IQ system and have consistently denied that it has any significance in measuring intelligence in the abstract. I have simply met too many high-IQ people whom I considered jackasses; and have met too many apparently low-IQ people who struck me as being quite intelligent. And I would much rather associate with the latter than with the former.

In fact, despite the fact that I am *still* International Vice-President of Mensa, after thirteen years, I rarely attend Mensa meetings. While some Mensans are wonderful human beings whom I dearly love, others—well, I can do without.

# 18

## Best Foot Backward

In my more self-pitying moods, I feel more and more as though I alone am defending the bastions of science against the onslaughts of the new barbarians. Therefore, although I may be repeating bits and pieces of statements I have made in previous articles, I would like to devote this one, in its entirety, to such a defense, which, I warn you, will be an entirely uncompromising one.

*Item 1*—You would think that in a publication like *New Scientist,* an excellent British weekly devoted to articles on scientific advance, there would be no space given to simpering antiscientific idiocy. —Not so!

In the May 16, 1974, issue, one of the magazine's feature writers, having delivered himself of a fairly incoherent defense of Velikovsky, went on to say: "Science in its 200-year flight has produced some neat tricks like canned food and long-playing records, but, truthfully, how much else of real value to man's threescore years and ten?"

I promptly wrote a letter in which I said, in part: ". . . one thing you might consider to be of real value *is* man's threescore years and ten. . . . Through most of history it has been more like onescore years and ten. May we expect a bit of gratitude from you for those extra forty years of life you have the chance of enjoying?"

The letter was published and, in no time at all, in the July 11, 1974, issue there came a blast from a gentleman from Herefordshire whom I shall call B. He felt, apparently, that longer life had its disadvantages, since it helped bring on the population explosion, for instance. He said also: ". . . those benighted times Mr. Asimov mentions that had a life expectancy a good deal less than threescore and ten did still manage to produce Chartres, Tintern, Raphael, and Shakespeare. What are the modern equivalents? —Centre Point, Orly, Andy Warhol, and SF?"

Noting the dig at science fiction and guessing from whom he meant to draw blood, I felt justified in removing the velvet gloves. In my answer I said, in part: "B. goes on to point out that short-lived men in centuries past produced great works of art, literature, and architecture. Is B. advancing this as an odd coincidence, or does he maintain the cultural advance of the past came about *because* men were short-lived?

"If, indeed, B. resents the extended lifetime science has made possible, and finds it destructive to humanity, what does he suggest? It would not be difficult, after all, to abandon the advances of science, to allow sewage to creep into our water supply, to eschew antiseptic surgery, to give up antibiotics, and then to watch the death rate rise to a level that will quickly produce (by B.'s novel line of argument) another Shakespeare.

"Should B. indeed welcome this, would he recommend that the benefits of a heightened death rate be applied only to the benighted heathen of other climes, the lesser breeds of darker color whose accelerating rate of passage might then make the globe more comfortable for the men of Herefordshire? Or does his rigid sense of fairness cause him to recommend that all nations, his own included, participate in this noble endeavor?

Does he, indeed, intend to set the example himself by manfully and nobly refusing to have his own life extended by science?

"Has it in fact occurred to B. that one answer to the population explosion brought on by the advance of science and medicine is to lower the birthrate? Or does he, perchance, find the lowering of the birthrate repugnant to his sense of morals, and does he much prefer the glamour of plague and famine as a cure for overpopulation?"

That letter too was printed and there came no answer.

*Item 2*—I get private communications, sometimes, that express an individual's dissatisfaction with the modern world of science and technology, and call for a quick retreat, best food backward, into a preindustrial world of nobility and happiness.

For instance, a letter arrived recently from a professor of something or other who had gotten himself a farm and was growing his own food. He told me jubilantly all about how great it was and how healthy and happy he felt now that he was freed of all that horrible machinery. He did use an automobile, he admitted, and he apologized for it.

He didn't apologize for the fact that he used a typewriter, however, and that the letter got to me by way of our modern system of transportation. He didn't apologize for the use of electric lights or the use of the telephone, so I assume he read by the light of a wood fire and sent messages by semaphore.

I simply wrote back a polite card wishing him all the joy of the medieval peasants, and that elicited a pretty angry reply that enclosed an unfavorable review of my book *Asimov's Annotated "Paradise Lost."* (Ah, yes, I remember now, he was a specialist on Milton and I think he objected to my invasion of the sacred precincts.)

*Item 3*—Once, during the question-and-answer session that followed one of my talks, a young man asked me if I honestly believed science had done anything to increase man's *happiness*.

"Do you think you would be just as happy if you had lived in the days of ancient Greece?" I asked.

"Yes," he replied firmly.

"How would you have enjoyed being a slave in the Athenian

silver mines?" I asked with a smile, and he sat down to think a bit about that.

Or consider the person who said to me once, "How pleasant it would be if only we lived a hundred years ago when it was easy to get servants."

"It would be horrible," I said at once.

"Why?" came the astonished answer.

And I said, quite matter-of-factly, "We'd be the servants."

Sometimes I wonder if the people who denounce the modern world of science and technology are precisely those who have always been comfortable and well off and who take it for granted that in the absence of machinery there would be plenty of people (*other* people) to substitute.

It may be that it is those who have never worked who are perfectly ready to substitute human muscles (not their own) for machinery. They dream of building the Chartres cathedral—as an architect and not as a peasant conscripted to drag stones. They fantasy life in ancient Greece—as Pericles and not as a slave. They long for Merrie Olde Englande and its nut-brown ale —as a Norman baron and not as a Saxon serf.

In fact, I wonder how much upper-class resistance to modern technology arises out of a petulant dissatisfaction over the fact that so many of the scum of the Earth (like me, for instance) now drive automobiles, have automatic washers, and watch television —thus reducing the difference between said scum and the various cultured aristocrats who moan that science has not brought anyone happiness. It has diminished the grounds of their self-esteem, yes.

Some years ago there was a magazine named *Intellectual Digest,* which was run by very nice people but, alas, didn't survive for more than a couple of years. They had run some articles denouncing science and felt that perhaps they ought to publish an article supporting science—and they asked me to write one.

I did and they bought it and paid for it—and then never published it. I suspect (but do not know) that they felt it would offend their clientele, who may have been, for the most part, members of that branch of soft-core intellectualism that considers it clever to know nothing about science.

That audience was, perhaps, impressed by an article by Robert Graves which was reprinted in the April 1972 issue of *Intellectual Digest* and which seemed to argue for the social control of science.*

Graves is a classicist, brought up in the British upper-class tradition in the years prior to World War I. He knows a great deal more about pre-Christian Hellenism, I am sure, than about post-industrial science, which makes him a dubious authority on the matter of scientific discovery, but this is what he says:

"In ancient times, the use of scientific discovery was closely guarded for social reasons—if not by the scientists themselves, then by their rulers. Thus the steam engine invented in Ptolemaic Egypt for pumping water to the top of the famous lighthouse on the Island of Pharos was soon abandoned, apparently because it encouraged laziness in slaves who had previously carried waterskins up the lighthouse stairs."

This, of course, is purest horseradish. The "steam engine" invented in Ptolemaic Egypt was a pretty little toy that couldn't have pumped water one foot, let alone to the top of the Pharos.

Yet never mind that. Graves' cautionary tale is true in essence even if it be false in detail. The Hellenistic Age (323–30 B.C.) did indeed see the bare beginnings of a kind of industrial age, and that this advance bumped to a quick halt may have been, in part at least, because slave labor was so available that there was no great demand for machines.

In fact, it is even possible to present a humanitarian argument against industrialization to the effect that if machines replaced slaves, what would one do with all the surplus slaves? Let them starve? Kill them? (Who says aristocrats aren't humane?)

Graves, then, and others like himself seem to be pointing to the social control of science in ancient times as being directed toward the preservation of slavery.

Is this, indeed, what we want? Are all the antiscience idealists to march bravely into battle under the banner of "Up with Slav-

---

* So am I, provided the control is exerted by those who know something about science.

ery"? Or, since most antiscience idealists think of themselves as artists, gentlemen farmers, philosophers, or whatever, and *never* as slaves, ought the banner read "Up with Slavery for Other People"?

Of course, some deep thinker may point out in rebuttal that the kind of factory life made possible by modern technology is not better than the lot of the ancient slave. Such arguments were used prior to the American Civil War to denounce the hypocrisy of free-state abolitionists, for instance.

This is not an altogether foolish argument and yet I doubt that any factory hand in Massachusetts would have voluntarily agreed to be a Black farm hand in Mississippi under the impression that the two professions were equivalent. —Or that a Black farm hand in Mississippi would have refused to become a factory hand in Massachusetts because he felt that was no improvement over slavery.

John Campbell, the late editor of *Analog Science Fiction,* used to go further. He believed (or pretended to believe) that slavery had its good points and that everyone was a slave anyway. He used to say, "You're a slave to your typewriter, aren't you, Isaac?"

"Yes, I am, John," I would reply, "if you want to use the term as a metaphor in my case and as a reality in the case of a Black man in the cotton fields of 1850."

He said, "You work just as long hours as the slaves did, and you don't take vacations."

I said, "But there's no foreman with a whip standing behind me to make *sure* I don't take vacations."

I never convinced him, but I sure convinced myself.

There are people who argue that science is amoral, that it makes no value judgments, that it is not only oblivious to the deepest needs of mankind but entirely irrelevant to them.

Consider the views of Arnold Toynbee, who, like Graves, is an upper-class Englishman who spent his formative years before World War I. In an article in the December 1971 issue of *Intellectual Digest,* he said: "In my belief, science and technology cannot satisfy the spiritual needs for which religion of all kinds does try to provide."

Please note that Toynbee is honest enough to say "try."

Well, then, which would you prefer, an institution that does not address itself to spiritual problems but solves them anyway, or an institution that talks about spiritual problems constantly but never does anything about them? In other words, do you want deeds or talk?

Consider the matter of human slavery. Surely that is a matter that should exercise those who are interested in the spiritual needs of mankind. Is it right, is it just, is it moral, for one man to be slavemaster and another man to be slave? Surely this is not a question for a scientist, since it is not something that can be solved by studying reactions in test tubes or by observing the shifting of needles on the dials of spectrophotometers. The question is for philosophers and theologians, and we all know they have had ample time to consider it.

Throughout the history of civilization, right down to modern times, the wealth and prosperity of a relatively small number of people has been built on the animallike labor and wretched existence of a large number of peasants, serfs, and slaves. What have our spiritual leaders had to say about it?

In our Western civilization, at least, the prime source of spiritual comfort is the Bible. Look through the Bible, then, from the first verse of Genesis to the last verse of Revelation and you will find not one word of condemnation of slavery as an institution. There are lots of generalizations about love and charity, but no practical suggestions as to governmental responsibility for the poor and unfortunate.

Look through all the writings of the great philosophers of the past and you will find no whisper of condemnation against slavery as an institution. To Aristotle, it seemed quite clear that there were people who seemed to be fitted by temperament to be slaves.

It was, indeed, quite the other way around. Spiritual leaders very often rallied to the support of slavery as an institution, either directly or indirectly. There were not wanting those who justified the forcible abduction of African Blacks into American slavery by saying that they were, in this way, made into Christians and that the salvation of their souls more than made up for the enslavement of their bodies.

Then, too, when religion caters to the spiritual needs of slaves and serfs by assuring them that their Earthly position is God's will and by promising them a life of eternal bliss after death if they do not commit the sin of rebelling against God's will, who is benefited more? Is it the slave whose life may be made more bearable in the contemplation of heaven? Or is it the slavemaster who need be that much less concerned with ameliorating the hard lot of the downtrodden and that much less fearful of revolt?

When, then, did slavery come to be recognized as a grievous and unjustifiable wrong? When did slavery come to an end?

Why, with the dawn of the Industrial Revolution, when machines began to replace muscles.

For that matter, when did democracy on a large scale become possible? When the means of transportation and communication in an industrial age made it possible to work out the mechanics of a representative legislature over wide areas, and when the flood of cheap machine-made goods of all kinds made the "lower classes" into valuable customers who deserved to be coddled.

And what do you suppose would happen if we turned away from science now? What if a noble young generation abandoned the materialism of an industry that seemed to be concerned with things rather than with ideals, and moved, best foot backward, into a world in which everyone moaned and whined about love and charity? Why, without the machinery of our materialistic industry, we would inevitably drift back to a slave economy and we could use love and charity to keep the slaves quiet.

Which is better? Amoral science which puts an end to slavery, or spirituality which in thousands of years of talk didn't?

Nor is slavery the only point we can make.

In the preindustrial age, mankind was subject to the constant onslaught of infectious disease. All the love of parents, all the prayers of congregations, all the lofty generalizations of philosophers could not prevent a child dying of diphtheria or half a nation dying of the plague.

It was the cold curiosity of men of science, working without value judgments, that magnified and studied the forms of life invisible to the unaided eye, that worked out the cause of infectious disease, that demonstrated the importance of hygiene, of clean food and water, of efficient sewage systems. It was that which worked out vaccines, antitoxins, chemical specifics, and antibiotics. It was that which saved hundreds of millions of lives.

It was scientists, too, who won the victory against pain and who discovered how to soothe physical anguish when neither prayer nor philosophy could. There are not many patients facing operations who would demand spiritual solace as a substitute for an anesthetic.

Is it *only* science that is to be praised?

Who can argue against the glories of art, music, and literature that existed long before science did? And what can science offer us to compare with such beauty?

For one thing, it is possible to point out that the vision of the Universe made apparent by the careful labor of four centuries of modern scientists far outweighs in beauty and majesty (for those who would take the trouble to look) all the creations of all human artists put together, or all the imaginings of mythologists, for that matter.

Beyond that, it is also a fact that before the days of modern technology, the full flower of art and of the human intellect was reserved for the few who were aristocratic and rich. It was modern science and technology that made books plentiful and cheap. It was modern science and technology that made art, music, and literature available to all and brought the marvels of the human mind and soul to even the meanest.

But haven't science and technology brought us all sorts of undesirable side effects, from the danger of nuclear war to the noise pollution of hard rock on transistor radios?

Yes, and that's nothing new. Every last technological advance, however primitive, has brought with it something undesirable. The stone-tipped axe brought mankind more food—and made war more deadly. The use of fire gave mankind light, warmth, more and better food—and the possibility of arson and of burning at the stake. The development of speech made mankind human—and liars, one and all.

But the choice between good and evil is man's—

In 1847, the Italian chemist Ascanio Sobrero produced nitroglycerine for the first time. He heated a drop of it and it exploded shatteringly. Sobrero realized, in horror, its possible application to warfare and stopped all research in that direction at once.

It didn't help, of course. Others followed up the work and it, along with other high explosives, were being used in warfare within half a century.

Did that make high explosives entirely bad? In 1866, the Swedish inventor Alfred Bernhard Nobel learned how to mix nitroglycerine with diatomaceous earth to produce a mixture that was completely safe to handle and which he called "dynamite." With dynamite, earth could be moved at a rate far beyond the pick-and-shovel efforts of all the ages before, and without brutalizing men at hard labor.

It was dynamite that helped forge the way for the railroads in the final decades of the nineteenth century, that helped construct dams, subways, building foundations, bridges, and a thousand other grand-scale constructions of the industrial age.

It is, after all, mankind's choice whether to use explosives to construct or to destroy. If he chooses the latter, the fault is not in the explosive but in mankind's folly.

Of course, you might argue that all the good that explosives can do isn't worth the harm they can do. You might argue that mankind is incapable of choosing the good and shunning the evil and therefore, as a pack of fools, must be denied explosives altogether.

In that case, let us think back to the medical advances that began with Jenner's discovery of vaccination in 1798, Pasteur's enunciation of the germ theory of disease in the 1860s, and so on. That has doubled man's average life-span, which is good, and has brought on the population explosion, which is bad.

As far as I can see, hardly anyone objects to advances in medicine. Even today, when so many people are concerned about the dangers of scientific and technological advance, I hear hardly any protests against research into the causes and cure of arthritis, circulatory disease, birth defects, or cancer.

And yet the population explosion is the most immediate danger mankind faces. If we avoid nuclear war, counteract pollution, learn to economize on our natural resources, and advance in every field of science, we will nevertheless be destroyed in a matter of decades if the population explosion continues unchecked.

Of all mankind's follies, that of allowing the death rate to drop faster than the birthrate is the worst.

So who's for the abolition of medical advance and a return to a high death rate? Who will march under the banner of "Up with Epidemics!"? (Of course, you may consider that epidemics are okay on some other continent—but they have a bad habit of spreading.)

Well, then, shall we pick and choose? Shall we keep medical advances and a few other noble examples of scientific progress and abandon the rest of technology? Shall we retire to farms and live in blameless rural splendor, forgetting the wicked city and its machines?

But the farms must have no machinery either—no powered tractors, reapers, binders, and all the rest. They must be without synthetic fertilizers and pesticides, which are the product of an advanced technology. They must be without irrigation machinery, modern dams, and so on. They must be without advanced genetic strains that require plenty of fertilizer and irrigation. —It has to be *that* way or you've got the entire mechanism of industrialization about your neck again.

In that case, however, world farming can support about one billion people on Earth and there happen to be four billion on Earth right now.

Three billion people, at least, have to be removed from the Earth if we're to become a planet of happy farmers. Any volunteers? No fair volunteering other people; is there anyone who wants to volunteer *himself* for removal. —I thought so.

In the same article, previously cited, in which Toynbee talked about spiritual needs, he also said: "The reason science does succeed in answering its questions is that these questions are not the most important ones. Science has not taken up religion's fundamental questions, or, if it has taken these up, it has not given genuine scientific answers to them."

What does Professor Toynbee want? Through advances in science we have ended slavery; brought more security, health, and creature comfort to more people than was dreamed of in all the centuries before science; made art and leisure available to hundreds of millions. All this is as a result of answering questions that "are not the most important ones." Maybe so, Professor, but I am a humble man and these unimportant questions seem pretty good to me if that's what they bring.

And how has religion answered its "fundamental questions." What are the answers? Is the mass of humanity more ethical, more virtuous, more decent and kindly because of the existence of religion, or is the state of humanity rather a testimonial to the failure of thousands of years of merely talking about goodness and virtue.

Is there any indication that some particular group of mankind under some particular religion is more moral or more virtuous or more decent than other groups of mankind under other particular religions or, for that matter, under no particular religion —either now or in the past. I have never heard of any such indication. If science could point to no better record of accomplishment than religion can point to, science would have vanished long ago.

The Emperor has no clothes, but superstitious awe seems to prevent the fact from being pointed out.

Let's summarize it, then—

You may not like the route taken by modern science and technology, but there is no other.

Name any world problem and I can tell you that, although science and technology *may not* solve it, anything else *cannot* solve it. So you have the choice: Possible victory with science and technology, or certain defeat without it.

Which do you choose?

## AFTERWORD

It is quite fashionable these days to blame science and scientists for our troubles. Thus, it's the scientists who discovered nuclear fission and are therefore to blame for nuclear bombs and the dangers of nuclear warfare. It is the scientists who produced the plastics that are not biodegradable, the poison gases and toxic chemicals that pollute the world, and so on.

However, it was scientists in mid-1945 who, horrified by the nuclear bombs, petitioned that it not be used on cities, and it was politicians and generals who insisted it should be and who won out. Why is it, then, that a number of scientists left the field of nuclear physics in disgust, and others had to contend with suicidal urges—while I never heard of any politician or general losing a night's sleep over the decision? Why are the scientists considered villains and the generals and politicians heroes?

Of course, there *are* scientists I consider villains, and there *are* generals and politicians I consider heroes, but in both cases they represent a small fraction of the whole. So if the foregoing essay seemed to have elements of bitterness in it, I hope you weren't surprised.

# 19

# The Subtlest Difference

Since I write on many subjects in these essays, and always with an insufferable air of knowledge and authority, it would probably do all my Gentle Readers a lot of good to have me own up to stupidity from time to time. I will gladly do so, since I have many examples to choose from.

About two weeks ago, for instance, I sat in the audience listening to a private detective talk about his profession. He was young, personable, intelligent, and a very good speaker. It was a pleasure to listen to him.

He told about the way in which he had helped get off an important wrong-doer by being able to show that the police had conducted an illegal search. He then explained that he felt perfectly justified in trying to get off people who were undoubtedly criminals because (1) they are constitutionally entitled to the best possible defense; (2) if the prosecution's tactics are faulty, the criminals will be released on appeal anyway; and (3) by insisting on due process to the last detail, we are protecting everybody, even ourselves, from a government that, without constant vigilance, can only too easily become a tyranny.

I sat there and nodded. Good stuff, I thought.

He then switched to humorous stories. One was about a professional man, separated from his wife and living with his secretary. Wanting to get rid of the secretary, the man asked the private detective to follow the secretary and let himself get caught at it by her. The secretary would then tell her lover she was being followed and he would say, "Oh, my goodness, my wife is on my trail. We must split up."

Although the private detective did everything he could to be caught, the secretary refused to be disturbed about it and the little plan failed.

Now my hand went up and, out of sheer stupidity, I asked a silly question. I said, "I understand the constitutional issues involved in working on the side of criminals. What, however, is the constitutional issue involved in helping some guy pull a dirty, sleazy trick on some poor woman? Why did you do that?"

The private detective looked at me with astonishment and said, "He *paid* me."

Everyone else in the audience snickered and nudged each other, and I realized I was the only person there who was so stupid that he had to have that explained to him.

In fact, so clearly was I being snickered at, that I didn't have the courage to ask the next question, which would have been, had I dared ask it, "But if being a private detective lays you open to the temptation to do filthy jobs for the money it brings you, why don't you choose some other profession?"

I suppose there's a simple answer to that question, too, which I'm too stupid to see.

—And now, having warned you all of my inability to understand simple things, I will take up a very difficult matter indeed, the question of life and death. In view of my confession, nothing I say need be taken as authoritative or as anything, indeed, but my opinion. Therefore, if you disagree with me, please feel free to continue to do so.

What is life and what is death and how do we distinguish between the two?

If we're comparing a functioning human being with a rock, there is no problem.

A human being is composed of certain types of chemicals intimately associated with living things—proteins, nucleic acids, and so on—while a rock is not.

Then, too, a human being displays a series of chemical changes that make up its "metabolism," changes in which food and oxygen are converted into energy, tissues, and wastes. As a result, the human being grows and can reproduce, turning simple substances into complex ones in apparent defiance of the second law of thermodynamics. A rock does not do this.

Finally, a human being demonstrates "adaptive behavior," making an effort to preserve life, to avoid danger and seek safety, both by conscious will and by the unconscious mechanisms of his physiology and biochemistry. A rock does not do this.

But the human/rock contrast offers so simple a distinction between life and death that it is trivial and doesn't help us out. What we should do is take a more difficult case. Let us consider and contrast not a human being and a rock, but a live human being and a dead human being.

In fact, let's make it as difficult as possible and ask what the essential difference is between a human being just a short time before death and the same human being just a short time after death—say, five minutes before and five minutes after.

What are the changes in those ten minutes?

The molecules are still all there—all the proteins, all the nucleic acids. Nevertheless, *something* has stopped being there, for where metabolism and adaptive behavior had been taking place (however feebly) before death, they are no longer taking place afterward.

Some spark of life has vanished. What is it?

One early speculation in this respect involved the blood. It is easy to suppose that there is some particular association between blood and life, one that is closer and more intimate than that between other tissues and life. After all, as you lose blood, you become weaker and weaker, and finally you die. Perhaps, then, it is blood which is the essence of life—and, in fact, life itself.

A remnant of this view will be found in the Bible, which in places explicitly equates life and blood.

Thus, after the Flood, Noah and his family, the only human survivors of that great catastrophe, are instructed by God as to what they might eat and what they might not eat. As part of this exercise in dietetics, God says: "But flesh with the life thereof, which is the blood thereof, shall ye not eat" (Genesis 9:4).

In another passage on nutrition, Moses quotes God as being even more explicit and as saying, "Only be sure that thou eat not the blood: for the blood is the life; and thou mayest not eat the life with the flesh" (Deuteronomy 12:23). Similar statements are to be found in Leviticus 17:11 and 17:14.

Apparently, life is the gift of God and cannot be eaten, but once the blood is removed, what is left is essentially dead and has always been dead and may be eaten.

By this view, plants, which lack blood, are not truly alive. They do not live, but merely vegetate and serve merely as a food supply.

In Genesis 1:29–30, for instance, God is quoted as saying to the human beings he has just created: "Behold, I have given you every herb bearing seed, which upon the face of all the earth, and every tree, in the which is the fruit of a tree yielding seed; to you it shall be for meat. And to every beast of the earth, and to every fowl of the air, and to everything that creepeth upon the earth, wherein there is life, I have given every green herb for meat . . ."

Plants are described as "bearing seed" and "yielding seed," but in animals "there is life."

Today we would not make the distinction, of course. Plants are as alive as animals, and plant sap performs the functions of animal blood. Even on a purely animal basis, however, the blood theory would not stand up. Although loss of blood in sufficient quantities inevitably leads to loss of life, the reverse is not true. It is quite possible to die without the loss of a single drop of blood; indeed, that often happens.

Since death can take place when, to all appearances, nothing material is lost, the spark of life must be found in something more subtle than blood.

What about the breath then? All human beings, all animals, breathe.

If we think of the breath, we see that it is much more appropriate as the essence of life than blood is. We constantly release the breath, then take it in again. The inability to take it in again invariably leads to death. If a person is prevented from taking in the breath by physical pressure on his windpipe, by a bone lodged in his throat, by being immersed in water—that person dies. The loss of breath is as surely fatal as the loss of blood; and the loss of breath is the more quickly fatal, too.

Furthermore, where the converse is not true for blood, (where people can die without loss of blood) the converse *is* true for air. People cannot die without loss of air. A living human being breathes, however feebly, no matter how close he is to death; but after death, he does not breathe, and that is always true.

Furthermore, the breath itself is something that is very subtle. It is invisible, impalpable, and, to early people, it seemed immaterial. It was just the sort of substance that would, and should, represent the essence of life and, therefore, the subtle difference between life and death.

Thus, in Genesis 2:7, the creation of Adam is described thus: "And the Lord God formed man of the dust of the ground, and breathed into his nostrils the breath of life; and man became a living soul."

The word for "breath" would be *ruakh* in Hebrew and that is usually translated as "spirit."

It seems a great stretch from "breath" to "spirit," but that is not so at all. The two words are literally the same. The Latin *spirare* means "to breathe" and *spiritus* is "a breath." The Greek word *pneuma* which means "breath," is also used to refer to "spirit." And the word "ghost" is derived from an Old English word meaning "breath." The word "soul" is of uncertain origin, but I am quite confident that if we knew its origin, it, too, would come down to breath.

Because, in English, we have a tendency to use words of Latin and Greek derivation and then forget the meaning of the classic terms, we attach grandiosity to concepts that don't belong there.

We talk of the "spirits of the dead." The meaning would be precisely the same, and less impressive, if we spoke of the "breath of the dead." The terms "Holy Ghost" and "Holy Spirit" are perfectly synonymous and mean, essentially, "God's breath."

It might well be argued that the literal meaning of words means nothing, that the most important and esoteric concepts must be expressed in lowly words, and that these words gather their meaning from the concept and not vice versa.

Well, perhaps if one believes that knowledge comes full-blown by supernatural revelation, one can accept that. I think, however, that knowledge comes from below, from observation, from simple and unsophisticated thinking that establishes a primitive concept that gradually grows complex and abstract as more and more knowledge is gathered. Etymology, therefore, is a clue to the *original* thought, overlain now by thousands of years of abstruse philosophy. I think that people noticed the connection of breath and life in a quite plain and direct way and that all the subtle philosophical and theological concepts of spirit and soul came afterward.

Is the human spirit as formless and impersonal as the breath that gave it its name? Do the spirits of all the human beings who have ever died commingle into one mixed and homogenized mass of generalized life?

It is difficult to believe this. After all, each human being is distinct and different in various subtle and not-so-subtle ways from every other. It would seem natural, then, to suppose that the essence of each one's life has, in some ways, to be different from every other. Each spirit, then, would retain that difference and would remain somehow reminiscent of the body it once inhabited and to which it lent the property and individuality of life.

And if each spirit retains the impress that gave the body its characteristic properties, it is tempting to suppose that the spirit possesses, in some subtle, airy, and ethereal manner, the form and shape of the human body it inhabited. This view may have been encouraged by the fact that it is common to dream of dead people as being still alive. Dreams were often given much significance in earlier times (and in modern times, too, for that matter) as messages from another world, and that would make it seem like strong evidence that the spirits resembled the bodies they had left.

For modesty's sake, if for no other reason, such spirits are usually pictured as clad in formless white garments, made of luminous cloud or glowing light, perhaps, and that, of course, gives rise to the comic-strip pictures of ghosts and spirits wearing sheets.

It is further natural to suppose a spirit to be immortal. How can the very essence of life die? A material object can be alive or dead, according to whether it contains the essence of life or not; but the essence of life can only be alive.

This is analogous to the statement that a sponge can be wet or dry depending on whether it contains water or not, but the water itself can only be wet; or that a room can be light or dark depending on whether the Sun's rays penetrate it or not, but the Sun's rays can only be light.*

If you have a variety of spirits or souls which are eternally alive and which enter a lump of matter at birth and give it life and then leave it and allow it to die, there must be a vast number of spirits, one for each human being who has ever lived or ever will live.

This number may be increased further if there are also spirits for various other forms of life. It may be decreased if the spirits can be recycled—that is, if a spirit, on leaving one dying body, can then move into a body being born.

Both these latter views have their adherents, sometimes in combination, so that there are some people who believe in transmigration of souls throughout the animal kingdom. A man who has been particularly misbehaved might be born again as a cockroach, whereas, conversely, a cockroach can be reborn as a man if it has been a very good and noble cockroach.

However the matter is interpreted, whether spirits are confined to human beings or spread throughout the animal kingdom or whether there is transmigration of souls or not, there must be a large number of spirits available for the purpose of inducing life and taking it away. Where do they all stay?

In other words, once the existence of the spirit is accepted, a

---

* You can argue both points and say that water at a temperature low enough to keep it non-melting ice, or water in the form of vapor, is not wet; and that the Sun's rays, if ultraviolet or infrared, are not light in appearance. However, I am trying to argue like a philosopher and not like a scientist—at least in this paragraph.

whole spirit world must be assumed. This spirit world may be down under the earth or up somewhere at great heights, on another world, or on another "plane."

The simplest assumption is that the spirits of the dead are just piled up underground, perhaps because the practice of burying the dead is a very ancient one.

The simplest underground dwelling place of the spirits would be one that is viewed as a gray place of forgetfulness, like the Greek Hades or the Hebrew Sheol. There the situation is almost like a perpetual hibernation. Sheol is described as follows in the Bible: "There the wicked cease from troubling; and there the weary be at rest. There the prisoners rest together; they hear not the voice of the oppressor. The small and great are there; and the servant is free from his master" (Job 3:17–19). And Swinburne describes Hades in *The Garden of Proserpine,* which begins:

> Here, where the world is quiet,
> Here, where all trouble seems
> Dead winds' and spent waves' riot
> In doubtful dreams of dreams.

This nothingness seems insufficient to many people and a rankling feeling of injustice in life tempts them to imagine a place of after-death torture where the people they dislike get theirs—the Greek Tartarus or the Christian Hell.

The principle of symmetry demands the existence of abodes of bliss as well for the people they like—Heaven, the Islands of the Blest, Avalon, the Happy Hunting Grounds, Valhalla.

All of this massive structure of eschatology is built up out of the fact that living people breathe and dead people don't and that living people desperately *want* to believe that they will not truly die.

Nowadays, we know, of course, that the breath has no more to do with the essence of life than blood does; that it, like blood, is merely the servant of life. Nor is breath insubstantial, immaterial, and mysterious. It is as material as the rest of the body and is composed of atoms no more mysterious than any other atoms.

Yet despite this, people still believe in life after death—even people who understand about gases and atoms and the role of oxygen. Why?

The most important reason is that regardless of evidence or the lack of it, people still want to believe. And because they do, there is a strong urge to believe even irrationally.

The Bible speaks of spirits and souls and life after death. In one passage, King Saul even has a witch bring up the spirit of the dead Samuel from Sheol (1 Samuel 28:7–20). This is enough for millions of people, but many of our secular and skeptical generation are not really inclined to accept, undiscriminatingly, the statements present in the collection of the ancient legends and poetry of the Jews.

There is, of course, eyewitness evidence. How many people, I wonder, have reported having seen ghosts and spirits? Millions, perhaps. No one can doubt that they have made the reports; but anyone can doubt that they have actually seen what they have reported they have seen. I can't imagine a rational person accepting these stories.

There is the cult of "spiritualism" which proclaims the ability of "mediums" to make contact with the spirit world. This has flourished and has attracted not only the uneducated, ignorant, and the unsophisticated, but, despite the uncovering of countless gross frauds, even such highly intelligent and thoughtful people as A. Conan Doyle and Sir Oliver Lodge. The vast majority of rational people, however, place no credence in spiritualism at all.

Then, too, over twenty years ago there was a book published called *The Search for Bridey Murphy,* in which a woman was supposedly possessed by the spirit of a long-dead Irishwoman, with whom one could communicate if her hostess were hypnotized. For a while, this was advanced as evidence of life after death, but it is no longer taken seriously.

But then is there *any* evidence of life after death that can be considered as scientific and rational?

Right now, there are claims that scientific evidence exists.

A physician named Elisabeth Kübler-Ross has been presenting statements she says she has received from people on their deathbeds that seem to indicate the existence of life after death —and a whole rash of books on this subject are being published, each book, of course, being guaranteed large sales among the gullible.

According to these reports now coming out, a number of people who have seemed to be "clinically dead" for a period of time have nevertheless managed to hang on to life, to have recovered, and then to have told of their experiences while they were "dead."

Apparently, they remained conscious, felt at peace and happy, watched their body from above, went through dark tunnels, saw the spirits of dead relatives and friends, and in some cases encountered a warm, friendly spirit, glowing with light, who was to conduct them somewhere.

How much credence can be attached to such statements?

In my opinion, none at all!

Nor is it necessary to suppose the "dead" people are lying about their experiences. A person who is near enough to death to be considered "clinically dead" has a mind that is no longer functioning normally. The mind would then be hallucinating in much the same way it would be if it were not functioning normally for any other reason—alcohol, LSD, lack of sleep, and so on. The dying person would then experience what he or she would expect to experience or want to experience. (None of the reports include Hell or devils, by the way.)

The life-after-deathers counter this by saying that people from all stations of life, and even from non-Christian India, tell similar stories, which lead them to believe there is objective truth to it. —I won't accept that for two reasons.

1. Tales of afterlife are widespread all over the world. Almost all religions have an afterlife, and Christian missionaries and Western communications technology have spread *our* notions on the subject everywhere.

2. Then, too, having experienced hallucinations of whatever sort, the recovered person, still weak perhaps and confused, must describe them—and how easy it must be to describe them in such a way as to please the questioner, who is usually a life-after-death enthusiast and is anxious to elicit the proper information.

All the experience of innumerable cases of courtroom trials makes it quite plain that a human being, even under oath and under threat of punishment, will, with all possible sincerity, mis-remember, contradict himself, and testify to nonsense. We also know that a clever lawyer can, by proper questioning, elicit al-most any testimony from even an honest, truthful, and intelli-gent witness. That is why the rules of evidence and of cross-examination have to be so strict.

Naturally, then, it would take a great deal to make me attach any importance to the statements of a very sick person elicited by an eager questioner who is a true believer.

But in that case what about my own earlier statement that some change must have taken place in the passage from human life to human death, producing a difference that is not a matter of atoms and molecules?

The difference doesn't involve blood or breath, but it has to involve *something!*

And it does. Something was there in life and is no longer there in death, and that something *is* immaterial and makes for a subtle difference—the subtlest difference of them all.

Living tissue consists not merely of complex molecules, but of those complex molecules *in complex arrangement.* If that arrange-ment begins to be upset, the body sickens; if that arrangement is sufficiently upset, the body dies. Life is then lost even though all the molecules are still there and still intact.

Let me present an analogy. Suppose one builds an intricate structure out of many thousands of small bricks. The structure is built in the form of a medieval castle, with towers and crenella-tions and portcullises and inner keeps and all the rest. Anyone looking at the finished product might be too far away to see the small individual bricks, but he will see the castle.

Now imagine some giant hand coming down and tumbling all the bricks out of which the castle is built, reducing everything to a formless heap. All the bricks are still there, with not one miss-ing. All the bricks, without exception, are still intact and undam-aged.

But where is the castle?

The castle existed only in the arrangement of the bricks, and when the arrangement is destroyed, the castle is gone. Nor is the castle anywhere else. It has no existence of its own. The castle was created out of nothing as the bricks were arranged and it vanished into nothing when the bricks were disarranged.

The molecules of my body, after my conception, added other molecules and arranged the whole into more and more complex form, and in a unique fashion, not quite like the arrangement in any other living thing that ever lived. In the process, I developed, little by little, into a conscious something I call "I" that exists only as the arrangement. When the arrangement is lost forever, as it will be when I die, the "I" will be lost forever, too.

And that suits me fine. No concept I have ever heard, of either a Hell or of a Heaven, has seemed to me to be suitable for a civilized rational mind to inhabit, and I would rather have the nothingness.

## AFTERWORD

There seem to be fads even in nonsense. In the foregoing essay, I make mention of Elisabeth Kübler-Ross and her contention that people on their deathbeds experience sensations that can be interpreted as having angels come to lead them to heaven—or something like that.

At the time, it seemed that this new form of afterlife nonsense, supported by something that *sounded* vaguely like science, might take over and produce a vast wave of heaven-and-hell mysticism. It was, in part, to combat this possibility that I wrote this article.

However, this particular variety of nonsense seems to have died down, which is a relief. However, nonsense in general does not. It is almost as though there is a law of conservation of nonsense, which states that nonsense cannot be destroyed; it only changes its form. Therefore, the Kübler-Ross nonsense simply changes form and, hocus pocus, it becomes the Shirley MacLaine inanity.

# 20

# The Floating
# Crystal Palace

Last month (as I write this) my wife, Janet, and I crossed the Atlantic on the *Queen Elizabeth 2;* then, after one day in Southampton, we crossed right back.

We did this for a number of reasons. I gave a pair of talks each way, Janet is crazy about ships, and both of us found ourselves in an island of peace away from the cares of the workaday world. (Actually I managed to write a small book while on board, but that's another story.)

In one respect, though, I was disenchanted on this particular voyage. It had always been my dim assumption that there was one word that is absolutely taboo on any liner. You might say something was "very large," "huge," "monstrous," "gigantic," but you would *never* say something was—well, the adjective begins with a "t."

I was wrong. One evening on the ship, a stand-up comedian said, "I hope you'll all be joining us at the big banquet tomorrow, folks. We're celebrating the anniversary of the *Titanic."*

I was shocked! Heaven knows I've never been accused of good

taste in my off-hand humor, but this, I thought, was going too far. Had I known he was going to say it, I might well have tried to round up a committee for the feeding of poor, deserving sharks by throwing the comedian overboard.

Did others feel the same way?

No, sir! The remark was greeted with general laughter, with myself (as far as I could tell) the only abstainer.

Why did they laugh? I thought about it, and an essay began to build itself in my mind. Here it is—

Let's start with St. Brendan, an Irish monk of the sixth century.

At that time, Ireland could fairly lay claim to being the cultural leader of the Western World. The West European provinces of the Roman Empire lay sunk and broken in gathering darkness, but the light of learning burned in Ireland (which had never been part of the Empire) and the knowledge of Greek was retained there, though nowhere else in the West. Until the Irish light was extinguished by the Viking invasions of the ninth century and the English incursions thereafter, there was a three-century golden age on the island.

Part of the golden age was a set of remarkable Irish explorations that reached to Iceland and perhaps even beyond. (An Irish colony may have existed on Iceland for a century, but was gone by the time the Vikings landed there in the ninth century.) One explorer we know by name was St. Brendan.

About 550, St. Brendan sailed northward from the west coast of Ireland and seems to have explored the islands off the northern Scottish coast—the Hebrides, the Orkneys, the Shetlands. It is possibie that he went still farther north, reaching the Faeroe Islands, about 750 kilometers (470 miles) north of the northern tip of Ireland. This was almost surely the record northward penetration by sea by any human being up to that time.

St. Brendan's voyage was remarkable enough for its time, but in later years tradition magnified it. In 800 a fictional account of his voyages was written and proved very popular. It was, in a way, a primitive example of science fiction, in that the writer drew liberally on his imagination but made careful use of traveler's tales as the supporting framework (just as modern science fiction writers would use scientific theory for the same purpose).

In the tale, for instance, St. Brendan is described as having sighted a "floating crystal palace."

Is there anything in oceanic exploration that could give rise to this particular fantasy?

Certainly. An iceberg. Assuming this interpretation to be correct, this is the first mention of an iceberg in world literature.

In later centuries when the northern ocean was systematically explored, icebergs came to be a common sight. Where did they come from?

To be sure, the sea tends to freeze near the poles, and the Arctic Ocean is covered with a more or less unbroken layer of ice in the winter months. This sea ice is not very thick, however. The average thickness is 1.5 meters (5 feet) and some parts may reach a thickness of as much as 4 meters (13 feet).

We can imagine pieces of that sea ice breaking off as the weather warms in the spring and then floating southward, but those pieces would scarcely be impressive. They would be flat slabs of ice, topping sea level by some 40 centimeters (15 inches) or less.

Compare this to an Arctic iceberg, the top of which can tower 30 meters (100 feet) above sea level. One iceberg has been reported as having a record height of 170 meters (560 feet) above sea level—almost half as tall as the Empire State Building. Counting the portion that was submerged, that piece of ice may have been 1.6 kilometers (1 mile) from top to bottom.

Such a huge chunk of ice could have been spawned only on land.

At sea, the liquid water below the ice layer acts as a heat sink which, even in the coldest polar winter, keeps the ice from growing too thick. On land, the solid surface, with less heat capacity than water and with no currents to bring warmer material from elsewhere, drops to low, subfreezing temperatures and exerts no melting effect. The snow simply piles up from year to year and is capable of forming great thicknesses of ice.

Long-lived ice forms and thickens on mountain heights all over the world. It also forms at sea level in polar regions. The largest piece of land in the Arctic which is wholly polar is Greenland and it is on that vast island that the ice is most extensive and thickest.

The Greenland ice sheet fills the interior of the island and is about 2,500 kilometers (1,500 miles) long, north to south, and up to 1,100 kilometers (700 miles) wide, east to west.

The area of the Greenland ice sheet is just over 1,800,000 square kilometers (700,000 square miles)—a single piece of ice, in other words, that is about 2.6 times the area of Texas. At its thickest point, the Greenland ice sheet is about 3.3 kilometers (2 miles) thick. Along most of the Greenland coast, however, is a fringe of bare land that, in places, is up to 300 kilometers (190 miles) wide.

(It is Greenland's southwestern fringe of bare land to which Viking colonists stubbornly clung for four centuries, from 980 to 1380.)

Each year more snow falls on the Greenland ice sheet and hardly any of it melts in the warmer months (and what does, tends to refreeze the next winter) yet the ice sheet does not get endlessly thicker. Ice, you see, is plastic under pressure.

As the ice sheet thickens, its own weight tends to flatten it and spread it out. The ice, driven by enormous pressure is forced, in the form of glaciers, to move, like solid creeping rivers, along the valleys and into the seas. These Greenland glaciers move at rates of up to 45 meters (150 feet) per day, which is an enormous speed when compared to the rate at which ordinary mountain glaciers (driven by far smaller pressures) move.

When the Greenland glaciers reach the sea, the ice does not melt appreciably. Neither the Greenland sun nor the cold seas surrounding Greenland will deliver enough heat to do much to them. The tips of the glaciers simply break off ("calve") and huge lumps of ice plop into the sea. It is these that are the icebergs. (*"Berg,"* by the way, is German for "mountain.")

In Arctic waters, some 16,000 icebergs are calved each year. About 90 percent of them originate from Greenland glaciers that enter the sea in Baffin Bay, which bathes the western shore of the island.

The largest glacier in the world, the Humboldt Glacier, lies in northwestern Greenland at latitude 80° N. It is 80 kilometers (50 miles) across its coastal foot, but it is too cold to break off icebergs at a record rate. Farther south, about two thirds of the length down the western coast of Greenland, the Jakobshavn Glacier calves 1,400 icebergs a year.

Since ice has a density of 0.9, most of any iceberg is below the surface. The exact quantity submerged depends on how pure the ice is. The ice usually contains a great many air bubbles which give it a milky appearance rather than the transparency of true ice, and this lowers its density. On the other hand, in approaching the sea, the glaciers may well scrape up gravel and rock which may remain with the iceberg and which would increase its overall density. On the whole, anything from 80 to 90 percent of the iceberg is submerged.

As long as icebergs remain in Arctic waters, they persist without much change. The freezing water of the Arctic Ocean will not melt them appreciably. The icebergs that form off the western coast of Greenland linger in Baffin Bay for a long time, but eventually begin to move southward through Davis Strait into the waters south of Greenland and east of Labrador.

Many icebergs are trapped along the bleak coast of Labrador and there they break up and slowly melt, but some persist, largely intact, as far south as Newfoundland, taking up to three years to make the 3,000-kilometer (1,800-mile) journey.

Once an iceberg reaches Newfoundland, however, its fate is sealed. It drifts past that island into the warm waters of the Gulf Stream.

In an average year some 400 icebergs pass Newfoundland and move into the shipping lanes of the North Atlantic. Most of them melt in two weeks in the warm embrace of the Gulf Stream, but the remnants of one giant were sighted on June 2, 1934, at the record southerly latitude of 30° N., the latitude of northern Florida.

At the start of the last stage of its journey, however, an iceberg is still massive and menacing and is even more dangerous than it looks, since the major portion of it is submerged and may jut outward considerably closer to some approaching vessel than the visible upper portion does.

In the years before radio, when ships were truly isolated and there was no way of knowing what lay beyond the horizon, icebergs were dangerous indeed. Between 1870 and 1890, for instance, fourteen ships were sunk and forty damaged by collision with icebergs.

Then came the *Titanic*. The *Titanic* was, when it was launched in 1911, the largest ship in the world. It was 270 meters (883 feet) long and had a gross tonnage of 46,000 metric tons. Its hull was divided into sixteen watertight compartments and four of them could be ripped open without sinking the ship. In fact, the ship was considered unsinkable and was proclaimed as such. In April 1912 it set off on its maiden voyage from Southampton to New York, carrying a glittering load of the rich and the socially prominent.

On the night of April 14–15, it sighted an iceberg at a point some 500 kilometers (300 miles) southeast of Newfoundland. The ship had been ignoring the possibility of icebergs and was going far too fast in its eagerness to set a world record for time of crossing. Consequently, by the time the iceberg was sighted, it was too late to avoid a collision.

The collision, when it came, opened a 90-meter (300-foot) gash on the ship's starboard side. A fatal five compartments were sliced open and even so the *Titanic* held out gamely. It took nearly three hours for it to sink.

That might have been enough to save the passengers, but there had been no lifeboat drills and, even if there had been, the lifeboats available had room for less than half the more than 2,200 people aboard.

By now, radio was in use on ships and the *Titanic* sent out a distress signal. Another ship, the *Californian*, was equipped to receive the signal and was close enough all night to speed to the rescue, but it had only one radio operator and a man has to sleep sometime. There was no one on duty when the signal came in.

More than 1,500 lives were lost when the *Titanic* went down. Because of the drama of that sinking, the number of lives lost, and the social position of many of the dead, the disaster revolutionized the rules governing sea travel. After the tragedy, all passenger ships were required to carry lifeboats with enough seats for everyone on board, lifeboat drills were to take place on every passage, radio receivers were operating twenty-four hours a day, with men taking shifts at the earphones, and so on.

In addition, in 1914 an International Ice Patrol was established and has been maintained ever since, to keep watch over the positions of these inanimate giants of the deep. It is supported by nineteen nations and is operated by the United States Coast Guard. The patrol supplies continuing information on all icebergs sighted below latitude 52° N., with a prediction of the movements of each over the next twelve hours.

Eventually, air surveillance and radar were added to the patrol and in the years since it has been established not one ship has been sunk by an iceberg within the area under guard. Indeed, modern liners stay so far away from icebergs that passengers never even see them on the horizon. It's no wonder, then, that the passengers on the *Queen Elizabeth 2* could afford to laugh at a tasteless reference to the *Titanic*.

The glaciers of western Greenland are the most dangerous iceberg formers in the world, but not the largest. They can't very well be the largest since the Greenland ice sheet, while the second largest in the world, is a very poor second.

The largest ice sheet is that of Antarctica. The Antarctica ice sheet is a roughly circular mass of ice with a diameter of about 4,500 kilometers (2,800 miles) and a shoreline of over 20,000 kilometers (12,500 miles). It has an area of about 14,000,000 square kilometers (5,500,000 square miles) and is about 7½ times the Greenland ice sheet in area—and about 1½ times the area of the United States. The average thickness of the Antarctica ice sheet is just about 2 kilometers (1¼ miles), and at its thickest, it is 4.3 kilometers (2⅔ miles).

The total volume of the Antarctica ice sheet is about 30,000,000 cubic kilometers (7,000,000 cubic miles) and this is 90 percent of all the ice in the world.

There are two deep indentations into the roughly circular continent, and these are Ross Sea and Weddell Sea. As the Antarctica ice sheet is flattened out and spreads outward, it reaches these seas first, but it doesn't calve there as the western Greenland ice sheet does. The Antarctica ice sheet is too thick and, instead, it moves out intact over the seas to form two ice shelves.

The ice shelves remain intact for a distance of up to 1,300 kilometers (800 miles) out to sea and form slabs of ice that are some 800 meters (½ mile) thick where they leave land and are still 250 meters (1/6 mile) thick at their seaward edge. The Ross Ice Shelf, the larger of the two, has an area equal to that of France.

The ice shelves do not push northward indefinitely, of course. Eventually, slabs of ice break off the seaward edge, to form huge "tabular icebergs," flat on top, up to 100 meters (330 feet) above sea level, and with lengths that can be measured in hundreds of kilometers.

In 1956 a tabular iceberg was sighted that was 330 kilometers (200 miles) long and 100 kilometers (60 miles) wide—a single piece of free-floating ice with an area half again that of the state of Massachusetts.

For the most part, Antarctic icebergs drift in the Antarctic Ocean and are carried round and round Antarctica, edging northward and slowly melting. Although representing a much larger mass of ice in total than the 400 Greenland icebergs that slip past Newfoundland each year, the Antarctic icebergs scarcely impinge upon the consciousness of mankind, since they are well away from the chief ocean trade routes of the world. Nowhere in the Southern Hemisphere are there shipping lanes as crowded as those of the North Atlantic.

An occasional Antarctic iceberg drifts quite far northward; in 1894 the last remnant of one was sighted in the western South Atlantic at latitude 26° S., not far south of Rio de Janeiro, Brazil.

Icebergs are not all bad. The vast Antarctica ice sheet and the huge icebergs it spawns serve as air-conditioners for the world and, by keeping the ocean depths cold, allow sea life to flourish.

Anything else? Well, let's start at another point.

The average American, drinking eight glasses of water a day, will consume 0.7 cubic meters (180 gallons) in a year. There is also water required for bathing, washing the dishes, watering the lawn, and so on, so the average American consumes, at home, 200 cubic meters (53,000 gallons) of water per year.

But Americans also need water for domestic animals, for growing crops, and for industry. To make a kilogram of steel requires 200 kilograms of water, for instance, and to grow a kilogram of wheat requires 8,000 kilograms of water.

All told, the water use of the United States comes to 2,700 cubic meters (710,000 gallons) per year per person.

In those regions of the world where industry is negligible and where agricultural methods are simple, water needs can be satisfied by 900 cubic meters (240,000 gallons) per person per year. The average figure for the world as a whole might come to 1500 cubic meters (400,000 gallons) per person per year.

How does this compare with the water supply of the world?

If all the water in the world were divided equally among the 4 billion people on Earth right now, it would amount to 320,000,000 cubic meters (85 billion gallons) for each person. That sounds like plenty. This is enough water, if efficiently recycled, to supply the needs of 210,000 times the present world population.

But wait! Fully 97.4 percent of all the water on Earth is the salt water of the ocean, and human beings don't use salt water, either for drinking, washing, agriculture, or industry. That 1500 cubic meters per person per year refers to fresh water only.

If all the *fresh* water on Earth were divided equally among the 4 billion people on Earth right now, it would amount to 8,300,000 cubic meters (2.2 billion gallons) for each person. Still not terrible. With efficient recycling, the fresh water supply could support 5,500 times the present world population.

But wait! Fully 98 percent of all the fresh water on Earth is locked up in the form of ice (mostly in the Antarctica ice sheet) and it isn't available for use by human beings. The only water that human beings can use is *liquid* fresh water, found in rivers, ponds, lakes, and ground water and replenished continually by rain and melting snow.

If all the *liquid* fresh water were divided equally among the 4 billion people on Earth right now, it would amount to 160,000 cubic meters (42,000,000 gallons) per person per year. That's still not fatal. With efficient recycling, that is enough to support 100 times the present population on Earth.

But wait! The recycling isn't 100 percent efficient. We can't very well use more liquid fresh water per year than is supplied each year by rain or by that portion of the snowfall that eventually melts. If all the *precipitated* liquid fresh water is divided among the 4 billion people on Earth right now, each would get

30,000 cubic meters (8,000,000 gallons) each year. That is enough to support 20 times the present population on Earth. But wait! The liquid fresh water of Earth is *not* evenly spread among the world's population. Nor does the rain fall evenly, either in space or in time. The result is that some areas of the world have too much water while other areas of the world have too little. There are rain forests and there are deserts; there are times when there are disastrous floods and other times when there are disastrous droughts.

Furthermore, most of the fresh water on Earth makes its way back to the sea without a reasonable chance of being used by human beings at all; and much of the fresh water that we could use is being polluted—more all the time. The result is that, amazing to say in this water-logged planet of ours, we are heading rapidly into a disastrous worldwide water shortage.

Well, then, what do we do?

1. Obviously, we must, most of all, control population. If we multiply the world's population by twenty times—something we can do in 150 years if we put our minds to it—our needs will outrun the total rain supply.

2. We must do nothing to destroy the fresh water available to us. We must minimize pollution and we must avoid destroying the soil by unwise agricultural practices that lower its ability to store water, thus promoting the spread of deserts.

3. We must minimize waste and must make use of our fresh water supply more efficiently. For instance, the Amazon River, the largest in the world, discharges into the sea in one year 7,200 cubic kilometers (1,700 cubic miles) of fresh water, enough to supply the needs of the present population of the world indefinitely—but virtually none of it is used by man. On the other hand, we mustn't overuse the fresh water, either. We mustn't tap ground water, for instance, at a rate faster than it can be replaced, for the dropping of the ground-water level or its invasion by salt water could be ruinous.

4. Water must be viewed as a global resource and efforts must be made to transfer it from points of excess to points of deficiency, as we routinely do for food and fuel, for instance.

So much for making do with what we have. Is there any way in which we can increase the supply? Well—

a. We can minimize the loss of fresh water by evaporation, by placing single-molecule films of certain solid alcohols, or layers of small plastic balls on exposed water surfaces. Such evaporation barriers are difficult to maintain, however, since wind and wave tend to break them up. And if they *are* maintained, they may interfere with the oxygenation of the water below.

b. Any rain that falls on the ocean is completely wasted. It might better fall on the land—it will then, in any case, return to the ocean, but it can be used en route. Any method of weather control we could devise that would shift the rain from sea to land would be helpful.

c. Since the ultimate source of rain is the evaporation of sea water by solar heat, we can add our human effort in that direction and get fresh water by desalinating ocean water artificially. This is not a blue-sky project but is done routinely today. Large ships get their fresh water by desalination, and energy-rich, water-poor nations such as Kuwait and Saudi Arabia do so, too— and are planning expansions of such equipment in the future. This *does* take energy in large amounts, however, and, at the moment, we are ill-equipped to commit those large amounts. Is there anything else?

Well, as I noted above, 98 percent of the fresh water supply on Earth is in the form of ice, which need only be melted, not distilled. Melting would take much less energy than desalination does.

The major trouble is that the ice is chiefly in Greenland and Antarctica and is not very accessible.

Some of the ice, however, is floating on the ocean. Can icebergs be dragged to where water is needed without increasing the cost to prohibitive levels?

The Arctic icebergs of the North Atlantic are relatively far away from most of those regions on Earth that are most in need of water. They would have to be moved around Africa, for instance, to reach the Middle East and around South America to reach the American West.

But what about the huge tabular icebergs of the Antarctic?

These could be moved directly northward to desiccated areas without having to dodge continental land masses. And even a relatively small iceberg of this type would represent 100,000,000 cubic meters of fresh water, or a year's supply for 67,000 people.

Such an iceberg would have to be dragged slowly northward to the Middle East, say, right through the warm waters of the tropics. The iceberg would have to be trimmed to a shiplike form to reduce water resistance; it would have to be insulated on the sides and bottom to reduce melting; and once it reached Middle East waters, it would have to be sliced up, each slice melted, and the water stored.

Can all this be done without making the expense of iceberg water greater than that of desalination water? Some experts think so, and I look forward to seeing the attempt made.

After all, how better to avenge the *Titanic* than to put icebergs to such a vital use?

## AFTERWORD

Writing these essays offers me a variety of pleasures.

One of them is to start with something very simple and well known and carry it through until we have something startling and contemporary—even science-fictional.

I like the foregoing essay because that is precisely the pleasure it gave me.

I must admit, though, that I haven't heard much, lately, about the towing of icebergs Equator-ward as a source of fresh water. But then there are fashions in huge engineering projects, too. They come and go. A generation ago, there was lots of talk of a tunnel under the English channel. Then—nothing. And now, without very much fanfare, it is actually under construction.

Again, there was once a big to-do about drilling holes right through the crust and into the mantle to sample the deeper layers of the Earth directly. Then it was decided that it was too expensive and difficult a project and it receded into silence. But someday (who knows) the notion may be revived and it may be done.

And someday people may be drinking icebergs.

# 21

## Alas, All Human

When I was doing my doctoral research back in medieval times, I was introduced to an innovation. My research professor, Charles R. Dawson, had established a new kind of data notebook that one could obtain at the university bookstore for a sizable supply of coin of the realm.

It was made up of duplicate numbered pages. Of each pair, one was white and firmly sewn into the binding, while the other was yellow, and was perforated near the binding so that it could be neatly removed.

You placed a piece of carbon paper between the white and yellow when you recorded your experimental data and, at the end of each day, you zipped out the duplicate pages and handed it in to Dawson. Once a week or so, he went over the pages with you in detail.

This practice occasioned me periodic embarrassment, for the fact is, Gentle Reader, that in the laboratory I am simply not deft. I lack manual dexterity. When I am around, test tubes drop and reagents refuse to perform their accustomed tasks. This was one of the several reasons that made it easy for me, in the fullness of time, to choose a career of writing over one of research.

When I began my research work, one of my first tasks was to learn the experimental techniques involved in the various investigations our group was conducting. I made a number of observations under changing conditions and then plotted the results on graph paper. In theory, those values ought to have fallen on a smooth curve. In actual fact, the values scattered over the graph paper as though they had been fired at it out of a shotgun. I drew the theoretical curve through the mess, labeled it "shotgun curve" and handed in the carbon.

My professor smiled when I handed in the sheet and I assured him I would do better with time.

I did—somewhat. Came the war, though, and it was four years before I returned to the lab. And there was Professor Dawson, who had saved my shotgun curve to show people.

I said, "Gee, Professor Dawson, you shouldn't make fun of me like that."

And he said, very seriously, "I'm not making fun of you, Isaac. I'm boasting about your integrity."

That puzzled me but I didn't let on. I just said, "Thank you," and left.

Thereafter, I would sometimes try to puzzle out what he had meant. He had deliberately set up the duplicate-page system so that he could keep track of exactly what we did each day and if my experimental technique turned out to be hopelessly amateurish, I had no choice but to reveal that fact to him on the carbon.

And then one day, nine years after I had obtained my Ph.D., I thought about it and it suddenly occurred to me that there had been no necessity to record my data directly in my notebook. I could have kept the data on any scrap of paper and then *transferred* the observations, neatly and in good order, to the duplicate pages. I could, in that case, have omitted any observations that didn't look good.

In fact, once I got that far in my belated analysis of the situation, it occurred to me that it was even possible to make changes in data to have them look better, or to invent data in order to prove a thesis and *then* transfer them to the duplicate pages.

Suddenly, I realized why Professor Dawson had thought that my handing him the shotgun curve was a proof of integrity, and I felt terribly embarrassed.

I like to believe that I have integrity, but that shotgun curve was no proof of it. If it proved anything, it proved only my lack of sophistication.

I felt embarrassed for another reason. I felt embarrassed over having thought it out. For all those years since the shotgun curve, scientific hanky-panky had been literally inconceivable to me, and now I had conceived it, and I felt a little dirty that I had. In fact, I was at this point in the process of changing my career over into full-time writing, and I felt relieved that this was happening. Having now thought of hanky-panky, could I ever trust myself again?

I tried to exorcise the feeling by writing my first straight mystery novel, one in which a research student tampers with his experimental data and is murdered as a direct result. It appeared as an original paperback entitled *The Death-Dealers* (Avon, 1958) and was eventually republished in hardcover under my own title of *A Whiff of Death* (Walker, 1967).

And lately, the subject has been brought to my attention again . . .

Science itself, in the abstract, is a self-correcting, truth-seeking device. There can be mistakes and misconceptions due to incomplete or erroneous data, but the movement is always from the less true to the more true.*

Scientists are, however, not science. However glorious, noble and supernaturally incorruptible science is, scientists are, alas, all human.

While it is impolite to suppose that a scientist may be dishonest, and heart-sickening to find out, every once in a while, that one of them is, it is nevertheless something that has to be taken into account.

No scientific observation is really allowed to enter the account

---

* Lest someone ask me "What is truth?" I will define the measure of "truth" as the extent to which a conception, theory or natural law fits the observed phenomena of the universe.

books of science until it has been independently confirmed. The reason is that every observer and every instrument has built-in imperfections and biases so that, even assuming perfect integrity, the observation may be flawed. If another observer, with another instrument, and with other imperfections and biases, makes the same observation, then that observation has a reasonable chance of possessing objective truth.

This requirement for independent confirmation also serves, however, to take into account the fact that the assumption of perfect integrity may not hold. It helps us counteract the possibility of scientific dishonesty.

Scientific dishonesty comes in varying degrees of venality; some almost forgivable.

In ancient times, one variety of intellectual dishonesty was that of pretending that what you had produced was actually the product of a notable of the past.

One can see the reason for this. Where books could be produced and multiplied only by painstaking hand copying, not every piece of writing could be handled. Perhaps the only way of presenting your work to the public would be to pretend it had been written by Moses, or Aristotle, or Hippocrates.

If the pretender's work is useless and silly, claiming it as the product of a great man of the past confuses scholarship and mangles history until such time as the matter is straightened out.

Particularly tragic, though, is the case of an author who produces a great work for which he forever loses the credit.

Thus, one of the great alchemists was an Arab named Abu Musa Jabir ibn Hayyan (721–815). When his works were translated into Latin, his name was transliterated into Geber and it is in that fashion he is usually spoken of.

Geber, among other things, prepared white lead, acetic acid, ammonium chloride and weak nitric acid. Most important of all, he described his procedures with great care and set the fashion (not always followed) of making it possible for others to repeat his work and see for themselves that his observations were valid.

About 1300, another alchemist lived who made the most important of all alchemical discoveries. He was the first to describe the preparation of sulfuric acid, the most important single industrial chemical used today that is not found as such in nature.

This new alchemist, in order to get himself published, attributed his finding to Geber and it was published under that name. The result? We can speak only of the False Geber. The man who made this great discovery is unknown to us by name, by nationality, even by sex, for the discoverer might conceivably have been a woman.

Much worse is the opposite sin of taking credit for what is not yours.

The classic case involved the victimization of Niccolo Tartaglia (1500–57), an Italian mathematician who was the first to work out a general method for solving cubic equations. In those days, mathematicians posed problems to each other, and upon their ability to solve these problems rested their reputations. Tartaglia could solve problems involving cubic equations and could pose problems of that sort which others found insoluble. It was natural in those days to keep such discoveries secret.

Another Italian mathematician, Girolamo Cardano (1501–76) wheedled the method from Tartaglia under a solemn promise of secrecy—and then published it. Cardano did admit he got it from Tartaglia, but not very loudly, and the method for solving cubic equations is still called Cardano's rule to this day.

In a way, Cardano (who was a great mathematician in his own right) was justified. Scientific findings that are known, but not published, are useless to science as a whole. It is the publishing that is now considered crucial and the credit goes, by general consent, to the first who publishes and not to the first who discovers.

The rule did not exist in Cardano's time, but reading it back in time, Cardano should get the credit anyway.

(Naturally, where publication is delayed through no fault of the discoverer, there can be a tragic loss of credit, and there have been a number of such cases in the history of science. That, however, is an unavoidable side effect of a rule that is, in general, a good one.)

You can justify Cardano's publication a lot easier than his having broken his promise. In other words, scientists might not actually do anything scientifically dishonest and yet behave in an underhanded way in matters involving science.

The English zoologist Richard Owen was, for instance, very much against the Darwinian theory of evolution, largely because Darwin postulated random changes that seemed to deny the existence of purpose in the universe.

To disagree with Darwin was Owen's right. To argue against Darwinian theory in speech and in writing was also his right. It is sleazy, however, to write on the subject in a number of anonymous articles and in those articles quote your own work with reverence and approval.

It is always impressive, of course, to cite authorities. It is far less impressive to cite yourself. To appear to do the former when you are really doing the latter is dishonest—even if you yourself are an accepted authority. There's a psychological difference.

Owen also fed rabble-rousers anti-Darwinian arguments and sent them into the fray to make emotional or scurrilous points that he would have been ashamed to make himself.

Another type of flaw arises out of the fact that scientists are quite likely to fall in love with their own ideas. It is always an emotional wrench to have to admit one is wrong. One generally writhes, twists and turns in an effort to save one's theory, and hangs on to it long after everyone else has given it up.

That is so human one need scarcely comment on it, but it becomes particularly important to science if the scientist in question has become old, famous and honored.

The prize example is that of the Swede Jöns Jakob Berzelius (1779–1848), one of the greatest chemists in history, who, in his later years, became a powerful force of scientific conservatism. He had worked up a theory of organic structure from which he would not budge, and from which the rest of the chemical world dared not deviate for fear of his thunders.

The French chemist Auguste Laurent (1807–53), in 1836, presented an alternate theory we now know to be nearer the truth. Laurent accumulated firm evidence in favor of his theory and the French chemist Jean Baptiste Dumas (1800–84) was among those who backed him.

Berzelius counterattacked furiously and, not daring to place himself in opposition to the great man, Dumas weaseled out of his former support. Laurent, however, held firm and continued to accumulate evidence. For this he was rewarded by being barred from the more famous laboratories. He is supposed to have contracted tuberculosis as a result of working in poorly heated provincial laboratories and therefore died in middle age.

After Berzelius died, Laurent's theories began to come into fashion and Dumas, recalling his own early backing of them, now tried to claim more than his fair share of the credit, proving himself rather dishonest after having proved himself rather a coward.

The scientific establishment is so often hard to convince of the value of new ideas that the German physicist Max Planck (1858–1947) once grumbled that the only way to get revolutionary advances in science accepted was to wait for all the old scientists to die.

Then, too, there is such a thing as overeagerness to make some discovery. Even the most staunchly honest scientist may be tempted.

Take the case of diamond. Both graphite and diamond are forms of pure carbon. If graphite is compressed very intensely, its atoms will transform into the diamond configuration. The pressure need not be quite so high if the temperature is raised so that the atoms can move and slip around more easily. How, then, to get the proper combination of high pressure and high temperature?

The French chemist Ferdinand Fréderic Moissan (1852–1907) undertook the task. It occurred to him that carbon would dissolve to some extent in liquid iron. If the molten iron (at a rather high temperature, of course) were allowed to solidify, it would contract as it did so. The contracting iron might exert a high pressure on the dissolved carbon and the combination of high temperature and high pressure might do the trick. If the iron were dissolved away, small diamonds might be found in the residue.

We now understand in detail the conditions under which graphite will change to carbon and we know, beyond doubt, that the conditions of Moissan's experiments were insufficient for the purpose. He could not possibly have produced diamonds.

Except that he did.

In 1893, he exhibited several tiny impure diamonds and a sliver of colorless diamond, over half a millimeter in length, which he said he had manufactured out of graphite.

How was that possible? Could Moissan have been lying? Of what value would that have been to him, since no one could possibly have confirmed the experiment and he himself would know he had lied?

Even so, he might have gone slightly mad on the subject, but most science historians prefer to guess that one of Moissan's assistants introduced the diamonds as a practical joke on the boss. Moissan fell for it, announced it, and the joker could not then back out.

More peculiar still is the case of the French physicist René Prosper Blondlot (1849–1930).

In 1895, the German physicist Wilhelm Konrad Roentgen (1845–1923) had discovered X rays and had, in 1901, received the first Nobel Prize in physics. Other strange radiations had been discovered in that period: cathode rays, canal rays, radioactive rays. Such discoveries led on to scientific glory and Blondlot craved some—which is natural enough.

In 1903, he announced the existence of "N rays" (which he named in this fashion in honor of the University of Nancy, where he worked). He produced them by placing solids such as hardened steel under strain. The rays could be detected and studied by the fact (Blondlot said) that they brightened a screen of phosphorescent paint, which was already faintly luminous. Blondlot claimed he could see the brightening, and some others said they could see it, too.

The major problem was that photographs didn't show the brightening and that no instrument more objective than the eager human eye upheld the claims of brightening. One day, an onlooker privately pocketed an indispensable part of the instrument Blondlot was using. Blondlot, unaware of this, continued to see the brightening and to "demonstrate" his phenomenon. Finally, the onlooker produced the part and a furious Blondlot attempted to strike him.

Was Blondlot a conscious faker? Somehow I think he was not. He merely wanted to believe something desperately—and he did.

Overeagerness to discover or prove something may actually lead to tampering with the data.

Consider the Austrian botanist Gregor Mendel (1822–84), for instance. He founded the science of genetics and worked out, quite correctly, the basic laws of heredity. He did this by crossing strains of green-pea plants and counting the offspring with various characteristics. He thus discovered, for instance, the three-to-one ratio in the third generation of the cross of a dominant characteristic with a recessive one.

The numbers he got, in the light of later knowledge, seem to be a little too good, however. There should have been more scattering. Some people think, therefore, that he found excuses for correcting the values that deviated too widely from what he found the general rules to be.

That didn't affect the importance of his discoveries, but the subject matter of heredity comes close to the heart of human beings. We are a lot more interested in the relationship between our ancestors and ourselves than we are in diamonds, invisible radiations and the structure of organic compounds.

Thus, some people are anxious to give heredity a major portion of the credit for the characteristics of individual people and of groups of people; while others are anxious to give that credit to the environment. In general, aristocrats and conservatives lean toward heredity; democrats and radicals lean toward environment.†

Here one's emotions are very likely to be greatly engaged—to the point of believing that one or the other point of view *ought* to be so whether it is so or not. It apparently takes distressingly little, once you begin to think like that, to lean against the data a little bit.

Suppose one is extremely environmental (far more than I myself am). Heredity becomes a mere trifle. Whatever you in-

---

† Since I never pretend to godlike objectivity myself, I tell you right now that I myself lean toward environment.

herit you can change through environmental influence and pass on to your children, who may again change them and so on. This notion of extreme plasticity of organisms is referred to as "the inheritance of acquired characteristics."

The Austrian biologist Paul Kammerer (1880–1926) believed in the inheritance of acquired characteristics. Working with salamanders and toads from 1918 onward, he tried to demonstrate this. For instance, there are some species of toads in which the male has darkly colored thumb-pads. The midwife toad doesn't, but Kammerer attempted to introduce environmental conditions that would cause the male midwife toad to develop those dark thumb-pads even though it had not inherited them.

He claimed to have produced such midwife toads and described them in his papers but would not allow them to be examined closely by other scientists. Some of the midwife toads were finally obtained by scientists, however, and the thumb-pads proved to have been darkened with India ink. Presumably, Kammerer had been driven to do this through the extremity of his desire to "prove" his case. After the exposure, he killed himself.

There are equally strong drives to prove the reverse—to prove that one's intelligence, for instance, is set through heredity and that little can be done in the way of education and civilized treatment to brighten a dumbbell.

This would tend to establish social stability to the benefit of those in the upper rungs of the economic and social ladder. It gives the upper classes the comfortable feeling that those of their fellow humans who are in the mud are there because of their own inherited failings and little need be done for them.

One psychologist who was very influential in this sort of view was Cyril Lodowic Burt (1883–1971). English upper class, educated at Oxford, teaching at both Oxford and Cambridge, he studied the IQs of children and correlated those IQs with the occupational status of the parents: higher professional, lower professional, clerical, skilled labor, semiskilled labor, unskilled labor.

He found that the IQs fit those occupations perfectly. The lower the parent was in the social scale, the lower the IQ of the child. It seemed a perfect demonstration that people should know their place. Since Isaac Asimov was the son of a shopkeeper, Isaac Asimov should expect (on the average) to be a shopkeeper himself, and shouldn't aspire to compete with his betters.

After Burt's death, however, doubts arose concerning his data. There were distinctly suspicious perfections about his statistics.

The suspicions grew and grew and in the September 29, 1978, issue of *Science,* an article appeared entitled, "The Cyril Burt Question: New Findings" by D. D. Dorfman, a professor of psychology at the University of Iowa. The blurb of the article reads: "The eminent Briton is shown, beyond reasonable doubt, to have fabricated data on IQ and social class."

And that's it. Burt, like Kammerer, wanted to believe something, so he invented the data to prove it. At least that's what Professor Dorfman concludes.

Long before I had any suspicions of wrongdoing in connection with Burt, I had written an essay called "Thinking About Thinking" (see Essay 17) in which I denounced IQ tests, and expressed my disapproval of those psychologists who thought IQ tests were good enough to determine such things as racial inferiority.

A British psychologist in the forefront of this IQ research was shown the essay by his son, and he was furious. On September 25, 1978, he wrote me a letter in which he insisted that IQ tests were culturally fair and that blacks fall twelve points below whites even when environments and educational opportunities are similar. He suggested I stick to things I knew about.

By the time I got the letter I had seen Dorfman's article in *Science* and noted that the psychologist who had written to me had strongly defended Burt against "McCarthyite character assassination." He also had apparently described Burt as "a deadly critic of other people's work when this departed in any way from the highest standards of accuracy and logical consistency" and that "he could tear to ribbons anything shoddy or inconsistent." It would appear, in other words, that not only was Burt dishonest, but he was a hypocrite in the very area of his dishonesty. (That's not an uncommon situation, I think.)

So, in my brief reply to X, I asked him how much of his work was based on the findings of Cyril Burt.

He wrote me a second letter on October 11. I expected another spirited defense of Burt, but apparently he had grown more cautious concerning him. He told me the question of Burt's work was irrelevant; that he had reanalyzed all the available data, leaving out entirely Burt's contribution; and that it made no difference to the final conclusion.

In my answer I explained that in my opinion Burt's work was totally relevant. It demonstrated that in the field of heredity versus environment, scientists' emotions could be so fiercely engaged that it was possible for one of them to stoop to falsifying results to prove a point.

Clearly, under such conditions, *any* self-serving results must be taken with a grain of salt.

I'm sure that my correspondent is an honest man and I would not for the world cast any doubts upon his work. However, the whole field of human intelligence and its measurement is as yet a gray area. There is so much uncertainty in it that it is quite possible to be full of honesty and integrity and yet come up with results of questionable value.

I simply don't think it is reasonable to use IQ tests to produce results of questionable value which may then serve to justify racists in their own minds and to help bring about the kind of tragedies we have already witnessed earlier in this century.

Clearly, my own views are also suspect. I may well be as anxious to prove what I want to prove as ever Burt was, but if I must run the (honest) chance of erring, then I would rather do so in opposition to racism.

And that's that.


## AFTERWORD

I am so strong a proponent of science and technology that my arguments in that direction might easily be considered suspect. I think of that frequently and cannot help but wonder how honest I am. How apt am I to ignore reports that run counter to my own strong beliefs? How ready am I to accept anything, without question, that supports them?

Someone once asked me what I would do if I were actually to see a "flying saucer" and were to observe that it was actually an alien spaceship. I replied that I would at once abandon my strong conviction that flying saucers were figments of the imagination or, sometimes, deliberate hoaxes, and would accept them as realities. But then I could not resist adding, "And on the day that happens, I will also go skating in hell which, by that time, will have frozen over."

However, I grew sufficiently uneasy as to wish to exorcise my gathering terrors by writing the foregoing essay in which I confronted them relentlessly. I wrote of cases in which scientists of note, and sometimes even of genius, allowed their emotions to overcome their reason. It happens!

It could happen to me, too, but I fight it constantly.

# 22

## Milton! Thou Shouldst Be Living at This Hour

Some time ago I was signing books at Bloomingdale's department store. I don't recommend this as a general practice if you are in the least bit shy or sensitive.

It involves sitting at some makeshift table with a pile of your books about you, amid a vast display of women's garments (that happened to be the section near which I was placed). People pass you with expressions varying from complete indifference to mild distaste. Sometimes they look at the books with an expression that might be interpreted as "What junk is this that meets my eye?" and then pass on.

And, of course, every once in a while someone comes up and buys a book, and you sign it out of sheer gratitude.

Fortunately, I am utterly without self-consciousness and can meet any eye without blushing, but I imagine that those who are more sensitive than I would experience torture. Even I would give it a miss were it not that my publisher arranges such things and I don't want to seem unreasonably uncooperative in measures designed to sell my books.

At any rate, there I was at Bloomingdale's and a tall woman, in her thirties (I should judge) and quite attractive, rushed up smiling, with a pretty flush mantling her cheeks and said, "I am *so* glad and honored to meet you."

"Well," said I, becoming incredibly suave at once, as I always am in the presence of attractive women, "that is as nothing to my pleasure in meeting *you.*"

"Thank you," she said, then added, "I want you to know I have just seen *Teibele and the Demon.*"

That seemed irrelevant, but I said the polite thing. "I hope you enjoyed it."

"Oh, I *did.* I thought it was wonderful, and I wanted to tell you that."

There was no real reason for her to do so, but politeness above all. "That's kind of you," I said.

"And I hope you make a billion dollars out of it," she said.

"That would be nice," I admitted, though privately I didn't think the owners of the play would let me share in the proceeds even to the extent of a single penny.

We shook hands and separated, and I never bothered to tell her that I was Isaac Asimov and not Isaac Bashevis Singer. It would merely have embarrassed her and spoiled her kindly good wishes.

My only concern is that someday she will meet Isaac Bashevis Singer and will say to him, "You impostor! I met the *real* Isaac Bashevis Singer and he's young and handsome."

On the other hand, she may not say that.

But then, it's easy to make mistakes.

For instance, most people who have heard of John Milton think of him as an epic poet second only to Shakespeare in renown and genius. As evidence, they point to *Paradise Lost.*

I, on the other hand, always think of Milton as something more than merely that.

The poet William Wordsworth, back in 1802, found himself in low spirits when he decided that England was a fen of stagnant waters and moaned, "Milton! thou shouldst be living at this hour."

Well, Bill, if Milton were living at *this* hour, here in the late twentieth century, I'm sure he would be that acme of art, a science fiction writer. As evidence, I point to *Paradise Lost.*

*Paradise Lost* opens as Satan and his band of rebellious angels are recovering in hell, after having been defeated in heaven. For nine days the stricken rebels have been unconscious, but now Satan slowly becomes aware of where he is (and, if you don't mind, I will quote without the use of lines of poetry, but as simple prose, to save space):

"At once, as far as Angel's ken, he views the dismal situation waste and wild, a dungeon horrible, on all sides round as one great furnace flamed; yet from those flames no light, but rather darkness visible served only to discover sights of woe."

Milton is, essentially, describing an extraterrestrial world. (As Carl Sagan has remarked, our present view of the planet Venus is not very far removed from the common conception of hell.)

The remark about "darkness visible" is surely modeled on the description of Sheol (the Old Testament version of hell) in the Book of Job: "A land of darkness, as darkness itself; and of the shadow of death, without any order, and where the light is as darkness."

Milton's phrase makes it graphic, however, and is a daring concept, one that is a century and a half in advance of science; for what Milton is saying is that there can be some radiation that is not visible as ordinary light and yet can be used to detect objects.

*Paradise Lost* was published in 1667, but it was not until 1800 that the German-English astronomer William Herschel (1738–1822) showed that the visible spectrum did not include all the radiation there was; that beyond the red there was "infrared" radiation that could not be seen but could be detected in other ways.

In other words, with remarkable prescience, Milton had hell lit by flames that gave off infrared light, but not visible light (at least we can interpret the passage so). To human eyes hell would be in darkness, but Satan's more-than-human retina could detect the infrared and to him it was "darkness visible."

Where is the hell that is occupied by Satan and his fallen angels? The common view of the location of hell, from ancient times on, is that it is somewhere deep in the Earth. The fact that bodies are buried underground contributes, I suppose, to this feeling. The fact that there are earthquakes and volcanoes gives rise to the thought that there is activity down there and that it is a place of fire and brimstone. Dante placed hell at the center of the Earth, and so would most unsophisticates of our culture today, I think.

Milton avoids that. Here's how he describes the location of hell:

"Such place Eternal Justice had prepared for those rebellious; here their prison ordained in utter darkness, and their portion set, as far removed from God and light of Heaven as from the centre thrice to the utmost pole."

It is logical to suppose the "centre" to be the center of the Earth, since that was also taken to be the center of the observable Universe in the Greek geocentric view of the Universe. This view was not shaken until Copernicus' heliocentric theory was published in 1543, but the Copernican view was not instantly accepted. Scientific and literary conservatives held to the Greek view. It took Galileo and his telescopic observations in 1609 and thereafter to establish the Sun at the center.

Milton, however, although writing a good half-century after the discoveries of Galileo, could not let go of the Greek view. After all, he was dealing with the biblical story, and the biblical picture of the Universe is a geocentric one.

Nor was this because Milton did not know about the telescopic findings. Milton had even visited Galileo in Italy in 1639 and refers to him in *Paradise Lost*. At one point, he finds it necessary to describe Satan's round and gleaming shield. (All the characters in *Paradise Lost* act and talk as much like Homeric heroes as possible and are armed just as Achilles would be; that's part of the epic convention.)

Milton says that Satan's shield is like the Moon, "whose Orb through optic glass the Tuscan artist views . . . to descry new lands, rivers or mountains in her spotty globe." There is no question but that the "Tuscan artist" is Galileo.

Nevertheless, Milton doesn't want to be involved in astronomical controversy and in book VIII of the epic he has the archangel Raphael respond to Adam's questions on the workings of the Universe in this way:

"To ask or search I blame thee not, for Heaven is as the Book of God before thee set, wherein to read his wondrous works, and learn his seasons, hours, or days, or months, or years: This to attain, whether Heaven move or Earth, imports not, if thou reckon right; the rest from man or angel the great Architect did wisely to conceal, and not divulge his secrets to be scanned by them who ought rather admire."

In other words, all that human beings need out of astronomy is a guide whereby to form a calendar; and to do this, it doesn't matter whether Earth moves or the Sun. I can't help but feel this to be a very cowardly evasion. Some of the pious of the world were willing to denounce, excommunicate, and even burn those who claimed the Earth moved—until the evidence began to show clearly that Earth *did* move, and when that came about, they then said, "Oh, well, it imports not; what's the difference?" If it "imports not," why did they make all that fuss earlier?

So the Miltonic Universe remains geocentric—the last important geocentric Universe in western culture. The "center" Milton speaks of in locating hell is the center of the Earth.

The distance from the center of the Earth to its pole, either the North Pole or the South Pole, is 4,000 miles, and this figure was known to Milton. The Earth had been several times circumnavigated by Milton's time and its size was well known.

In that case, "thrice" that distance would be 12,000 miles, and if this is the interpretation of "from the centre thrice to the utmost pole," then hell would be 12,000 miles from heaven.

It seems reasonable to suppose that Earth is equidistant from hell and heaven. If, then, heaven were 2,000 miles from Earth in one direction and hell 2,000 miles from Earth in the opposite direction, that would allow hell to be 12,000 miles from heaven if we count in Earth's 8,000 miles diameter.

But this is ridiculous. If heaven and hell were each 2,000 miles away, surely we would see them. The Moon is 240,000 miles away (something the Greeks, and therefore Milton, knew) and we see it without trouble. To be sure, the Moon is a large body, but surely heaven and hell would be large also.

Something is wrong. Let's reconsider:

The line in Milton reads, "from the centre thrice to the utmost pole." What is the *utmost* pole? Surely, it is the celestial pole, the point in the sky that is directly overhead when you stand on a terrestrial pole.

No one in Milton's time knew how far away the celestial pole was. Astronomers knew the Moon was a quarter of a million miles away and the best guess the Greeks had been able to make where the distance of the Sun was concerned was 5 million miles. Since the Sun was the middle planet of the seven (in the Greek view, which listed them in order of increasing distance as the Moon, Mercury, Venus, the Sun, Mars, Jupiter, and Saturn), it would be fair to consider the farthest planet, Saturn, to be 10 million miles away. The sky itself, with the stars painted upon it, would be immediately beyond Saturn.

A reasonable guess, then, for the shape of the universe in Milton's time would be that of a large sphere about 10 million miles in radius and therefore 20 million miles in diameter. Such a size would be acceptable to the astronomers of the day whether they thought the Earth was at the center or the Sun.

If, then, we imagine heaven to lie outside the celestial sphere in one direction and hell outside it in another, we have a vision of three separate universes, each enclosed in a spherical "sky." In book II, Milton speaks of "this firmament of Hell" so that he must be thinking of hell as having a sky of its own (with planets and stars of its own, I wonder?). Presumably, so would heaven.

Milton doesn't indicate anywhere in the epic just how large he thinks the celestial sphere is, or how large heaven and hell are, or exactly what their spatial relationship to each other is. I suppose that the simplest setup would be to have the three of them arranged in an equilateral triangle so that, center to center, each is 30 million miles from the other two. If all are equal in size and each is 10 million miles in radius, then each is 10 million miles from the other two, firmament to firmament. This is an un-Miltonic picture but at least it is consistent with what he says and with the state of astronomy at the time.

Milton, having postulated three separate universes, each neatly enclosed in a solid, thin curve of metal, called the "firmament," invites the question, what lies outside these three universes?

This question arises in modern science, too, which visualizes our Universe as expanding from a small condensed body some 15 billion years ago. What lies beyond the volume to which it has now expanded? ask the questioners.

Scientists might speculate, but they have no answer and it may even be that there will prove no conceivable way in which they can find an answer.

Milton was more fortunate, for he knew the answer.

Later, Milton has Satan point out that the storm is over; that the divine attack which hurled the rebelling angels out of heaven and down a long, long fall into hell has now died away:

"And the thunder, winged with red lightning and impetuous rage, perhaps hath spent his shafts, and ceases now to bellow through the vast and boundless Deep."

In the biblical story of creation, it is stated that, to begin with, "darkness was on the face of the deep." The biblical writers apparently saw the Universe at its beginning as a formless waste of waters.

Milton must accept the word, for he cannot deny the Bible, but he grafts onto it Greek notions. The Greeks believed that the Universe was originally chaos—that is, "disorder"—with all its fundamental building blocks ("elements") randomly mixed. The Divine Creation, in this view, consisted not in bringing matter into existence out of nothing, but in sorting out those mixed elements and creating cosmos (an ordered universe) out of chaos.

Milton, in the epic, equates the biblical "deep" with the classical "chaos" and has it "boundless."

In other words, in the Miltonic view, God, who is eternal, existed to begin with, but for countless eons was surrounded by an infinite waste of chaos.

At some time, presumably, he created heaven, along with hordes of angels who were given the job of singing the praises of their Creator. When some of the angels got bored with the task and rebelled, God created the companion world of hell and hurled the rebels into it. Immediately thereafter, he created a celestial sphere within which a new experiment might be housed —humanity.

All three, then, are embedded in the still infinite sea of chaos in which, if God chose, innumerable more celestial spheres might be formed, though Milton nowhere says so.

Milton goes on to describe how the fallen angels, in their new home, so different from their old and so much worse, nevertheless get to work to try to make it as livable as possible. "Soon had his crew opened into the hill a spacious wound and digged out ribs of gold."

Although gold is an entirely unsuitable structural metal (too soft and too dense) and is valued only for its beauty and rareness, human beings, completely mistaking a subjective, assigned value for the real thing, have unimaginatively dreamed of golden buildings and golden streets (studded with equally unsuitable precious stones) as the highest form of luxury. They have imagined heaven to consist of such structures, and apparently the fallen angels want to make their new habitation as much like home as possible.

They build a city, which they call All-Demons in a democratic touch that contrasts with the absolute autocracy of heaven. Of course, the name is given in Greek, so that it is Pandemonium. Because all the denizens of hell meet there in conference, the word has entered the English language from Milton's epic to mean the loud, confused noise that would seem characteristic, in our imaginings, of a hellish gathering.

There follows a democratic conference in which Satan, who has rebelled against God's dictatorship, welcomes the views of anyone who wishes to speak. Moloch, the most unreconstructed of the angelic rebels, advocates renewed war: meeting God's weapons with an armory drawn from hell—

"To meet the noise of his Almighty Engine he shall hear Infernal thunder, and for lightning see black fire and horror shot with equal rage among his angels; and his Throne itself mixt with Tartarean sulfur, and strange fire."

The "black fire" is the "darkness visible" of hell. "Strange fire" is an expression from the Bible. Two sons of Aaron burned "strange fire" at the altar and were struck dead in consequence. The Bible doesn't explain what is meant by *strange fire*. One can guess that the unfortunates didn't use the proper ritual in starting the fire or in blessing it.

Here, however, we can't help think in the hindsight of our recent knowledge that infrared is not the only direction in which we can step out of the visible spectrum. There is also ultraviolet at the energetic end, along with X rays and gamma rays. Is Moloch suggesting that the demons counter the lightning with energetic radiation (black fire) and nuclear bombs (strange fire)?

After all, Milton can't be thinking merely of gunpowder when he speaks of strange fire. As is explained later in the epic, the rebelling angels used gunpowder in their first battle and were defeated anyway. So it has to be something beyond gunpowder!

(What a science fiction writer was lost in Milton by virtue of his being born too soon!)

Once the various rebels have spoken, each arguing a different point of view, Satan makes a decision. He is not for outright war, nor for surrendering to defeat either. Suppose, though, that someone were to make his way to the human celestial sphere. There that someone might try to corrupt the freshly created human beings and thus spoil at least part of God's plan.

It would not be an easy task. In the first place, whoever essayed it would have to break through hell's firmament, which "immures us round ninefold, and gates of burning Adamant barred over us prohibit all egress."

Then, even if someone managed to break out, "the void profound of unessential Night receives him next."

This is an amazing line. Consider:

There had been stories of trips from Earth to the Moon even in ancient times. In 1638, an English clergyman, Francis Godwin, had written *Man in the Moone* about such a trip, and it had been a great success. Milton may well have known about the book, so that the notion of travel between worlds was not absolutely new.

Yet all previous tales of trips to the Moon had assumed that air existed everywhere within the celestial sphere. Godwin's heroes had gotten to the Moon by hitching wild swans to a chariot and having the birds fly him there.

Milton, however, was talking not about interplanetary travel nor even about interstellar travel. He was speaking of travel from one universe to another and he was the first writer on the subject to realize he would *not* be traveling through air.

The Italian physicist Evangelista Torricelli, by weighing air in 1643, had shown that the atmosphere had to be limited in height and that the space between worlds was a vacuum, but this stunning new concept was for the most part ignored by otherwise imaginative writers for a long time (just as so many of them ignore the speed-of-light limit today).

Milton reached out for the concept, however, when he speaks of a "void profound" and "unessential Night."

Night is the synonym for chaos (*"darkness* brooded over the face of the deep") and "unessential" means "without essence," without the fundamental elements. And yet, as we shall see, Milton reached out but only partly grasped the notion.

Satan, scorning to propose a dangerous task for someone else to fulfill, undertakes the journey himself. He makes his way to the bounds of hell, where he encounters a hag (Sin) and her monstrous son (Death). There he persuades the hag, who holds the key, to open the barrier. Satan then looks out upon the "void profound."

What Satan now sees is a "hoary deep, a dark illimitable ocean without bound, without dimension, where length, breadth, and height, and time and place are lost; where eldest Night and Chaos, ancestors of Nature, hold eternal anarchy, amidst the noise of endless wars, and by confusion stand. For hot, cold, moist, and dry, four champions fierce strive here for mastery, and to battle bring their embryon atoms."

This is not a vacuum that Satan describes, but it is a concept equally daring, for Milton's imaginative description of chaos comes quite close to the modern view of the state of maximum entropy.

If everything is a random mixture and if there are no substantial differences in properties from point to point in space, then there is no way of making any measurement for there is nothing to seize upon as a reference point. Length, breadth, and height, the three spatial dimensions, no longer have meaning. Furthermore, since the flow of time is measured in the direction of increasing entropy, when that entropy has reached its maximum, there is no longer any way of measuring time. Time has no meaning any more than position does: "time and place are lost."

The Greeks divided matter into four elements, each with its characteristic properties. Earth was dry and cold, fire was dry and hot, water was wet and cold, air was wet and hot. In chaos, these properties are thrown into total confusion, and, indeed, maximum entropy is equivalent to total disorder.

Suppose the Universe is in a state of maximum entropy, so that (in Greek terms) chaos exists. Once total randomness exists, continuing random shiftings of properties may, after an incredibly long interval (but then, since time doesn't exist at maximum entropy, an incredibly long interval might as well be a split second, for all anyone can say)—chance may just happen to produce order and the Universe may begin again. (If a well-shuffled deck of cards is shuffled further, then eventually, all the spades, hearts, clubs, and diamonds may just happen to come back into order.) The role of God would then be to hasten this random event and make it certain.

In describing chaos in Greek terms, Milton, however, does not entirely let go of the notion of a vacuum. If chaos has all matter mixed, there must be fragments of nonmatter mixed into it as well, or it would not be true chaos. Every once in a while, then, Satan might encounter a bit of vacuum, as an airplane may strike a downdraft, or a swimmer an undertow.

Thus, Satan meets "a vast vacuity: all unawares fluttering his pennons vain plumb-down he drops ten thousand fathom deep, and to this hour down had been falling, had not by ill chance the strong rebuff of some tumultuous cloud instinct with fire and nitre hurried him as many miles aloft."

I believe this is the first mention of vacuum between worlds in literature. (To be sure, Milton did not have the notion of gravity straight. He wrote twenty years before Newton's great book on the subject was published.)

Satan makes it. By the end of book II of *Paradise Lost,* he has reached Earth, having performed as daring and imaginative a journey as any in modern science fiction.

There's just one other touch, I want to mention. In book VIII, Adam asks the archangel Raphael how the angels make love.

"To whom the Angel with a smile that glowed celestial rosy red, Love's proper hue, answered, 'Let it suffice thee that thou knowest us happy, and without Love no happiness. Whatever pure thou in the body enjoyest (and pure thou wert created) we enjoy in eminence, and obstacle find none of membrane, joint, or limb exclusive bars: Easier than air with air, if Spirits embrace, total they mix, union of Pure with Pure desiring . . ."

When *I* wanted to write about another universe and about a group of living organisms totally different from ourselves, I needed one thing that was really strange about which to build all else.

I had my organisms make love totally and "obstacle find none." I arranged three sexes as a further difference and "total they mix." Out of that came the second section of my novel *The Gods Themselves,* which won a Hugo and a Nebula in 1973 and of which everyone said the second part was best.

So if you want to know where I get my crazy ideas—well sometimes I borrow them from the best science fiction writers I can find—like John Milton.

And if by some chance you suddenly feel interested in reading *Paradise Lost* for yourself, I suggest you find a copy of *Asimov's Annotated "Paradise Lost."* Some people think it's pretty good; *I* think it's extremely good.

## AFTERWORD

There's a huge advantage in being so cheerfully appreciative that one carelessly undertakes the task of writing about almost anything. I rarely allow the question "But do I *know* anything about the subject?" to deter me. I just assume I know enough.

Thus, having written large volumes on the Bible and on Shakespeare, and having had an enormous amount of fun in the process, I cast about for something else to do that would give me pleasure. So I thought, "Why not annotate *Paradise Lost?*" I promptly did, and enjoyed it so well that before I could manage to skid to a halt when I had completed the twelfth and last book, I found that I had also done *Paradise Regained.* I would have gone on to *Samson Agonistes* but I felt that Doubleday would draw the line there.

The result is that I had no hesitation in using the expertise I had gained in my Miltonic endeavors to go further and write the foregoing essay in which I interpret Milton's epic in a fashion (I am quite confident) no one has ever tried before. In short, I treated Milton as a science fiction writer and, frankly, I think I proved my case completely. Don't you think so, too?

# 23

## And After Many a Summer Dies the Proton

If any of you aspire to the status of Very Important Person, let me warn you sulkily that there are disadvantages. For myself, I do my best to avoid VIP-dom by hanging around my typewriter in a state of splendid isolation for as long as possible. And yet—the world intrudes.

Every once in a while, I find myself slated to attend a grand function at some elaborate hotel, and the instructions are "black tie." That means I've got to climb into my tuxedo. It's not really very difficult to do so and once I'm inside it, with the studs and links in place, with the tie hooked on and the cummerbund adjusted, I don't feel very different. It's just the principle of the thing. I'm not a tuxedo person; I'm a baggy-old-clothes person.

Just the other night I was slated to appear, tuxedo-ablaze-in-glory at the Waldorf-Astoria. I had been invited—but I had not received any tickets.

Whereupon I said to Janet (who made her usual wifely suggestion that she seize her garden shears and cut great swatches out of my luxuriant sideburns and received my usual husbandly refusal), "Listen, if we get there and they won't let us in without tickets, please don't feel embarrassed. We'll just leave our coats in the checkroom, go down two flights to the Peacock Alley and eat there."

In fact, I was hoping we'd be turned away. Of all the restaurants I've tried in New York, the Peacock Alley is my favorite. The closer we got to the hotel, the more pleasant was my mind's-eye picture of myself wreaking havoc with the comestibles at the Peacockian festive board.

Finally, there we were, standing before a group of fine people who barred the way to the Grand Ballroom, with instructions to keep out the riffraff.

"I'm sorry," I said, firmly, "but I don't have any tickets."

Whereupon a clear whisper sounded from one young woman on the other side of the table, "Oh, my goodness! Isaac Asimov!"

And instantly, Janet and I were hustled into the VIP room and my hopes for the Peacock Alley went a-glimmering.*

So let us turn, by an easy progression of thought, to that VIP of the subatomic particles: the proton.

Fully 90 percent of the mass of that portion of the Universe of which we are most aware—the stars—consists of protons. It is therefore apparently fair to say that the proton is the very stuff of the Universe and that if anything deserves the rating Very Important, it is the proton.

Yet the proton's proud position on the throne of subatomic VIP-dom is now being shaken.

In the first place, there is the possibility that it is not the proton after all that is the stuff of the universe, but the neutrino, and that the proton makes up only a very inconsiderable portion of the universal mass.

In the second place, it is possible that the proton is not even immortal, as has long been thought, but that after many a summer each one of the little things faces decay and death even as you and I.

But let's start from the beginning.

---

* It was all right. It was a very good banquet and a lot of fun.

At the moment, there seem to be two fundamental varieties of particle: leptons and quarks.

There are different sorts of leptons. First, there are the electron, the muon, and the tauon (or tau electron). Then there are the mirror-image particles, the antielectron (or positron), the antimuon, and the antitauon. Then there is a neutrino associated with each of the above: the electron neutrino, the muon neutrino, and the tauon neutrino, plus, of course, an antineutrino for each.

That means twelve leptons altogether that we know of, but we can simplify the problem somewhat by ignoring the antiparticles, since what we have to say about the particles will hold just as firmly for the antiparticles. Furthermore, we will not try to distinguish between the neutrinos since there is a chance that they may oscillate and swap identities endlessly.

Therefore let us speak of four leptons—the electron, the muon, the tauon, and the neutrino.

Different particles have different rest masses. For instance, if we set the rest mass of the electron at 1, the rest mass of the muon is about 207, and that of the tauon is about 3,600. The rest mass of the neutrino, on the other hand, may be something like 0.0001.

Mass represents a very concentrated form of energy and the general tendency seems to be for massive particles to change, spontaneously, into less massive particles.

Thus, tauons tend to break down into muons, electrons, and neutrinos and to do it quickly, too. The half-life of a tauon (the period of time during which half of them will have broken down) is only about five trillionths of a second ($5 \times 10^{-12}$ seconds).

Muons, in turn, break down to electrons and neutrinos, but since muons are less massive than tauons they seem to last a bit longer and have half-lives of all of 2.2 millionths of a second ($2.2 \times 10^{-6}$ seconds).

You might expect that electrons, then, might live a little longer still, and break down to neutrinos, and that neutrinos, after a perhaps quite respectable lifetime, might melt away to complete masslessness, but that's not the way it works.

Leptons can't disappear altogether, provided we are dealing with particles only or antiparticles only, and not a mixture of the two. An electron and an antielectron can combine and mutually annihilate, converting themselves into zero-mass photons (which are not leptons), but that's another thing and we're not dealing with it.

As long as we have only particles (or only antiparticles), leptons must remain in existence; they can shift from one form to another, but cannot disappear altogether. That is the *law of conservation of lepton number,* which also means that a lepton cannot come into existence out of a nonlepton. (A lepton *and* its corresponding antilepton can simultaneously come into existence out of nonleptons, but that's another thing.) And don't ask *why* lepton number is conserved; it's just the way the universe seems to be.

The conservation of lepton number means that the neutrino, at least, should be immortal and should never decay, since no still-less-massive lepton exists for it to change into. This fits the facts, as nearly as we can tell.

But why should the electron be stable, as it seems to be? Why doesn't it break down to neutrinos? That would not violate the law of conservation of lepton number.

Ah, but leptons may possess another easily measurable characteristic—that of electric charge.

Some of the leptons, the various neutrinos and antineutrinos, have no electric charge at all. The others—the electron, the muon, and the tauon—all have an electric charge of the same size, which, for historical reasons, is considered to be negative and is usually set equal to unity. Each electron, muon and tauon has an electric charge of $-1$; while every antielectron, antimuon, and antitauon has an electric charge of $+1$.

As it happens, there is a *law of conservation of electric charge,* which is a way of saying that electric charge is never observed to disappear into nothing, or appear out of nothing. No lepton decay can affect the electric charge. (Of course, an electron and an antielectron can interact to produce photons, and the opposite charges, $+1$ and $-1$, will cancel. What's more, a lepton and an antilepton can be formed simultaneously, producing both a $+1$ and a $-1$ charge where no charge existed before—but these are different things from those we are discussing. We are talking about particles and antiparticles as they exist separately.)

The least massive of the leptons with charge is the electron. That means that though more massive leptons can easily decay to the electron, the electron cannot decay because there is nothing less massive which can hold an electric charge, and that electric charge *must* continue to exist.

To summarize, then:

Muons and tauons can come into existence under conditions where the general energy concentration is locally very high, say, in connection with particle accelerators or cosmic ray bombardment; but once formed, they cannot last for long. Under ordinary conditions, removed from high-energy events, we would find neither muons nor tauons and the universal content of leptons is restricted to the electron and the neutrino. (Even the antielectron does not exist in significant numbers.)

Let us pass on next to the other basic variety of particle, the quark. Quarks, like leptons, exist in a number of varieties, but with a number of important differences.

For one thing, quarks carry fractional electric charges, such as $+2/3$ and $+1/3$. (Antiquarks have charges of $-2/3$ and $-1/3$, naturally.)

Furthermore, the quarks are subject to the "strong interaction," which is enormously more intense than the "weak interaction" to which leptons are subject. The intensity of the strong interaction makes it unlikely (even, perhaps, impossible) for quarks to exist in isolation. They seem to exist only in bound groups that form according to rules recently worked out by scientists. One very common way of grouping is to have three quarks associate in such a way that the overall electric charge is either 0, 1, or 2 (positive in the case of some, negative in the case of others).

These three-quark groups are called *baryons,* and there are large numbers of them.

Again, however, the more massive baryons decay quickly into less massive baryons, which decay into still less massive baryons, and so on. As side products of this decay, mesons are produced which are particles made up of only two quarks. There are no stable mesons. All break down more or less rapidly into leptons; that is, into electrons and neutrinos.

There is, however, a *law of conservation of baryon number,* so that whenever a baryon decays, it must produce another baryon, whatever else it produces. Naturally, when you get to the baryon of the lowest possible mass, no further decay can take place.

The two baryons of lowest mass are the proton and the neutron, so that any other baryon, of the many dozens that can exist, quickly slides down the mass scale to become either a proton or a neutron. These two baryons are the only ones that exist in the universe under the ordinary conditions that surround us. They tend to combine in varying numbers to form the atomic nuclei.

The proton and neutron differ, most obviously in the fact that the proton has an electric charge of +1, while that of the neutron is 0. Naturally, atomic nuclei, which are made up of protons and neutrons, all carry a positive electric charge of a quantity equal to the number of protons present. (There are also such things as antiprotons with a charge of −1, and antineutrons which differ from neutrons in magnetic properties, and these can group together to form negatively charged nuclei and antimatter, but never mind that right now.)

The positively charged nuclei attract negatively charged electrons in numbers that suffice to neutralize the particular nuclear charge, thus forming the different atoms with which we are familiar. Different atoms, by transferring or sharing one or more electrons, form molecules.

But the proton and neutron differ slightly in mass, too. If we call the electron's mass 1, then the proton's mass is 1,836 and the neutron's mass is 1,838.

When the two exist in combination in nuclei, they tend to even out their properties and to become, in effect, equivalent particles. Inside nuclei, then, they can be lumped together and referred to as *nucleons.* The entire nucleus is then stable, although there are nuclei where the proton-neutron mixture is not of the proper ratio to allow a perfect evening out of properties, and which are therefore radioactive—but that's another story.

When the neutron is in isolation, however, it is not stable. It tends to decay into the slightly less massive proton. It emits an electron, which carries off a negative charge, leaving a positive charge behind on what had been a neutron. (This simultaneous production of a negative *and* a positive charge does not violate the law of conservation of electric charge.) A neutrino is also formed.

The mass difference between proton and neutron is so small that the neutron doesn't decay rapidly. The half-life of the isolated neutron is about twelve minutes.

This means that the neutron can exist for a considerable length of time only when it is in combination with protons, forming an atomic nucleus. The proton, on the other hand, can exist all by itself for indefinite periods and can, all by itself, form an atomic nucleus, with a single electron circling it—forming the ordinary hydrogen atom.

The proton is thus the only truly stable baryon in existence. It, along with the electron and the neutrino (plus a few neutrons that exist in atomic nuclei), makes up virtually all the rest mass of the universe. And since protons outshine the others in either number or individual rest mass, the proton makes up 90 percent of the mass of such objects as stars. (The neutrinos may be more massive, in total, but they exist chiefly in interstellar space.)

Consider the situation, however, if matters were the other way around and if the neutron were slightly less massive than the proton. In that case, the proton would be unstable and would decay to a neutron, giving up its charge in the form of a positively charged antielectron (plus a neutrino). The antielectrons so formed would annihilate the electrons of the universe, together with the electric charge of both, and left behind would be only the neutrons and neutrinos. The neutrons would gather, under the pull of their overall gravitational field, into tiny neutron stars, and those would be the sole significant structures of the universe.

Life as we know it, would, of course, be utterly impossible in a neutron-dominated universe, and it is only our good fortune that the proton is slightly less massive than the neutron, rather than vice versa, that gives us expanded stars, and atoms—and life.

Everything, then, depends on the proton's stability. How stable is it? Our measurements show no signs of proton decay, but our measurements are not infinitely delicate and precise. The decay might be there but might be taking place too slowly for our instruments to catch it.

Physicists are now evolving something called the Grand Unified Theory (GUT) by which one overall description will cover the electromagnetic interaction (affecting charged particles), the weak interaction (affecting leptons), and the strong interaction (affecting quarks and quark groupings such as mesons, baryons, and atomic nuclei).

According to GUT, each of the three interactions is mediated by *exchange particles* with properties dictated by the necessity of making the theory fit what is already known. The electromagnetic exchange particle is the photon, which is a known particle and very well understood. In fact, the electromagnetic interaction is well described by quantum electrodynamics, which serves as a model for the rest of the GUT.

The weak interaction is mediated by three particles symbolized as $W^+$, $W^-$, and $Z^0$, which have not yet been detected. The strong interaction is mediated by no less than eight "gluons," for whose existence there is reasonable evidence, albeit indirect.

The more massive an exchange particle is, the shorter its range. The photon has a rest mass of zero, so electromagnetism is a very long-range interaction and falls off only as the square of the distance. (The same is true of the gravitational interaction, which has the zero-mass graviton as the exchange particle, but the gravitational interaction has so far resisted all efforts to unify it with the other three.)

The weak-exchange particles and the gluons have considerable mass, however, and therefore the intensity of their influence falls off so rapidly with distance that that influence is measurable only at distances comparable in size to the diameter of the atomic nucleus, which is only a tenth of a trillionth of a centimeter ($10^{-13}$ centimeters) across or so.

GUT, however, in order to work, seems to make necessary the existence of no fewer than twelve more exchange particles, much more massive than any of the other exchange particles, therefore extremely short-lived and difficult to observe. If they *could* be observed, their existence would be powerful evidence in favor of GUT.

It seems quite unlikely that these ultramassive exchange particles can be directly detected in the foreseeable future, but it would be sufficient to detect their effects, if those effects were completely unlike those produced by any other exchange particles. And such an effect does (or, at any rate, *might*) exist.

If one of these hypermassive exchange particles should happen to be transferred from one quark to another within a proton, a quark would be changed to a lepton, thus breaking both the law of conservation of baryon number and the law of conservation of lepton number. The proton, losing one of its quarks, becomes a positively charged meson that quickly decays into antielectrons, neutrinos, and photons.

The hypermassive exchange particles are so massive, however, that their range of action is roughly $10^{-29}$ centimeters. This is only a tenth of a quadrillionth ($10^{-16}$) the diameter of the atomic nucleus. This means that the point-sized quarks can rattle around inside a proton for a long, long time without ever getting sufficiently close to one another to exchange a proton-destroying exchange particle.

In order to get a picture of the difficulty of the task of proton decay, imagine that the proton is a hollow structure the size of the planet Earth, and that inside that vast planetary hollow are exactly three objects, each about a hundred-millionth of a centimeter in diameter—in other words, just about the size of an atom in our world. Those "atoms" would have diameters that represent the range of action of the hypermassive exchange particles.

These "atoms," within that Earth-sized volume, moving about randomly, would have to collide before the proton would be sent into decay. You can easily see that such a collision is not likely to happen for a long, long time.

The necessary calculation makes it seem that the half-life for such proton decay is ten million trillion trillion years ($10^{31}$ years). After many a summer, in other words, dies the proton—but after many, many, *many* a summer.

To get an idea of how long a period of time the proton's half-life is, consider that the lifetime of the Universe to this point is usually taken as 15,000,000,000 years—fifteen billion in words, $1.5 \times 10^{10}$ years in exponential notation.

The expected lifetime of the proton is roughly 600 million trillion ($6 \times 10^{20}$) times that.

If we set the mighty life of the Universe as the equivalent of one second, then the expected half-life of the proton would be the equivalent of 200 trillion years. In other words, to a proton, the entire lifetime of the Universe so far is far, far less than an eye blink.

Considering the long-lived nature of a proton, it is no wonder that its decay has not been noted and that scientists have not detected the breakage of the laws of conservation of baryon number and lepton number and have gone on thinking of those two laws as absolutes.

Might it not be reasonable, in fact, to ignore proton decay? Surely a half-life of $10^{31}$ years is so near to infinite, in a practical sense, that it might as well be taken as infinite and forgotten.

However, physicists can't do that. They must try to measure the half-life of proton decay, if they can. If it turns out to be indeed $10^{31}$ years, then that is powerful support for GUT; and if it turns out that the proton is truly stable then GUT is invalid or, at the very least, would require important modification.

A half-life of $10^{31}$ years doesn't mean that protons will all last for that long and then just as the last of those years elapses, half of them will decay at once. Those atom-sized objects moving about in an Earth-sized hollow could, by the happenstance of random movement, manage to collide after a single year of movement, or even a single second. They might, on the other hand, just happen to move about for $10^{100}$ or even $10^{1,000}$ years without colliding.

Statistically, though, since there are many, many protons, some decays should take place all the time. In fact, if the half-life of the proton were merely ten thousand trillion years ($10^{16}$ years) there would be enough proton decays going on within our bodies to kill us with radioactivity.

Even with a half-life of $10^{31}$ years, there would be enough proton decays going on right now to destroy something like thirty thousand trillion trillion trillion protons ($3 \times 10^{40}$) *every second* in the universe as a whole, or three hundred thousand trillion trillion ($3 \times 10^{29}$) every second in our Galaxy alone, or three million trillion ($3 \times 10^{18}$) every second in our Sun alone, or three thousand trillion ($3 \times 10^{15}$) every second in Jupiter alone, or three billion ($3 \times 10^9$) every second in Earth's oceans.

This begins to look uncomfortably high, perhaps. Three billion proton decays every second in our oceans? How is that possible with an expected lifetime so long that the entire life of the Universe is very nearly nothing in comparison?

We must realize how small a proton is and how large the Universe is. Even at the figures I've given above it turns out that only enough protons decay in the course of a billion years throughout the entire Universe to be equivalent to the mass of a star like our Sun. This means that in the total lifetime of our Universe so far, the Universe has lost through proton decay the equivalent of fifteen stars the mass of the Sun.

Since there are 10,000,000,000,000,000,000,000 (ten billion trillion, or $10^{22}$) stars in the Universe as a whole, the loss of fifteen through proton decay can easily be ignored.

Put it another way. In one second of the hydrogen fusion required to keep it radiating at its present rate, the Sun loses six times as much mass as it has lost through proton decay during the entire five-billion-year period during which it has been shining.

The fact that, despite the immensely long half-life of the proton, decays go on steadily at all times, raises the possibility of the detection of those decays.

Three billion decays every second in our oceans sounds as though it should be detectable—but we can't study the ocean as a whole with our instruments and we can't isolate the ocean from other possibly obscuring phenomena.

Nevertheless, tests on considerably smaller samples have fixed the half-life of the proton as no shorter than $10^{29}$ years. In other words, experiments have been conducted where, if the proton's half-life were shorter than $10^{29}$ years, protons would have been caught in the act of decaying—and they weren't. And $10^{29}$ years is a period of time only one one-hundredth the length of $10^{31}$ years.

That means that our most delicate detecting devices combined with our most careful procedures need only be made a hundred times more delicate and careful in order just barely to detect the actual decay of protons if the GUT is on the nose. Considering the steady manner in which the field of subatomic physics has been advancing this century, this is a rather hopeful situation.

The attempt is being made, actually. In Ohio, the necessary apparatus is being prepared. Something like ten thousand tons of water will be gathered in a salt mine deep enough in the Earth to shield it from cosmic rays (which could produce effects that might be confused with those arising from proton decay).

There would be expected to be 100 decays per year under these conditions, and a long meticulous watch *may,* just possibly *may,* produce results that will confirm the Grand Unified Theory and take us a long step forward indeed in our understanding of the Universe.

### AFTERWORD

Alas, in the seven years that have elapsed since the foregoing essay was written, no proton decays have been detected that can be attributed to the conditions described by the Grand Unified Theory. This, I think, has disheartened scientists, and they have turned to other theories involving "strings" and "superstrings" and "supersymmetry" that I might write about in this essay-series some day—but only after I get to understand them sufficiently myself.

This is bothersome. There are some far-out suggestions that I am instantly out of sympathy with, like those involving tachyons. When such suggestions seem to lose popularity and be dismissed, it bothers me not at all. Rather, I pride myself on having the kind of intuition that tells me at once when something won't work.

There are, however, suggestions with which I *am* in sympathy, and when these seem to lose popularity, my lower lip quivers and I feel distressed. My tendency then is to cling to them as long as I can and as long as observations don't rule them out *completely.* The possibility of proton decay is an example of something that I was eager to accept.

But why do I instantly accept some suggestions and reject others? Ah, that I don't know.

# 24

## The Circle of the Earth

Once, Janet and I were in a hotel room during the course of one of my lecture engagements, and a chambermaid knocked on the door to ask if we needed any towels. It seemed to me we had towels, so I said that no, we didn't need towels.

I had scarcely closed the door, when Janet called from the bathroom saying that we did, too, need towels, and to call her back.

So I opened the door, called her back, and said, "Miss, the woman I have here in my hotel room with me says we do, too, need more towels. Would you bring some?"

"Sure," said she, and went off.

Out came Janet, with that expression of exasperation she wears whenever my sense of humor escapes her a bit. She said, "Now why did you say that?"

"It was a literally true statement."

"You know you said that deliberately, in order to imply we're not married. When she comes back, you just tell her we're married, you hear?"

Back came the chambermaid with the towels and I said, "Miss, the woman I have here in my hotel room with me wants me to say to you that we're married."

And over Janet's cry of "Oh, *Isaac,*" the chambermaid said, haughtily, "I couldn't care less!"

So much for modern morality.

I thought of this incident recently in the aftermath of an essay I wrote for *Science Digest* in which I made the casual statement that the Bible assumes the Earth to be flat.

You'd be surprised at the indignant letters I got from people who denied vigorously that the Bible assumed the Earth to be flat.

Why? After all, the Bible was written in the day when *everyone* assumed the Earth was flat. To be sure, by the time the latest biblical books were written, a few Greek philosophers thought otherwise, but who listened to *them?* I thought it was only reasonable that the men who wrote the various books of the Bible should know no more about astronomy than anyone else at the time and that we should all be charitable and kind to them, therefore.

However, the Fundamentalists are not like the chambermaid in that hotel. When it comes to any suggestion of a biblical flat Earth, they couldn't care *more.*

Their thesis, you see, is that the Bible is literally true, every word, and what's more, that it is "inerrant"; that is, that it cannot be wrong. (This follows clearly from their belief that the Bible is the inspired word of God; that God knows everything; and that, like George Washington, God cannot tell a lie.)

In support of this thesis, the Fundamentalists deny that evolution has taken place; they deny that the Earth and the Universe as a whole are more than a few thousand years old, and so on.

There is ample scientific evidence that the Fundamentalists are wrong in these matters, and that their notions of cosmogony have about as much basis in fact as the Tooth Fairy has, but the Fundamentalists won't accept that. By denying some scientific findings and distorting others, they insist that their silly beliefs have some value, and they call their imaginary constructions "scientific" creationism.

At one point, however, they draw the line. Even the most Fundamental of Fundamentalists would find it a little troublesome to insist that the Earth is flat. After all, Columbus didn't fall off the end of the world, and the astronauts have actually seen the world to be a sphere.

If, then, the Fundamentalists were to admit that the Bible assumes a flat Earth, their entire structure of the inerrancy of the Bible falls to the ground. And if the Bible is wrong in so basic a matter, it can be wrong anywhere else, and they might as well give up.

Consequently, the merest mention of the biblical flat Earth sends them all into convulsions.

My favorite letter, arriving in this connection, made the following three points:

1. The Bible specifically says the Earth is round (and a biblical verse is cited), yet despite this biblical statement, human beings persisted in believing the Earth to be flat for two thousand years thereafter.

2. If there seem to have been Christians who insisted the Earth was flat, it was only the Catholic Church that did so, not Bible-reading Christians.

3. It was a pity that only nonbigots read the Bible. (This, it seemed to me, was a gentle remark intended to imply that I was a bigot who didn't read the Bible and therefore spoke out of ignorance.)

As it happened, my letter-writing friend was well and truly wrong on all three points.

The biblical verse he cited was Isaiah 40:22.

I doubt that my correspondent realized it, or would believe it if he were told, but the fortieth chapter of Isaiah begins that section of the book which is called "the Second Isaiah" because it was not written by the same hand that wrote the first thirty-nine chapters.

The first thirty-nine chapters were clearly written about 700 B.C., in the time of Hezekiah, king of Judah, at the time when the Assyrian monarch Sennacherib was threatening the land. Beginning with Chapter Forty, however, we are dealing with the situation as it was about 540 B.C. in the time of the fall of the Chaldean Empire to Cyrus of Persia.

This means that the Second Isaiah, whoever he might have been, grew up in Babylonia, in the time of the Babylonian captivity and was undoubtedly well educated in Babylonian culture and science.

The Second Isaiah, therefore, thinks of the Universe in terms of Babylonian science, and to the Babylonians the Earth was flat.

Well, then, how does Isaiah 40:22 read? In the Authorized Version (better known as the King James Bible), which is *the* Bible to the Fundamentalists, so that every last mistranslation it contains is sacred to them, the verse, which is part of the Second Isaiah's attempt to describe God, reads:

"It is he that sitteth upon the circle of the earth . . ."

There you have it—"the circle of the earth." Is that not a clear indication that the Earth is "round"? Why, oh why, did all those bigots who don't read the Bible persist in thinking of the Earth as flat, when the word of God, as enshrined in the Bible, spoke of the Earth as a "circle"?

The catch, of course, is that we're supposed to read the King James Bible as though it were written in English. If the Fundamentalists want to insist that every word of the Bible is true, then it is only fair to accept the English meanings of those words and not invent new meanings to twist the biblical statements into something else.

In English, a "circle" is a two-dimensional figure; a "sphere" is a three-dimensional figure. The Earth is very nearly a sphere; it is certainly *not* a circle.

A coin is an example of a circle (if you imagine the coin to have negligible thickness). In other words, what the Second Isaiah is referring to when he speaks of "the circle of the earth" is a flat Earth with a circular boundary; a disk; a coin-shaped object.

The very verse my correspondent advanced as proof that the Bible considered the Earth to be a sphere is the precise verse that is the strongest evidence that the Bible assumes the Earth to be flat.

If you want another verse to the same effect, consider a passage in the Book of Proverbs, which is part of a paean of praise to personified Wisdom as an attribute of God:

"When he prepared the heavens, I was there: when he set a compass upon the face of the depth." (Proverbs 8:27).

A compass, as we all know, draws a circle, so we can imagine God marking out the flat, circular disk of the world in this fashion. William Blake, the English artist and poet, produced a famous painting showing God marking out the limits of the Earth with a compass. Nor is "compass" the best translation of the Hebrew. The Revised Standard Version of the Bible has the verse read, "When he established the heavens, I was there, when he drew a circle on the face of the deep." That makes it clearer and more specific.

Therefore, if we want to draw a schematic map of the world as it seemed to the Babylonians and Jews of the sixth century B.C. (the time of the Second Isaiah) you will find it in Figure 1. Although the Bible nowhere says so, the Jews of the late biblical period considered Jerusalem the center of the "circle of the

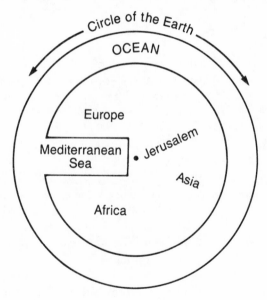

Figure 1

world"—just as the Greeks thought of Delos as the center. (A spherical surface, of course, has no center.)

Now let us quote the entire verse:

"It is he that sitteth upon the circle of the earth, and the inhabitants thereof are as grasshoppers; that stretcheth out the heavens as a curtain, and spreadeth them out as a tent to dwell in." (Isaiah 40:22).

The reference to Earth's inhabitants as "grasshoppers" is merely a biblical cliché for smallness and worthlessness. Thus, when the Israelites were wandering in the wilderness, and sent spies into the land of Canaan, those spies returned with disheartening stories of the strength of the inhabitants and of their cities.

The spies said:

". . . we were in our own sight as grasshoppers, and so we were in their sight." (Numbers 13:33).

Observe, however, the comparison of the heavens with a curtain, or a tent. A tent, as it is usually pictured, is composed of some structure that is easily set up and dismantled: hides, linen, silk, canvas. The material is spread outward above and then down on all sides until it touches the ground.

A tent is *not* a spherical structure that surrounds a smaller spherical structure. No tent in existence has ever been that. It is, in most schematic form, a semisphere that comes down and touches the ground in a circle. And the ground underneath a tent is *flat.* That is true in every case.

If you want to see the heavens and Earth, in cross section, as pictured in this verse, see Figure 2. Inside the tent of the heav-

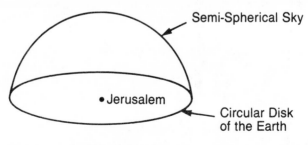

Figure 2

ens, upon the flat-Earth base, the grasshoppers that are human-ity dwell.

Such a concept is reasonable for people who have not been very far from home; who have not navigated the oceans; who have not observed the changing positions of the stars during travels far north or south, or the behavior of ships as they ap-proach the horizon; who have been too terrified of eclipses to observe closely and dispassionately the shadow of the Earth upon the Moon.

However, we have learned a lot about the Earth and the Uni-verse in the last twenty-five centuries, and we know very well that the picture of the Universe as a tent curtain draped over a flat disk does not match reality. Even Fundamentalists know that much, and the only way they can avoid coming to the conclusion that the Bible is in error is to deny plain English.

And that shows how hard it is to set limits to human folly.

If we accept a semispherical sky resting on a flat-disk Earth, we have to wonder what it rests upon.

The Greek philosophers, culminating in Aristotle (384–322 B.C.), who were the first to accept a spherical Earth, were also the first who did not have to worry about the problem. They realized that gravity was a force pointing to the center of the spherical Earth, so they could imagine the Earth to be suspended in the center of the larger sphere of the Universe as a whole.

To those who came before Aristotle, or who had never heard of Aristotle, or who dismissed Aristotle, "down" was a cosmic direction independent of Earth. As a matter of fact, this is so tempting a view that, in every generation, youngsters have to be cajoled out of it. Where is the youngster in school who, on first encountering the notion of a spherical Earth, doesn't wonder why the people on the other side, walking around, as they do, upside down, don't simply fall off?

And if you deal with a flat Earth, as the biblical writers did, you have to deal with the question of what keeps the whole shebang from falling.

The inevitable conclusion for those who are not ready to con-sider the whole thing divinely miraculous is to assume the Earth must rest on something—on pillars, for instance. After all, doesn't the roof of a temple rest on pillars?

But then, you must ask what the pillars rest on. The Hindus had the pillars resting on giant elephants, who in turn stood upon a supergiant turtle, which in turn swam across the surface of an infinite sea.

In the end, we're stuck with either the divine or the infinite. Carl Sagan tells of a woman who had a solution simpler than that of the Hindus. She believed the flat Earth rested on the back of a turtle. She was questioned . . .

"And what does the turtle rest on?"

"On another turtle," said the woman, haughtily.

"And what does that other turtle—"

The woman interrupted, "I know what you're getting at, sir, but it's no use. It's turtles *all the way down.*"

But does the Bible take up the matter of what the Earth rests on?—Yes, but only very casually.

The trouble is, you see, that the Bible doesn't bother going into detail in matters that everyone may be assumed to know. The Bible, for instance, doesn't come out and describe Adam when he was first formed. It doesn't say specifically that Adam was created with two legs, two arms, a head, no tail, two eyes, two ears, one mouth, and so on. It takes all this for granted.

In the same way, it doesn't bother saying right out "And the Earth is flat" because the biblical writers never heard anyone saying anything else. However, you can see the flatness in their calm descriptions of Earth as a circle and of the sky as a tent.

In the same way, without saying specifically that the flat Earth rested on something, when everyone *knew* it did, that something is referred to in a very casual way.

For instance, in the thirty-eighth chapter of Job, God is answering Job's complaints of the injustice and evil of the world, not by explaining what it's all about, but by pointing out human ignorance and therefore denying human beings even the right to question (a cavalier and autocratic evasion of Job's point, but never mind). He says:

"Where wast thou when I laid the foundations of the earth? declare, if thou hast understanding. Who hath laid the measures thereof, if thou knowest? or who hath stretched the line upon it? Whereupon are the foundations thereof fastened? or who laid the corner stone thereof." (Job 38:4–6).

What are these "foundations"? It's hard to say because the Bible doesn't describe them specifically.

We might say that the "foundations" refer to the lower layers of the Earth, to the mantle and the liquid iron core. However, the biblical writers never heard of such things, any more than they ever heard of bacteria—so that they had to use objects as large as grasshoppers to represent insignificance. The Bible *never* refers to the regions under the Earth's surface as composed of rock and metal, as we shall see.

We could say that the Bible was written in a kind of double-talk; in verses that meant one thing to the unsophisticated contemporaries of the biblical writers, but that meant something else to the more knowledgeable readers of the twentieth century, and that will turn out to mean something else still to the still more knowledgeable readers of the thirty-fifth century.

If we say that, however, then the entire Fundamentalist thesis falls to the ground, for everything the Bible says can then be interpreted to be adjusted to a fifteen-billion-year-old Universe and the course of biological evolution, and this the Fundamentalists would flatly reject.

Hence, to argue the Fundamentalist case, we must assume the King James Bible to be written in English, so that the "foundations" of the Earth are the objects on which the flat Earth rests.

Elsewhere in the Book of Job, Job says, in describing the power of God:

"The pillars of heaven tremble and are astonished at his reproof." (Job 26:11).

It would seem these pillars are the "foundations" of the Earth. Perhaps they are placed under the rim of the Earth where the sky comes down to meet it, as in Figure 3. These structures are then both the pillars of heaven and the foundations of the Earth.

What do the pillars in turn rest on? Elephants? Turtles? Or is it pillars "all the way down"? Or do they rest on the backs of angels who eternally fly through space? The Bible doesn't say.

And what is the sky that covers the flat Earth like a tent?

In the Bible's creation tale, the Earth begins as a formless waste of water. On the first day, God created light and somehow,

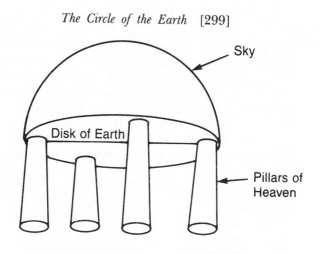

Figure 3

without the presence of the Sun, caused it to be intermittent, so that there existed the succession of day and night.

Then, on the second day, he placed the tent over the formless waste of waters:

"And God said, Let there be a firmament in the midst of the waters, and let it divide the waters from the waters." (Genesis 1:6).

The first syllable of the word "firmament" is "firm" and that is what the biblical writers had in mind. The word is a translation of the Greek *stereoma,* which means "a hard object" and which is, in turn, a translation of the Hebrew *rakia,* meaning "a thin, metal plate."

The sky, in other words, is very much like the semispherical metal lid placed over the flat serving dish in our fancier restaurants.

The Sun, Moon, and stars are described as having been created on the fourth day. The stars were viewed as sparks of light pasted on the firmament, while the Sun and Moon are circles of light that move from east to west across the firmament, or perhaps just below it.

This view is to be found most specifically in Revelation, which was written about A.D. 100 and which contains a series of apocalyptic visions of the end of the Universe. At one point it refers to a "great earthquake" as a result of which:

". . . the stars of heaven fell unto the earth, even as a fig tree casteth her untimely figs, when she is shaken of a mighty wind. And the heaven departed as a scroll when it is rolled together . . ." (Revelation 6:13–14).

In other words, the stars (those little dots of light) were shaken off the thin metal structure of the sky by the earthquake, and the thin metal sky itself rolled up like the scroll of a book.

The firmament is said "to divide the waters from the waters." Apparently there is water upon the flat base of the world structure, the Earth itself, and there is also a supply of water *above* the firmament. Presumably, it is this upper supply that is responsible for the rain. (How else account for water falling from the sky?)

Apparently, there are openings of some sort that permit the rain to pass through and fall, and when a particularly heavy rain is desired, the openings are made wider. Thus, in the case of the Flood:

". . . the windows of heaven were opened." (Genesis 7:11).

By New Testament times, Jewish scholars had heard of the Greek multiplicity of spheres about the Earth, one for each of the seven planets and then an outermost one for the stars. They began to feel that a single firmament might not be enough.

Thus, St. Paul, in the first century A.D., assumes a plurality of heavens. He says, for instance:

"I knew a man in Christ above fourteen years ago . . . such an one caught up to the third heaven." (2 Corinthians 12:2).

What lies under the flat disk of the Earth? Certainly not a mantle and a liquid iron core of the type geologists speak of today; at least not according to the Bible. Under the flat Earth, there is, instead, the abode of the dead.

The first mention of this is in connection with Korah, Dathan, and Abiram, who rebelled against the leadership of Moses in the time of the wandering in the wilderness:

"And it came to pass . . . that the ground clave asunder that was under them: And the earth opened her mouth, and swallowed them up, and their houses, and all the men that appertained unto Korah, and all their goods. They, and all that appertained to them, went down alive into the pit, and the earth closed upon them: and they perished . . ." (Numbers 16:31–33).

The pit, or "Sheol," was viewed in Old Testament times rather like the Greek Hades, as a place of dimness, weakness, and forgetfulness.

In later times, however, perhaps under the influence of the tales of ingenious torments in Tartarus, where the Greeks imagined the shades of archsinners to be confined, Sheol became hell. Thus, in the famous parable of the rich man and Lazarus, we see the division between sinners who descend into torment and good people who rise into bliss:

"And it came to pass, that the beggar died, and was carried by the angels into Abraham's bosom: the rich man also died, and was buried; And in hell he lift up his eyes, being in torments, and seeth Abraham afar off, and Lazarus in his bosom. And he cried and said, Father Abraham, have mercy on me, and send Lazarus, that he may dip the tip of his finger in water, and cool my tongue; for I am tormented in this flame." (Luke 16:22–24).

The Bible doesn't describe the shape of the pit, but it would be interesting if it occupied the other semisphere of the sky, as in Figure 4.

It may be that the whole spherical structure floats on the infinite waste of waters out of which heaven and Earth were created, and which represents primeval chaos, as indicated in Figure 4. In that case, perhaps we don't need the pillars of heaven.

Thus, contributing to the waters of the Flood, were not only the windows of heaven opened wide but, at that time also:

". . . were all the fountains of the great deep broken up . . ." (Genesis 7:11).

In other words, the waters of chaos welled upward and nearly overwhelmed all of creation.

Naturally, if the picture of the Universe is indeed according to the literal words of the Bible, there is no chance of a heliocentric system. The Earth cannot be viewed as moving at all (unless it is viewed as floating aimlessly on the "great deep") and certainly it cannot be viewed as revolving about the Sun, which is a small circle of light upon the solid firmament enclosing Earth's flat disk.

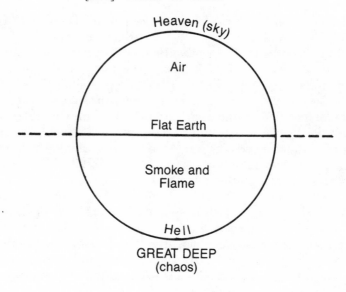

Figure 4

Let me emphasize, however, that I do not take this picture seriously. I do not feel compelled by the Bible to accept this view of the structure of Earth and sky.

Almost all the references to the structure of the Universe in the Bible are in poetic passages of Job, of Psalms, of Isaiah, of Revelation, and so on. It may all be viewed as poetic imagery, as metaphor, as allegory. And the creation tales at the beginning of Genesis must also be looked upon as imagery, metaphor, and allegory.

If this is so, then there is nothing that compels us to see the Bible as in the least contradictory to modern science.

There are many sincerely religious Jews and Christians who view the Bible in exactly this light, who consider the Bible to be a guide to theology and morality, to be a great work of poetry—but *not* to be a textbook of astronomy, geology, or biology. They have no trouble in accepting both the Bible and modern science, and giving each its place, so that they:

". . . Render therefore unto Caesar the things which be

Caesar's, and unto God the things which be God's." (Luke 20:25).

It is the Fundamentalists, the Literalists, the Creationists with whom I quarrel.

If the Fundamentalists insist on foisting upon us a literal reading of the Genesis creation tales; if they try to force us to accept an Earth and Universe only a few thousand years old, and to deny us evolution, then I insist that they accept as literal every other passage in the Bible—and that means a flat Earth and a thin, metal sky.

And if they don't like that, what's that to me?

## AFTERWORD

I imagine that it must annoy the creationists to have me so at home with the Bible, and to have me be able to quote it so freely. But why not? I haven't written a two-volume *Asimov's Guide to the Bible* for nothing.

Of course, it is perfectly true that the Bible is so long and so complex that it is possible to find quotations to support almost any thesis you like. History is full of violent disputations, and burnings at the stake, and even wars, in which the opposing forces hurled biblical texts at each other.

Shakespeare points out in *The Merchant of Venice* that "The devil can cite Scripture for his purpose" and I keep waiting for some of my opponents to tell me that—but they never have.

You see, the trouble with that particular quotation is that there is no objective way of deciding which of two conflicting sides the devil represents. In the history of theological disputation, each side has always insisted that the devil is represented by the other side.

So I intend to continue to cite the Bible and show that it says the Earth is flat, and I defy the creationists to find a citation anywhere in the Bible that will show the Earth to be a sphere.

# 25

# What Truck?

I am not a very visual person. What's more, I have a very lively inner life so that things are jumping about inside my cranium all the time and that distracts me. Other people are therefore astonished at the things I don't see. People change their hairstyles and I don't notice. New furniture comes into the house and I sit on it without comment.

Once, however, I seem to have broken the record in that respect. I was walking up Lexington Avenue, speaking animatedly (as is my wont) to someone who was walking with me. I walked across a roadway, still talking, my companion crossing with me with what seemed to be a certain reluctance.

On the other side, my companion said, "That truck missed us by one inch."

And I said, in all innocence, "What truck?"

So I got a rather long dull lecture, which didn't reform me, but which got me to thinking about the ease with which one can fail to see trucks. For instance . . .

Some time ago a reader sent me a copy of the October 1903 issue of *Munsey's Magazine* and I looked through it with considerable interest. The enormous advertising section was like a window into another world. The item of particular fascination, however, which the reader had called to my attention was an article entitled "Can Men Visit the Moon?" by Ernest Green Dodge, A.M.

It was the kind of article I myself might have written eighty years ago.

As it happens, I have often had occasion to wonder whether my own attempts to write about the technology of the future might seem less than inspired in the brilliant light of hindsight. I have usually felt, rather woefully, that it would—that it would turn out that there would be trucks I didn't see, or trucks I saw that weren't really there.

I can't expect to live eighty more years and check on myself, but what if I look at remarks I might have made eighty years ago and see how they would sound in the light of what we now know?

Mr. Dodge's article is the perfect way of doing this, for he was clearly a rational man with a good knowledge of science, and with a strong but disciplined imagination. In short, he was as I like to imagine that I am.

In some places he hits the target right in the bull's-eye.

Concerning a trip to the Moon, he says: ". . . it is not, like perpetual motion or squaring the circle, a logical impossibility. The worst that can be said is that it now looks as difficult to us as the crossing of the great Atlantic must once have appeared to the naked savage upon its shore, with no craft but a fallen tree and no paddle but his empty hands. The impossibility of the savage became the triumph of Columbus, and the day-dream of the nineteenth century may become the achievement even of the twentieth."

Exactly! Human beings were standing on the Moon only sixty-six years after Dodge's article had appeared.

Dodge goes on to list the difficulties of space travel, which, he points out, arise primarily out of the fact that "space is indeed empty, in a sense which no man-made vacuum can approach. . . . a portion of outer space the size of the Earth contains absolutely nothing, so far as we know, but a few flying grains of meteoric stone, weighing perhaps ten or fifteen pounds in all."

Dodge is a careful man. Although the statement seemed irrefutable in 1903, he inserts that cautious phrase "so far as we know" and was right to do so.

In 1903 subatomic particles were just becoming known. Electrons and radioactive radiations had been discovered less than a decade before. These were only earthbound phenomena, however, and cosmic rays were not discovered until 1911. Dodge could not, therefore, have known that space was filled with energetic electrically charged particles of insignificant mass, but considerable importance.

On the basis of what he did know in 1903, Dodge lists four difficulties that could arise in traveling from Earth to Moon through the vacuum of outer space.

The first is, of course, that there is nothing to breathe. He dismisses that, quite correctly, by pointing out that a spaceship would be airtight and would carry its own internal atmosphere, just as it would bring along supplies of food and drink. Breathing is therefore no problem.

The second difficulty is that of "the terrible cold" of outer space. This Dodge takes more seriously.

It is, however, a problem that tends to be overestimated. To be sure, any piece of matter that is in deep space and far from any source of radiation would reach an equilibrium temperature of about 3 degrees absolute, so this can be viewed as "the temperature of space." Anything traveling from the Earth to the Moon is, however, not far from a source of radiation. It is in the vicinity of the Sun, just as much as the Earth and Moon are, and is bathed in solar radiation all the way.

What's more, the vacuum of space is an excellent heat insulator. This was well known in 1903, for James Dewar had invented the equivalent of the thermos bottle eleven years before the article was written. There is sure to be internal heat within the spaceship, if only the body heat of the astronauts themselves, and this will be lost very slowly by way of radiation through vacuum. (This is the only way of losing heat in space.)

Dodge thinks that the ships would have to be guarded against heat loss by "having the walls . . . heavily padded." He also suggests a heat supply in the form of "large parabolic mirrors outside [which] would throw concentrated beams of Sunlight through the window."

This is a sizable overestimate, since nothing of the sort is necessary. Insulation must be placed on the outside of the ships, but that is for the purpose of avoiding the *gain* of too much heat during passage through the atmosphere. The *loss* of heat is of no concern to anyone.

The third difficulty arises from the fact that the ship will be in free fall during most or all the passage from the Earth to the Moon so that the astronauts will experience no gravitational pull. This Dodge very reasonably shrugs off, pointing out that "dishes could be fastened to the table, and people could leap and float, even if they could not walk."

He does not speculate on possible deleterious physiological changes arising from exposure to zero gravity, and this might be considered shortsighted. Still, this has turned out not to be a problem. In recent years people have remained under zero gravity conditions continuously for more than half a year and have apparently shown no permanent ill-effects.

The fourth and last danger that Dodge considers is that of the possibility of meteoric collisions but (despite the fact that science fiction writers continued to view that as a major danger for half a century longer) Dodge dismisses this, too, as statistically insignificant. He was right to do so.

He does not mention the fifth danger, that of the cosmic rays and other electrically charged particles, something he simply could not have known about in 1903. There were some misgivings about this after the discovery of the radiation belts in 1958 but, as it turns out, they did not materially interfere with humanity's reach to the Moon.

Dodge thus decided that there were no dangers in space that would prevent human beings from reaching the Moon, and he was right. If anything, he had overestimated the danger of the supposed cold of space.

The next question was exactly how to go about actually traversing the distance from Earth to Moon. In this connection, he mentions five possible "plans." (One gets the impression, though Dodge does not actually say so, that these five plans are the only ones that are conceivable.)

The simplest is "the Tower Plan." This would involve the construction of an object tall enough to reach the Moon, something like the scheme of the builders of the biblical tower of Babel. Dodge mentions the Eiffel Tower, which had been built fourteen years before, and which, at a height of 984 feet, was the tallest structure in the world at the time the article was written (and for twenty-seven years longer).

He says: "the combined wealth of all nations might construct an edifice of solid steel eight or ten miles in height, but not much more, for the simple reason that the lower parts could not be made strong enough to bear the weight that must rest upon them." To reach the Moon, there would have to be "a building material about five hundred times tougher than armor-plate, and such may never be discovered." (Note the "may." Dodge is a careful man.)

There are many other deficiencies to the plan that Dodge does not mention. The Moon, having an elliptical orbit at an angle to Earth's equatorial plane, would approach the top of the tower only once in a long while, and when it did so, the lunar gravity would produce a huge strain on it. Air would remain only at the bottom of the tower, thanks to the pull of Earth's gravity, and there would still be the problem of traversing the 300,000 kilometers or so to the Moon's perigee distance after the tower had been built (let alone traversing it in the process of building the tower). Scratch the "Tower Plan."

Dodge doesn't mention the variant possibility of a "skyhook," a long vertical structure in such a position between Earth and Moon that the combined gravitational pull holds it in place, and that can be used as a help in negotiating the Earth-Moon passage. Personally, I don't think that's anywhere near practical, either.

Dodge's second scheme is "the Projectile Plan." This involves shooting a ship out of a giant cannon and having it emerge with speed enough to reach the Moon (if correctly aimed). This is the method used by Jules Verne in *From the Earth to the Moon*, published thirty-eight years before, in 1865.

Dodge points out that to reach the Moon, the projectile must leave the muzzle of the cannon at a speed of 11.2 kilometers per second (the escape velocity from Earth) plus a little extra to make up for air-resistance losses in passing through the atmosphere. The spaceship would have to accelerate from rest to 11.2 kilometers per second in the length of the cannon barrel, and this would neatly crush all passengers on board, leaving not a bone unbroken.

The longer the cannon, the lower the acceleration, but, says Dodge, ". . . even if the gun barrel had the impossible length of forty miles, the poor passenger would be subjected for eleven seconds to a pressure equivalent to a hundred men lying upon him."

But suppose we could overcome that difficulty and somehow picture the spaceship leaving the cannon's mouth with the passengers on it still alive. The spaceship would then be a projectile, moving in response to the force of gravity and nothing more. It would be as unable to alter its course as any other cannonball would.

If the ship were aimed at the Moon and were eventually to land on it, it would have to strike with a speed of not less than 2.37 kilometers per second (the Moon's escape velocity). And that, of course, would mean instant death. Or, as Dodge says, ". . . unless our bullet-ship can carry on its nose a pile of cushions two miles high on which to light, the landing will be worse than the starting!"

Of course, the ship need not land on the Moon. Dodge does not pursue this plan farther, but the cannon may be aimed with such superhuman nicety as to miss the Moon by just the right amount and at just the right speed to cause it to move around the Moon in response to the lunar gravity and race back to a rendezvous with Earth.

If the ship then hit the Earth squarely, it would strike at no less than 11.2 kilometers per second, so the passengers would be fried to death on the passage through the atmosphere before being blasted to death on collision with the solid ground or (very little better at such a speed) the ocean. And if the spaceship hit a city, it would kill many thousands of innocents as well.

The original superhuman aim might have brought the ship

back to Earth just sufficiently off-center to trap it in Earth's gravity and put it into an orbital path within the upper reaches of Earth's atmosphere. The orbit would gradually decay. Furthermore, some parachute arrangement might then be released to hasten the decay and bring the ship down safely.

But to expect all that of one aim is to expect far too much even if the initial acceleration were not murderous. Scratch the Projectile Plan.

The third scheme is "the Recoil Plan."

Dodge points out that a gun can fire in a vacuum and, in the process, undergo recoil. We can imagine a spaceship that is a kind of mighty gun which could eject a projectile downward, so that it would itself recoil upward. While recoiling, it could eject another projectile downward and give itself another kick upward.

If the ship fired projectiles rapidly enough, it would recoil upward faster and faster and, in fact, recoil itself all the way to the Moon.

Dodge, however, argues that the recoil is increasingly great as the mass of the bullet increases, and that "to be effective its weight [mass, really] should equal or exceed that of the gun itself."

We must imagine, then, an object that would fire away half of itself, leaving the other half to move upward—and fire half of what is left of itself as it rises, thus moving upward faster—and then fire half of what is now left of itself—and so on, until it reaches the Moon.

But how big must a spaceship be to begin with, if it has to fire away half of itself, then half of what is left, then half of what is left and so on? Dodge says, "An original outfit as big as a mountain chain would be necessary in order to land even a small cage safe upon the lunar surface." He feels that the Recoil Plan is therefore even less practical than the Projectile Plan.

On to the fourth scheme, "the Levitation Plan."

This involves nothing less than the screening, somehow, of the force of gravity. Dodge admits that no such gravity-screen is known, but supposes that it might be possible to discover one at some time in the future.

In a way, a hydrogen-filled balloon seems to nullify gravity. Indeed, it seems to fall upward through the atmosphere and to exhibit levitation (from a Latin word meaning "light") rather than gravitation (from a Latin word meaning "heavy").

Edgar Allan Poe, in his story "The Unparalleled Adventure of One Hans Pfaall," published sixty-eight years before, in 1835, made use of a balloon to travel to the Moon. A balloon, however, merely floats on the denser layers of the atmosphere and does not truly neutralize gravity. When it rises to a height where the thinning atmosphere is no denser than the gas contained within the balloon, there is no further rise. Poe imagined a gas far less dense than hydrogen (something we now know does not, and cannot, exist) but even that could not have lifted a balloon more than a fraction of one percent of the distance to the Moon. Dodge knew that and did not so much as mention balloons.

What Dodge meant was a true gravity neutralization, such as H. G. Wells used in his story "The First Men in the Moon," published two years before, in 1901.

Of course if you neutralized gravity you would have zero weight, but would that alone carry you to the Moon? Would a spaceship with zero weight not merely be subject to the vagaries of every puff of air? Would it not simply drift this way and that in a sort of Brownian motion and even if, eventually (a long eventually, perhaps), it got to the top of the atmosphere and went beyond, might it not then be moving away from Earth in a random direction that would only come within reach of the Moon as a result of an unusually long-chance coincidence?

Dodge, however, has a better notion. Imagine yourself in a spaceship resting on Earth's equator. Earth is rotating on its axis so that each point on the equator, including the spaceship, is moving about the axis at a speed of just about 0.46 kilometers per second. This is a supersonic speed (about 1.5 Mach) and if you were trying to hold on to an ordinary object that was whirling you about at that speed, you would not be able to hold on for the barest fraction of a second.

However, the Earth is very large, and the change in direction from the straight line in the time of one second is so small that the acceleration inward is quite moderate. The force of gravity upon the ship is strong enough to hold it to Earth's surface despite the speed with which it is whirled. (It would have to be whirled about the Earth at seventeen times the speed before gravity would cease being strong enough to hold it.)

But suppose the spaceship has a gravity screen plastered all over its hull, and at a particular moment the screen is activated. Now, with no gravitation to hold it down, it is cast off from the Earth like a clod of mud from a spinning flywheel. It would move in a straight line tangent to the curve of the Earth. The Earth's surface would drop below it, very slowly at first, but faster and faster, and if you were careful to activate the screen at just the right time, the ship's flight would eventually intersect the Moon's surface.

Dodge does not mention that the Earth's curved motion about the Sun would introduce a second factor, and that the Sun's motion among the stars would add a third component. These would represent comparatively minor adjustments, however.

The landing on the Moon would be better than in the previous plans, for a spaceship unaffected by the Moon's gravity need not approach it at anything like its escape velocity. Once the ship is almost touching the Moon, the gravity screen can be turned off and the ship, suddenly subject to the Moon's relatively weak gravity, can drop a few feet, or inches, with a slight jar.

How about the return, though? The Moon rotates on its axis very slowly, and a point on its equator travels at $1/100$ the speed of a point on Earth's equator. Using the gravity screen on the Moon will lend the spaceship only $1/100$ the velocity it had on leaving Earth, so that it will take 100 times as long to travel from Moon to Earth as from Earth to Moon.

However, we can dismiss the whole notion. Albert Einstein promulgated his general theory of relativity thirteen years after Dodge's article was written, so Dodge can't be faulted for not knowing that a gravity screen is simply impossible. Scratch the Levitation Plan.

Dodge is most hopeful about his fifth scheme, "the Repulsion Plan." Here it is not just a matter of neutralizing gravity he hopes for, but some form of repulsive force that would actively overbalance gravitational attraction.

After all, there are two kinds of electrical charge and two kinds of magnetic pole, and in either case, like charges, or like poles, repel each other. Might there not be a gravitational repulsion as well as a gravitational attraction, and might not spaceships someday use a combination of the two, sometimes pushing away from an astronomical body and sometimes pulling toward it, and might this not help take us to the Moon?

Dodge does not actually say there might be such a thing as gravitational repulsion, and his caution is good, for, from the later Einsteinian view, it would seem that gravitational repulsion is impossible.

Dodge does mention light pressure, though, pointing out that it can, in some cases, counteract the force of gravity. He uses comets' tails as an example. Gravity would be expected to pull the tails toward the Sun but the solar light pressure pushes them in the opposite direction, overcoming gravitation.

Actually, he is wrong here, for solar light pressure, it turns out, is too weak to do the job. It is the solar wind that does it.

Light pressure might be used as a motive force, to be sure, but it would be too weak to work against the nearby pull of a sizable body or, for that matter, against air resistance. A spaceship would have to be in fairly deep space to begin with, and it would have to have sails that were extremely thin and many square kilometers in area.

As a way of lifting a spaceship from the Earth's surface toward the Moon, light pressure, or anything like it, is hopeless. Scratch the Repulsion Plan.

And that's all. Dodge is an intelligent, knowledgeable man who clearly understands science (as of 1903); yet if we consider only his five plans as he describes them, *not one* has the faintest hope of ever allowing human beings to travel from Earth to Moon.

Yet it has been done! My father was alive when that article was written and he lived to see human beings stand on the Moon.

How is that possible?

Well, have you noticed the word that Dodge omitted? Have

you noticed that *he didn't see the truck?* He did not mention the rocket!

There was no reason for him to omit it. Rockets had been known for eight centuries. They had been used in peace and in war. Newton, in 1687, had thoroughly explained the rocket principle. Even earlier, in 1656, Cyrano de Bergerac in his story "A Voyage to the Moon" listed seven ways of reaching the Moon, and he *did* include rocketry as one of the methods.

How, then, did Dodge come to leave it out? Not because he wasn't sharp. In fact at the tail end of his article he was sharp-sighted enough to see, in 1903, the possibility of using the Moon's surface for the collection of solar energy.

No, he didn't mention the rocket because the best of us don't see the truck sometimes. (I wonder, for instance, what trucks all of us are missing right now.)

Dodge *almost* got it with his recoil plan, but for the fact that he made an odd blooper. He thought that in order to get a decent recoil, the gun must fire a bullet that had a mass at least equal to itself, and that is wrong.

What counts in shot and recoil, action and reaction, is momentum. When a bullet leaves a gun with a certain momentum, the gun must gain an equal momentum in the opposite direction, and momentum is equal to mass *multiplied by velocity*. In other words, a small mass would produce sufficient recoil if it moved with sufficient velocity.

In rockets, the hot vapors that are ejected move downward with great velocity and do so continuously, so that the body of the rocket moves up with surprising acceleration considering the small mass of the ejected vapor. It still takes a large mass to begin with to deliver a comparatively small object to the Moon, but the disparity is far, far less than Dodge had feared.

Furthermore, the recoil effect is continuous for as long as the fuel is being burned and the vapors ejected, and that is equivalent to a projectile being moved along a cannon tube for hundreds of miles. The acceleration becomes small enough to be borne.

The possession of a reserve supply of fuel once the rocket is well on its way to the Moon means the rocket can be maneuvered; its descent to the Moon can be braked; it can take off for

Earth again at will; and it can maneuver properly for entry into Earth's atmosphere.

And that is all, really, except for two coincidences, one mild and one wild—and you know how I love to find coincidences.

The mild coincidence is this: In the very year that this article was written for *Munsey's Magazine,* Konstantin Tsiolkovsky began a series of articles in a Russian aviation magazine that went into the theory of rocketry, as applied to space travel specifically. It was the very first scientific study of the sort, so that modern astronautic rocketry had its start just at the time that Dodge was speculating about everything *but* rocketry.

The wild coincidence is this: Immediately after Dodge's article, in which he fails to mention the word "rocket" or to realize that it was the rocket, and the rocket alone, that would afford human beings the great victory of reaching the Moon, there is, of course, another article, and what do you think the title of that article is?

Don't bother guessing. I'll tell you.

It is "Rocket's Great Victory."

No, it isn't somebody else correcting Dodge's omission. It is a piece of fiction with the subtitle "The stratagem by which Willie Fetherston won a race and a bride."

"Rocket," in this story, is the name of a horse.

## AFTERWORD

After the first year or so of this series of essays, I settled down into the habit of beginning each article with a personal anecdote, usually funny. Partly, it's because I want to put the reader into a relaxed mood before I start shoving cerebral argumentation at him, and partly it's because I like to talk about myself.

The question arises, and is sometimes asked, as to whether I make up these anecdotes. The answer is (hand on heart) that I don't. Every one of them happened to me more or less exactly as I describe it. I sometimes put them into a slightly more literary form, refining the raw material, so to speak, but never in such a way that the truth is in the slightest bit distorted.

I say this now because people can't believe that I can walk

across the street without noticing that I was nearly hit by a huge truck. However, it's so. I have this power of concentration.

Of course, then they decide that they can't believe that with such a power of concentration, I haven't been crushed flat by some vehicle many years ago. Well, I would like to believe that I have a fairy godmother who keeps watch over me but, since I don't really think I have (and, believe me, I regret that), I have no explanation.

# 26

## More Thinking
## About Thinking

In Essay 17, "Thinking About Thinking," I expressed my dissatisfaction with intelligence tests and gave my reasons therefor. I presented arguments for supposing that the word "intelligence" stood for a subtle concept that could not be measured by a single figure such as that represented by an "intelligence quotient" (IQ).

I was very pleased with the essay all the more so since it was attacked by a psychologist for whose work I have little respect (see Essay 21, "Alas, All Human").

Nor did I think I would ever have to add to it. In fact, I rather suspected I had emptied myself of all possible thought I might have on the subject of intelligence.

And then, not long ago as I write this, I found myself sitting at a dinner table with Marvin Minsky of M.I.T. on my right hand and Heinz Pagels of Rockefeller University on my left.

Pagels was conducting a three-day conference on computers and earlier that day had moderated a panel discussion entitled

"Has artificial intelligence research illuminated human thinking?"

I did not attend the panel (various deadlines precluded that) but my dear wife, Janet, did, and from her account it would seem that Minsky, one of the panelists, and John Searle of the University of California engaged in a dispute on the nature of artificial intelligence. Minsky, the leading proponent of that field of research, opposed Searle's view that consciousness was a purely biological phenomenon and that no machine could ever have consciousness or intelligence.

At the dinner Minsky continued to maintain his view that artificial intelligence was *not* a contradiction in terms, while Pagels was supporting the legitimacy of Searle's view. Since I was sitting between, the polite but intense argument was being conducted over my head both literally *and* figuratively.

I listened to the arguments with increasing anxiety for I had carelessly agreed, months before, to give an after-dinner talk that night. It now seemed to me that the Minsky-Searle debate was the only topic on the collective mind of the high-powered dinner attendees and that it would be absolutely necessary for me to talk on that subject if I were to have any chance of holding their attention.

It meant that I had to go back to thinking about thinking, and that I had less than half an hour in which to do it. I managed, of course, or I wouldn't be telling you this. In fact, I was told that during the rest of the conference I was occasionally quoted with approval.

I can't give you my talk word for word, since I spoke off the cuff as I always do, but here is a reasonable facsimile.

Suppose we start with the easy assumption that *Homo sapiens* is the most intelligent species on Earth, either living now or in the past. It should not be surprising, therefore, that the human brain is so large. We tend, with considerable reason, to associate the brain with intelligence and vice versa.

The brain of the adult human male has a mass of about 1.4 kilograms, on the average, and is far larger than any nonmammalian brain, past or present. This is not surprising, considering that mammals as a class have larger brains and are more intelligent than any other kinds of living organisms.

Among the mammals themselves it is not surprising that the larger the organism as a whole, the larger the brain, but the human brain is out of line in this respect. It is larger than those of mammals far more massive than humans are. The human brain is larger than that of the horse, the rhinoceros, or the gorilla, for instance.

And yet the human brain is not the largest there is. The brains of elephants are larger. The largest elephant brains have been found to have masses of about 6 kilograms, or roughly 4 1/4 times that of the human brain. What's more, the brains of the large whales have been found to be more massive still. The most massive brain ever measured was that of a sperm whale, and it had a mass of about 9.2 kilograms—6 1/2 times that of the human brain.

Yet elephants and large whales, while more intelligent than most animals, are never thought to compare even remotely with human beings in intelligence. Quite clearly, brain mass is not all there is to be considered where intelligence is concerned.

The human brain makes up about 2 percent of the mass of the total human body. An elephant with a 6-kilogram brain, however, would have a mass of 5,000 kilograms, so that his brain would make up only about 0.12 percent of the mass of its body. As for a sperm whale, which can attain a mass of 65,000 kilograms, its 9.2-kilogram brain would make up only about 0.014 percent of the mass of its body.

In other words, per unit of body mass the human brain is 17 times as large as that of the elephant, and 140 times as large as that of the sperm whale.

Is it fair to put brain/body mass ratio ahead of mere brain mass?

Well, it seems to give us a truthful answer, since it points up the apparently obvious fact that human beings are more intelligent than the larger-brained elephants and whales. Besides, we might argue it out (probably in a simplistic manner) in this fashion—

The brain controls the workings of the body, and what is left over from these low-thought-control duties can be reserved for activities such as imagination, abstract reasoning, and creative fancy. Though the brains of elephants and whales are large, the bodies of those mammals are enormous, so that their brains, large though they are, are fully preoccupied with all the routine of running those vast masses, and have very little left over for "higher" functions. Elephants and whales are therefore less intelligent than human beings despite the size of their brains.

(And that's why women can have brains 10 percent less massive than those of men, on the average, and not be 10 percent less intelligent. Their bodies are smaller, too, and their brain/body mass rations are, if anything, a trifle higher than those of men.)

Still, the brain/body mass ratio can't be everything either. Primates (the apes and monkeys) all have high brain/body mass ratios and, on the whole, the smaller the primate, the higher the ratio. In some small monkeys the brain makes up 5.7 percent of the body mass, and that is nearly three times the ratio in human beings.

Why, then, aren't these small monkeys more intelligent than human beings?—Here the answer may be that their brains are just too small to serve the purpose.

For really high intelligence, you need a brain massive enough to provide the thought power necessary, and a body small enough not to use up the entire brain and leave nothing for thinking. This combination of large brain and small body seems to meet its best balance in the human being.

But wait! Just as primates tend to have a higher brain/body ratio as they grow smaller, so do the cetaceans (the whale family). The common dolphin is no more massive than a man, on the whole, but it has a brain that is about 1.7 kilograms in mass, or 1/5 more massive than the human brain. The brain/body ratio is 2.4 percent.

In that case, why isn't the dolphin more intelligent than the human being? Can there be some qualitative difference between the two kinds of brains that condemns the dolphin to relative stupidity?

For instance, the actual brain cells are located at the surface of the cerebrum and make up the "gray matter." The interior of the brain is made up, to a large extent, of the fat-swathed processes extending from the cells and (thanks to the color of the fat) this is the "white matter."

It is the gray matter that is associated with intelligence, and therefore the surface area of the brain is more important than its mass. As we consider species in order of increasing intelligence, we find that the surface area of the brain increases more rapidly than the mass does. One way this becomes apparent is that the surface area increases to the point where it cannot be spread out smoothly over the brain's interior, but wrinkles into convolutions. A convoluted brain would have a larger surface area than a smooth brain of the same mass.

Therefore we associate convolutions with intelligence and, to be sure, mammalian brains are convoluted while nonmammalian brains are not. A monkey's brain is more convoluted than a cat's brain. A human brain, not surprisingly, is more convoluted than that of any other land mammal, even including such relatively intelligent ones as chimpanzees and elephants.

And yet the dolphin's brain is more massive than the human brain, has a higher brain/body mass ratio, and *in addition* is more convoluted than the human brain is.

*Now* why aren't dolphins more intelligent than human beings? To explain that, we have to fall back on the supposition that there is some shortcoming in the structure of the dolphin's brain cells, or in its cerebral organization—points for which there is no evidence.

Let me, however, suggest an alternative view. How do we know dolphins are not more intelligent than human beings?

To be sure, they don't have a technology, but that's not surprising. They live in water where fire is impossible, and the skillful use of fire is the fundamental basis of human technology. What's more, life in water makes streamlining essential, so that dolphins lack the equivalent of the human being's delicately manipulative hands.

But is technology alone a sufficient measure of intelligence? When it suits us, we dismiss technology. Consider the structures built by such social insects as bees, ants, and termites, or the delicate tracery of the spider web. Do these accomplishments make a bee, ant, termite, or spider more intelligent than the gorilla, which builds a crude tree nest?

We say "No" without a moment's hesitation. We consider that the lower animals, however marvelous their accomplishments, proceed only on instinct, and that this is inferior to conscious thought. Yet that may be only our self-serving judgment.

Might it not be conceivable that dolphins would consider our technology the result of a lower form of thinking, and dismiss it as evidence of intelligence, in a self-serving judgment of their own?

Of course, human beings have the power of speech. We make use of complex modulations of sound to express infinitely subtle ideas, and no other species of living thing does that or comes anywhere near it. (Nor can they communicate with equivalent complexity, versatility, and subtlety by any other means, as far as we know.)

Yet the humpback whale sings complex "songs," while the dolphin is capable of producing a greater variety of different sounds than we can. What makes us so sure that dolphins can't or don't speak?

But intelligence is such a noticeable thing. If dolphins are so smart, why isn't it *obvious* that they are so smart?

I maintained in "Thinking About Thinking" that there are different kinds of intelligence among human beings and that IQ tests are misleading for that reason. Even if this were so, however, all the human intelligential (I have to invent that word) varieties clearly belong to the same genus. It is possible for us to recognize such varieties even though they are quite different. We can see that Beethoven had one kind of intelligence, Shakespeare another, Newton still another, and Peter Piper (the pickle-picking expert) yet another, and we can understand the value of each.

Yet what of an intelligential variety altogether different from anything any human being has? Would we even recognize it as intelligence at all, no matter how we studied it?

Suppose a dolphin, with its enormous, convoluted brain and its vast armory of sounds, had a mind that could consider complex ideas and a language that could express them with infinite subtlety. But suppose those ideas and that language were so different from anything to which we were accustomed that we could not even grasp the fact that they were ideas and language, let alone understand their content.

Suppose a colony of termites, all together, had a community brain that could react in a way so different from our individual ones that we would not see the community intelligence no matter how glaringly "obvious" it might be.

The trouble may be partially semantic. We insist on defining "thinking" in such a way that we come to the automatic conclusion that only human beings think. (In fact, bigots throughout history have been certain that only males rather similar in appearance to themselves could think, and that women and "inferior races" could not. Self-serving definitions can do a great deal.)

Suppose we defined "thinking" as being that sort of action that led to a species taking those measures that would best ensure its own survival. By that definition, every species thinks in some fashion. Human thinking becomes but one more variety, and one that is not necessarily better than others.

In fact, if we consider that the human species, with the full capacity for forethought, and knowing exactly what it is doing and what may happen, nevertheless has a very good chance of destroying itself in a nuclear holocaust—the only logical conclusion we can come to, by my definition, is that *Homo sapiens* thinks more poorly, and is less intelligent, than any species that lives, or has ever lived, on Earth.

It may be, then, that just as the IQ-niks achieve their results by carefully defining intelligence in such a way as to make themselves and people like themselves "superior," so humanity as a whole does the same by its careful definition of what constitutes thinking.

To make this plainer, let's consider an analogy.

Human beings "walk." They do so on two legs with their mammalian body tipped upward so as to produce a backward bend to the spine in the lumbar region.

We might define "walking" as motion on two legs with the body balanced on a recurved spine. By this definition, walking would be unique to the human being and we might well be proud of this fact, and with reason. This sort of walking freed our forelimbs from all necessity to help us move about (except under certain emergency conditions) and gave us permanently available hands. This development of upright posture preceded the development of our large brain and may, indeed, have led to it.

Other animals don't walk. They move on four legs or on six, eight, dozens, or none. Or they fly, or swim. Even those quadrupeds who can rise to their hind legs (such as bears and apes) do so only temporarily and are most comfortable on all fours.

There are animals that are strictly bipedal, such as kangaroos and birds, but they often hop rather than walk. Even birds that walk (as pigeons and penguins do) are primarily fliers or swimmers. And birds that never do anything but walk (or—its faster cousin—run), such as the ostrich, still lack the recurved spine.

Suppose, then, that we insisted on making "walking" totally unique and did so to the point where we lacked words for ways in which other species progressed. Suppose we were content to say that human beings were "walkative" and all other species were not, and refused to stretch our vocabulary beyond that.

If we insisted on doing so with sufficient fervor we would not need to pay any attention to the beautiful efficiency with which some species hop, or leap, or run, or fly, or sail, or dive, or slither. We would develop no phrase such as "animal locomotion" to cover all these varieties of progression.

And if we dismissed all forms of animal locomotion but our own as simply "non-walkative," we might never have to face the fact that human locomotion is, in many ways, not as graceful as that of a horse or a hawk, and is, indeed, one of the least graceful and admirable forms of animal locomotion.

Suppose, then, we invent a word to cover all the ways in which living things might behave in such a way as to meet a challenge or to promote survival. Call it "zorking." Thinking, in the human sense, might be one form of zorking, while other species of living things might display other forms of zorking.

If we approach zorking without preconceived judgments, we might find that thinking is not always the best way of zorking, and we might stand a slightly better chance of understanding the zorking of dolphins or of termite communities.

Or suppose we consider the problem of whether machines can

think; whether a computer can ever have consciousness; whether robots can possibly feel emotion; where, in short, we are to attain, in future, such a thing as true "artificial intelligence."

How can we argue such a thing, if we don't first stop to consider what intelligence might be? If it is something only a human being can have by definition, then, of course, a machine can't have it.

But any species can zork, and it may be that computers will be able to, also. Computers won't zork, perhaps, in a fashion that any biological species will, so we need a new word for what they do, too. In my impromptu talk at the computer force, I used the word "grotch" and I suppose that will do as well as any other.

Among human beings there are an indefinite number of different ways of zorking; different ways that are sufficiently alike for all to be included under the general heading of "thinking." And among computers, too, there are liable to be an indefinite number of different ways of zorking, but ways so different from those found in human beings as to be included under the general heading of "grotching."

(And nonhuman animals may zork in different ways still, so that we would have to invent dozens of different words for zork varieties and classify them in complicated fashion. What's more, as computers developed, we might find that "grotching" wasn't sufficient, so that we would have to work up subheadings. —But all that's for the future. My crystal ball isn't infinitely clear.)

To be sure, we design our computers in such a way that they can solve problems that are of interest to us, and therefore they give us the illusion that they think. We must recognize, though, that even when a computer solves a problem that we ourselves would have to solve in the absence of a computer, it and we nevertheless solve it by totally different processes. They grotch and we think, and it may be useless to sit about and debate whether computers think. Computers might as well sit around and debate whether human beings grotch.

But is it reasonable to suppose that human beings would create an artificial intelligence so different from human intelligence as to require a recognition of computer grotching as independent of human thinking?

Why not? It's happened before. For countless thousands of

years, human beings transported objects by tucking them under their arms or balancing them on their heads. In doing so, they could only transport so much mass, at most.

If human beings piled objects on the backs of donkeys, horses, oxen, camels, or elephants, they could transport larger masses. That, however, is just the substitution of the direct use of larger muscles for smaller ones.

Eventually, however, human beings invented an artificial device that made transportation easier. How did the machine bring this about? Did it do it by producing an artificial walk, run, fly, swim, or any of the myriad of other forms of animal locomotion?

No. Some human being in the dim days of prehistory invented the wheel and axle. As a result, a much larger mass could be placed in a cart and dragged by human or animal muscles than could be carried by those muscles directly.

The wheel and axle is the most astonishing invention ever made by human beings, to my way of thinking. The human use of fire was at least preceded by the observation of natural fires set by lightning. But the wheel and axle had no natural ancestry. It does not exist in nature; no life-form has evolved it to this day. Thus, "machine-aided locomotion" was, from its inception, utterly different from all forms of animal locomotion; and, in the same way, it would not be surprising if mechanical zorking were different from all forms of biological zorking.

Of course, primitive carts couldn't move by themselves, but eventually the steam engine was invented, and then later the internal combustion engine and the rocket—none of which acts anything like muscles.

Computers are, as yet, at the pre–steam-engine stage. Computers can work but can't do so "by themselves." Eventually the equivalent of a steam engine will be developed and the computers will be able to solve problems by themselves, but still by a process totally different from that of the human brain. They will still be grotching rather than thinking.

All this seems to rule out fears that computers will "replace" us, or that human beings will become superfluous and die out.

After all, wheels haven't made legs superfluous. There are times when walking is more convenient and more useful than rolling. Picking one's way over rough ground is easy when walking, very difficult by automobile. And I wouldn't think of getting from my bed to the bathroom by any process other than walking.

But can't computers eventually do anything human beings can do, even if they grotch rather than think? Can't computers grotch up symphonies, dramas, scientific theories, love affairs—anything you care to name?

Maybe. Every once in a while I see a machine designed to lift legs over obstructions so that it walks. However, the machine is so complicated and the motions so ungraceful that it strikes me that no one is ever going to take the huge trouble to try to produce and use such things as anything but a tour de force (like the airplane that flew the English Channel by bicycle power—and will never be used again).

Grotching, whatever it is, is quite obviously best adapted to the exceedingly rapid and inerrant manipulation of arithmetical quantities. Even the simplest computer can grotch the multiplication and division of huge numbers much faster than human beings can think their way through to the solution.

That doesn't mean grotching is superior to thinking; it just means that grotching is better adapted to that particular process. As for thinking, that is well adapted to processes that involve insight, intuition, and the creative combination of data to produce unexpected results.

Computers can perhaps be designed to do such things after a fashion, just as mathematical prodigies can grotch after a fashion —but either is a waste of time.

Let thinkers and grotchers work at their specialties and pool the results. I imagine that human beings *and* computers, working together, can do far more than either could alone. It is the symbiosis of the two that represents the shape of the future.

One more point: If grotching and thinking are widely different things, can one expect the study of computers ever to illuminate the problem of human thought?

Let us go back to the problem of locomotion.

A steam engine can power machines to do work that is ordinarily done by muscles, and to do it more intensely and tirelessly, but that steam engine is in no way similar to the muscle in structure. In the steam engine, water is heated to steam and the expanding steam pushes pistons. In the muscle, a delicate protein named actomyosin undergoes molecular changes which cause the muscle to contract.

It might seem that you could study boiling water and expanding steam for a million years and not be able to deduce one thing about actomyosin from that. Or, conversely, that you could study every molecular change actomyosin can undergo and not learn one thing about what makes water boil.

In 1824, however, a young French physicist, Nicolas L. S. Carnot (1796–1832) studied the steam engine in order to determine what factors controlled the efficiency with which it worked. In the process, he was the first to begin the line of argument that, by the end of the century, had fully developed the laws of thermodynamics.

These laws are among the most powerful generalizations in physics and it was found that they applied in full rigor to living systems as well as to such simpler things as steam engines.

Muscular action, however complicated its innermost workings, must labor under the constraints of the laws of thermodynamics just as steam engines must, and this tells us something about muscles that is enormously important. What's more we learned it from steam engines, and might never have learned it from a study of muscles alone.

Similarly, the study of computers may never tell us, directly, anything at all about the intimate structure of the human brain, or of the human brain cell. Nevertheless, the study of grotching may lead to the determination of the basic laws of zorking, and we may find that these laws of zorking apply to thinking as well as to grotching.

It may be, then, that even though computers are nothing like brains, computers may teach us things about brains that we might never discover by studying brains alone—so, in the last analysis, I am on Minsky's side.

## AFTERWORD

I must admit that in my science fiction I do not necessarily practice what I preach in my science essays.

In my science essays, I am firm in my belief that the speed of light is an ultimate limit that will not and cannot be surpassed, but in my science fiction stories, I always use faster-than-light travel.

Again, in my science essays, I am firm in my belief that in the end robotic "artificial intelligence" will be quite different in form from the "natural intelligence" that we have; and that the two kinds of intelligence will be complementary, rather than competitive.

In my robot stories, however, which I have been writing for about half a century, my robots have been evolving steadily, becoming more complex, more capable, and more and more resembling human beings. Finally, my supreme robotic creation, R. Daneel Olivaw, has ended up being indistinguishable from a human being both physically and intellectually. In fact, he only gives away his robothood by the fact that he is far more intelligent, far more decent, far more virtuous and moral than any human being can possibly be.

Does that mean I contradict myself? Yes.

# 27

# Far as Human Eye Could See

I received a communication from a tax-gathering department the other day, and such communications are marked by two unfailing characteristics. First, they are tremble-inducing (What are they after? What have I done wrong?). Second, they are written in High Martian. It is simply impossible to interpret what they are saying.

As nearly as I could make out, something was wrong with one of my minor taxes of 1979. I had underpaid by $300 and was being soaked that, plus $122 in interest and so the total came to $422. Somewhere among the rank and sprouting verbiage there was a collection of words that sounded like the threat of my being strung up by one big toe for twenty years if I didn't pay in five minutes.

I called my accountant, who, as always, was utterly calm at this threat to someone else's existence. "Send it to me," he said, stifling a yawn. "I'll look at it."

"I think," I said, nervously, "I had better pay it first."

"If you wish," he said, "since you can afford it."

So I did. I wrote out the check, put it in an envelope, and sprinted to the post office to make the deadline and save my big toe.

Then I took the document to my accountant, who used his special accountant's magnifying glass to study the small print. Finally, he was ready with his diagnosis.

He said, "They're telling you *they* owe *you* money."

"Then why are they charging me interest?"

"That's the interest *they* owe *you.*"

"But they threaten me if I don't pay."

"I know, but tax collecting is a dull job and you can't blame them for trying to inject a little harmless fun into it."

"But I paid them already."

"It doesn't matter. I will simply write to them and explain that they terrorized an honest citizen and they will eventually send you a check for $844, covering their debt to you, plus your unnecessary payment." Then he added, with a jovial smile, "But don't hold your breath."

That gave me my opportunity for the last word. "A person who deals with publishers," I said, austerely, "is accustomed to not holding his breath for payment."*

And now, having established my credentials as a keen-eyed, far-seeing individual, let us do a little keen-eyed farseeing.

Suppose I dip into the future far as human eye could see (to coin a phrase Alfy Tennyson once used). If I do that, what will I see happening to Earth? Let us assume, to begin with, that Earth is alone in the Universe, albeit with its present age and structure.

Naturally, if it is alone in the Universe, there is no Sun to light and warm it, so its surface is dark and at a temperature near absolute zero. It is, in consequence, lifeless.

Its interior, however, is hot because of the kinetic energy of the smaller bodies that coalesced to form it 4.6 eons ago ("eon" being taken to be 1,000,000,000—one billion—years). The inner heat would escape only slowly through the insulating rock of its crust, and, besides, would be continually renewed by the

---

* Actually, the tax people sent me back my check within ten days, saying they had no right to it.

breakdown of such radioactive constituents of earthly matter as uranium-238, uranium-235, thorium-232, potassium-40, and so on. (Of these, uranium-238 contributes about 90 percent of the heat.)

We might assume, then, that Earth, alone in the Universe, would endure for a long time in its condition of cold outside and hot inside. The uranium-238, however, slowly decays, with a half-life of 4.5 eons. As a result half of the original supply has already disappeared, and half of what remains will disappear in the next 4.5 eons, and so on. In about 30 eons from now, the uranium-238 remaining in the Earth will be only about 1 percent of the present content.

We may expect, then, that with time, the Earth's internal heat will leak away and will be less and less efficiently replaced by the shrinking supply of radioactive materials. By the time the Earth is 30 eons older than it is now, it will be merely lukewarm inside. It would continue to lose heat (at a slower and slower rate) for an indefinite period, getting even closer to absolute zero, and, of course, never quite reaching it.

But the Earth is not the only body in existence. In our Solar System alone, there are countless other objects of planetary and subplanetary size, from mighty Jupiter down to tiny dust particles and even down to individual atoms and subatomic particles. There might be similar collections of such nonluminous objects circling other stars to say nothing of such objects wandering through the interstellar spaces of our Galaxy. Suppose, then, that the entire Galaxy was made up of such nonluminous objects only. What would be their ultimate fate?

The larger the body, the higher the internal temperature and the greater the internal heat gathered together in the process of formation; and, in consequence, the longer the time it would take to cool off. My rough guess is that Jupiter, with a little over three hundred times the mass of the Earth, would take at least a thousand times as long to cool as Earth would—say, 30,000 eons.

In the course of this vast length of time, however (two thousand times the present age of the Universe), other things would happen that would outweigh the mere process of cooling off.

There would be collisions between bodies. In the periods of time we're used to, such collisions would not be common, but over the space of 30,000 eons, there would be very many. Some collisions would result in breakups and disintegrations into still smaller bodies. Where a small body collides with a much larger one, however, the smaller body is trapped by the larger, and remains with it. Thus, Earth sweeps up trillions of meteorites and micrometeorites each day, and its mass slowly, but steadily, increases as a result.

We may consider it a general rule, in fact, that as a result of collisions, large bodies grow at the expense of small bodies, so that, with time, small bodies tend to grow rare, while large bodies grow ever larger.

Each collision that adds to the mass of a larger body also adds kinetic energy that is converted into heat, so that the cooling-off rate of the larger body is further slowed down. In fact, particularly large bodies, which are especially effective in gathering up smaller ones, gain energy at a rate that will cause them to warm up rather than cool down. This higher temperature, plus the greater central pressures that come with increasing mass, will eventually (when the body is at least ten times the mass of Jupiter) bring about nuclear reactions at the center. The body will undergo "nuclear ignition," in other words, and its overall temperature will rise even higher until, finally, the surface grows faintly luminous. The planet will have become a feeble star.

One can then imagine our Galaxy as consisting of planetary and subplanetary nonluminous bodies that gradually develop, here and there, into faint specks of light. It is useless to do so, however, because in actual fact, the Galaxy, in forming, condensed into bodies massive enough to undergo nuclear ignition to begin with. It consists of as many as 300 billion stars, many of them quite brilliant and a few of them thousands of times as luminous as our Sun.

What we must ask, then, is what will become of the stars, for their fate will far outweigh anything that will happen to the smaller nonluminous bodies that, for the most part, circle in orbit about the various stars.

Nonluminous bodies can exist without serious change (except for the cooling process, and occasional collision) for indefinite periods, because their atom structure resists the inward pull of gravity. The stars, however, are in a different situation.

Stars, being far more massive than planets, have far more intense gravitational fields and their atomic structure smashes under the inward pull of those fields. As a result, stars, on formation, would at once shrink to planetary size and gain enormous densities, if gravity were all that need be taken into account. However, the vast temperatures and pressures at the center of such massive objects result in nuclear ignition, and the heat, developed by the nuclear reactions at the core, succeeds in keeping the stars' volumes expanded even against the pull of their enormous gravities.

The heat of stars, however, is developed at the expense of nuclear fusion that converts hydrogen to helium, and, eventually, to more complicated nuclei still. Since there is a finite amount of hydrogen in any star, the nuclear reactions can continue only for so long. Sooner or later, as the content of nuclear fuel diminishes, there is a gradual failure of the ability of nuclear-developed heat to keep stars expanded against the inexorable and forever continuing inward pull of gravity.

Stars no more massive than our Sun eventually consume enough of their fuel to be forced to undergo a rather quiet gravitational collapse. They contract to "white dwarfs" the size of Earth or less (though retaining virtually all their original mass). White dwarfs consist of shattered atoms, but the free electrons resist compression through their mutual repulsion, so that a white dwarf, left to itself, will remain unchanged in structure for indefinite periods.

Stars that are more massive than the Sun undergo more drastic changes. The more massive they are, the more violent the events. Beyond a certain mass, they will explode into "supernovas" that are capable of radiating, for a brief period, as much energy as 100 billion ordinary stars. Part of the mass of the exploding star is blown off into space and what is left can collapse into a "neutron star." To form a neutron star, the force of collapse must break through the electron sea that would maintain it in the form of a white dwarf. The electrons are driven into combination with atomic nuclei, producing neutrons which, lacking electrical charge, do not repel each other but are forced together in contact.

Neutrons are so tiny, even compared to atoms, that the entire mass of the Sun could be squeezed into a sphere no more than 14 kilometers in diameter. The neutrons themselves resist breakdown, so that a neutron star, left to itself, will remain unchanged in structure for indefinite periods.

If the star is particularly massive, the collapse will be so catastrophic that even neutrons will not be able to resist the in-pulling effect of gravity, and the star will collapse past the neutron-star stage. Past that there is nothing to prevent the star from collapsing indefinitely toward zero volume and infinite density and a "black hole" is formed.

The amount of time it takes a star to use up its fuel to the point of collapse varies with the mass of the star. The larger the mass, the more quickly its fuel is used up. The largest stars will maintain an extended volume for only a million years, or even less, before collapsing. Stars the size of the Sun will remain extended for perhaps 10 to 12 billion years before collapsing. The least massive red dwarfs may shine up to 200 billion years before the inevitable.

Most stars of our Galaxy were formed not long after the Big Bang some 15 billion years ago, but a scattering of new stars (including our own sun) have been forming steadily ever since. Some are forming now, and others will continue to form for billions of years to come. The new stars that will form out of dust clouds are, however, limited in number. The dust clouds of our Galaxy amount to only 10 percent of its total mass, so that 90 percent of all the stars that can form have already formed.

Eventually, the new stars will also collapse and while the occasional supernova will add to the interstellar dust, the time will come when no new stars can form. All the mass of our Galaxy will have been collected into stars that will exist in collapsed form only, and in three different varieties: white dwarfs, neutron stars, and black holes. In addition, there will be various nonluminous planetary and subplanetary bodies here and there.

Black holes, left to themselves, give out no light and are as nonluminous as planets. White dwarfs and neutron stars do give off radiation, including visible light, possibly even more per unit surface than ordinary stars do. However, white dwarfs and neutron stars have such small surfaces compared to ordinary stars that the total light they emit is insignificant. A galaxy composed of only collapsed stars and planetary bodies would therefore be essentially dark. After about 100 eons (six or seven times the present age of the Galaxy) there would be only insignificant sparks of radiation to relieve the cold and darkness that would have fallen everywhere.

What's more, what specks of light do exist will slowly diminish and vanish. White dwarfs will slowly dim and become black dwarfs. Neutron stars will slow their rotations and emit weaker and weaker pulses of radiation.

These bodies, however, will not be left to themselves. They will all still make up a galaxy. The 200 or 300 billion collapsed stars will still have the shape of a spiral galaxy and will still revolve majestically about the center.

Over the eons, there will be collisions. Collapsed stars will collide with bits of dust, gravel, even sizable planetary bodies. At long intervals, collapsed stars will even collide with each other (releasing quantities of radiation that will be large in human terms but insignificant against the dark mass of the Galaxy). In general, the tendency, in such collisions, will be for the more massive body to gain at the expense of the less massive body.

A white dwarf that gains in mass will eventually become too massive to remain one and will reach the point where it collapses suddenly into a neutron star. Similarly, a neutron star will reach the point of collapsing into a black hole. Black holes, which can collapse no further, will slowly gain in mass.

In a billion eons ($10^{18}$ years), it may be that our Galaxy will consist almost entirely of black holes of varying sizes—with a smattering of non-black-hole objects, from neutron stars down to dust, making up but a very small fraction of the total mass.

The largest black hole would be the one that was originally at the center of the Galaxy, where the mass concentration has always been the greatest. Indeed, astronomers suspect there is already a massive black hole at the Galaxy's center, one with a mass of perhaps a million suns, and steadily growing.

The black holes making up the Galaxy in this far future will be revolving about the central black hole in orbits of varying radii and eccentricity and two will every now and then pass each other comparatively closely. Such near misses might well allow a transfer of angular momentum, so that one black hole will gain energy and will loop farther out from the galactic center, while the other will lose energy and will drop in closer to the center.

Little by little, the central black hole will swallow up one smaller black hole after another, as the small ones lose enough energy to approach the center too closely.

Eventually, after a billion billion eons ($10^{27}$ years), the Galaxy may consist essentially of a "galactic black hole," surrounded by a scattering of smaller black holes that are far enough away to be virtually independent of the gravitational influence of the center.

How large would the galactic black hole be? I have seen an estimate for its mass as a billion suns, or 1 percent of the total mass of the Galaxy. The remaining 99 percent would be made up (almost entirely) of the smaller black holes.

Yet I feel uneasy about that. I can't offer any evidence, but my instinct tells me that the galactic black hole should be more like 100 billion suns in mass, or half the mass of the Galaxy, while isolated black holes make up the other half.

Our Galaxy does not, however, exist in isolation. It is part of a cluster of some two dozen galaxies, called the "Local Group." Most of the members of the Local Group are considerably smaller than our Galaxy, but at least one, the Andromeda Galaxy, is larger than ours.

In the $10^{27}$ years that would suffice to convert our Galaxy into a galactic black hole surrounded by smaller ones, the other galaxies of the Local Group would each be converted into the same. Naturally, the various galactic black holes would vary in size according to the original mass of the galaxy in which they formed. The Local Group, then, would consist of two dozen or so galactic black holes, with the Andromeda black hole the largest and our Milky Way black hole next.

All these galactic black holes would be revolving about the center of gravity of the Local Group, and various galactic black holes would undergo near misses with a transfer of angular momentum. Again, some would be forced far from the center of gravity and some would sink closer to it. Eventually, a super-galactic black hole would form that might have a mass (my guess) equal to 500 billion suns—a mass equal to about twice the mass of our own Galaxy—with smaller galactic black holes and sub-galactic black holes circling in enormous orbits about the super-galactic black hole, or actually drifting off in space, altogether independent of the Local Group. This should be a better picture of the situation after $10^{27}$ years than the one drawn earlier from our Galaxy alone.

The Local Group is not all there is in the Universe, either. There are other clusters, perhaps as many as a billion of them, some of them large enough to include a thousand individual galaxies or more.

The Universe, however, is expanding. That is, the clusters of galaxies are receding from each other at large velocities. By the time $10^{27}$ years have passed and the Universe consists of super-galactic black holes, those individual supergalactic black holes will be receding from each other at such speeds that it is not likely they will ever interact significantly.

What's more, the smaller black holes that will have escaped from the clusters and will be wandering about through inter-cluster space are not likely to encounter major black holes in the ever expanding space through which they move.

We might come to the conclusion, then, that there is not much to say of the Universe after the $10^{27}$-year mark is reached. It will consist merely of supergalactic black holes in endless recession from each other (assuming, as most astronomers now think, that we live in an "open universe"; one, that is, that will expand forever) with a scattering of smaller black holes wandering through intercluster space. And, it might seem to us, there will be no significant change other than that expansion.

If so, we would probably be wrong.

The original feeling about black holes was that they were an absolute dead end—everything in, nothing out.

It seems, however, that is not so. The English physicist Stephen William Hawking (1942– ), applying quantum-mechanical considerations to black holes, showed that they could evaporate.

Every black hole has the equivalent of a temperature. The smaller the mass, the higher the temperature and the faster they will evaporate.

In fact, the rate of evaporation is inversely proportional to the cube of the mass, so that if black hole A is ten times as massive as black hole B, then black hole A will take a thousand times as long to evaporate. Again, as a black hole evaporates and loses mass, it evaporates faster and faster, and when it gets to be small enough, it evaporates explosively.

The temperature of sizable black holes is within a billionth of a billionth of a degree above absolute zero, so that their evaporation is dreadfully slow. Even after $10^{27}$ years, very little evaporation has yet taken place. Indeed, what evaporation does take place is overwhelmed by the absorption of matter by the black holes as they swing through space. Eventually, though, little will remain to be absorbed and evaporation will slowly begin to dominate.

Very slowly, over eons and eons of time, the black holes shrink in size, the smaller ones shrinking faster. Then, one by one, in inverse order of size, they shrivel and pop explosively into oblivion. The really large black holes take $10^{100}$, or even $10^{110}$, years to do this.

In evaporating, black holes produce electromagnetic radiation (photons) and neutrino/antineutrino pairs. These possess no rest-mass, but only energy (which, of course, is a form of thinly spread-out mass).

Even if particles remain in space, they will not necessarily be permanent.

The mass of the Universe is made up almost entirely of protons and neutrons, with a minor contribution from electrons. Until recently, protons (which make up about 95 percent of the mass of the Universe right now) were thought to be completely stable, as long as they were left to themselves.

Not so, according to current theory. Apparently, protons can, very slowly, decay spontaneously into positrons, photons, and neutrinos. The half-life of a proton is something like $10^{31}$ years, which is an enormous interval, but not enormous enough. By the time all the black holes have evaporated, a so much longer time has elapsed that something like 90 percent of all the protons existing in the Universe will have broken down. By the time $10^{32}$ years have passed, more than 99 percent of the protons will have broken down, and perhaps the black holes will also be gone by way of proton annihilation.

The neutrons, which can exist stably in association with protons, are liberated when protons break down. They are then unstable and, in the space of minutes, break down to electrons and protons. The protons then break down in their turn to positrons and massless particles.

The only particles remaining in quantity will then be electrons and positrons and in time they will collide, annihilating each other in a shower of photons.

By the time, then, that $10^{100}$ years have passed, the black holes will be gone, one way or the other. The Universe will be a vast ball of photons, neutrinos, and antineutrinos, and nothing more, expanding outward indefinitely. Everything will spread out more and more thinly, so that space will more and more approximate a vacuum.

One current theory, the so-called inflationary Universe, begins with a total vacuum, one that contains not only no matter, but no radiation. Such a vacuum, according to quantum theory, can undergo random fluctuations to produce matter and antimatter in equal or nearly equal proportions. Generally, such matter/antimatter annihilates itself almost at once. Given time enough, however, a fluctuation may take place that will produce an enormously massive quantity of matter/antimatter, with just enough unbalance to create a universe of matter in a sea of radiation. A superrapid expansion will then prevent annihilation and will produce a universe large enough to accommodate galaxies.

Perhaps, then, by the time, say, $10^{500}$ years pass, the Universe will be close enough to a vacuum to allow fluctuations on a large scale to become possible again.

Then, amid the dead ashes of an old, old universe, a totally new one may be conceived, rush outward, form galaxies, and begin another long adventure. In that view (which I must admit I've made up myself and which has not been advanced by any reputable astronomer that I know of), the forever expanding Universe is not necessarily a "one-shot" universe.

It may be that outside our Universe (if we could reach outside to observe) there are the dregs of an enormously tenuous, enormously older universe, that faintly encloses us; and outside that a still more tenuous, far, far older one, that encloses both; and beyond that—forever and forever without end.

But what if we live in a "closed universe," one with a high enough density of matter in it to supply the gravitational pull required to bring the expansion to an end some day, and to begin a contraction, a falling together, of the Universe?

The general astronomic view is that the density of matter in the Universe is only about a hundredth of the minimum quantity required to close the Universe, but what if astronomers are wrong? What if the overall density of matter in the Universe is actually twice the critical value?

In that case, it is estimated that the Universe will expand till it is 60 eons old (four times its present age), at which time the slowing rate of expansion will have finally come to a halt. At that time, the Universe will have reached a maximum diameter of about 40 billion light-years.

The Universe will then slowly start to contract and do so faster and faster. After another 60 eons, it will pinch itself into a Big Crunch, and finally disappear into the vacuum from which it originated.

Then, after a timeless interval, another such universe will form out of the vacuum—expand—and contract—over and over again without end. Or perhaps universes are formed in succession, some of which are open and some closed in random order.

No matter how we slice it, however, if we look far enough, we can end up with a vision of universe after universe, in infinite numbers through eternity—far as human eye could see.

## AFTERWORD

There is always a chance that I will make a scientific error in one of these essays and that it will escape my eye and appear in print in *Fantasy and Science Fiction*. What happens then, if I am lucky, and I usually am, is that one of my readers will catch it and point it out to me and I will have a chance to fix it up before it appears in one of my book collections.

In one essay, which happens not to appear in this retrospective volume, no other than the famous chemist, Linus Pauling, caught a beauty. He wrote to me with great satisfaction that I had made an error of 23 orders of magnitude (coming up with a number a hundred billion trillion times too large—or too small). He didn't tell me where the error was and I had to find it by myself in an absolute panic. (I found it.)

I thought I would never do anything quite that egregious again, but I was wrong. In the foregoing essay, as it appeared originally in the magazine, I made an error of more than 100 orders of magnitude, and I won't even try to put that into words. This time, my friend Harry C. Stubbs (who writes science fiction under the name of Hal Clement) pointed it out, and told me where it was. I corrected it.

# 28

# The Relativity
# of Wrong

I received a letter from a reader the other day. It was handwritten in crabbed penmanship so that it was very difficult to read. Nevertheless, I tried to make it out just in case it might prove to be important.

In the first sentence, he told me he was majoring in English Literature, but felt he needed to teach me science. (I sighed a bit, for I knew very few English Lit majors who are equipped to teach me science, but I am very aware of the vast state of my ignorance and I am prepared to learn as much as I can from anyone, however low on the social scale, so I read on.)

It seemed that in one of my innumerable essays, here and elsewhere, I had expressed a certain gladness at living in a century in which we finally got the basis of the Universe straight.

I didn't go into detail in the matter, but what I meant was that we now know the basic rules governing the Universe, together with the gravitational interrelationships of its gross components, as shown in the theory of relativity worked out between 1905 and 1916. We also know the basic rules governing the subatomic particles and their interrelationships, since these are very neatly described by the quantum theory worked out between 1900 and 1930. What's more, we have found that the galaxies and clusters of galaxies are the basic units of the physical Universe, as discovered between 1920 and 1930.

These are all twentieth-century discoveries, you see.

The young specialist in English Lit, having quoted me, went on to lecture me severely on the fact that in *every* century people have thought they understood the Universe at last, and in *every* century they were proved to be wrong. It follows that the one thing we can say about our modern "knowledge" is that it is *wrong*.

The young man then quoted with approval what Socrates had said on learning that the Delphic oracle had proclaimed him the wisest man in Greece. "If I am the wisest man," said Socrates, "it is because I alone know that I know nothing." The implication was that I was very foolish because I was under the impression I knew a great deal.

Alas, none of this was new to me. (There is very little that is new to me; I wish my correspondents would realize this.) This particular thesis was addressed to me a quarter of a century ago by John Campbell, who specialized in irritating me. He also told me that all theories are proven wrong in time.

My answer to him was, "John, when people thought the Earth was flat, they were wrong. When people thought the Earth was spherical, they were wrong. But if *you* think that thinking the Earth is spherical is *just as wrong* as thinking the Earth is flat, then your view is wronger than both of them put together."

The basic trouble, you see, is that people think that "right" and "wrong" are absolute; that everything that isn't perfectly and completely right is totally and equally wrong.

However, I don't think that's so. It seems to me that right and wrong are fuzzy concepts, and I will devote this essay to an explanation of why I think so.

First, let me dispose of Socrates because I am sick and tired of this pretense that knowing you know nothing is a mark of wisdom.

No one knows *nothing*. In a matter of days, babies learn to recognize their mothers.

Socrates would agree, of course, and explain that knowledge of trivia is not what he means. He means that in the great abstractions over which human beings debate, one should start without preconceived, unexamined notions, and that he alone knew this. (What an enormously arrogant claim!)

In his discussions of such matters as "What is justice?" or "What is virtue?" he took the attitude that he knew nothing and had to be instructed by others. (This is called "Socratic irony," for Socrates knew very well that he knew a great deal more than the poor souls he was picking on.) By pretending ignorance, Socrates lured others into propounding their views on such abstractions. Socrates then, by a series of ignorant-sounding questions, forced the others into such a mélange of self-contradictions that they would finally break down and admit they didn't know what they were talking about.

It is the mark of the marvelous toleration of the Athenians that they let this continue for decades and that it wasn't till Socrates turned seventy that they broke down and forced him to drink poison.

Now where do we get the notion that "right" and "wrong" are absolutes? It seems to me that this arises in the early grades, when children who know very little are taught by teachers who know very little more.

Young children learn spelling and arithmetic, for instance, and here we tumble into apparent absolutes.

How do you spell sugar? Answer: s-u-g-a-r. That is *right*. Anything else is *wrong*.

How much is 2 + 2? The answer is 4. That is *right*. Anything else is *wrong*.

Having exact answers, and having absolute rights and wrongs, minimizes the necessity of thinking, and that pleases both students and teachers. For that reason, students and teachers alike prefer short-answer tests to essay tests; multiple-choice over blank short-answer tests; and true-false tests over multiple-choice.

But short-answer tests are, to my way of thinking, useless as a measure of the student's understanding of a subject. They are merely a test of the efficiency of his ability to memorize.

You can see what I mean as soon as you admit that right and wrong are relative.

How do you spell "sugar?" Suppose Alice spells it p-q-z-z-f and Genevieve spells it s-h-u-g-e-r. Both are wrong, but is there any doubt that Alice is wronger than Genevieve? For that matter, I think it is possible to argue that Genevieve's spelling is superior to the "right" one.

Or suppose you spell "sugar": s-u-c-r-o-s-e, or $C_{12}H_{22}O_{11}$. Strictly speaking, you are wrong each time, but you're displaying a certain knowledge of the subject beyond conventional spelling.

Suppose then the test question was: how many different ways can you spell "sugar." Justify each.

Naturally, the student would have to do a lot of thinking and, in the end, exhibit how much or how little he knows. The teacher would also have to do a lot of thinking in the attempt to evaluate how much or how little the student knows. Both, I imagine, would be outraged.

Again, how much is $2 + 2$? Suppose Joseph says: $2 + 2 =$ purple, while Maxwell says: $2 + 2 = 17$. Both are wrong but isn't it fair to say that Joseph is wronger than Maxwell.

Suppose you said: $2 + 2 =$ an integer. You'd be right, wouldn't you? Or suppose you said: $2 + 2 =$ an even integer. You'd be rather righter. Or suppose you said: $2 + 2 = 3.999$. Wouldn't you be *nearly* right?

If the teacher wants 4 for an answer and won't distinguish between the various wrongs, doesn't that set an unnecessary limit to understanding?

Suppose the question is, how much is $9 + 5$?, and you answer 2. Will you not be excoriated and held up to ridicule, and will you not be told that $9 + 5 = 14$?

If you were then told that 9 hours had passed since midnight and it was therefore 9 o'clock, and were asked what time it would be in 5 more hours, and you answered 14 o'clock on the grounds that $9 + 5 = 14$, would you not be excoriated again, and told that it would be 2 o'clock? Apparently, in that case, $9 + 5 = 2$ after all.

Or again suppose Richard says: $2 + 2 = 11$, and before the

teacher can send him home with a note to his mother, he adds, "To the base 3, of course." He'd be right.

Here's another example. The teacher asks: "Who is the fortieth President of the United States?" and Barbara says, "There isn't any, teacher."

"Wrong!" says the teacher, "Ronald Reagan is the fortieth President of the United States."

"Not at all," says Barbara, "I have here a list of all the men who have served as President of the United States under the Constitution, from George Washington to Ronald Reagan, and there are only thirty-nine of them, so there is no fortieth President."

"Ah," says the teacher, "but Grover Cleveland served two nonconsecutive terms, one from 1885 to 1889, and the second from 1893 to 1897. He counts as both the twenty-second and twenty-fourth President. That is why Ronald Reagan is the thirty-ninth person to serve as President of the United States, and is, at the same time, the fortieth President of the United States."

Isn't that ridiculous? Why should a person be counted twice if his terms are nonconsecutive, and only once if he served two consecutive terms. Pure convention! Yet Barbara is marked wrong—just as wrong as if she had said the fortieth President of the United States is Fidel Castro.

Therefore, when my friend the English Literature expert tells me that in every century scientists think they have worked out the Universe and are *always wrong*, what I want to know is *how* wrong are they? Are they always wrong to the same degree? Let's take an example.

In the early days of civilization, the general feeling was that the Earth was flat.

This was not because people were stupid, or because they were intent on believing silly things. They felt it was flat on the basis of sound evidence. It was *not* just a matter of "That's how it looks," because the Earth does *not* look flat. It looks chaotically bumpy, with hills, valleys, ravines, cliffs, and so on.

Of course, there are plains where, over limited areas, the Earth's surface *does* look fairly flat. One of those plains is in the

Tigris-Euphrates area where the first historical civilization (one with writing) developed, that of the Sumerians.

Perhaps it was the appearance of the plain that may have persuaded the clever Sumerians to accept the generalization that the Earth was flat; that if you somehow evened out all the elevations and depressions, you would be left with flatness. Contributing to the notion may have been the fact that stretches of water (ponds and lakes) looked pretty flat on quiet days.

Another way of looking at it is to ask what is the "curvature" of Earth's surface. Over a considerable length, how much does the surface deviate (on the average) from perfect flatness. The flat-Earth theory would make it seem that the surface doesn't deviate from flatness at all, that its curvature is 0 to the mile.

Nowadays, of course, we are taught that the flat-Earth theory is *wrong;* that it is all wrong, terribly wrong, absolutely. But it isn't. The curvature of the Earth is *nearly* 0 per mile, so that although the flat-Earth theory is wrong, it happens to be *nearly* right. That's why the theory lasted so long.

There were reasons, to be sure, to find the flat-Earth theory unsatisfactory and, about 350 B.C., the Greek philosopher Aristotle summarized them. First, certain stars disappeared beyond the southern horizon as one traveled north, and beyond the northern horizon as one traveled south. Second, the Earth's shadow on the Moon during a lunar eclipse was always the arc of a circle. Third, here on Earth itself, ships disappeared beyond the horizon hull-first in whatever direction they were traveling.

All three observations could not be reasonably explained if the Earth's surface were flat, but could be explained by assuming the Earth to be a sphere.

What's more, Aristotle believed that all solid matter tended to move toward a common center, and if solid matter did this, it would end up as a sphere. A given volume of matter is, on the average, closer to a common center if it is a sphere than if it is any other shape whatever.

About a century after Aristotle, the Greek philosopher Eratosthenes noted that the Sun cast a shadow of different lengths at different latitudes (all the shadows would be the same length if the Earth's surface were flat). From the difference in shadow length, he calculated the size of Earth's sphere and it turned out to be 25,000 miles in circumference.

The curvature of such a sphere is about 0.000126 per mile, a quantity very close to 0 per mile as you can see, and one not easily measured by the techniques at the disposal of the ancients. The tiny difference between 0 and 0.000126 accounts for the fact that it took so long to pass from the flat Earth to the spherical Earth.

Mind you, even a tiny difference, such as that between 0 and 0.000126, can be extremely important. That difference mounts up. The Earth cannot be mapped over large areas with any accuracy at all if the difference isn't taken into account and if the Earth isn't considered a sphere rather than a flat surface. Long ocean voyages can't be undertaken with any reasonable way of locating one's own position in the ocean unless the Earth is considered spherical rather than flat.

Furthermore, the flat Earth presupposes the possibility of an infinite Earth, or of the existence of an "end" to the surface. The spherical Earth, however, postulates an Earth that is both endless and yet finite, and it is the latter postulate that is consistent with all later findings.

So although the flat-Earth theory is only slightly wrong and is a credit to its inventors, all things considered, it is wrong enough to be discarded in favor of the spherical-Earth theory.

And yet is the Earth a sphere?

No, it is *not* a sphere; not in the strict mathematical sense. A sphere has certain mathematical properties—for instance, all diameters (that is, all straight lines that pass from one point on its surface, through the center, to another point on its surface) have the same length.

That, however, is not true of the Earth. Various diameters of the Earth differ in length.

What gave people the notion the Earth wasn't a true sphere? To begin with, the Sun and the Moon have outlines that are perfect circles within the limits of measurement in the early days of the telescope. This is consistent with the supposition that the Sun and Moon are perfectly spherical in shape.

However, when Jupiter and Saturn were observed by the first

telescopic observers, it became quickly apparent that the outlines of those planets were not circles, but distinct ellipses. That meant that Jupiter and Saturn were not true spheres.

Isaac Newton, toward the end of the seventeenth century, showed that a massive body would form a sphere under the pull of gravitational forces (exactly as Aristotle had argued), but only if it were not rotating. If it were rotating, a centrifugal effect would be set up which would lift the body's substance against gravity, and this effect would be greater the closer to the equator you progressed. The effect would also be greater the more rapidly a spherical object rotated and Jupiter and Saturn rotated very rapidly indeed.

The Earth rotated much more slowly than Jupiter or Saturn so the effect should be smaller, but it should still be there. Actual measurements of the curvature of the Earth were carried out in the eighteenth century and Newton was proved correct.

The Earth has an equatorial bulge, in other words. It is flattened at the poles. It is an "oblate spheroid" rather than a sphere. This means that the various diameters of the Earth differ in length. The longest diameters are any of those that stretch from one point on the equator to an opposite point on the equator. This "equatorial diameter" is 12,755 kilometers (7,927 miles). The shortest diameter is from the North Pole to the South Pole and this "polar diameter" is 12,711 kilometers (7,900 miles).

The difference between the longest and shortest diameters is 44 kilometers (27 miles), and that means that the "oblateness" of the Earth (its departure from true sphericity) is $44/12,755$, or 0.0034. This amounts to $1/3$ of 1 percent.

To put it another way, on a flat surface, curvature is 0 per mile everywhere. On Earth's spherical surface, curvature is 0.000126 per mile everywhere (or 8 inches per mile). On Earth's oblate spheroidical surface, the curvature varies from 7.973 inches to the mile to 8.027 inches to the mile.

The correction in going from spherical to oblate spheroidal is much smaller than going from flat to spherical. Therefore, although the notion of the Earth as sphere is wrong, strictly speaking, it is not *as* wrong as the notion of the Earth as flat.

Even the oblate-spheroidal notion of the Earth is wrong, strictly speaking. In 1958, when the satellite *Vanguard I* was put into orbit about the Earth, it was able to measure the local gravitational pull of the Earth—and therefore its shape—with unprecedented precision. It turned out that the equatorial bulge south of the equator was slightly bulgier than the bulge north of the equator, and that the South Pole sea level was slightly nearer the center of the Earth than the North Pole sea level was.

There seemed no other way of describing this than by saying the Earth was pearshaped and at once many people decided that the Earth was nothing like a sphere but was shaped like a Bartlett pear dangling in space. Actually, the pearlike deviation from oblate-spheroid perfect was a matter of yards rather than miles and the adjustment of curvature was in the millionths of an inch per mile.

In short, my English Lit friend, living in a mental world of absolute rights and wrongs, may be imagining that because all theories are *wrong,* the Earth may be thought spherical now, but cubical next century, and a hollow icosahedron the next, and a doughnut shape the one after.

What actually happens is that once scientists get hold of a good concept they gradually refine and extend it with greater and greater subtlety as their instruments of measurement improve. Theories are not so much wrong as incomplete.

This can be pointed out in many other cases than just the shape of the Earth. Even when a new theory seems to represent a revolution, it usually arises out of small refinements. If something more than a small refinement were needed, then the old theory would never have endured.

Copernicus switched from an Earth-centered planetary system to a Sun-centered one. In doing so, he switched from something that was obvious to something that was apparently ridiculous. However, it was a matter of finding better ways of calculating the motion of the planets in the sky and, eventually, the geocentric theory was just left behind. It was precisely because the old theory gave results that were fairly good by the measurement standards of the time that kept it in being so long.

Again, it is because the geological formations of the Earth change *so* slowly and the living things upon it evolve *so* slowly that it seemed reasonable at first to suppose that there was *no* change and that Earth and life always existed as they do today. If that were so, it would make no difference whether Earth and life were billions of years old or thousands. Thousands were easier to grasp.

But when careful observation showed that Earth and life were changing at a rate that was very tiny but *not* zero, then it became clear that Earth and life had to be very old. Modern geology came into being, and so did the notion of biological evolution.

If the rate of change were more rapid, geology and evolution would have reached their modern state in ancient times. It is only because the difference between the rate of change in a static Universe and the rate of change in an evolutionary one is that between zero and very nearly zero that the creationists can continue propagating their folly.

Again, how about the two great theories of the twentieth century—relativity and quantum mechanics?

Newton's theories of motion and gravitation were very close to right, and they would have been absolutely right if only the speed of light were infinite. However, the speed of light is finite, and that had to be taken into account in Einstein's relativistic equations, which were an extension and refinement of Newton's equations.

You might say that the difference between infinite and finite is itself infinite, so why didn't Newton's equations fall to the ground at once? Let's put it another way, and ask how long it takes light to travel over a distance of a meter.

If light traveled at infinite speed, it would take light 0 seconds to travel a meter. At the speed at which light actually travels, however, it takes it 0.0000000033 seconds. It is that difference between 0 and 0.0000000033 that Einstein corrected for.

Conceptually, the correction was as important as the correction of Earth's curvature from 0 to 8 inches per mile was. Speeding subatomic particles wouldn't behave the way they do without the correction, nor would particle accelerators work the way they do, nor nuclear bombs explode, nor the stars shine. Nevertheless, it was a tiny correction and it is no wonder that Newton, in his time, could not allow for it, since he was limited in his observations to speeds and distances over which the correction was insignificant.

Again, where the prequantum view of physics fell short was that it didn't allow for the "graininess" of the Universe. All forms of energy had been thought to be continuous and to be capable of division into indefinitely smaller and smaller quantities.

This turned out to be not so. Energy comes in quanta, the size of which is dependent upon something called Planck's constant. If Planck's constant were equal to 0 erg-seconds, then energy would be continuous, and there would be no grain to the Universe. Planck's constant, however, is equal to 0.0000000000000-000000000000066 erg-seconds. That is indeed a tiny deviation from zero, so tiny that ordinary questions of energy in everyday life need not concern themselves with it. When, however, you deal with subatomic particles, the graininess is sufficiently large, in comparison, to make it impossible to deal with them without taking quantum considerations into account.

Since the refinements in theory grow smaller and smaller, even quite ancient theories must have been sufficiently right to allow advances to be made; advances that were not wiped out by subsequent refinements.

The Greeks introduced the notion of latitude and longitude, for instance, and made reasonable maps of the Mediterranean basin even without taking sphericity into account, and we still use latitude and longitude today.

The Sumerians were probably the first to establish the principle that planetary movements in the sky exhibit regularity and can be predicted, and they proceeded to work out ways of doing so even though they assumed the Earth to be the center of the Universe. Their measurements have been enormously refined but the principle remains.

Newton's theory of gravitation, while incomplete over vast distances and enormous speeds, is perfectly suitable for the Solar System. Halley's Comet appears punctually as Newton's theory of gravitation and laws of motion predict. All of rocketry is based on Newton, and *Voyager II* reached Uranus within a second of the predicted time. None of these things were outlawed by relativity.

In the nineteenth century, before quantum theory was dreamed of, the laws of thermodynamics were established, including the conservation of energy as first law, and the inevitable increase of entropy as the second law. Certain other conservation laws such as those of momentum, angular momentum, and electric charge were also established. So were Maxwell's laws of electromagnetism. All remained firmly entrenched even after quantum theory came in.

Naturally, the theories we now have might be considered wrong in the simplistic sense of my English Lit correspondent, but in a much truer and subtler sense, they need only be considered incomplete.

For instance, quantum theory has produced something called "quantum weirdness" which brings into serious question the very nature of reality and which produces philosophical conundrums that physicists simply can't seem to agree upon. It may be that we have reached a point where the human brain can no longer grasp matters, or it may be that quantum theory is incomplete and that once it is properly extended, all the "weirdness" will disappear.

Again, quantum theory and relativity seem to be independent of each other, so that while quantum theory makes it seem possible that three of the four known interactions can be combined into one mathematical system, gravitation—the realm of relativity—as yet seems intransigent.

If quantum theory and relativity can be combined, a true "unified field theory" may become possible.

If all this is done, however, it would be a still finer refinement that would affect the edges of the known—the nature of the Big Bang and the creation of the Universe, the properties at the center of black holes, some subtle points about the evolution of galaxies and supernovas, and so on.

Virtually all that we know today, however, would remain untouched and when I say I am glad that I live in a century when the Universe is essentially understood, I think I am justified.

# AFTERWORD

In the introduction to the foregoing essay I mention John W. Campbell, Jr. (1910–71), the greatest editor the field has ever seen or is ever likely to see.

I met him in 1938 and we grew very close. For years, he carefully studied my writing and discussed my stories with me at length, making suggestions for the revision of old stories and for the writing of new ones. I learned from him more about science fiction than I learned from everyone else put together, and I have never hesitated to say that I owe my career to him.

He was important to me in another way, too, and one that I less frequently talk about. Perhaps I should mention it here. John Campbell knew everything there was to know about science fiction, but he also knew everything there was to know about twisted misapprehensions concerning science and society. As soon as he got away from science fiction, he was always wrong— but was so clever and persuasive that it was all but impossible to *prove* him wrong, no matter how ridiculous his point of view.

I got an incredible amount of practice in argumentation as a result of forever trying to set him straight, and he sharpened my ability to argue logically to a nearly infinite extent. It's conceivable he did it on purpose.

# 29

## A Sacred Poet

I heard, once, that the oratory of William Jennings Bryan, the populist leader of the Democratic party in the first decade of this century, was likened to the North Platte River of his home state, Nebraska. His oratory, they said, like the river, "was two miles wide and a foot deep."

Well, last night I met a very amiable and likable gentleman who had spent decades in researching a particular subject and the result was that his knowledge was, in my opinion, two miles deep, but only a foot wide.

He gave a talk and, in the question-and-answer session that followed, I had a little set-to with him. Twice I tried to make my point, and twice he drowned me in irrelevant chatter. When I tried a third time, with a ringing "Nevertheless," the moderator stopped me for fear I would forget my manners and offend the man.

In the course of the few things I *did* have a chance to say, however, I quoted the Latin poet Horace. No, I didn't quote him in Latin because I am not that kind of scholar, but I quoted him in English, which was good enough. The quotation goes as follows:

"Many brave men lived before Agamemnon, but all are overwhelmed in eternal night, unwept, unknown, because they lack a sacred poet."

By this (which, by the way, was quite apropos of the point I was trying to make) Horace meant that not all Agamemnon's deeds and heroisms and high rank would have helped him live in memory had it not been that Homer wrote the *Iliad.* It was the poet's work and not the hero's that lived in memory.

Though I didn't get to make my point as I wished, the quote remained in my mind and it led me to the following essay, which will be quite unlike any I have offered you for, lo, these many years. Be patient with me, for I am going to discuss poetry.

Let me make a few things plain, first. I am no expert on poetry. I have a certain facility with parodies and limericks, but there it stops.

Nor do I pretend to any ability at judging the worth of poetry. I can't tell a good poem from a bad one, and I have never had the impulse to be a "critic."

So what am I going to talk about when I discuss poetry? Why, something that doesn't require judgment or poetic understanding, or even critical ability (if there should be such a thing.)

I want to talk about the *effect* of poetry. Some poems have an effect on the world and some poems don't. It has nothing to do with being good or bad. That is a subjective decision and I imagine there will always and eternally be disagreements on such a matter. But there can't be any disagreement about a poem's effectiveness. Let me give you an example.

In 1797, the infant United States built its first warships. One of them, built in Boston, was the *Constitution.* The ship had a brief workout when France and the United States had a minor, unofficial naval war in 1798.

The real test came in 1812, when the United States went to war with Great Britain for a second time. This war started with a humiliation on land. General William Hull, an utter incompetent, surrendered Detroit to the British virtually without a blow. (Hull was court-martialed and condemned to death for this, but was granted a reprieve because of his services in the Revolutionary War.)

What saved American morale in those difficult first months was the feats of our small Navy, which took on the proud British men-of-war and knocked them for a loop. The *Constitution* was under the command of William Hull's younger brother, Isaac Hull. On July 18, 1812, the *Constitution* met up with the British *Guerrière* ("Warrior"), and in two and a half hours riddled it into a Swiss cheese so that it had to be sunk.

On December 19, the *Constitution*, under a new captain, destroyed another British warship off the coast of Brazil. In this second battle, the British cannonballs bounced off the seasoned timbers of the *Constitution*'s hull, doing no damage, and the crew cheered the sight. One cried out that the ship's sides were made of iron. The ship was at once named "Old Ironsides," and it has been known by that name ever since, to the point where I imagine few people remember its real name.

Well, ships grow old, and by 1830 Old Ironsides was obsolete. It had done its work and it was going to be scrapped. The Navy was ready to scrap it, for it had far better ships now. Congress wasn't anxious to spend any more money on it so the scrapping looked good. There were some sentimentalists who thought the ship ought to be preserved as a national treasure, but who cares about a few soft-headed jerks. Besides, you can't fight City Hall, as the saying goes.

In Boston, however, there lived a twenty-one-year-old youngster named Oliver Wendell Holmes. He had just graduated from Harvard, he was planning to study medicine, and he had dashed off reams of poetry. In fact, his fellow students had named him "class poet."

So Holmes wrote a poem entitled "Old Ironsides." Perhaps you know it. Here's the way it goes:

> Ay, tear her tattered ensign down!
>   Long has it waved on high,
> And many an eye has danced to see
>   That banner in the sky;
> Beneath it rung the battle shout,
>   And burst the cannon's roar—

The meteor of the ocean air
　　Shall sweep the clouds no more.

Her deck, once red with heroes' blood,
　　Where knelt the vanquished foe,
When winds were hurrying o'er the flood,
　　And waves were white below,
No more shall feel the victor's tread,
　　Or know the conquered knee—
The harpies of the shore shall pluck
　　The eagle of the sea!

Oh, better that her shattered hulk
　　Should sink beneath the wave;
Her thunders shook the mighty deep,
　　And there should be her grave;
Nail to the mast her holy flag,
　　Set every threadbare sail,
And give her to the god of storms,
　　The lightning and the gale!

The poem was published on September 14, 1830, and was quickly reprinted everywhere.

Is the poem a good one? I don't know. For all I know, critics will say it is mawkish and overblown, and that its images are melodramatic. Perhaps. I only know that I have never been able to read it aloud with a steady voice, particularly when I get to the parts about the harpies and about the threadbare sails. I can't even read it to myself, as I did just now, without gulping and finding it difficult to see the paper.

To critics, that may make me an object of scorn and derision, but the fact is that I'm not, and wasn't, the only one. Wherever that poem appeared, a sudden roar of protest arose from the public. Everyone began contributing money to help save Old Ironsides. The school children brought their pennies to school. There was no stopping it. The Navy and the Congress found itself facing an aroused public and discovered that it wasn't Old Ironsides that was battling the god of storms; *they* were.

They gave in at once. Old Ironsides was *not* scrapped. It was *never* scrapped. It still exists, resting in Boston Harbor, where it will continue to exist indefinitely.

It was not Old Ironsides' feats of war that saved it. It was that it had a sacred poet. Good or bad, the poem was *effective*.

The War of 1812 gave us a poem called "The Defense of Fort McHenry," which was published on September 14, 1814, and was quickly renamed "The Star-Spangled Banner."

It's our national anthem, now. It's difficult to sing (even professional singers have trouble, sometimes) and the words don't flow freely. Most Americans, however patriotic, know only the first line. (I am rather proud of the fact that I know, and can sing without hesitation, all four stanzas.)

All *four* stanzas? Every Fourth of July, the *New York Times* prints the music and all the words of the anthem, and try as you might, you will count only three stanzas. Why? Because during World War II, the government abolished the third stanza as too bloodthirsty.

Remember that the poem was written in the aftermath of the British bombardment of Fort McHenry in Baltimore Harbor. If the fort's guns had been silenced, then the British ships could have disembarked the soldiers they carried. Those soldiers would surely have taken Baltimore and split the nation (which was still hugging the seacoast) in two. Those soldiers had already sacked Washington, which was a small hick town of no importance. Baltimore was an important port.

In the course of the night the ships' guns fell silent, and to Francis Scott Key, on board one of the British ships (trying to get the release of a friend), the whole question was whether the American guns had been silenced and knocked out, or whether the British ships had given up the bombardment. Once the dawn came, the answer would be plain—it would depend on whether the American flag or the British flag was flying over the fort.

The first stanza asks, then, whether the American flag is still flying. The second stanza tell us it *is* still flying. The third stanza is a paean of unashamed triumph and here it is:

And where is that band who so vauntingly swore
　　That the havoc of war and the battle's confusion
A home and a country should leave us no more?

Their blood has washed out their foul footsteps'
   pollution.
No refuge could save the hireling and slave
From the terror of flight, or the gloom of the grave:
   And the star-spangled banner in triumph doth wave
   O'er the land of the free and the home of the brave.

Good poetry? Who knows? Who cares? If you know the tune,
sing it. Get the proper scorn into "foul footsteps," the proper
hatred into "hireling and slave," the proper sadistic glee into the
"terror of flight, or the gloom of the grave" and you'll realize
that it rouses passions a little too strongly. But who knows, there
are times when you may want those passions.

I should point out that music plays its part, too. Sing a poem
and the effect is multiplied manifold.

Consider the American Civil War. For over two years, the
Union suffered one disaster after another in Virginia. The mut-
tonheads who ran the Union army were, one after the other, no
match for Robert E. Lee and Thomas J. "Stonewall" Jackson.
Those were the best soldiers the United States ever produced
and, as Fate would have it, they fought their greatest battles
against the United States.

Why did the North continue to fight? The South was ready to
stop at any time. The North needed only to agree to leave the
South alone, and the war would be over. But the North continued to fight through one bloody debacle after another. One of
the reasons for that was the character of President Abraham
Lincoln, who would not quit under any circumstances—but another was that the North was moved by a religious fervor.

Think of "The Battle Hymn of the Republic". It's a march, yes,
but not a war march. It is God, not man, who is marching. The
key word in the title is "hymn," not "battle," and it is (or should
be) always sung slowly and with the deepest emotion.

Julia Ward Howe, who wrote the words (to the well-known
tune of "John Brown's Body"), had just visited the camps of the
Army of the Potomac in 1862, and was very moved. The hymn
must surely have expressed a great deal of what many Northerners felt. There are five stanzas to the poem and most Americans,

today, barely know the first, but during the Civil War it was all five that were known. Here is the fifth:

In the beauty of the lilies Christ was born across the sea,
With a glory in His bosom that transfigures you and me:
As he died to make men holy, let us die to make men free,
   While God is marching on.

"Let us die to make men free!" I don't say that everyone in the North had that fervor, but some did, and the words may have swayed those on the borderline. After all, *something* kept the Northern armies fighting through disaster after disaster, and "The Battle Hymn" was surely one of the factors.

And if slavery moved some Northerners as an evil that must be fought and destroyed at any cost, there were other Northerners to whom the Union was a benefit that must be supported and preserved at any cost, and there was a song for that, too.

The worst defeat suffered by the Union was in December, 1862, when the unspeakable General Ambrose Burnside, perhaps the most incompetent general ever to lead an American army into battle, sent his soldiers against an impregnable redoubt manned by the Confederate army. Wave after wave of the Union army surged forward, and wave after wave was cut down.

It was after that battle that Lincoln said, "If there is a worse place than Hell, then I am in it." He also remarked of Burnside on a later occasion that he "could snatch defeat from the very jaws of victory."

But, the story goes, as the Northern army lay in camp that night trying to recover, someone struck up a new song that had been written by George Frederick Root, who had already written "Tramp! Tramp! Tramp! The Boys Are Marching." This time he had come up with something called "The Battle Cry of Freedom."

Here is one of the stanzas:

Yes, we'll rally round the flag, boys, we'll rally once again,
   Shouting the battle cry of Freedom.
We will rally from the hillside, we'll gather from the plain,
   Shouting the battle cry of Freedom.
The Union forever! Hurrah, boys, hurrah!

Down with the traitor, and up with the star!
And we'll rally round the flag, boys, we'll rally once again,
    Shouting the battle cry of Freedom.

Even I, with my tin ear, have a sneaking suspicion that this is a
good song but not great poetry, or even adequate poetry, but
(the story continues) a Confederate officer hearing those distant
strains from the defeated army, gave up hope at that moment.
He felt that a defeated army that could still sing that song about
"the Union forever" would never be finally defeated, but would
keep coming back to the assault again and again, and would
never give up till the Confederacy was worn out and could fight
no more. And he was right.

There's something about words and music together that have
an amazing effect.

There's an ancient Greek story, for instance, that may conceivably be true (the Greeks never spoiled a story by worrying over
the facts of the case). According to it, the Athenians, fearful of a
loss in a forthcoming battle, sent to the oracle at Delphi for
advice. The oracle advised them to ask the Spartans to lend them
one soldier.

The Spartans did not like to defy the oracle so they gave the
Athenians one soldier, but, not particularly anxious to help a
rival city to victory, were careful not to give Athens a general or a
renowned fighter. They handed the Athenians a lame regimental
musician. And at the battle, the Spartan musician played and
sang such stirring music that the Athenians, cheering, advanced
on the enemy at a run and swept the field.

Then there's the story (probably also apocryphal) of an event
that took place in the Soviet Union, during the Nazi invasion,
when a group of German soldiers, meticulously dressed in Soviet uniforms, marched into Soviet-held territory in order to
carry out an important sabotage mission. A young boy, seeing
them pass, hastened to the nearest Soviet army post and reported a group of German soldiers dressed in Soviet uniforms.
The Nazis were rounded up and, I presume, given the treatment
routinely accorded spies.

The boy was then asked, "How did you know those were
German soldiers, and not Soviet soldiers?"

And the boy replied, "They weren't singing."

For that matter, did you ever see John Gilbert in *The Big Parade*, a silent movie about World War I? Gilbert has no intention of being caught up in war hysteria and joining the army, but his car is stopped by a parade passing by—men in uniform, the flag flying, instruments blowing and banging away.

It's a silent movie, so you don't hear any words, you don't hear any music (except for the usual piano accompanist), you don't hear any cheering. You see only Gilbert's face behind the wheel, cynically amused. But he has to stay there till the parade is done, and after a moment one of Gilbert's feet is tapping out the time, then both feet are, then he's beginning to look excited and eager and—of course—he gets out of the car to enlist. Without hearing a thing, you find it completely convincing. That *is* how people get caught up and react.

I can give you a personal experience of my own. As you probably can guess from what I've already said, I am not only a Civil War buff, but with respect to that war, I'm an ardent Northern patriot. "The Union forever," that's me.

But once when I was driving from New York to Boston, alone in my car, I was listening to a series of Civil War songs on the car radio. One song I had never heard before and I've never heard since. It was a Confederate song from a desperate time in the war and it was pleading for the South to unite and, with all its strength, throw back the Yankee invaders. And by the time the song was over I was in utter distress, knowing that the war had ended over a century before and that there was no Confederate recruiting station to which I could run and volunteer.

Insidious, the power these things have.

During the Crimean War, with Great Britain and France fighting Russia, the British commanding general, Baron Raglan, gave a command that was so ambiguous and was accompanied by a gesture that was so uncertain that nobody knew exactly what he meant. Because no one dared say, "That's crazy," the order ended by sending 607 men and horses of the Light Brigade charging pell-mell into the main Russian army. In twenty minutes, half the men and horses were casualties and, of course, nothing was accomplished.

The commander of the French contingent, Pierre Bosquet,

stared in disbelief as the men rode their horses into the mouths of cannon and said, "C'est magnifique, mais ce n'est pas la guerre." Freely translated, he was saying, "That's all very nice, but that's not the way you fight a war."

However, Alfred, Lord Tennyson wrote a poem about it, that starts with the familiar:

> Half a league, half a league
> Half a league onward;
> All in the valley of Death
> Rode the six hundred.

He wrote a total of fifty-five lines in a rhythm that mimicked perfectly the sound of galloping horses. Read it properly, and you'll think you're one of the horsemen careening forward on that stupid charge.

Tennyson didn't actually hide the fact that it was a mistake. He says:

> Forward the Light Brigade!
> Was there a man dismayed?
> Not though the soldier knew
> Someone had blundered:
> Theirs not to make reply,
> Theirs not to reason why,
> Theirs but to do and die:
> Into the valley of Death
> Rode the six hundred.

The result is that, thanks to the poem, everyone thinks of the Charge in its heroic aspect, and no one thinks of it as an example of criminally inept generalship.

Sometimes a poem totally distorts history and keeps it distorted, too.

In 1775, the British controlled Boston while dissident colonials were concentrated at Concord. General Gage, the British commander, sent a contingent of soldiers to confiscate the arms and powder that was being stored at Concord and to arrest Samuel Adams and John Hancock, who were the ringleaders of dissent.

Secrets weren't kept well, and colonial sympathizers in Boston set out to ride through the night to warn Adams and Hancock to make themselves scarce, and to warn the people in Concord to hide the arms and powder. Two of the riders were Paul Revere and William Dawes. They took different routes but got to Lexington. Adams and Hancock were staying there and, on hearing the news, quickly rode out of town.

Revere and Dawes then went on toward Concord, but were stopped by a British patrol and were arrested. That was it for both of them. Neither one of them ever got to Concord. Neither of them gave the vital warning to the men of Concord.

*However,* in Lexington, Revere and Dawes had been joined by a young doctor named Samuel Prescott, who was still awake because he had been with a woman, doing what I suppose a man and woman would naturally do when alone late at night.

He buttoned his pants and joined the two. *He* avoided the British patrol and managed to get to Concord. *He* got the Concord people roused and ready, with the arms parceled out for defense.

The next day, when the British stormed their way through Lexington and got to Concord, the "minute-men" were waiting for them behind their trees, guns in hand. The British just barely made it back to Boston and the War of the American Revolution had begun.

Lexington-and-Concord remained famous forever after, but the business about people riding to give warning was drowned out somehow. No one knew of it.

In 1863, however, the Civil War was at its height and the North was still looking for its great turning-point victory (which was to come at Gettysburg in July of that year). Henry Wadsworth Longfellow felt the urge to write a patriotic ballad to hearten the Union side, so he dug up the old tale no one remembered and wrote a poem about the warning ride in the night.

And he ended it with a mystical evocation of the ghost of that rider:

> Through all our history, to the last,
> In the hour of darkness and peril and need,
> The people will waken and listen to hear

The hurrying hoof-beats of that steed,
And the midnight message of Paul Revere.

The poem proved immensely popular, and very heartening to its readers, with its implication that the ghosts of the past were fighting on the side of the Union.

But there was an important flaw in it. Longfellow mentioned only Paul Revere, who after all, had never completed the job. It was *Preston* who warned Concord.

And did you ever hear of Preston? Did anyone ever hear of Preston? Of course not. Preston's role is no secret. Any reasonable history book, any decent encyclopedia will tell you all about it.

But what people know is not history, not encyclopedias, but:

Listen, my children, and you shall hear
Of the midnight ride of Paul Revere. . . .

That's the power of a poem, even (if you'll forgive my tin ear and let me make a judgment) of a rotten poem like "Paul Revere's Ride"!

## AFTERWORD

In my first thirty years as a science columnist for *Fantasy and Science Fiction,* I wrote, naturally, 360 essays, one for each month. If I were asked which of all those was my favorite, I would not hesitate. It is the foregoing—my discussion of effective poetry.

It is strange that this should be so, for poetry is not my forte and I will cheerfully agree that I know nothing about it.

However, I was lying awake one night (I am a poor sleeper, and have always been—I *hate* sleeping) and I got to thinking about "Old Ironsides" which, in my younger days, I knew by heart, and from there I went on to other poems that I knew well (virtually all of them nineteenth-century verses by the Romantic poets) and by morning I was exhausted with the various emotions to which they had subjected me.

There was no way in which I could fail to write an essay on the subject. I had never used my column for anything quite as far removed from science as this one was, and I had the feeling that, for the *first time,* the magazine would object to one of my columns. Ed Ferman, the editor, surprised me, however, by going out of his way to tell me how much he liked it.

Then I thought that the readers would storm with disapproval. They didn't. In fact, the essay received more letters and more *approving* letters than any other I had ever published. Go know!

# 30

# The Longest River

One way of achieving an act of creativity is to look at something in an unexpected way.

Thus, for thousands of years, the hole in the needle was put at the blunt end, so that the thread followed like a long tail after the needle had pierced the cloth. But when people tried to invent a sewing machine, nothing worked until Elias Howe had the brilliant turnabout idea of putting the hole near the point of the needle.

We who write science fiction find a particular necessity in looking at things differently, for we must deal with societies other than those that exist. A society that looks at everything in the same way we do is not a different society. After nearly half a century of science fiction writing, that sort of sideways squint has therefore become second nature to me.

Thus, at a meeting over which I was presiding, a couple of weeks ago, a member rose to introduce his two guests.

He said, "Let me introduce, first, Mr. John Doe, who is a

brilliant lawyer and an absolute expert in bridge. Let me also introduce Dr. Richard Roe, who is a great psychiatrist and a past master at poker." He then smiled bashfully, and said, "So you see where my interest lies."

Whereupon I said, quite automatically, "Yes, in working up lawsuits against psychotics," and brought the house down.

But to get to the point . . .

More than twenty years ago, I wrote an essay on the great rivers of the world ("Old Man River," *F&SF*, November, 1966).* Ever since then, I've had it in my mind to devote an entire essay to just one river. Naturally, it would have to be the largest river of them all, the one that drains the greatest territory, the one that delivers the most water to the sea, the one that is so mighty that all other rivers are merely rivulets compared to it. The river I speak of is, of course, the Amazon.

Now the time has come, and even as I sit down, with satisfaction, to write the essay, the kaleidoscope I call my mind suddenly heaves, rattles, and changes shape. I think: Why should I be impressed merely by size, by gigantism? Why shouldn't I devote myself to a river that has done most for humanity?

And which should that be but the Nile.

In one respect, the Nile *is* an example of gigantism. It is much smaller than the Amazon in that it delivers far less water to the sea, but it is *longer* than the Amazon. It is, indeed, the longest river in the world, for it is 6,736 kilometers (4,187 miles) long compared to a length of about 6,400 kilometers (4,000 miles) for the Amazon, which is second longest.

The difference between them is that the Amazon flows west to east along the equator, through the largest rain forest in the world. It is constantly being rained on and has, in addition, a dozen tributaries that are mighty rivers in their own right. By the time it reaches the Atlantic, then, it is delivering some 200,000 cubic meters (7,000,000 cubic feet) of water per second, and its outflow can be detected over 300 kilometers (200 miles) out into the sea. The Nile, on the other hand, flows south to north, beginning in tropical Africa, but with its northern half flowing

* See my book *Science, Numbers, and I* (Doubleday, 1968)

through the Sahara Desert without tributaries, so that it receives no water at all, but merely evaporates. No wonder it finally discharges into the Mediterranean only a small fraction of the water discharged by the mighty Amazon.

But the Sahara was not always a desert region. Twenty thousand years ago, glaciers covered much of Europe and cool winds brought moisture to northern Africa. What is now desert was then a pleasant land with rivers and lakes, forests and grassland. Human beings, as yet uncivilized, roamed the area and left behind their stone tools.

Gradually, however, as the glaciers retreated, and the cool winds drifted ever farther north year by year, the climate of North Africa grew hotter and drier. Droughts came and slowly grew worse. Plants died and animals retreated to regions that were still wet enough to support them. Human beings retreated also, many toward the Nile which, in that long-distant time, was a wider river, one that snaked lazily through broad areas of marsh and swamp and delivered far more water to the Mediterranean. Indeed the valley of the Nile was not at all an inviting place for human occupancy until after it had dried out somewhat.

When the Nile was still too wet and swampy to be entirely enticing, there was a lake that existed to its west, about 210 kilometers (130 miles) south of the Mediterranean. In later times, this body of water came to be called Lake Moeris by the Greeks. It existed as a last reminder of a northern Africa that had once been much better watered that it was in later times. There were hippopotami in Lake Moeris and other, smaller game. From 4500 to 4000 B.C., flourishing villages of the late Stone Age lined its shores.

The lake suffered, however, from the continued drying out of the land. As its level fell, and the animal life it supported grew sparser, the villages along its shore withered. At the same time, though, population grew along the nearby Nile, which became more manageable.

By 3000 B.C., Lake Moeris could only exist in decent size if it were somehow connected with the Nile and was able to draw water from the river. It required increasing exertion, however, to keep the ditch between the two dredged and working.

The battle to do so was finally lost and the lake is now almost gone. In its place is a depression, mostly dry, at the bottom of which is a shallow body of water, now called Birket Qarun. It is about 50 kilometers (30 miles) long west to east and 8 kilometers (5 miles) long north to south. Near the shores of this last remnant of old Lake Moeris is the city of El Fayum that gives it name to the entire depression.

To go on to the next step requires a small digression. . . .

In 8000 B.C., human beings the world over were hunters and gatherers, as they had been for ages. The total population of the Earth may then have been only eight million, or about as many people as there are in New York City today.

But at about that time, some people in what is now called the Middle East learned how to plan for the future where food was concerned.

Instead of hunting animals and killing them on the spot, human beings kept some alive, cared for them, encouraged them to breed, and killed a few, now and then, for food. They also got milk, eggs, wool, skins, and even work, out of them.

Again, instead of just gathering what plant food they came across, human beings learned to sow plants and care for them, so that eventually they could be harvested and eaten. Clearly, human beings could sow a much greater concentration of edible plants than they were likely to find in a state of nature.

By herding animals and farming plants, groups of human beings vastly increased their food supply, and their population grew rapidly. Increasing population meant that more plants could be grown and more animals cared for, so that in general there was a surplus of food, something that had never happened (except for brief periods immediately after a large kill) in the old hunting and gathering days.

This meant that not everyone had to labor at growing food. Some could make pottery and exchange it for food. Some could be metalworkers. Some could be tellers of tales. In short people could begin to specialize, and society began to gain variety and sophistication.

Of course, farming had its penalty. As long as one merely hunted and gathered, one could avoid conflict. If a stronger band encroached on a tribe's territory, it could prudently retreat to some safer place. Not much was lost in the process. The tribe only owned what it could carry and they would take that along.

Farmers, however, owned land, and that was immovable. If marauding bands, intent on stealing the farmers' food stores, swooped down, the farmers had no choice but to fight. To retreat and give up their farms would mean starvation, since there were now too many of them to be supported by any means other than farming.

This meant that farmers had to band together, for in union there was strength. Their houses were built in clusters. They would choose some site with a good natural water supply, and surround their houses by a wall for security. They then had what we would today call a "city" (from the Latin "civis"). The inhabitants of cities are "citizens," and the kind of social system in which cities are prevalent is called "civilization."

In a city in which first hundreds and then thousands of human beings clustered, it would be difficult to live without people stepping all over each other. Rules of living had to be set up. Priests had to be appointed to make those rules, and kings to enforce them. Soldiers had to be trained to fight off marauders. (See how easily we recognize the coming of civilization.)

It is hard to tell now just exactly where agriculture got its very first start. Possibly this was on the borders of the modern nations of Iraq and Iran (the very border over which both nations have now been fighting a useless war for eight years).

One reason for supposing that area was the place where farming (or agriculture, as it is commonly called) began, is that barley and wheat grow wild there, and it is just those plants that lend themselves to cultivation.

There is a site called Jarmo in northern Iraq that was uncovered in 1948. The remains of an old city were found there, revealing the foundations of houses built of thin walls of packed mud and divided into small rooms. The city may have held from one hundred to three hundred people. In the lowest and oldest layer, dating back to 8000 B.C., the evidence of very early farming was uncovered.

Once discovered, of course, the techniques for agriculture spread out slowly from the original center.

What was needed for farming, first and foremost, was water. Jarmo is at the edge of a mountain range, where rising air cools and where the water vapor it holds condenses out as rain. However, even at best, rain can be unreliable, and a dry year will mean a lean harvest and hunger, if not starvation.

A supply of water that is more dependable than rain is that which you get out of a river. For that reason, farms and cities grew up along the banks of rivers, and civilization began to center there.

The nearest rivers to the original farming communities are the twin rivers of the Tigris and Euphrates in what is modern Iraq, and this may therefore have been the site of the earliest large-scale civilization, but it soon spread westward to the Nile and by 5000 B.C. both were flourishing. (Agriculture also spread to the Indus. Some thousands of years later, it began independently in the Hwang-ho region of northern China. Some thousands of years later still, it began among the Mayans of North America and the Incas of South America.)

The crucial discovery of writing, which took place not long before 3000 B.C., was made by the Sumerians, who then lived along the lower reaches of the Tigris-Euphrates valley. Since the use of writing is the boundary line between prehistory and history, the Sumerians were the first people to have a history. The technique was quickly picked up by the Egyptians, however.

Living on a river may mean that farmers have an unfailing source of water whether it rains or not, but the water won't come to the farmer of its own accord. It must be brought there. To do so in pails is clearly ineffective, so one must dig a ditch into which river water can run of its own accord and maintain that ditch to keep it from silting up. In the end a whole network of such irrigation ditches must be built up, with raised banks along them, and along the river, to prevent too-easy flooding.

Taking care of such an irrigation network requires a careful and well-coordinated community effort. This places a premium on good government and capable leadership. It also places a premium on cooperation between the various cities along a river, since if a city upstream is wasteful of water, or pollutes it, or allows flooding, that will harm all the cities downstream.

There is a certain pressure, therefore, to develop a river-wide government, or what we would refer to as a nation.

Nationhood came first to Egypt, and the reason is the Nile.

The Nile is a placid river, not given at all to violent moods. This means that even primitive boats, inefficient in design and fragile in structure, can float on the Nile without trouble. There is no fear of storms.

What's more, the water flows northward and the wind usually blows southward. This means that one can hoist a simple sail if one wishes to be blown upriver (south) and then take it down if you wish the current to carry you downriver (north). Thanks to the quality of the Nile, then, people and goods could easily move from city to city.

Such movement up and down the river insured that the city-states would share a language and a culture and feel a certain economic interdependence and communal understanding.

As for the Sumerians, they had two rivers. One, the Tigris, was too turbulent to be navigable by simple means (hence its name, "tiger"). The Euphrates is more easily handled and the major Sumerian cities therefore lined its banks. Still, it was not quite the placid highway that the Nile was, and the Sumerian cities felt more isolated than the Egyptians did and were therefore less prone to cooperation.

Furthermore, while the Nile was bounded on both sides by deserts that kept outsiders at bay, the Euphrates was less well-protected and more open to raids and to settlement by surrounding peoples. This meant that the Tigris-Euphrates valley contained also Akkadians, Arameans, and other peoples whose language and culture was different from that of the Sumerians, while the population along the Nile, on the other hand, was quite uniform.

Consequently, it is not surprising that Egypt was unified before the peoples of the Tigris-Euphrates were. Somewhere around 2850 B.C., a ruler named Narmer (known as Menes to the Greeks) united the cities of the Nile under his rule and established the nation of Egypt. We don't know the details of how this was done, but it seems to have been a relatively peaceful process.

The Sumerian cities, however, fought each other viciously and the region was not unified till 2360 B.C., five centuries after the

Egyptians had been. What's more, the Sumerians had fought themselves into war-weary weakness, so that the union was brought about by a non-Sumerian, Sargon of Agade. He established his rule by harsh conquest and brought under his banner a variety of languages and cultures, so that Sargon's unified kingdom was not a nation but, rather, an empire.

An empire tends to be less stable than a nation, as the dominated ethnic groups feel resentment against the dominating one. The Tigris-Euphrates valley therefore saw a succession of upsets as first one group and then another gained predominance, or as raiders from outside took advantage of internal disunion to establish themselves. Egypt, in contrast, was an extraordinarily stable society for its first twelve centuries of nationhood.

Then there is the matter of the calendar.

Primitive people use the Moon for the purpose, since the Moon's phases repeat themselves every 29½ days. That is a period that is short enough to handle and long enough to be useful. It gives us the "lunar month," which can be 29 and 30 days long in alternation.

Eventually, it was noted that every 12 months or so the seasons went through their cycle. Twelve lunar months after sowing time, it was sowing time again, in other words. Of course, the seasons are not as reliable as the phases of the Moon. Springs can be cold and late, or mild and early. In the long run, it was clear, however, that 12 lunar months (which have a total of 354 days) was not quite long enough to mark the cycle of the seasons. After two or three years, a lunar calendar of this sort would indicate sowing time so much earlier than it should be that it would lead to disaster.

For that reason a 13th month had to be added to the year every now and then if the lunar calendar was to be kept even with the seasonal cycle. Eventually, a 19-year cycle was established within which 12 years had, in a certain fixed order, 12 lunar months, or 354 days, and seven had 13 lunar months, or 383 days. This meant that, on the average, the year was 365 days long.

This calendar was awfully complicated but it worked and it spread to other peoples, including the Greeks and the Jews. The

Jewish liturgical calendar to this day is the one developed by the people of the Tigris-Euphrates.

The early Egyptians were aware of and used the lunar months, but they were also aware of something else. The Nile (as we know, but they did not) rises among the mountains of east central Africa. When the rainy season comes to that distant region, water tumbles into the lakes and rivers, and surges down the Nile. The level of the Nile rises and the river floods over its banks for a period of time, leaving a deposit of rich, fertile silt behind. It is the Nile flood which insures the harvest, and the Egyptians awaited it eagerly, for in the years when it was late, scanty, or both, they would see hard times.

The close attention Egyptians paid to the flooding of the Nile made them realize that it came, on the average, every 365 days, and it seemed to them that it was this period that was of overwhelming importance. They, therefore, adopted a solar calendar. They made every month 30 days long, so that twelve of them marked 360 days, and added five monthless holidays at the end before starting another cycle of twelve months. In this way the months were "calendar months" that were out of step with the Moon, but in step with the seasons.

Actually, it was not quite in step with the seasons. The year is not 365 days long, but very close to 365¼. The Egyptians could not help but understand this, for every year the Nile flood came six hours later (on the average) according to the Egyptian calendar. This meant that the date of the flood wandered through the entire calendar and returned to the original date only after 365 × 4, or 1,460 years.

This wandering could have been prevented by adding a 366th day to the year every four years, but the Egyptians never bothered to do this. However, when the Romans finally adopted the Egyptian calendar in 46 B.C., they spread those five extra days through the year, giving some months 31 days, and added an extra day every four years. That (with very minor modifications) is the calendar the whole world uses today—for secular purposes, anyway.

The Nile flood sometimes wiped away the markings that separated the holdings of one family from those of another. Methods had to be devised to redetermine those boundaries. It is thought that this slowly gave rise to the methods of calculation that we know as "geometry" (from Greek words meaning "to measure the Earth").

Those same floods assured Egypt of so much food that it could afford to trade the surplus to surrounding peoples not blessed with the Nile and to get in exchange foreign artisanry. The Nile thus encouraged international trade.

What's more, with the large food surplus, it was not necessary to put every pair of hands to work growing food. There was an ample labor supply to be put to the task of what we would today call "public works." The prize example, of course, was the raising of the Pyramids between 2600 and 2450 B.C.

It may be that the Pyramids set the example of gigantism in architecture in the Western world. The latest manifestation of this I can see from my apartment windows—the total conversion of Manhattan into light-dimming skyscrapers.

To my way of thinking, then, the Nile has given us one of the two earliest civilizations, the first nation, the solar calendar, geometry, international trade, and public works. It has also given us a mystery that has intrigued human beings for thousands of years. Where does the Nile originate? What is its source?

The ancient world of western Asia and the Mediterranean knew of seven rivers with lengths of 1,900 kilometers (1,180 miles) or more. Leaving out the Nile, the other six, together with their lengths, are:

> Euphrates—3,600 kilometers (2,235 miles)
> Indus—2,900 kilometers (1,800 miles)
> Danube—2,850 kilometers (1,770 miles)
> Oxus—2,540 kilometers (1,580 miles)
> Jaxartes—2,200 kilometers (1,370 miles)
> Tigris—1,900 kilometers (1,180 miles)

The Persian Empire included the Tigris and Euphrates in their totality. The Oxus and the Indus were at the eastern extremity of that Empire and the Jaxartes was just beyond the northeastern boundary. The Danube formed the northern boundary of much of the European dominions of the Roman Empire. The source of each of these rivers was known as a matter of public knowledge, or, in the case of the Oxus and Jaxartes, from travelers' reports.

That left the Nile. It was the core of Egypt from the beginning and was included eventually in the Persian Empire and, still later, in the Roman Empire. The Nile, however, was twice as long (as we now know) as the longest of the other rivers, and it extended outside the limits of civilization right down into modern times, so that in all that time no one knew where the source was.

The Egyptians were the first to wonder. About 1678 B.C., the land was invaded by Asians who were using the horse and chariot for warfare—something the Egyptians had not encountered before. The Egyptians finally managed to throw them out about 1570 B.C.

In reaction, the Egyptians invaded Asia in its turn and established the "Egyptian Empire." For nearly four centuries, Egypt was the strongest power in the world.

Under the Empire, the Egyptians also expanded up the Nile. The Nile has occasional sections of rough water ("cataracts") that are numbered from the north to the south. The First Cataract is at the city known as Syene to the ancient Greeks and as Aswan to us today. This is 885 kilometers (550 miles) south of the Mediterranean. It was a navigation problem, and Egypt proper did not extend south of the First Cataract. Even today modern Egypt extends only about 225 kilometers (140 miles) south of the Cataract.

South of the First Cataract was a nation called Nubia. Today it is called Sudan. Occasionally, strong Egyptian monarchs had attempted to extend their dominion beyond the First Cataract, and, under the Empire, that effort reached its maximum. The Empire's greatest conqueror, Thutmose III, penetrated, about 1460 B.C., to the Fourth Cataract, where the Nubian capital of Napata stood.

Napata is about 2,000 kilometers (1,250 miles) upstream from the mouth of the Nile and the river is still going strong, still mighty, showing no signs of dwindling to its source.

The later conquerors of Egypt—the Ptolemies, the Romans, and the Muslims—made no effort to extend their political control south of the First Cataract. If anyone explored southward, no coherent account of their travels remain.

The first modern European to venture south of Aswan was a Scottish explorer, James Bruce (1730–94). In 1770 he traveled to Khartoum (the modern capital of Sudan) which is about 640 kilometers (400 miles) upstream from the ruins of Napata. There two rivers join to form the Nile. One (the Blue Nile) comes in from the southeast; the other (the White Nile) comes in from the southwest.

Bruce followed the Blue Nile upstream for something like 1,300 kilometers (800 miles) and finally came to Lake Tana in northwest Ethiopia. He felt that to be the source of the Nile, but he was wrong. The Blue Nile is merely a tributary. It is the White Nile that is the main stream.

Arab traders had brought back vague tales of great lakes in East Africa, and some European explorers thought that those might well be the source of the White Nile. Two English explorers, Richard Francis Burton (1821–90) and John Hanning Speke (1827–64), started from Zanzibar on the east African coast in 1857 and by February, 1858, reached Lake Tanganyika, a long, narrow body of water 1,000 kilometers (620 miles) from the African coast.

By then, Burton had had enough and left. Speke, however, moved northward on his own and, on July 30, 1858, reached Lake Victoria. This is 69,500 square kilometers (26,818 square miles) in area, so that it is a little larger than West Virginia. It is the largest lake in Africa and the only fresh-water lake that is larger is Lake Superior, which has an area one-fifth greater than that of Victoria.

The White Nile issues from the northern rim of Lake Victoria, which can thus represent the source of the river. However, the longest river that flows *into* Lake Victoria is the Luvironza, which is 1,150 kilometers (715 miles) long, and flows into the lake from the west.

A drop of water from the headwaters of the Luvironza could flow into Lake Victoria and out again into the White Nile and from there to the Mediterranean, traveling 6,736 kilometers (4,187 miles).

The source of the Luvironza is, therefore, the source of the

Nile, and it is located in the modern nation of Burundi, about 55 kilometers (35 miles) east of Lake Tanganyika. When Burton broke away, he was almost at the source of the Nile.

But, then, how was he to know?

## AFTERWORD

This essay is a rather quiet and non-controversial one, but it approaches history from my own, somewhat unusual, point of view.

History, like mathematics, is something I love more than it loves me. When I was in college, as a matter of fact, I debated with myself whether to major in history or in chemistry. I decided on chemistry, because I felt that as a historian I would be condemned to the academic life, whereas as a chemist, I might go out into industry or into a research institute.

This was unbelievably foolish of me, for when I finally became a chemist, I realized that industry was not for me, and I remained in the academic life.

I have, however, never forgotten history, for I have written many history books as well as many scientific books, and even when I discuss science I tend to approach it historically. I am so grateful that my publishers tend to humor me and publish whatever I write so that I can indulge *all* my various penchants—chemistry *and* history (and everything else that catches my fancy as well).

# 31

## The Secret of the Universe

Paradoxes, in the sense of self-contradictory statements, have always irritated me. It's my firm belief that the Universe works in such a way that self-contradictions do not occur. If, then, it seems we have a paradox, it can only because we have perversely insisted on saying something we should not say.

Here, for instance, is an example of a paradox. Suppose that a certain town contains only one barber and that he shaves every man in the town except those who shave themselves. The question is: Who shaves the barber?

The barber cannot shave himself because he shaves only those who do not shave themselves. On the other hand, if he doesn't shave himself, he is bound, by the terms of the statement, to shave himself.

The paradox only arises, however, if we insist on making statements that already possess the seeds of self-contradiction. The proper way of making a *sensible* statement about the situation is to say: "The barber shaves himself and, in addition, every other man in the town except those who shave themselves." Then there is no paradox.

Here's another one: A certain despotic monarch has decreed that anyone crossing a certain bridge must declare his destination and his purpose for going there. If he lies, he must be hanged. If he tells the truth, he must be left in peace.

A certain man, crossing the bridge, is asked his destination and answers, "I am going to the gallows for the purpose of being hanged."

Well, then, if he is now hanged, he was telling the truth and should have been left in peace. But if he is left in peace, he told a lie and should have been hanged. Back and forth. Back and forth.

Again, that answer must be anticipated and must be ruled out of bounds or the decree is senseless. (In real life, I imagine the despotic monarch would say, "Hang him for being a wise guy," or "He hasn't told the truth till after he was hanged, whereupon you can allow his corpse to go in peace.")

In mathematics, there *is* the tendency to forbid the sources of paradox. For instance, if division by zero were allowed, it could be easily proved that all numbers of any kind were equal. So, to prevent that, mathematicians arbitrarily forbid division by zero, and that's all there is to that.

More subtle paradoxes in mathematics have their uses, since they stimulate thought and encourage the increase of mathematical rigor. Back in 450 B.C., for instance, a Greek philosopher, Zeno of Elea, advanced four paradoxes, all of which tended to show that motion, as it was sensed, was impossible.

The best-known of these paradoxes is usually known as "Achilles and the Tortoise" and this is the way it goes:

Suppose that Achilles (the fleetest of the Greek heroes involved in the siege of Troy) could run ten times as fast as a tortoise, and suppose the two take part in a race, with the tortoise given a ten-yard head start.

In that case, it can be argued that Achilles cannot possibly overtake the tortoise, for by the time Achilles has covered the ten yards between himself and the tortoise's original position, the tortoise has advanced one yard. When Achilles covers the additional yard, the tortoise has advanced another tenth of a yard, and by the time Achilles runs that distance the tortoise has advanced a hundredth of a yard, and so on forever. Achilles comes ever closer, but he can't ever quite catch up.

The reasoning is impeccable, but we all know that, in actual truth, Achilles would quickly pass the tortoise. In fact, if two people, A and B, are having a race, and if A can run faster than B by even the smallest measure, A will eventually overtake and pass B, even if B has a very large (but finite) head start, provided both parties travel at a constant best speed for an indefinitely prolonged period.

There's the paradox, then. Logical reasoning shows that Achilles cannot overtake the tortoise, and simple observation shows that he can and does.

This stumped mathematicians for two thousand years, partly because it seemed to be taken for granted that if you have an infinite series of numbers, such as $10 + 1 + \frac{1}{10} + \frac{1}{100} \ldots$ , then the sum must be infinite and the time it takes to cross a distance represented by such numbers must also be infinite.

Eventually, though, mathematicians realized that this apparently obvious assumption—that an infinite set of numbers, however small, must have an infinite sum—was simply wrong. The Scottish mathematician James Gregory (1638–75) is usually given credit for making this clear about 1670.

In hindsight, this is surprisingly easy to show. Consider the series $10 + 1 + \frac{1}{10} + \frac{1}{100}. \ldots$ Add 10 and 1 and you have 11; add $\frac{1}{10}$ to that and you have 11.1; add $\frac{1}{100}$ to that and you have 11.11; add $\frac{1}{1,000}$ to that and you have 11.111. If you add an infinite number of such terms, you end up with $11.111111 \ldots$ $\ldots$ But such an infinite decimal number is only $11\frac{1}{9}$ in fractions.

Consequently, the entire infinite set of ever-decreasing numbers that represents the lead of the tortoise over Achilles has a total sum of $11\frac{1}{9}$ yards and Achilles overtakes the tortoise in the time it takes him to run $11\frac{1}{9}$ yards.

An infinite series with a finite sum is a "converging series," and the simplest example, by my judgment, is $1 + \frac{1}{2} + \frac{1}{4} + \frac{1}{8}. \ldots$ , where each term is half the one before. If you start adding together the terms of such a series you will have no trouble convincing yourself that the sum of the entire infinite set is, simply, 2.

An infinite series with an infinite sum is a "diverging series." Thus, the series $1 + 2 + 4 + 8$. . . . clearly grows larger and larger without limit, so that the sum can be said to be infinite.

It isn't always easy to tell if a series is divergent or convergent. For instance, the series $1 + 1/2 + 1/3 + 1/4 + 1/5$. . . . is divergent. If you add the terms, the sum grows continually larger. To be sure, the growth in the value of the sum becomes slower and slower, but if you take enough terms you can get a sum that is higher than 2, or 3, or 4, or any higher number you care to name.

I believe that this series is the most gently divergent it is possible to have.

I learned about convergent series, if I recall correctly, in my high school course in intermediate algebra, when I was fourteen, and it really struck me in a heap.

Unfortunately, I am not a natural mathematician. There were those who, even in their teenaged years, could grasp truly subtle mathematical relationships; men like Galois, Clairaut, Pascal, Gauss, and so on; but I was not one of them by several light-years.

I struggled with converging series and managed to see something in a vague, unsystematic way and now, over half a century later, with a great deal more experience, I can present those teenage thoughts in a much more sensible way.

Let's consider the series $1 + 1/2 + 1/4 + 1/8 + 1/16$ . . . and try to find a way of representing them by something we can easily visualize. Imagine a series of squares, for instance, the first one being 1 centimeter on each side, the second 1/2 centimeter, the third 1/4 centimeter, the fourth 1/8 centimeter, and so on.

Imagine them all shoved tightly together so that you have the largest square on the left, the second largest adjoining it on the right, then the third largest, the fourth and so on. You have a line of an infinite number of smaller and smaller squares, side by side.

All of them taken together, *all* of them, would stretch across a total length of two centimeters. The first one would take up half the total length, the next one would take up half of what's left, the next half of what now remains, and so on *forever.*

Naturally, the squares become extremely tiny very rapidly. The 27th square is roughly the size of an atom and once it is placed all that is left of the two-centimeter total is about the width of another atom. Into the second atom's-width, however, an infinite number of further squares still rapidly decreasing in size is squeezed.

The 27th square is roughly 1/100,000,000th of a centimeter on each side, so let's imagine that it and all the squares that follow are magnified a hundred million times. The 27th square would now appear to be one centimeter on each side, followed by another square that was 1/2 centimeter on each side, followed by one that was 1/4 centimeter, and so on.

In short, the magnification would produce a series just equal, both in size and in number of squares, to the one we began with.

What's more, the 51st square is so small that it is only about the width of a proton. Nevertheless, if *it* were expanded to a one-centimeter square, it would have a tail of still smaller squares equal both in size and in number to what we had at the beginning.

We could keep this up *forever,* and never run out. No matter how far we went, millions of ever-decreasing squares, trillions, duodecillions, we would have left a tail precisely similar to the original. Such a situation is said to show "self-similarity."

And all of it, *all* of it, fits into a two-centimeter width. Nor is there anything magic about the two-centimeter wide. It can all be made to fit into a one-centimeter width, or a 1/10-centimeter width—or the width of a proton, for that matter.

It's no use trying to "understand" this in the same sense that we understand that there are 36 inches in a yard. We have no direct experience with infinite quantities and we can't have. We can only try to imagine the consequences of the existence of infinite quantities, and the consequences are so utterly different from anything we *can* experience that they "make no sense."

For instance, the number of points in a line is a higher infinity than that of the infinite number of integers. There is no conceivable way in which you can match those points with numbers. If you were to try to arrange the points in such a way as to line them up with numbers, you would invariably find that some points had no numbers attached to them. In fact, an infinite number of points would have no numbers attached to them.

On the other hand, you can match the points in a line one centimeter long, with the points in another line two centimeters long, so that you must conclude that the shorter line has as many points as the longer one. In fact, a line one centimeter long has as many points as can be squeezed into the entire three-dimensional Universe. You want that explained? Not by me, and not by anyone. It can be proven, but it can't be made to "make sense" in the ordinary way.

Let's get back to self-similarity. We can find that not only in a series of numbers, but in geometrical shapes. In 1906, for instance, a Swedish mathematician, Helge von Koch (1870–1924), invented a kind of super-snowflake. This is how he got it.

You start with an equilateral triangle (all sides equal), divide each side into thirds, and construct a new, smaller equilateral triangle on the middle third of each of the sides. This gives you a six-pointed star. You then divide each of the sides of the six equilateral triangles of the star into thirds and build a new, still smaller equilateral triangle on each middle third. You now have a figure rimmed by eighteen equilateral triangles. You divide each of the sides of these eighteen triangles into thirds—and so on and so on, *forever.*

Naturally, no matter how large your original triangle and how meticulous your draughtsmanship, the new triangles quickly become too small to draw. You have to draw them in imagination and try to work out the consequences.

If, for instance, you built up the super-snowflake forever, the length of the perimeter bounding the snowflake at each stage forms a diverging series. In the end, therefore, the perimeter of the snowflake is of infinite length.

On the other hand, the area of the snowflake at each stage forms a converging series with a finite sum. That means even at the end, with an infinite perimeter, the snowflake has an area of no more than 1.6 times the original equilateral triangle.

Suppose now that you study one of the relatively large triangles on one of the sides of the original triangle. It is infinitely complex as smaller and smaller and smaller triangles sprout off it, without end. If you take one of those smaller triangles, however, one so small that it can be seen only under a microscope, and imagine it expanded for easy viewing, it is just as complex as the larger triangle had been. If you consider a still smaller and an even smaller one, indefinitely, the complexity does not decrease. The super-snowflake shows self-similarity.

Here is another example. Imagine a tree, with a trunk that is divided into three branches. Each of those branches divides into three smaller branches and each of those smaller branches divides into three still smaller branches. You can easily imagine a real tree having a branching arrangement like that.

However, to have a mathematical super-tree, you must imagine that all the branches divided into three smaller branches, and each of these into three still smaller branches, and each of these into yet smaller branches, *forever*. Such a super-tree also shows self-similarity and each branch, however small, is as complex as the entire tree.

Such curves and geometrical figures were called "pathological" at first because they didn't follow the simple rules that governed the polygons, circles, spheres, and cylinders of ordinary geometry.

In 1977, however, a French-American mathematician, Benoit Mandelbrot, began to study such pathological curves systematically, and showed that they didn't fit even the most fundamental properties of geometric figures.

We are all taught, as soon as we are exposed to geometry, that a point is zero-dimensional, a line is one-dimensional, a plane is two-dimensional, and a solid is three-dimensional. Eventually, we find that if we consider a solid that possesses duration and exists in time, it is four-dimensional. We may even learn that geometers can handle still higher dimensions as a matter of course.

All these dimensions, however, are whole numbers—0, 1, 2, 3, and so on. How can we have anything else?

Mandelbrot, however, showed that the boundary of the super-snowflake was so fuzzy and made such sharp turns at every point that there was no use considering it to be a line in the ordinary sense. It was something that was not quite a line and yet not quite a plane, either. It had a dimension that was *in between* 1 and 2. In fact, he showed that it made sense to consider its dimension to be equal to the logarithm of 4 divided by the logarithm of 3. This comes to about 1.26186. Thus, the boundary of the super-snowflake has a dimension of just over 1¼.

Other such figures also had fractional dimensions, and because of this, they came to be called "fractals."

It turned out that fractals were not pathological examples of geometric shapes that were dreamed up through the fevered imaginations of mathematicians. Rather, they were closer to the real objects of the world than were the smooth, simple curves and planes of idealized geometry. It was these latter that were the products of imagination.

In consequence, Mandelbrot's work became more and more important.

Now let's change the subject slightly. Several years ago, I had occasion to hang about Rockefeller University now and then and I met Heinz Pagels there. He was a tall fellow with white hair and a smooth, unlined face. He was exceedingly pleasant and bright.

He was a physicist and knew much more about physics than I did. This was no surprise. Everyone knows more than I do about something or other. It also seemed to me that he was more intelligent than I was.

You might think, if you share the general opinion that I have a giant ego, that I would hate people who seemed more intelligent than I do, but I don't. I have discovered that people more intelligent than I am (and Heinz was the third of the sort I had met) are extremely kindly and pleasant, and besides I have found that if I listen carefully to them, I am stimulated sufficiently to work up useful ideas; and ideas, after all, are my stock in trade.

I remember that in our first conversation, Heinz talked about the "inflationary Universe," a new idea to the effect that the Universe, in the first instant after its formation, expanded at enormous speed, thus explaining some points that bothered astronomers, who had assumed the initial moments of the Big Bang to be non-inflationary.

What particularly interested me was that Heinz told me that

according to this theory, the Universe started as a quantum fluctuation of the vacuum, and was thus created out of nothing.

This got me excited, because in the September 1966 issue of *F&SF,* years before the inflationary Universe had been thought up, I had published an essay called "I'm Looking over a Four-Leaf Clover" (see Essay 8) in which I suggested that the Universe was created out of nothing at the time of the Big Bang. In fact, a key statement in the essay was my definition of what I called Asimov's Cosmogonic Principle; i.e., "In the Beginning, there was Nothing."

This does *not* mean I anticipated the inflationary Universe. I just get these intuitional thrusts, but I lack the ability to carry through. Thus, at fourteen, I had the vague intuitional notion of self-similarity in connection with converging series, but neither then, nor at any time thereafter, could I possibly have duplicated what Mandelbrot did. And though I grasped the concept of creation out of nothing, I couldn't in a million years have worked out the detailed theory of an inflationary Universe. (However, I'm not a total failure. I early realized that my intuitional grasp made it possible for me to write science fiction.)

I met Heinz periodically thereafter, all the more so after he became the Director of the New York Academy of Sciences.

One time, a bunch of us, including Heinz and myself, were sitting about discussing this and that, and Heinz raised an interesting question.

He said, "Is it possible, do you suppose, that someday, all the questions of science will be answered and there will be nothing left to do? Or is it impossible to get all the answers? And is there any way we can conceivably decide, right now, which of these two situations is correct?"

I was the first to speak. I said, "I believe we can decide right now, Heinz, and easily."

Heinz turned to me and said, "How, Isaac?"

And I said, "It's my belief that the Universe possesses, in its essence, fractal properties of a very complex sort and that the pursuit of science shares these properties. It follows that any part of the Universe that remains un-understood, and any part of scientific investigation that remains unresolved, however small that might be in comparison to what is understood and resolved, contains within it all the complexity of the original. Therefore, we'll never finish. No matter how far we go, the road ahead will be as long as it was at the start, and that's the secret of the Universe."

I reported all this to my dear wife, Janet, who looked at me thoughtfully and said, "You'd better write up that idea."

"Why?" I said. "It's just an idea."

She said, "Heinz might use it."

"I hope he does," I said. "I don't know enough physics to do anything with it, and he does."

"But he might forget he heard it from you."

"So what? Ideas are cheap. It's only what you do with them that counts."

Then came July 22, 1988, when Janet and I headed out to the Rensselaerville Institute in upstate New York to conduct our sixteenth annual seminar, which on that occasion was to be centered about biogenetics and its possible side effects—scientific, economic and political.

Something extra was added, however. Mark Chartrand (whom I had met years ago when he was Director of the Hayden Planetarium in New York) is a perennial faculty member at these seminars, and he had brought with him a thirty-minute TV-cassette featuring fractals.

In just the last few years, you see, computers have become powerful enough to produce a fractal figure and slowly expand it millions and millions of times. They can do this with very complex fractals, not merely things as simple (and, therefore, uninteresting) as super-snowflakes and super-trees.) What's more, the whole thing is made more brilliant with false color.

We began to watch the cassette at 1:30 P.M. on Monday, July 25, 1988.

We started with a dark cardioid (heart-shaped) figure, that had small subsidiary figures about it, and little by little it grew larger on the screen. One subsidiary figure would slowly be centered and grow larger until it filled the screen and it could be seen that it was surrounded by subsidiary figures, too.

The effect was that of slowly sinking into complexity that never stopped being complex. Little objects that looked like tiny dots grew larger and revealed complexity while new little objects formed. It *never stopped*. For half an hour, we watched it as different parts of the figure were expanded into new visions of unceasing beauty.

It was absolutely hypnotic. I watched and watched, and after a while, I simply couldn't withdraw my attention. The whole was as close as I ever came, or could come, to *experiencing* infinity, instead of merely imagining it and talking about it.

When it was over, it was a wrench to come back to the real world.

I said dreamily to Janet afterward, "I'm sure I was right in what I said to Heinz that time. That's the Universe and science— endless—endless—endless. The job of science will never be done, it will just sink deeper and deeper into never-ending complexity."

Janet frowned. "You still haven't written up that idea, though, have you?"

And I said, "No, I haven't."

But while we were at the Institute, we were isolated from the world. There were no newspapers, no radio, no television, and we were too busy with the details of the seminar to worry about that.

It wasn't until we got back to our apartment on the 27th, and I was leafing my way through the accumulated newspapers, that I found out what had happened.

While we were in Rensselaerville, Heinz Pagels was attending an extended meeting on physics in Colorado. Pagels was also an enthusiastic mountain-climber and, during the weekend break, on Sunday, July 24, he climbed Pyramid Peak, fourteen thousand feet high, along with a companion. He had lunch there, and at 1:30 P.M. (just twenty-four hours before I started watching the TV-cassette) he started down the mountain.

He stepped on a rock that was loose. It trembled under him and he lost his balance. He went sliding down the mountainside and was killed. He was forty-nine years old.

I, totally unprepared, turned to one of the obituary pages and saw the scare headline. It was a bad and unexpected shock, and

I'm afraid I must have cried out in unhappiness for Janet came running and read the obituary over my shoulder.

I looked up at her, sorrowfully, and said, "Now he'll never have a chance to use my idea."

So now, at last, I have written it up. Partly, this was so I could say something about Heinz, whom I so admired. And partly, it's because I wanted to put the notion on paper so that (just possibly) someone—if not Heinz, *someone*—might be able to use it and do something with it.

After all, I can't. Just getting the idea represents my total ability. I can't move an inch beyond that.

## AFTERWORD

I included a thirty-first essay on the principle of "the baker's dozen"—add another one to be sure of giving full measure. Besides, this particular essay was inspired by the death of a friend, and deals with a contribution I made to the philosophy of science rather than to science itself, and I'm rather pleased with it.

But let me use this final space to say something about my essays as a whole.

Of all the things I write, my essays for this series are perhaps the least well paid. It's understandable. *Fantasy and Science Fiction* is not a wealthy magazine, and I knew that from the start.

However, of all the things I write, my essays for this series give me the most pleasure and that far more than makes up for the fact that I am not munificently compensated therefor. I have told Ed Ferman over and over again, and do not hesitate to say it now in print, that, if the time came when he simply could not afford to pay me for my essays at all, I would cheerfully continue to write them for nothing. He assures me, though, it won't come to that.

I also know that I cannot live forever and that there is not likely to be any way in which I can write another 360 essays. Someday the last essay will be written and what its number will be I don't know. But when that day comes I suppose there will be very little I will regret, in the leaving of life, as much as the loss of the chance to keep on writing these essays forever.

## About the Author

Isaac Asimov is the author of over 400 books of fiction and nonfiction, including his latest bestselling novel, *Prelude to Foundation*. The essays in this book were first published in *The Magazine of Fantasy and Science Fiction* during the years 1958–1988.